# REA's Test Prep Books Are The Best!

**(a sample of the <u>hundreds of letters</u> REA** ~~...ives~~ **each year)**

*(more on next page)*

*(continued from front page)*

" I just wanted to thank you for helping me get a great score
on the AP U.S. History exam... Thank you for making great test preps! "
*Student, Los Angeles, CA*

" Your Fundamentals of Engineering Exam book was the absolute best
preparation I could have had for the exam, and it is one of the major
reasons I did so well and passed the FE on my first try. "
*Student, Sweetwater, TN*

" I used your book to prepare for the test and found that the advice and the
sample tests were highly relevant... Without using any other material, I earned
very high scores and will be going to the graduate school of my choice. "
*Student, New Orleans, LA*

" What I found in your book was a wealth of information sufficient to shore up
my basic skills in math and verbal... The section on analytical ability was
excellent. The practice tests were challenging and the answer explanations most
helpful. It certainly is the Best Test Prep for the GRE! "
*Student, Pullman, WA*

" I really appreciate the help from your excellent book. Please keep up
the great work. "
*Student, Albuquerque, NM*

" I am writing to thank you for your test preparation... your book helped me
immeasurably and I have nothing but praise for your GRE preparation. "
*Student, Benton Harbor, MI*

*(more on back page)*

# THE BEST TEST PREPARATION FOR THE

# MAT

# MILLER ANALOGIES TEST

**Tracy Budd**
Instructor of English
Rutgers University
New Brunswick, NJ

**Heather Craven**
Library Sciences Consultant
Morristown, NJ

**Marc Davis**
English Consultant
Somerset, NJ

**Mitchel Fedak, M.S.**
Instructor of Chemistry,
Physics, and Mathematics
Community College of Allegheny County
North Versailles, PA

**John P. Frade**
Social Sciences Consultant
Hillsborough, NJ

**Dr. Bernice Goldberg, Ph.D.**
Educational Consultant
Falmouth, ME

**Gary Land, Ph.D.**
Instructor and Chair
Department of History
Andrews University
Berrien Springs, MI

**Carol Rush, Ph.D.**
Instructor of Science
La Roche College
Pittsburgh, PA

***Research & Education Association***
61 Ethel Road West
Piscataway, New Jersey 08854

The Best Test Preparation for the
MILLER ANALOGIES TEST (MAT)

Year 2002 Printing

Printed in the United States of America

Library of Congress Control Number 99-75141

International Standard Book Number 0-87891-864-7

Research & Education Association
61 Ethel Road West
Piscataway, New Jersey 08854

# CONTENTS

# ABOUT RESEARCH & EDUCATION ASSOCIATION

Research & Education Association (REA) is an organization of educators, scientists, and engineers specializing in various academic fields. Founded in 1959 with the purpose of disseminating the most recently developed scientific information to groups in industry, government, high schools, and universities, REA has since become a successful and highly respected publisher of study aids, test preps, handbooks, and reference works.

REA's Test Preparation series includes study guides for all academic levels in almost all disciplines. Research & Education Association publishes test preps for students who have not yet completed high school, as well as high school students preparing to enter college. Students from countries around the world seeking to attend college in the United States will find the assistance they need in REA's publications. For college students seeking advanced degrees, REA publishes test preps for many major graduate school admission examinations in a wide variety of disciplines, including engineering, law, and medicine. Students at every level, in every field, with every ambition can find what they are looking for among REA's publications.

While most test preparation books present practice tests that bear little resemblance to the actual exams, REA's series presents tests that accurately depict the official exams in both degree of difficulty and types of questions. REA's practice tests are always based upon the most recently administered exams, and include every type of question that can be expected on the actual exams.

REA's publications and educational materials are highly regarded and continually receive an unprecedented amount of praise from professionals, instructors, librarians, parents, and students. Our authors are as diverse as the fields represented in the books we publish. They are well-known in their respective disciplines and serve on the faculties of prestigious high schools, colleges, and universities throughout the United States and Canada.

# ACKNOWLEDGMENTS

In addition to our authors, we would like to thank Dr. Max Fogiel, President, for his overall guidance, which brought this publication to completion; John Paul Cording, Manager of Educational Software Publishing, for coordinating production of this book; Larry B. Kling, Quality Control Manager of Books in Print, for his supervision of revisions; Omar J. Musni, Editorial Assistant, for coordinating revisions to this edition; and Marty Perzan and Michael C. Cote for typesetting the manuscript.

# MAT INDEPENDENT STUDY SCHEDULE

The following study schedule allows for thorough preparation for the MAT. Although it is designed for eight weeks, it can be condensed into a four week course by condensing two weeks into one. If you are not enrolled in a structured course, be sure to set aside enough time, at least two or three hours each day, to study. But no matter which study schedule works best for you, the more time you spend studying, the more prepared and relaxed you will feel on the day of the exam.

| Week | Activity |
|---|---|
| 1 | Take the first exam as a diagnostic exam. Your score will be an indication of your strengths and weaknesses. Carefully review all explanations, because although a piece of information may be wrong in one analogy, it may be useful in another. |
| 2 | Study REA's Main Analogy Review to familiarize yourself with the analogy format. Take the second practice test, and pay close attention to the types of analogies that are difficult for you. |
| 3 and 4 | Study REA's Subject Reviews. Use any other supplementary information that may help you absorb as much information as possible. This includes reference books, encyclopedias, trivia questions, etc. Take the third and fourth practice tests. |
| 5 | Create tests for yourself using index cards. These cards will be particularly helpful in learning vocabulary words and word parts. Take the fifth practice test. |
| 6 | Continue testing yourself using your index cards. You may want to have a friend or colleague quiz you on key facts and items. Take the sixth practice test. Track your progress over all your practice tests and determine which types of analogies are still difficult for you. |
| 7 | Study any areas you consider to be your weaknesses by using your study materials, references, and notes. Take the seventh practice test. Remember to study the explanations for all the questions, because they may provide valuable information. |
| 8 | Take the final practice test. Review all explanations and continue to study using your index cards and REA's Subject Reviews. |

**MILLER ANALOGIES TEST**

# SECTION ONE

# *About the MAT*

# Chapter 1

# SCORING HIGH
# ON THE MAT

## ABOUT THIS BOOK

This book provides a complete and accurate representation of the Miller Analogies Test (MAT). A comprehensive review details specific strategies for attacking analogy questions, and glossary type subject reviews provide the information you will need to achieve a high score on this unique and challenging exam. You are allowed fifty minutes to take the actual exam, and the same amount of time is allotted for each of our practice tests. These tests contain every type of question you can expect to see on the actual exam, and following each practice test are detailed explanations of every analogy to help you better understand the test material.

## ABOUT THE TEST

### Who Takes the Test and What is it Used For?

The Miller Analogies Test is a graduate admissions and scholarship exam required by over 2,300 schools in both the United States and Canada. In addition, some corporations use the test to place their executives.

### Who Administers the Test?

The Psychological Corporation of San Antonio, Texas, administers the Miller Analogies Test. This is the oldest commercial test publisher in the nation, that publishes and administers tests for a variety of academic and business oriented applications.

### When Should the MAT be taken?

The MAT is usually taken shortly after a candidate graduates from college. You may be applying to a number of graduate schools that require the MAT, or a prospective employer may ask that you take the test. You should determine whether or not the exam will be required of you so that you have enough time to prepare. You may also wish to allow yourself time to take the MAT again, in case you are not pleased with your initial score. Give yourself enough time to carefully study our review material, and familiarize yourself with the format of the exam. This will spare you the anxiety of having to learn about the MAT during the actual exam.

## When and Where is the Test Given?

The MAT is administered through a network of Controlled Testing Centers licensed by the Psychological Corporation. These testing centers comply with the Psychological Corporation's rigorous standards for test administration; however, they are free to set their own fees and schedules. To apply for the test, you must apply directly to the testing center.

For more information regarding Controlled Testing Centers, their fees, and schedules, you may contact:

Miller Analogies Test Coordinator
The Psychological Corporation
555 Academic Ct.
San Antonio, Texas 78204-3956
Phone: (800) 622-3231
Website: www.hbtpc.com/mat/

## Is There a Registration Fee?

Yes, you must pay a fee to take the MAT. As stated above, fees are set by individual testing centers. A complete list of Controlled Testing Centers is available in the Miller Analogies Test registration bulletin, available from the Psychological Corporation.

# HOW TO USE THIS BOOK

## What Should I Study First?

Your first step to a high score on the MAT is a comprehensive under-standing of the analogy format, and the challenges it presents. For this reason, a careful reading of our Main Analogies Review is essential. When you have completed this section, take the first practice test. This will help you get a clear idea of those areas that are most challenging to you. From there, you will be able to devise the plan of study that will be most beneficial to you.

### When Should I Start Studying?

It is never too early to begin studying for the MAT. Do not procrastinate! Last minute studying and cramming are not effective ways to learn. The more time you allow yourself to study for the MAT, the better your chances of achieving a high score. Give yourself enough time to become familiar with the format of the test and the material it covers. This will allow you to arrive at the testing center with confidence.

## FORMAT OF THE MILLER ANALOGIES TEST

The format of the MAT is very straightforward. You are given 50 minutes to complete 100 analogies. The test has no sectional divisions, and there are no breaks. Three of the four elements of an analogy are given to you, and you must complete the analogy by choosing the best answer from the four multiple-choice options provided.

## ABOUT THE REVIEW SECTIONS

There are two main sections to our MAT review material. The first section covers the nature of the analogy itself, and specific strategies for answering problems posed in the analogy format. This section is very important because unless you have a very clear understanding of the analogy format, you may mistakenly choose answers that seem correct, but are in fact only meant to confuse you. Verisimilitude will be your greatest challenge when taking the MAT.

The second section of the MAT review material contains numerous glossary type skills reviews, designed to provide you with as much information as possible to prepare for the wide variety of subject matter that you are likely to encounter on the Miller Analogies Test. The MAT is unlike most other standardized tests in that it not only tests your ability to critically analyze the relationships between given items, but also on the amount of information you bring to the test. Nothing will be more helpful to you in preparing for the MAT than a well-rounded education.

## SCORING AND SCORE REPORTS

Approximately 10 to 15 working days after you take the MAT, you will receive your personal score report. This report will list your name, address, and social security number as you entered them on your answer document, your raw score, your percentile scores, and your score recipient codes. When you take our practice tests, you will only be able to determine your raw score, because your percentile scores are based on your performance compared to other MAT candidates. One percentile score will be based on the current normative data of the general population of MAT candidates. The other percentile score is based on current normative data of MAT candidates with whom you share an intended major.

There is one important difference between your personal score report and the official score report submitted to those institutions that you specify when you take the MAT. The official score report will list your MAT scores for any administration taken in the last five years. Scores for tests taken longer than five years ago will not be reported.

If, while you are taking the MAT, you decide that you are truly unhappy with your performance, you may exercise the no score option. How to exercise this option will be explained to you at the Controlled Testing Center. If you choose not to have your exam scored, no score reports will be sent to your specified recipients, and there will be no reportable record of you ever having taken the MAT. However, before you exercise this option, consider the ramifications carefully. No refunds are available to candidates who choose the no score option, and once this decision is made, it is irrevocable. You will be sent a personal score report, however it will not show any score. Any future requests to have your test scored and your scores reported will be denied.

## STUDYING FOR THE MAT

It is very important that you choose the time and place for studying that works best for you. Some candidates set aside a few hours in the morning to study, while others retain more information by studying just before going to sleep. Some students require absolute silence while studying, and some others are undisturbed by what many candidates would consider intolerable distractions. Only you can determine when and where your study time will be most effective, but you must be consistent and use your time wisely. Work out a routine and stick to it.

You may study our review material under any circumstances you like, however when you are taking our practice tests, you should try to duplicate the actual testing conditions as closely as possible. Turn off the stereo or television, and sit at a clean table free from distractions. Be sure to accurately time yourself so that you will be used to working at a set pace.

As you complete each practice test, score your test and thoroughly review each explanation. You may even want to review the explanations for the analogies you completed correctly, because whenever possible, each analogy imparts up to eight pieces of information. An answer choice that is incorrect for one analogy may turn out to be correct for another, so no bit of knowledge should be wasted.

## TEST-TAKING TIPS

While the subject matter of the MAT may be unlike any other standardized test that you may have encountered in the past, there are several ways to acclimate yourself to this type of exam that will help alleviate any test-taking anxiety that you may feel. Listed below are a few of these methods that will help you take the MAT with confidence.

**Become comfortable with the format of the MAT.** When you take our practice tests, simulate actual testing conditions as closely as possible. Stay calm and pace yourself. Remember that you have less than a minute for each analogy, so get used to working at a steady pace. You will probably notice that pacing becomes much easier after only a few practice tests. This will boost your confidence, and greatly increase your chances of doing well on the actual exam.

**Read all of the possible answers.** This is more important on the MAT than virtually any other standardized test, because relationships between MAT analogy items can be very subtle. If you ignore even minor nuances in word meanings, you are more likely to choose an answer that is only partially correct. Be sure to choose the best answer, rather than one that looks correct immediately.

**Use the process of elimination.** If you are having difficulty with a particular analogy, go through all the possible answer choices and eliminate as many as possible. Even if you can only eliminate one answer choice, you have increased your chance of picking a correct answer by 25 percent.

**Work on the easiest analogies first.** Remember, time spent on one analogy is time not spent on another. Go through the entire test answering questions in those subject areas that come easiest to you, then return to the more difficult ones. If you spend too much time working on difficult analogies, time may run out before you've had the opportunity to answer easier ones.

**Guess.** Your score on the MAT will be expressed as the number of questions answered correctly. Therefore, you should never leave a question blank. Even if you have absolutely no idea what the correct answer to a given analogy might be, guessing gives you a 25 percent chance of responding correctly. If you leave a question blank, that chance has been eliminated.

**Be sure that the oval you are marking on your answer sheet corresponds to the number of the analogy in the test booklet.** The graders of the MAT, whether your answer sheets are hand scored or machine scored, have no sympathy for clerical errors. One incorrectly placed answer could disrupt your entire answer sheet, and even if you are fortunate enough to discover the problem early, you will waste valuable time correcting your answer sheet. Be extremely careful when filling in your answer choices.

## THE DAY OF THE TEST

### Before the Test

On the day of the test, you should wake up early after a good night's rest, and have a good breakfast. Dress comfortably, and in layers that can be added or removed as conditions in the testing center require. You should make sure that you will not be distracted by hunger, or by being too hot or too cold. In addition, plan to arrive at the testing center early. No one will be permitted into the testing center after the test has begun, and arriving early will allow you to become acclimated to the surroundings of the testing center. This will minimize the chance of distraction during the test.

To facilitate your early arrival, you may want to prepare everything you will need the night before the test. Be sure that you have your admission ticket, two forms of identification (at least one with a recent photograph), and several sharpened number 2 pencils with erasers, as none will be provided at the testing center.

If you like, you may wear a watch to the testing center, however be sure to disable any alarms or signals that may be present. These might distract you and the other candidates. No dictionaries, calculators, notebooks, briefcases, or packages may be taken into the testing center. Drinking, smoking, and eating are also prohibited.

### During the Test

Once you have entered the testing center, follow all directions of the test supervisor carefully. If you do not, you risk being dismissed from the testing center, forfeiting your testing fees, and having your scores canceled.

When all of the testing materials have been distributed, the test supervisor will give you instructions for filling out the answer sheet. You must fill out this sheet carefully, because any errors may affect your score reports.

You may be asked to take a short test of experimental analogy questions called a tryout test before the actual exam. The test administrators use the results of these tryout tests to compile future exams. Your score on the tryout tests will not be reported, and have no effect on your actual exam score. This is a requirement of the test administrators, and you will not be permitted to chose whether or not to take the tryout test.

When the actual MAT has begun, be sure to fill in your answer choices carefully, completely, and neatly. You may change your answer, but be sure to completely erase your previous choice. Any stray marks or incompletely erased answer choices may be misinterpreted as your response.

## After the Test

Once you have finished the test, turn in your testing materials and proceed to the exit in an orderly fashion. Your score report will arrive in approximately 10 working days.

# Chapter 2

# MAIN ANALOGY REVIEW

## INTRODUCTION

The Miller Analogies Test is unlike any test you have taken previously, and probably unlike any test you will ever encounter again. Although you may have been introduced to verbal analogies on the P.S.A.T. or the S.A.T., they were relatively easy compared to the ones you will find on the Miller Analogies Test. The P.S.A.T. and S.A.T. analogies were tests of your reasoning ability with vocabulary words of varying difficulty. By contrast, the Miller Analogies Test contains analogy questions that test your reasoning ability in a multitude of subject areas.

SOCIAL SCIENCES — Sociology, Psychology, Anthropology, Philosophy, Economics, Geography

NATURAL SCIENCES — Chemistry, Botany, Biology, Physics, Geology, Health Sciences

FINE ARTS AND HUMANITIES — Art, Art History, Music, Literature

MATHEMATICS — ability to perform mathematical operations such as multiplication, division, square roots, etc., in order to analyze numerical relationships, knowledge of Roman numerals

HISTORY — American History, Government, World History

VOCABULARY — words that would be considered difficult

GENERAL INFORMATION — this is a catchall category which contains information not included in the previous categories, but which may be considered common information

At this point you should be awestruck at the diversity and number of subject areas covered in the Miller Analogies Test. After all, you probably didn't study some of these courses in your career as a student so far. What's more, you might not have any interest in them at all.

Don't let the types or quantity of subjects deter you. You are not expected to have in-depth knowledge in all these subjects. Rather, the Miller Analogies Test expects you to have a superficial acquaintance with these topics.

In fact, the Miller Analogies Test contains what you could consider trivial information about these subjects. If you can answer Jeopardy quiz show questions, or play a decent game of Trivial Pursuit, you have about as much knowledge as you need in the subject areas. Remember, that this is an ANALOGY test. You need to show that you can discern the RELA-TIONSHIP between the words in the questions.

Within any of the various topics, there are certain ideas that would be known to you even if you didn't study the course. For example,

- You don't have to be a History major to know that Ceylon is the former name of the nation now known as Sri Lanka.

- You don't have to be a Chemistry major to know that a pH of 7 is neutral.

- You don't have to be an English major to know that Mark Twain was the pseudonym for Samuel Clemens.

- You don't have to be a Music major to know that "fortissimo" means "very loudly."

- You don't have to be a Math major to know that 3 squared is 9 or that the Roman numeral I is one and X is ten.

- You don't have to be an English major to know that Candide is a character in a novel by Voltaire.

These are examples of the types of information that are demanded by the Miller Analogies Test. As you can tell by these few examples, although there are many subjects tested, there is little esoteric or profound knowledge required within the subject area.

The major difficulty that you will encounter on the test is the same as any test that contains analogies — in each question, you must determine the relationship between the given words and then decide which word in the answer choices best maintains that relationship.

# FORMAT

An analogy is a relationship between two things which may be unlike in some respects, but are similar in at least one way. It is this similarity that is the key to the analogy. It is therefore important that you know the definitions of the words to be compared, because what you will be doing on the Miller Analogies Test is finding how the definitions of these words relate to each other.

Actually, an analogy can be considered the verbal equivalent of a proportion in mathematics. In math, you recall that a colon between a pair of numbers indicates that the numbers are a ratio; as, for example, 4:1 means that "the odds are 4 to 1." The relationship 4 to 1 is the same as the relationship 8 to 2. If we translate the ratio 4:1 into words, we can say that: for every four times that something happens in one case, it happens one time in the other case.

In a verbal comparison, a colon also separates two words that can be compared. We would read a verbal comparison as: Word A has a relationship to Word B — A : B. A double colon between two such comparisons means that the relationship Word A to Word B is the same as the relationship Word C to Word D — A : B :: C : D.

It is essential that you identify the relationship between Word A and Word B in order to complete the pattern that exists between C and D.

DESOLATE : JOYOUS — The relationship between these words can be stated as DESOLATE is the opposite of JOYOUS. Similarly, the relationship between DESPAIR : HOPE can be stated as DESPAIR is the opposite of HOPE. Therefore, we could write these analogies as: DESOLATE : JOYOUS :: DESPAIR : HOPE.

In the Miller Analogies Test, one word in the verbal equation has been replaced by four choices. Only one choice accurately completes the relationship. The analogy may appear in the test as any one of the following combinations:

(a, b, c, d) : B :: C : D

A : (a, b, c, d) :: C : D

A : B :: (a, b, c, d) : D

A : B :: C : (a, b, c, d)

CASSETTE : AUDITORY :: BOOK : (a. tactile, b. visual, c. olfactory, d. savory)

The answer that best expresses the relationship is (b) visual. A CAS-SETTE provides an AUDITORY experience, and a BOOK provides a VISUAL experience.

Any one of the terms in the analogy may be replaced in the question.

HOUSE : SHELTER :: (a. animal, b. friendship, c. food, d. job: SUSTENANCE

The correct answer is (c) food. A HOUSE provides a person with SHEL-TER, and FOOD provides a person with SUSTENANCE.

KEYBOARD : (a. typewriter, b. screen, c. puzzle, d. element) :: DASHBOARD : CAR

The correct answer is (a) typewriter. A KEYBOARD is part of a TYPE-WRITER, and a DASHBOARD is part of a CAR.

(a. campus, b. building, c. tribe, d. army) : REGIMENTS :: SCHOOL : GRADES

The correct answer is (d) army. An ARMY unit is organized by REGI-MENTS, and a SCHOOL unit is organized by GRADES.

No matter how you rearrange the words, a relationship exists between their definitions. An ARMY and a SCHOOL are both institutions, and REGIMENTS and GRADES are both methods of organization within them. The key to completing analogies is to recognize the pattern within them.

## PARITY OF PARTS OF SPEECH

The Miller Analogy Test is essentially a test of your ability to recognize the relationship between the meanings of words. Parts of speech are always consistent within individual analogies. If the choices in the question are ADJECTIVE : NOUN, then the answer must be ADJECTIVE : NOUN. Some words can be used as both verbs and nouns. Don't get confused. The specific parts of speech that are given will remain constant.

(a. drill, b. string, c. board, d. nail) : HAMMER :: FLUTE : PIANO

The correct answer is (a) drill. If you look at the total question, FLUTE and PIANO are both nouns. The relationship between them can be stated as the following: Both a FLUTE and a PIANO are instruments. The word we would be seeking is a noun also, and would be related to HAMMER in the same way. Both a DRILL and a HAMMER are tools (instruments).

DRILL is also a verb, but by looking over the total analogy, we know that we are looking for a noun.

Although INAUGURATE : PRESIDENT :: CORONATION : KING seems to be correct on the surface, this is not a valid analogy. "Inaugurate" is a verb and "coronation" is a noun. The two words are not the same part of speech. Don't be fooled by words that seem to go together.

## TYPES OF ANALOGIES

### 1. Word : Synonym

This type of analogy is the relationship between a word and its synonym. You could say that any given word can be replaced by the other.

HABITATION : (a. nest, b. earth, c. dome, d. abode) :: VOID : BLANK

First, we establish the relationship between the given words. VOID (emptiness) is a synonym for BLANK: therefore, we are looking for a word which is a synonym for HABITATION. The correct answer is (d) abode. A HABITATION is an ABODE. The words are synonyms of each other.

### 2. Word : Antonym

This analogy type is the relationship between a word and its opposite.

FRAGMENT : ASSEMBLE :: IMPOVERISH : (a. enrich, b. money, c. egocentric, d. humble)

The first thing to do is establish the relationship between the given words. What is the relationship between FRAGMENT and ASSEMBLE. We know that FRAGMENT can be either a noun meaning "a part broken off," or a verb meaning "to break into fragments." In order to determine which part of speech we will be working with, it's necessary to check the part of speech of its verbal equivalent, which is IMPOVERISH. IMPOVERISH is a verb, and therefore FRAGMENT must also be a verb. We can then say, that FRAGMENT (break into fragments) is the opposite of ASSEMBLE (put together.) The correct answer is (a) enrich. IMPOVERISH (make poor) is the opposite of ENRICH (make rich).

A similar analogy is word extension : antonym. In this case the words have opposite meanings, but different parts of speech.

PASSIVE : ACTIVITY :: OBJECTIVE: (a. prejudice, b. humor, c. envy, d. elegance)

The correct answer is (a) PREJUDICE. Looking at the given words, we determine, that if you are PASSIVE, then you don't show any ACTIVITY. The correct answer would maintain that relationship. If you are OBJECTIVE, then you don't show any PREJUDICE. PASSIVE and OBJECTIVE are adjectives describing a condition, and ACTIVITY and PREJUDICE are nouns.

### 3. Cause : Effect (or Effect : Cause)

This type of analogy involves a word and the outcome it causes. However, the analogy could reverse the relationship by starting with the outcome and following with the word itself.

BACTERIA : DISEASE :: (a. planet, b. sun, c. noon, d. day) : HEAT

The relationship between the given words can be stated as BACTERIA causes DISEASE. We then have to determine which of the words best fits that same relationship to HEAT. The correct answer is (b) sun. BACTE-RIA is a cause of DISEASE and SUN is a cause of HEAT.

The reverse pattern is EFFECT to CAUSE. Examples are:

FOOD : AGRICULTURE    LAUGHTER : JOKE

Here, FOOD is the result of AGRICULTURE which causes it to be produced. LAUGHTER is the result that follows (or should follow), a JOKE.

### 4. Part : Whole (or Whole : Part)

This analogy type represents the relationship between a segment and the whole entity.

SONG : (a. tune, b. repertory, c. instrument, d. conductor) ::
CHAPTER : BOOK

The correct answer is (b) repertory. If we establish the relationship between the given words, we would say that a SONG is part of a whole REPERTORY, and a CHAPTER is part of a whole BOOK. The pattern can also be reversed.

BANK : VAULT    ZOO : CAGE

If we assume that a BANK is a whole building or organization, then a VAULT is a smaller part of it. Also, in the organization we call a ZOO, a CAGE is a part of this whole.

SPECTRUM : RED :: ELEMENTS : (a. hydrogen, b. zinc, c. copper, d. oxygen)

The relationship between the given words can be stated that the SPEC-TRUM contains RED as the first color of the group of colors in the passage of light through a prism. Therefore, the correct answer is (a) HYDROGEN. Of all the ELEMENTS in the chemical chart we would find that HYDROGEN is the first element listed in the group. This is a difficult analogy. Not only are we looking for a word that is part of the whole, but we are also seeking its relative position within the group.

## 5. Condition : Greater or Lesser Degree

This analogy compares one situation and its greater or lesser degree of intensity.

> HAPPY : EXHILARATED :: (a. punish, b. hit, c. respond, d. relate) : CASTIGATE

The correct answer is (a) punish. If we create a sentence using the given words, we could say that HAPPY is a less extreme feeling than EXHILA-RATED, and (a) PUNISH is a less severe action than CASTIGATE which means "to punish severely." The pattern can also be reversed.

> FORTIFY : BUILD :: SANITIZE : (a. germs, b. building, c. clean, d. length)

The correct answer is (c). If you FORTIFY something, you build it with strength so FORTIFY is a greater degree than BUILD. If you SANITIZE something, you clean it with more emphasis than normal.

## 6. Person or Thing : Characteristic (or Characteristic : Person or Thing)

This analogy type requires that you establish a relationship between a given person or thing and the characteristic that it represents.

> PREVARICATOR: (a. builds, b. travels, c. lies, d. sings) :: THIEF : STEALS

The correct answer is (c) LIES. If we work from the given words, the sentence would be a THIEF is a person who STEALS. We are then look-ing for a word that describes a PREVARICATOR. A PREVARICATOR is a person who deviates from the truth when speaking, therefore, a PRE-VARICATOR is a person who LIES.

This category is similar to the one in which a thing or person is compared with the action or job that they perform.

> ACTOR : PORTRAYS :: JURY : (a. evaluates, b. convenes, c. rules, d. influences)

The correct answer is (a) evaluates. An ACTOR is a person whose job it is to PORTRAY a character, and a JURY is made up of people whose job it is to EVALUATE evidence. The pattern can also be reversed. For example: REVOLTS : REBEL or DECORATES : GARNISH.

> GEOPHYSICS : (a. solids, b. stars, c. motion, d. earth) :: GEOLOGY : MATTER

Using the given analogy, we would create a sentence that states GEOLOGY is the study of MATTER. We then need to find which word represents the study of GEOPHYSICS. The correct answer is (d) earth. GEOPHYSICS is the study of the EARTH.

## 7. Group : Member (or Member : Group)

This analogy represents the relationship between a group and a member or representative of that group. It is similar to part : whole in that one word represents a piece of the other.

> (a. pride, b. flock, c. coven, d. pack) : LION :: SENATE : SENATOR

The correct answer is (a) pride. A PRIDE is the group to which a LION belongs, and the SENATE is the group to which a SENATOR belongs. The pattern can also be reversed as member : group, for example CAT : FELINE, or SALMON : FISH, or GRAPE : FRUIT.

> DATA : CENSUS :: (a. symposium, b. congregation, c. resort, d. retreat) : OPINIONS

Using the given words, we would create a sentence that states that DATA is a piece of information that comes from a CENSUS. We are then looking for a word that represents many opinions. The correct answer is (a) symposium. A SYMPOSIUM is a collection of opinions about a topic.

## 8. User : Tool (or Tool : User)

This analogy type represents a name of a person who uses a specific tool.

> (a. doctor, b. singer, c. captain, d. dentist) : DRILL :: CARPENTER : HAMMER

The correct answer is (d) dentist. Using the given words, we could say that a CARPENTER is a person who uses a HAMMER. Therefore, we would be looking for an answer that represents the type of person who would use a DRILL. A DENTIST uses a DRILL.

The pattern can also be reversed.

Tool : Person

BOBBIN : (a. musician, b. equestrian, c. weaver, d. radiologist) ::
LATHE : MACHINIST

The correct answer is (c) weaver. Using the given words, we would create a sentence that states a LATHE is used by a MACHINIST. We are then looking for the name of the person who would use a BOBBIN. A BOBBIN is a cylinder or spindle for dispensing thread. Therefore, A BOBBIN is used by a WEAVER. A variation of this pattern might be instrument : application or tool : application, and its reversal. For example,

WORD PROCESSOR : WRITING     TROWEL : GARDENING

A WORD PROCESSOR is used in WRITING and a TROWEL is used in GARDENING.

## 9. Trait : Example (or Example : Trait)

This type of analogy states the relationship between a distinguishing quality and an example of that quality.

INGENIOUS : (a. convoluted, b. intelligent, c. dishonest,
d. courageous) :: BRAZEN : EXTROVERTED

The correct answer is (b) intelligent. Using the given words, we would say that a BRAZEN (marked by boldness) person is EXTROVERTED (a person interested in things outside the self). If a person is INGENIOUS (has skill or cleverness), then that person has to be INTELLIGENT. The pattern can also be reversed.

Trait : Example

TUNELESS : DISCORDANT :: FRAGRANT : (a. ambrosial,
b. pungent, c. rancid, d. lackluster)

Using the given words, we would say that TUNELESS is an example of something that is DISCORDANT (a harsh combination of musical sounds). We are then seeking a word of which FRAGRANT is an example. The correct answer is (a) ambrosial (capable of being a food for a god). An example of something that is FRAGRANT would be an example of a food that is AMBROSIAL.

## 10. Object : Material (or Material : Object)

This analogy type represents an object and the material it is made of.

> SKIRT : (a. book, b. gabardine, c. picture, d. window) :: SHIRT :
> COTTON

The correct answer is (b) gabardine. GABARDINE is a material that SKIRTS can be made of, and COTTON is a material that SHIRTS can be made of. The pattern can also be reversed.

> Material : Object

> SILK : PARACHUTE :: METAL : (a. coins, b. money, c. currency,
> d. debt)

The correct answer is (a) coins. Using the given words, we would say that SILK is the material that a PARACHUTE is made out of. METAL is the material that (a) COINS are made out of. Remember, that although (b) money and (c) currency are plausible choices, they are not the correct answers. Not all money is made of metal, nor is all currency.

## 11. Symbol : Institution (or Institution : Symbol)

This analogy type represents the relationship between a specific symbol and the institution it represents.

> (a. pamphlet, b. vote, c. flag, d. bouquet) : GOVERNMENT :: CROWN
> : MONARCHY

The correct answer is (c) flag. Using the given words, a CROWN is the symbol of a MONARCHY (a nation or state governed by a monarch). A FLAG is the symbol of institutional GOVERNMENT. The pattern can also be reversed.

> Institution : Symbol

> HAWAII : HIBISCUS :: NEW YORK : (a. pansy, b. rose, c. carnation,
> d. lily)

Using the given words, we would state that HAWAII is a state whose flower symbol is represented by the HIBISCUS flower. We are then looking for the flower that represents the state of NEW YORK. The correct answer is (b) rose. The ROSE is the state flower of NEW YORK.

# TOPICS

The Miller Analogies Test challenges you to reason the relationships between words in the following subject areas: Social Sciences, Natural Sciences, Fine Arts and Humanities, Mathematics, History, Vocabulary, and General Information.

## Social Sciences

This category includes subjects within the area considered social sciences. These types of subjects could include: sociology, psychology, anthropology, philosophy, economics, and geography. Although these are wide ranging categories, you don't have to be a social science major to be able to answer the questions. For the most part the questions will be on general topics that pertain to the subject area. Look at the following examples.

### *Sociology*

> (a. society, b. role, c. action, d. government) : INDIVIDUAL ::
> POPULATION : UNIT

The correct answer is (a) society. A SOCIETY is comprised of INDIVIDUALS, and a POPULATION contains UNITS. This is an example of whole : part.

### *Psychology*

> PIAGET: COGNITIVE :: (a. Kohlberg, b. Skinner, c. Freud, d. Dewey) :
> MORAL

The correct answer is (a) Kohlberg. PIAGET studied the COGNITIVE development in children, and KOHLBERG studied the moral development of children. This is an example of person : characteristic.

### *Anthropology*

> EVOLUTION : DARWIN :: (a. culture, b. fossils, c. language, d.
> conflict) : MEAD

Using the given analogy words, we would say that the study of EVOLUTION was pursued by DARWIN. Therefore, we need to choose which aspect of anthropology was studied by MEAD. The correct answer is (a) culture. The CULTURE of primitive societies was studied by Margaret Mead. This is an example of person : characteristic.

### Philosophy

(a. realism, b. naturalism, c. pluralism, d. hedonism) : SCIENTIFIC
EXPLANATION :: EMPIRICISM : SENSE PERCEPTIONS

The correct answer is (b) naturalism. Using the given words, we would create a sentence that states EMPIRICISM (a philosophical term that means that all knowledge is derived from experience by way of sense perception) is based on sense perceptions. We are then looking for the philosophical term on which SCIENTIFIC EXPLANATION is based. The answer is NATURALISM. This is a philosophical term that says that because all objects in nature are regular and not haphazard, they are all subject to a scientific explanation. This is an example of a trait : example type of analogy.

### Economics

Washington : 1 :: (a. 5, b. 10, c. 20, d. 50) : Lincoln

The correct answer is (a) 5. Using the given analogy we would create the following sentence: The portrait of Washington is on the $1 bill. Therefore, we are looking for the denomination of the bill on which Lincoln is depicted. The correct answer is that Lincoln is on the $5 bill. This is an example of part to whole. The portrait of Lincoln is part of the $5 bill.

### Geography

ALASKA : RHODE ISLAND :: MAINE : (a. Alabama, b. Pennsylvania,
c. Florida, d. Virginia)

The correct answer is (c) Florida. If we look at the given words in the analogy, we could say that ALASKA is the largest state in land area while RHODE ISLAND is the smallest state in land area. Therefore, we are looking for opposites. We are looking for a state that has an opposite relationship to MAINE. Since MAINE is the northernmost state on the eastern seaboard, what is the southernmost state? The correct answer is FLORIDA. This analogy type is closest to word : antonym.

## Natural Sciences

This category includes subjects from the following areas: chemistry, botany, biology, physics, geology, and health sciences. The types of analogy questions that you will be asked are based on information from these topics. As before, it is not necessary for you to be an expert in these areas. Look at the following examples. The information necessary for you to know is of a general type, and doesn't require much in-depth knowledge of all the subjects.

## Chemistry

ATOM : ELEMENT :: MOLECULE : (a. compound, b. mass, c. mixture, d. energy)

The correct answer is (a) compound. When we look at the given words, we can say that an ATOM is the smallest part of an ELEMENT that retains the element's properties. Therefore, we are looking for a word that can complete the following sentence: A MOLECULE is the smallest part of a ? that contains the properties of it. A COMPOUND is the correct answer. A molecule is the smallest part of a compound that retains that compound's properties. This is an example of a part : whole analogy.

## Botany

GENUS : (a. division, b. class, c. order, d. kingdom) :: MISTLETOE : PLANT

The correct answer is (d) kingdom. Using the given words, we would say that MISTLETOE is a part of the whole category of PLANTS. In botany, plants are placed in categories from the most to the least specific. GENUS is the most specific name (the part) and KINGDOM is the least specific (the whole category). If we rearrange the analogy, we could say that the GENUS is MISTLETOE, and the KINGDOM is PLANT.

## Biology

(a. cellulose, b. water, c. chlorophyll, d. carbon dioxide) : PLANT CELL :: PROTEIN : ANIMAL CELL

The correct answer is (a) cellulose. The given analogy could be stated as PROTEIN is the material that makes up the membrane of an ANIMAL CELL. We are then looking for a word which makes up the membrane of a PLANT CELL. The cell membrane of a typical PLANT CELL is made up of CELLULOSE. This analogy type is mostly related to trait : characteristic. Because the membrane has cellulose it must be a plant cell.

## Physics

ROBOTS : MACHINES :: CONSTELLATIONS : (a. planets, b. gravity, c. moons, d. stars)

The correct answer is (d) stars. Using the given words, we could create a sentence which states that ROBOTS are MACHINES made up of many machines arranged in a specific way. Therefore, we would need a word that retains this relationship. CONSTELLATIONS are made up of many STARS arranged in a specific way. This analogy is closest to whole : part.

### Geology

> LAPIDARY : (a. concrete, b. glass, c. stone, d. plant) :: SCULPTOR : CLAY

The correct answer is (c) stone. A LAPIDARY is a person who turns a common, rough STONE into a gem. If we use the given words, we would create a sentence that states that a SCULPTOR turns CLAY into a work of art. This is an example of a person : job type of analogy.

### Health Sciences

> ANEMIA : IRON :: SCURVY : (a. beta carotene, b. calcium, c. vitamin A, d. vitamin C)

The correct answer is (d) vitamin C. Using the given words, the relationship can be stated as ANEMIA is a disease caused by a lack of IRON in your diet. We are then looking for a word that would fit into the sentence SCURVY is a disease caused by a lack of ? in your diet. SCURVY is caused by a lack of vitamin C. This analogy type is most similar to extension : antonym. If you have SCURVY then you don't have any vitamin C in your diet.

## Fine Arts and Humanities

This category can be broken down into four general areas: art, art history, music, and literature. As with the previous subject areas, it is not necessary to be an expert in the individual subject areas. It is important for you to have a general conceptual understanding of the topics.

### Art

> (a. easel, b. canvas, c. palette, d. brush) : COLORS :: BOWL : INGREDIENTS

The correct answer is (c) palette (an oval board used by an artist to mix colors). If we use the original words, we could say that a BOWL is what a cook uses to mix INGREDIENTS. Therefore we are looking for an object that is used to mix COLORS. PALETTE is the only correct choice. This is an example of a thing : action analogy.

### Art History

> GILBERT STUART : PORTRAITS :: CLAUDE MONET : (a. abstract
> shapes, b. impressionistic art, c. fantasy, d. realism)

The correct answer is (b) impressionistic art. Using the given analogy we can state the relationship between the words as GILBERT STUART painted mostly PORTRAITS. Therefore we would have to find the type of art that CLAUDE MONET was most famous for. That would be Impressionism. This would be a type of person : characteristic analogy.

### Music

> APPALACHIAN SPRING : UNITED STATES :: SWAN LAKE :
> (a. Austria, b. England, c. Italy, d. Russia)

The correct answer is (d). Using the given words, we could state the relationship in a sentence that says: APPALACHIAN SPRING is music composed in the UNITED STATES by Aaron Copeland. Therefore, in what country was SWAN LAKE composed? The correct answer is SWAN LAKE was composed in RUSSIA by Peter Tchaikovksy. This is an example of a thing : characteristic analogy.

### Literature

> *MACBETH* : *HAMLET* :: *TAMING OF THE SHREW* : (a. *The Little
> Foxes*, b. *Cyrano de Bergerac*, c. *King Lear*, d. *The Iliad*)

The correct answer is (c) *King Lear*. The relationship between *MACBETH* and *HAMLET* is that they are both plays written by Shakespeare. *TAMING OF THE SHREW* is also a play written by Shakespeare; therefore, we are looking for an answer which would also be a Shakespearean play. In a way, this could be considered a synonym analogy. *MACBETH, HAMLET, TAMING OF THE SHREW,* and *KING LEAR* are all plays written by the same author.

## Mathematics

This category contains mathematically-oriented analogy questions that could include knowledge of mathematical operations, such as your ability to do multiplication, division, and square roots. You have to determine the relationships between numbers. You might also be tested on your knowledge of Roman numerals. Included in this category could be a type of question testing your general knowledge of math related information. This topic would be found in the following analogies.

(a. troy, b. gram, c. ton, d. yard) : LENGTH :: QUART : CAPACITY

The correct answer is (d) yard. Using the given words, we would state that a QUART is a measure of CAPACITY. Therefore, which word would indicate a measure of LENGTH? The YARD is a measure of LENGTH. This could be considered a thing : characteristic analogy. A YARD characterizes LENGTH and a QUART characterizes CAPACITY.

MILLION : 6 :: TRILLION : (a. 9, b. 10, c. 11, d. 12)

The correct answer is (d) 12. A MILLION is represented by 6 zeros, and a TRILLION is represented by 12 zeros. This could be considered a characteristic : thing analogy. A MILLION is represented, or characterized by 6 zeros.

Other types of analogy questions may require that you perform mathematical operations in order to determine the relationship between the given numbers.

3 : 81 :: (a. 4, b. 5, c. 6, d. 7) : 625

The correct answer is (b) 5. The relationship of 3 and 81 is that the number 3 is multiplied by itself four times. Therefore, you have to determine which number multiplied by itself four times equals 625.

Another type of mathematical analogy may be:

(a. 0.35, b. 1.45, c. 0.75, d. 1.00) : 0.25 :: 1.56 : 0.52

The correct answer is (c) 0.75. If you look at the given numbers, you will determine that by dividing 1.56 by 3, you will get 0.52. Therefore, you need to figure out which number divided by 3 will give you 0.25.

Another type of mathematically oriented question you may encounter on the Miller Analogies Test is based on your knowledge of Roman numerals:

L : C :: (a. X , b. M, c. D, d. V) : XX

The correct answer is (a) X. If you know that V = 5, X = 10, XX = 20, L = 50, C = 100, D = 500, and M = 1,000, then you can determine that the relationship between L and C could be stated as follows: L is one-half of C. Therefore you will need a number that is one-half of XX. Since 10 (X) is one-half of 20 (XX), that is the correct answer.

## History

The Miller Analogies Test requires you to have some general knowledge of American History and Government, as well as some knowledge of

World History. You don't have to be a History major in order to answer the types of questions found on the test. The types of questions are so general that you've probably studied the topics throughout your school career.

## American History

> (a. Casey Jones, b. Paul Revere, c. Franklin Roosevelt, d. Martin Luther King, Jr.) : PATRICK HENRY :: HARRY TRUMAN : DOUGLAS MacARTHUR

The correct answer is (b) Paul Revere. If you look at the given relationship, you may determine that the most obvious one is that DOUGLAS MacARTHUR was a general who served under President HARRY TRUMAN. Therefore, they were contemporaries. You then need to find which of the choices was a contemporary of PATRICK HENRY.

PAUL REVERE and PATRICK HENRY were contemporaries, just as HARRY TRUMAN and DOUGLAS MacARTHUR were. This could be considered a type of synonymous analogy. Both parts of the analogy are similar in that the people were contemporaries.

## American Government

> INTERNAL REVENUE : TREASURY :: (a. prisons, b. consumer affairs, c. public affairs, d. mint) : JUSTICE

The correct answer is (a) prisons. The INTERNAL REVENUE service is part of the TREASURY department and the PRISONS are part of the JUSTICE department in American government. This could be considered a whole : part analogy.

## World History

> FRENCH REVOLUTION : NAPOLEON BONAPARTE :: RUSSIAN REVOLUTION : (a. Lenin, b. Stalin, c. Khruschev, d. Nicholas)

The correct answer is (a) Lenin. After the French Revolution, NAPOLEON BONAPARTE came to power as a dictator over France, and after the RUSSIAN REVOLUTION the person who came to rule Russia was LENIN. This could be considered a person : characteristic analogy. NAPOLEON BONAPARTE is associated with the FRENCH REVOLUTION as LENIN is associated with the RUSSIAN REVOLUTION.

## Vocabulary

As with most of the analogies you are familiar with, those on the Miller Analogies Test require your knowledge of relationships between vocabulary words. These words may be considered difficult for two reasons. One, because they are not the common types of words that you would normally use in everyday language, and two, because they may be related in a way that is not obvious.

> PUERILE : SUBTLETY :: INJUDICIOUS : (a. sagacity, b. repentance, c. candor, d. uncertainty)

The correct answer is (a) sagacity. The relationship between PUERILE (childish, silly) and SUBTLETY (shrewd, keen), may be stated as follows: Someone who acts in a PUERILE manner will show no SUBTLETY. Someone who behaves in an INJUDICIOUS (not exercising sound judgment) manner will have no SAGACITY (wisdom, prudence). This could be considered a trait : example type of analogy.

> ALIENATION : ENMITY :: (a. examination, b. rejoicing, c. depression, d. repentance) : BLITHE

The correct answer is (b) rejoicing. The analogy between the given words can be stated as follows: During a time of ALIENATION (estrangement) you might feel ENMITY (hatred) towards something. In order to complete the analogy, we need to find a word that tells you when you would feel BLITHE (happy, lighthearted) toward something. During a time of REJOICING you would feel BLITHE towards something. This could be considered a thing : characteristic type of analogy.

## General Information

This is a catchall category. It applies to any information not covered in the aforementioned categories. General information is knowledge that you have picked up from various and diverse places, such as magazines, textbooks, recreational readings, etc. It is the kind of general knowledge that you would assume any educated person would know.

> JACK NICKLAUS : (a. tennis racket, b. golf club, c. boxing gloves, d. basketball) :: GEORGE GERSHWIN : PIANO

The correct answer is (b) golf club. The given analogy contains the relationship between GEORGE GERSHWIN and PIANO. GEORGE GERSHWIN is a famous pianist, and therefore his talent lies in playing the PIANO. You then have to determine what field JACK NICKLAUS is famous in. Unless you have been totally hidden away in a dark cave for years, you have to know that JACK NICKLAUS is a famous golfer. So the correct answer has to be GOLF CLUB. This is a user : tool type of analogy.

CITIZEN : VISA :: SOLDIER (a. gun, b. uniform, c. pass, d. detention)

The correct answer is (c) pass. Using the given analogy, we can say that a CITIZEN requires a VISA to gain entry to or leave a country. In order to maintain the relationship we need to determine what a SOLDIER needs in order to go into or out of his/her base. A SOLDIER requires a PASS to facilitate movement. This would be considered a thing : characteristic type of analogy.

As you can tell by the examples, these types of questions do not fall into any particular subject category, and yet they require you to have an understanding of the given words in order to determine the relationship and complete the analogy.

ROBIN HOOD : ENGLAND :: (a. George Washington, b. Eugene O'Neill, c. Johnny Appleseed, d. Paul Revere) : AMERICA

The correct answer is (c) Johnny Appleseed. The relationship that you should have determined from the given words is that ROBIN HOOD was or was not a myth in ENGLAND. You then have to find the person who has the same status in America. JOHNNY APPLESEED may or may not have been a myth.

## TEST-TAKING STRATEGIES

Sometimes words can have more than one meaning. When looking over the test question, you may be confused at first by the word choices.

(a. pride, b. flock, c. coven, d. pack) : LION :: SENATE : SENATOR

PRIDE may be a verb (meaning to indulge in pride) or it may be a noun (meaning conceit or a group of lions). If you look over the total analogy, you will realize that the verb form cannot be correct because all the words in the analogy are nouns. Therefore, you have to decide if any of the noun definitions fit into the analogy. It then becomes obvious that PRIDE is the correct answer because one of the definitions of PRIDE refers to a group of LIONS. The relationship that the analogy is testing is that of group : member.

The same reasoning can also apply to the word : synonym analogy PIECE : (a. bowl, b. text, c. handle, d. fragment) :: GLINT : GLEAM. PIECE is a versatile word. It can be used as either a noun (meaning fragment, a written work, a coin, or a gun) or a verb (meaning to repair by adding pieces). If you establish that the relationship between GLINT : GLEAM is that GLINT is a synonym of GLEAM, then you need the word that would be a synonym to PIECE. All the words in the analogy are nouns; therefore, we have to consider the noun meaning of PIECE. Using process of elimination on all PIECE definitions, you will discover that the correct meaning of PIECE in the analogy is that of FRAGMENT.

## Word Parts

Some of the words used in the Miller Analogies Test may be unfamiliar to you. If this happens, then it is necessary for you to make the best educated guess you can. Learning the meaning of prefixes, roots, and suffixes may make this task a lot easier. Study the following lists of the most commonly used prefixes, roots, and suffixes. Be sure to use index cards for the items you don't know or find unusual. Look over the examples given, and then try to think of your own. Testing yourself in this way will allow you to see if you really do know the meaning of each item.

## How to Answer Miller Analogy Questions

The questions on the Miller Analogies Test are not as straightforward as those you've encountered on other tests that include analogy questions. Other analogy tests rely on your knowledge of the definitions of vocabulary words. The Miller Analogies Test relies not only on your knowledge of words, but also of names in various subjects or fields. In addition, you will be required to perform mathematical computations.

Although the diversity of topics you are tested on may seem to make it impossible for you to study for the MAT, that isn't the case. Most of the information you are required to know is so general and trivial that you probably are already knowledgeable in the subject. The questions are designed to test your familiarity with words or numbers and their relationships — that's all. You will not be expected to know detailed amounts of information. Just be able to establish the relationship between the given analogy words or numbers and maintain that relationship to determine the answer to each question.

Individual questions on the Miller Analogy Test are written in the following way: A : B :: C : D. Any one of these variables may be omitted. On either side of the equation there will be a complete set of words. You have to determine the relationship between the two words on the completed side. It is then necessary for you to choose which would be the best word out of the four choices, which when inserted into the equation, would make both sides have similar relationships.

If an analogy question seems difficult or unclear, you have the option of rearranging the words. Because an analogy is comparable to a mathematical equation, it is feasible for you to rearrange the items so that they might make more sense. For example, a given analogy is A : B :: C : D, and it can be reordered without losing validity, so that B : A :: D : C.

| | |
|---|---|
| Given Analogy: | ITINERARY : TRIP :: AGENDA : MEETING |
| Reordered: | TRIP : ITINERARY :: MEETING : AGENDA |

This can be interpreted as follows:

| | |
|---|---|
| Given: | An ITINERARY is used to plan a TRIP, and an AGENDA is used to plan a MEETING. |
| Reordered: | An ITINERARY is a plan used on a TRIP and an AGENDA is a plan used at a MEETING. |

The best way to approach analogy questions is to create a sentence that states a clear and direct relationship between the two given capitalized words on either side of the equation. Substitute the choices into a sentence you create between the choices and the given capitalized word on the other side of the equation. Make sure you look at all the choices before you choose an answer. Eliminate any choice which does not make sense in your answer. Sometimes, there may be two or more possible choices that seem to fit the analogy. In this case, you must go back to your original relationship sentence and revise it.

SHELL : WALNUT :: (a. section, b. juice, c. rind, d. fruit) : ORANGE

The first question you have to ask yourself, is "What is the relationship between the two given capitalized words SHELL and WALNUT?" The most obvious sentence is: SHELL is part of the WALNUT. You then substitute the words in the answer choices and see if they relate to ORANGE in the same way.

(a)  SECTION is part of the ORANGE.

(b)  JUICE is part of the ORANGE.

(c)  RIND is part of the ORANGE.

(d)  FRUIT is part of the ORANGE.

So far, choices (a), (b), and (c) are correct. It is therefore necessary to revise our initial sentence to make it more precise.

The SHELL is the outer covering of a WALNUT.

(a) SECTION is the outer covering of an ORANGE.

(b) JUICE is the outer covering of an ORANGE.

(c) RIND is the outer covering of an ORANGE.

(d) FRUIT is the outer covering of an ORANGE.

When the initial sentence is revised, the logical choice is (c) RIND.

## GUESSING STRATEGIES

Unlike some other standardized tests, there is no penalty for guessing. Therefore, it is to your advantage to guess intelligently on every question. You will not be penalized for getting an answer wrong. After you have established a relationship between the two given words, you should then eliminate the obviously incorrect choices, and guess from the remaining ones. If you immediately choose an answer, you have a one in four chance of getting it correct. If you eliminate one choice, you then have a one in three chance, and if you can eliminate two choices, you have a one in two, or 50%, chance of getting it correct. If you leave a question blank, then you will automatically get it wrong.

If you know the meaning of both capitalized words on one side, form a sentence with a clear relationship and then insert the choices to form a relationship with the given word on the other side of the question.

(a. ape, b. fish, c. zoo, d. swim) : MINNOW :: GEM : AGATE

A sentence that states the relationship between two given words on the same side is: group : member — A GEM is the group of which AGATE is a member. You then have to find the word which relates to MINNOW in the same way.

(a) APE is a group of which MINNOW is a member.

(b) FISH is a group of which MINNOW is a member.

(c) ZOO is a group of which MINNOW is a member.

(d) SWIM is a group of which MINNOW is a member.

The correct answer is (b) FISH.

Always look for options to eliminate. Occasionally you can save a lot of time if you just happen to note the perfect match from the start. In that case, you should quickly review the other options, just to be sure you are correct.

If you don't know all the words in the question, use the sentence you have already formed, and substitute the answer whose meanings you do know, and eliminate those which don't fit. It's possible that you may be able to use your knowledge of prefixes, roots, and suffixes to help you arrive at the correct answer.

> BIOLOGY : (a. plants, b. life, c. planets, d. death) :: PSYCHOLOGY : MIND

"OGY" is a suffix meaning "the study of," and therefore if you know that "BIO" is a root word meaning "life," then BIOLOGY is the study of life. "PSYCH" is a root word meaning "mind," and so PSYCHOLOGY means the study of the mind. The relationship between the two given words on the same side of the analogy can be expressed as: PSYCHOLOGY is the study of the MIND. You now have to choose which of the following choices is correct.

(a) BIOLOGY is the study of PLANTS.

(b) BIOLOGY is the study of LIFE.

(c) BIOLOGY is the study of PLANETS.

(d) BIOLOGY is the study of DEATH.

The correct answer is (b) LIFE.

If you do not know the meanings of some of the words, and knowledge of prefixes, roots, and suffixes isn't appropriate, then try to recall in what context you might have heard the words used. Keep in mind that you are looking for a match with the same relationship as the capitalized given word pair, you are not looking for a word that matches in meaning.

> (a. stratosphere, b. environment, c. gravity, d. technology) : JET STREAM :: CRUST : GEOLOGIC FAULT

If you can't recall the meaning of STRATOSPHERE, try and recall some sentence you might have heard in the past that could provide a context for you. "His head is never here on Earth. It's always in the stratosphere." or "That kite flew so high it reached the stratosphere." These sentences give you an idea that "stratosphere" is a word meaning very high up. As before, we follow the first step in approaching an analogy question by creating a relationship between the two given words on one side of the verbal equation:

Within the Earth's CRUST is found GEOLOGIC FAULT.

(a)   Within the Earth's STRATOSPHERE is found JET STREAM.

(b)   Within the Earth's ENVIRONMENT is found JET STREAM.

(c)   Within the Earth's GRAVITY is found JET STREAM.

(d)   Within the Earth's TECHNOLOGY is found JET STREAM.

The correct answer is (a) STRATOSPHERE. If you are looking for a word that means "high up" then ENVIRONMENT, GRAVITY, and TECH-NOLOGY can be eliminated. STRATOSPHERE is the choice that is left, and happens to be the most precise relationship for the analogy.

Sometimes prefix, root, suffix or context knowledge can't be used. In this case, try to work backwards from the answer choices.

STORMY : TEMPESTUOUS :: SCARED : (a. compassionate, b. soothing, c. frightened, d. elegant)

If you don't know the meaning of TEMPESTUOUS, try working the analogy this way:

(a)   Is there a relationship between SCARED and COMPASSION-ATE?

(b)   Is there a relationship between SCARED and SOOTHING?

(c)   Is there a relationship between SCARED and FRIGHTENED?

(d)   Is there a relationship between SCARED and ELEGANT?

There are two possible choices: (b) SCARED and SOOTHING and (c) SCARED and FRIGHTENED. If you are SCARED, then something SOOTHING would calm you down. In (c), if you are SCARED, then you are FRIGHTENED. There are logical relationships within these two an-swer choices.

Look back at the word STORMY. You know that there are many definitions, among them, to rain or snow with violence, or to have rage. Since the choices for SCARED are adjectives, the best definition of STORMY would be an adjective also.

Let's reorder the analogy.

STORMY : SCARED :: TEMPESTUOUS : (b. soothing, c. frightened)

If it is STORMY, then you might be SCARED. Therefore:

If it is TEMPESTUOUS, then you might be SOOTHING

If it is TEMPESTUOUS, then you might be FRIGHTENED

Reordered this way, your best guess would be FRIGHTENED. FRIGHTENED is an adjective describing a feeling. By the way, TEMPESTUOUS means full of storm. So the original analogy STORMY : TEMPESTUOUS describes a word : synonym relationship. SCARED and FRIGHTENED are also synonyms.

## REMEMBER

- Always establish a relationship between the given words and use that relationship to complete the analogy.

- Make an educated guess even if you are not sure of the answer. This means using your knowledge of prefixes, roots, suffixes, and context. Sometimes you have to work backwards from the answer.

- Sometimes an uncommon meaning of a word fits the analogy better than a common one. Always be flexible enough to revise your original relationship sentence.

- Look for parts of speech. The part of speech of a word in an analogy is always the same as the part of speech of the corresponding answer choices.

- Look for the relationships between the given numbers. Be flexible enough to work all sorts of mathematical computations on them. Be prepared to work with squares and cubes.

## TIME MANAGEMENT

The Miller Analogies Test is a timed test. You will have 50 minutes to answer 100 questions. This means you have 30 seconds to answer each analogy question. All of the analogy questions have the same value. Therefore, you do not want to spend your time deliberating over questions that you don't know at first. Get all your sure points. Do not spend a lot of time deliberating over analogy questions that you are unsure of.

The best way to approach this is to quickly go through each question, answering those which you know the answer to. By following this strategy, you will be skipping over some questions that you don't know immediately. Make sure that you circle those questions in your question booklet. Skip the corresponding questions on your answer sheet. You do not want to lose points for putting answers in the wrong spaces. After you have answered all the questions that you can, go back to the ones you have skipped, and try working them out by using the strategies mentioned previously. Do not leave any answers blank. Make your best educated guess.

# MAT

## MILLER ANALOGIES TEST

# SECTION TWO

# *Practice Tests*

# MAT – Practice Test 1 Answer Sheet

1. (a) (b) (c) (d)
2. (a) (b) (c) (d)
3. (a) (b) (c) (d)
4. (a) (b) (c) (d)
5. (a) (b) (c) (d)
6. (a) (b) (c) (d)
7. (a) (b) (c) (d)
8. (a) (b) (c) (d)
9. (a) (b) (c) (d)
10. (a) (b) (c) (d)
11. (a) (b) (c) (d)
12. (a) (b) (c) (d)
13. (a) (b) (c) (d)
14. (a) (b) (c) (d)
15. (a) (b) (c) (d)
16. (a) (b) (c) (d)
17. (a) (b) (c) (d)
18. (a) (b) (c) (d)
19. (a) (b) (c) (d)
20. (a) (b) (c) (d)
21. (a) (b) (c) (d)
22. (a) (b) (c) (d)
23. (a) (b) (c) (d)
24. (a) (b) (c) (d)
25. (a) (b) (c) (d)
26. (a) (b) (c) (d)
27. (a) (b) (c) (d)
28. (a) (b) (c) (d)
29. (a) (b) (c) (d)
30. (a) (b) (c) (d)
31. (a) (b) (c) (d)
32. (a) (b) (c) (d)
33. (a) (b) (c) (d)
34. (a) (b) (c) (d)

35. (a) (b) (c) (d)
36. (a) (b) (c) (d)
37. (a) (b) (c) (d)
38. (a) (b) (c) (d)
39. (a) (b) (c) (d)
40. (a) (b) (c) (d)
41. (a) (b) (c) (d)
42. (a) (b) (c) (d)
43. (a) (b) (c) (d)
44. (a) (b) (c) (d)
45. (a) (b) (c) (d)
46. (a) (b) (c) (d)
47. (a) (b) (c) (d)
48. (a) (b) (c) (d)
49. (a) (b) (c) (d)
50. (a) (b) (c) (d)
51. (a) (b) (c) (d)
52. (a) (b) (c) (d)
53. (a) (b) (c) (d)
54. (a) (b) (c) (d)
55. (a) (b) (c) (d)
56. (a) (b) (c) (d)
57. (a) (b) (c) (d)
58. (a) (b) (c) (d)
59. (a) (b) (c) (d)
60. (a) (b) (c) (d)
61. (a) (b) (c) (d)
62. (a) (b) (c) (d)
63. (a) (b) (c) (d)
64. (a) (b) (c) (d)
65. (a) (b) (c) (d)
66. (a) (b) (c) (d)
67. (a) (b) (c) (d)
68. (a) (b) (c) (d)

69. (a) (b) (c) (d)
70. (a) (b) (c) (d)
71. (a) (b) (c) (d)
72. (a) (b) (c) (d)
73. (a) (b) (c) (d)
74. (a) (b) (c) (d)
75. (a) (b) (c) (d)
76. (a) (b) (c) (d)
77. (a) (b) (c) (d)
78. (a) (b) (c) (d)
79. (a) (b) (c) (d)
80. (a) (b) (c) (d)
81. (a) (b) (c) (d)
82. (a) (b) (c) (d)
83. (a) (b) (c) (d)
84. (a) (b) (c) (d)
85. (a) (b) (c) (d)
86. (a) (b) (c) (d)
87. (a) (b) (c) (d)
88. (a) (b) (c) (d)
89. (a) (b) (c) (d)
90. (a) (b) (c) (d)
91. (a) (b) (c) (d)
92. (a) (b) (c) (d)
93. (a) (b) (c) (d)
94. (a) (b) (c) (d)
95. (a) (b) (c) (d)
96. (a) (b) (c) (d)
97. (a) (b) (c) (d)
98. (a) (b) (c) (d)
99. (a) (b) (c) (d)
100. (a) (b) (c) (d)

# MILLER ANALOGIES

# PRACTICE TEST 1

**TIME:**    50 Minutes
             100 Analogies

---

**DIRECTIONS**: Read each of the following analogies carefully, and choose the BEST answer to each item. Fill in your responses in the answer sheets provided.

---

1. MINERVA : THE ARTS :: (a. Pomona b. Flaura c. Gaia d. Demeter) : FRUITS

2. COW : HEIFER :: FOX : (a. vixen b. gander c. bitch d. ewe)

3. HALIFAX : CANADA :: O'HARE : (a. New York b. Ireland c. Chicago d. England)

4. SCOPES : DARROW :: MCCARTHY : (a. Bailey b. Cohn c. Hutz d. Slotnick)

5. EARL : JIMMY CARTER :: (a. Wilson b. Milhous c. Baines d. Herbert) : RONALD REAGAN

6. BETTY : ELIZABETH :: (a. Jeremy b. Jeffrey c. Sean d. James) : JOHN

7. UPI : AP :: Press Association : (a. Courier b. IPS c. AT&T d. Reuters)

8. (a. Tar heel b. Garden c. Buckeye d. Sunshine) : OHIO :: EMPIRE : NEW YORK

9. MAGYAR : (a. Hungary b. China c. Madagascar d. Morocco) :: GAELIC : IRELAND

10. SAHARA : (a. Gobi b. Mojave c. Patagonia d. Arabian) :: AUSTRA-
    LIA : GREENLAND

11. SUPERIOR : CASPIAN :: (a. Mediterranean b. Coral c. Bering
    d. North) : ARABIAN SEA

12. MERCURY : JUPITER :: (a. Atlantic b. Indian c. Antarctic d. Arctic)
    : PACIFIC

13. CALF : WHALE :: (a. foal b. fawn c. chick d. cygnet) : SWAN

14. TALLAHASSEE : FLORIDA :: (a. Dover b. Newark c. Concord
    d. Annapolis) : DELAWARE

15. JUSTINIAN : (a. Macedonia b. Byzantium c. Athens d. Franks) ::
    AUGUSTUS : ROME

16. GINSBERG : KEROUAC :: HUGHES : (a. Hurston b. Walker
    c. Morrison d. Lee)

17. GALAPAGOS : (a. Greece b. Italy c. Ecuador d. India) :: AZORES :
    PORTUGAL

18. MARCO POLO : CHINA :: COLUMBUS : (a. North America
    b. Caribbean c. Central America d. Pacific Islands)

19. 1865 : EMANCIPATION OF AMERICAN SLAVES :: 1861 :
    (a. French Revolution b. Alaskan purchase c. emancipation of Rus-
    sian serfs d. the passage of the Eighteenth Amendment)

20. 1799 : WASHINGTON :: 1865 : (a. Lincoln b. Buchanan
    c. McKinley d. Arthur)

21. LATITUDE : PARALLELS :: LONGITUDE : (a. line b. equator
    c. degree d. meridians)

22. LEIBNIZ : RATIONALISM :: LOCKE : (a. empiricism b. atomism
    c. idealism d. phenomenologism)

23. ORNITHOLOGY : BIRDS :: ICHTHYOLOGY : (a. cancer b. cur-
    rency c. metals d. fish)

24. EIFFEL TOWER : GUSTAVE EIFFEL :: GUGGENHEIM MU-
    SEUM : (a. Solomon Guggenheim b. Frank Lloyd Wright c. Walter
    Gropius d. Egon Schiele)

25. POUND : 16 OUNCES :: TROY POUND : (a. 8 oz. b. 24 oz. c. 12
    oz. d. 17 oz.)

26. CHRONOMETER : TIME :: ANEMOMETER : (a. weight b. atmo-
    spheric pressure c. wind speed d. distance)

27. EUROPE/RUSSIA : 13% OF THE WORLD POPULATION ::
    CHINA : (a. 35% b. 20% c. 29% d. 17%)

28. ENGLISH : 460 MILLION SPEAKERS :: SPANISH : (a. 400
    million b. 80 million c. 125 million d. 357 million)

29. PRIMARY ECONOMIC ACTIVITY : FARMING :: SECONDARY
    ECONOMIC ACTIVITY : (a. service b. information and research
    c. manufacturing d. mining)

30. DONATELLO : BRONZE :: DÜRER : (a. copper b. titanium c. iron
    d. plaster)

31. BUONARROTI : MICHELANGELO :: REMBRANDT :
    (a. Donatello b. Munch c. Lichtenstein d. Van Rijn)

32. PRIDE : LIONS :: (a. gaggle b. flock c. rafter d. herd) : TURKEYS

33. SWARM : BEES :: BUSINESS : (a. bears b. eagles c. ferrets d. elks)

34. ERATO : LOVE :: (a. Urania b. Terpsichore c. Euterpe d. Calliope) :
    DANCING

35. LAKOTA : SIOUX NATION :: (a. Mohawk b. Cherokee c. Navaho
    d. Lenape) : IROQUOIS CONFEDERACY

36. *COMMON SENSE* : THOMAS PAINE :: (a. *Civil Disobedience*
    b. *Origin of Species* c. *Wealth of Nations* d. *Poor Richard's Almanac*)
    : ADAM SMITH

37. HERTZ : FREQUENCY :: (a. joule b. tesla c. watt d. newton) : FORCE

38. FIRST ANNIVERSARY : SECOND ANNIVERSARY :: PAPER : (a. cotton b. leather c. linen d. crystal)

39. VENTRICLE : AURICLE :: OCCIPITAL : (a. pylorous b. temporal c. thoracic d. nevus)

40. FEMUR : SKELETON :: (a. stomach b. brain c. skin d. heart) : ORGANS

41. BAROMETER : ATMOSPHERIC PRESSURE :: (a. anemometer b. bolometer c. galvanometer d. densitometer) : ELECTRICAL CURRENTS

42. BELL : TELEPHONE :: (a. Davy b. Deere c. Fitch d. Fulton) : STEAMBOAT

43. AMETHYST : OPAL :: LIMESTONE : (a. loam b. marble c. lava d. obsidian)

44. LEMONS : (a. vinegar b. aspirin c. batteries d. soap) :: ACID : BASE

45. POSITIVE : NEGATIVE :: CATION : (a. neutron b. anion c. proton d. electron)

46. 0° LATITUDE : EQUATOR :: 23.5° NORTH LATITUDE : (a. prime meridian b. tropic of Capricorn c. middle latitudes d. tropic of Cancer)

47. SPHYGMOMANOMETER : (a. doctor b. engineer c. photographer d. astronomer) :: COMPASS : NAVIGATOR

48. ENTOMOLOGIST : ARACHNOLOGIST :: GEOGRAPHER : (a. cartographer b. geologist c. archaeologist d. botanist)

49. *SANTA MARIA* : FRANCESO PINEDO :: *SPIRIT OF ST. LOUIS* : (a. Richard Byrd b. Charles Lindbergh c. Clarence Chamberlain d. Albert "Putty" Reed )

50. BARBARY COAST : NORTH AFRICA :: GOLD COAST : (a. Zimbabwe b. Chad c. South Africa d. Ghana)

51. ENDOCRINOLOGIST : (a. teeth b. eyes c. glands d. intestines) :: DERMATOLOGIST : SKIN

52. STRATFORD-ON-AVON : SHAKESPEARE :: BERDICHEV, UKRAINE : (a. Conrad b. Tolstoy c. Nabokov d. Solzhenitsyn)

53. JULIUS : REPUBLIC :: AUGUSTUS : (a. democracy b. aristocracy c. empire d. monarchy)

54. CORONATION : INAUGURATION :: (a. cardinal b. monarch c. bishop d. pope) : PRESIDENT

55. SAXOPHONE : (a. brass b. woodwind c. percussion d. horn) :: VIOLIN: STRING

56. SONNET : (a. 14 b. 16 c. 18 d. 10) :: HAIKU : THREE

57. KAFKA : SAMSA :: CAMUS : (a. Gregor b. Meursault c. *The Stranger* d. Franz)

58. APHRODITE : VENUS :: ZEUS : (a. Apollo b. Hecate c. Jupiter d. Mercury)

59. MICHELANGELO : LEONARDO :: (a. Dali b. Goya c. Cassatt d. Monet) : RENOIR

60. BOVARY : FLAUBERT :: CHATTERLY : (a. D.H. Lawrence b. V.S. Naipaul c. E.M. Forester d. Wyndham Lewis)

61. ELEANOR ROOSEVELT : FDR :: CLYTAEMNESTRA : (a. Lysistrata b. Antigone c. Agammemnon d. Caligula)

62. THATCHER : MAJOR :: AUGUSTUS : (a. Claudius b. Julius c. Tiberius d. Nero)

63. K2 : EVEREST :: (a. Australia b. Africa c. Antarctica d. South America) : ASIA

64. TWAIN : CLEMENS :: (a. Eliot b. Dennisen c. Woolf d. Sand) : EVANS

65. VAN GOGH : *LUST FOR LIFE* :: (a. Frost b. Dali c. Bukowski d. Kerouac) : *BARFLY*

66. BYRON : ROMANTICISM :: (a. Melville b. Salinger c. Eliot d. Shelley) : TRANSCENDENTALISM

67. DEMOCRACY : CITIZENRY :: THEOCRACY : (a. church b. state c. populace d. monarch)

68. URSINE : BEAR :: CERVINE : (a. deer b. reptile c. fowl d. mule)

69. POSITIVE : NEGATIVE :: SHARP : (a. tone b. flat c. bass d. treble)

70. CONSTANTINE : CHRISTIANITY :: ASOKA : (a. Taoism b. Jainism c. Hinduism d. Buddhism)

71. FIBULA : TIBIA :: RADIUS : (a. sternum b. ulna c. femur d. mandibular)

72. CLAUSTRO : CLOSED SPACES :: (a. geno b. hydro c. mastigo d. xeno) : STRANGERS

73. MARAT : SADE :: JEFFERSON : (a. Robespierre b. Thoreau c. Franklin d. Hudson)

74. $\pi r^2$ : AREA :: $2\pi r$ : (a. circumference b. width c. volume d. depth)

75. CALORIE : (a. pressure b. volume c. heat d. force) :: ACRE : AREA

76. SUNUNU : (a. Bush b. Reagan c. Meese d. Ford) :: PANETTA : CLINTON

77. Ag : SILVER :: Fe : (a. magnesium b. fermium c. iron d. zinc)

78. PLATO : THE ACADEMY :: GROPIUS : (a. Bauhaus b. Citadel c. Cambridge d. Montessori)

79. GODDARD : ROCKET :: BABBAGE: (a. Xerox b. fountain pen
    c. computer d. electric typewriter)

80. NILE : AFRICA :: (a. Yangtze b. Hwang Ho c. Yellow d. Ashikaga)
    : CHINA

81. LIVY : POLIO :: TURNER : (a. Limerick b. Influenza c. Prescott
    d. Moffit)

82. MAORI : NEW ZEALAND :: YANOMAMI : (a. Argentina b. Egypt
    c. Micronesia d. Brazil)

83. PLANCK : (a. rocketry b. physics c. quantum physics d. calculus) ::
    EUCLID : GEOMETRY

84. PLUTO : HADES :: (a. Vulcan b. Frigg c. Loki d. Isis) :
    HEPHAESTUS

85. MONTICELLO : (a. Adams b. Franklin c. Jackson d. Jefferson) ::
    FALLING WATER : WRIGHT

86. PRADO : (a. Rome b. Madrid c. Sante Fe d. Prague) ::
    GUGGENHEIM : NEW YORK

87. FRANKLIN : AMERICA :: (a. Goethe b. Baudelaire c. Corbiseur
    d. Voltaire) : FRANCE

88. CONRAD : (a. Scotland b. England c. Ukraine d. Ireland) :: TWAIN
    : UNITED STATES

89. PHILATELIST : STAMPS :: LEPIDOPTERIST : (a. minerals
    b. butterflies c. coins d. clocks)

90. GEORGE BUSH : RONALD REAGAN :: ANDREW JOHNSON :
    (a. John Q. Adams b. Abe Lincoln c. Rutherford Hayes
    d. Andrew Jackson)

91. HINDI : INDIA :: (a. Spanish b. English c. Portuguese d. French) :
    PERU

92. RUPEE : INDIA :: LIRA : (a. Egypt b. Greece c. Italy d. Spain)

93. BIBLIOPHILE : (a. bibles b. religion c. books d. music) :: ANGLO-PHILE : ENGLAND

94. SLEUTH : (a. zebras b. horses c. worms d. bears) :: GAGGLE : GEESE

95. GYNOPHOBE : WOMAN :: ANDROPHOBE : (a. man b. homo-sexuals c. germs d. animals)

96. REFLECT : ABSORB :: CONVEX : (a. bend b. scatter c. converge d. concave)

97. SRI LANKA : CEYLON :: (a. Zimbabwe b. Zaire c. Ghana d. Uru-guay) : BELGIAN CONGO

98. MELODIOUS : CACOPHONOUS :: (a. dry b. petulant c. sweet d. succulent) : ARID

99. 2 : 8 :: 4 : (a. 12 b. 17 c. 64 d. 24)

100. AVIARY : BIRDS :: FORMICARY : (a. fish b. reptiles c. insects d. ants)

# Practice Test 1

## ANSWER KEY

| | | | |
|---|---|---|---|
| 1. (a) | 26. (c) | 51. (c) | 76. (a) |
| 2. (a) | 27. (b) | 52. (a) | 77. (c) |
| 3. (c) | 28. (d) | 53. (c) | 78. (a) |
| 4. (b) | 29. (c) | 54. (b) | 79. (c) |
| 5. (a) | 30. (a) | 55. (b) | 80. (a) |
| 6. (c) | 31. (d) | 56. (a) | 81. (c) |
| 7. (d) | 32. (c) | 57. (b) | 82. (d) |
| 8. (c) | 33. (c) | 58. (c) | 83. (c) |
| 9. (a) | 34. (b) | 59. (d) | 84. (a) |
| 10. (d) | 35. (a) | 60. (a) | 85. (d) |
| 11. (b) | 36. (c) | 61. (c) | 86. (b) |
| 12. (d) | 37. (d) | 62. (c) | 87. (d) |
| 13. (d) | 38. (a) | 63. (b) | 88. (c) |
| 14. (a) | 39. (b) | 64. (a) | 89. (b) |
| 15. (b) | 40. (c) | 65. (c) | 90. (b) |
| 16. (a) | 41. (c) | 66. (a) | 91. (a) |
| 17. (c) | 42. (c) | 67. (a) | 92. (c) |
| 18. (b) | 43. (b) | 68. (a) | 93. (c) |
| 19. (c) | 44. (d) | 69. (b) | 94. (d) |
| 20. (a) | 45. (b) | 70. (d) | 95. (a) |
| 21. (d) | 46. (d) | 71. (b) | 96. (d) |
| 22. (a) | 47. (a) | 72. (d) | 97. (b) |
| 23. (d) | 48. (a) | 73. (c) | 98. (d) |
| 24. (b) | 49. (b) | 74. (a) | 99. (c) |
| 25. (c) | 50. (d) | 75. (c) | 100. (d) |

# DETAILED EXPLANATIONS
# OF ANSWERS

1. **(a)**    (a) is correct because Pomona is the Roman goddess of fruits as Minerva is the Roman goddess of the Arts and knowledge. (b) is incorrect because Flaura is the Roman goddess of flowers. (c) is incorrect because Gaia is the Greek goddess of the Earth. (d) is incorrect because Demeter, who is a goddess of fruits, is Greek, not Roman.

2. **(a)**    (a) is correct because a vixen is a female fox as a heifer is a female bovine. (b) is incorrect because a gander is a male goose. (c) is incorrect because a bitch is a female dog. (d) is incorrect because an ewe is a female sheep.

3. **(c)**    (c) is correct because Chicago's international airport is named O'Hare, as Canada's international airport is named Halifax. (a) is incorrect because New York is home to JFK and Laguardia international airports. (b) is incorrect because Ireland's international airport is Belfast. (d) is incorrect because England's international airport is Heathrow.

4. **(b)**    (b) is correct because Roy Cohn defended Joseph McCarthy as Clarence Darrow defended John Scopes. (a) is incorrect because F. Lee Bailey is famous for defending the Boston Strangler. (c) is incorrect because Lionel Hutz is a fictional attorney. (d) is incorrect because Barry Slotnick is famous for defending Bernhard Goetz.

5. **(a)**    (a) is correct because Wilson is Ronald Reagan's middle name as Earl is Jimmy Carter's. (b) is incorrect because Milhous is the middle name of Richard Nixon. (c) is incorrect because Baines is the middle name of Lyndon Johnson. (d) is incorrect because Herbert is the middle name of George Bush.

6. **(c)**    (c) is correct because Sean is a form of John as Betty is a form of Elizabeth. (a) is incorrect because Jeremy is a form of Henry. (b) is incorrect because Geoff is the German form of Jeffrey. (d) is incorrect because James is a Latin form of Jacob.

7. **(d)**    (d) is correct because Reuters and Press Association are based in London, just as United Press International and Associated Press are based in New York. (a) is incorrect because Courier is not an English

news service. (b) is incorrect because IPS (International Press Service) is based in Rome. (c) is incorrect because AT&T is an American telecommunications firm.

8. **(c)** (c) is correct because Buckeye is the nickname for Ohio just as Empire is the nickname for New York. (a) is incorrect because Tar heel is the nickname for North Carolina. (b) is incorrect because Garden is the nickname for New Jersey. (d) is incorrect because Sunshine is the nickname for Florida.

9. **(a)** (a) is correct because Magyar is the main language of Hungary just as Gaelic is the main language of Ireland. (b) is incorrect because Mandarin and Cantonese are the main languages of China. (c) is incorrect because Malagasy is the main language of Madagascar. (d) is incorrect because Arabic is the official language of Morocco.

10. **(d)** (d) is correct because the Arabian Desert is the second largest desert to the Sahara as Greenland is the second largest island to Australia. (a) is incorrect because Gobi is the third largest desert. (b) is incorrect because Mojave is the sixth largest. (c) is incorrect because Patagonia is the fourth.

11. **(b)** (b) is correct because the Coral Sea is the largest sea with the Arabian Sea being the second largest, just as Superior is the second largest lake to the Caspian Sea (actually a lake). (a) is incorrect because the Mediterranean is the fourth largest sea. (c) is incorrect because the Bering is the fifth largest sea. (d) is incorrect because the North is the twenty-second largest sea.

12. **(d)** (d) is correct because the Arctic Ocean is the smallest and the Pacific Ocean is the largest as Mercury is the smallest planet and Jupiter is the largest. (a) is incorrect because the Atlantic is the second largest ocean. (b) is incorrect because the Indian is the third largest ocean. (c) is incorrect because there is no Antarctic Ocean.

13. **(d)** (d) is correct because a cygnet is a baby swan just as a calf is a baby whale. (a) is incorrect because a foal is a baby horse. (b) is incorrect because a fawn is a baby deer. (c) is incorrect because a chick is a baby chicken.

14. **(a)** (a) is correct because Dover is the capital of Delaware just as Tallahassee is the capital of Florida. (b) is incorrect because while Newark

is a major city in both Delaware and New Jersey, it is the capital of neither state. (c) is incorrect because Concord is the capital of New Hampshire. (d) is incorrect because Annapolis is the capital of Maryland.

15. **(b)**    (b) is correct because Justinian was the greatest ruler of Byzantium just as Augustus was the greatest ruler of Rome. (a) is incorrect because Philip was the greatest ruler of Macedonia. (c) is incorrect because the greatest ruler of Athens was Pericles. (d) is incorrect because the greatest ruler of the Frankish kingdom was Clovis I.

16. **(a)**    (a) is correct because Zora Neale Hurston and Langston Hughes both emerged from the Harlem Renaissance just as Ginsberg and Kerouac both emerged from the Beat Movement. (b) and (c) are incorrect because both Alice Walker and Toni Morrison were born after the Harlem Renaissance. (d) is incorrect because Harper Lee was not part of the Harlem Renaissance.

17. **(c)**    (c) is correct because the Galapagos Islands belong to Ecuador just as the Azores belong to Portugal. (a) is incorrect because the major island group of Greece is the Cyclades. (b) is incorrect because the major island group of Italy is the Aeloian. (d) is incorrect because the main island group of India is Andaman.

18. **(b)**    (b) is correct because Columbus was the first non-indigenous person to land in the Caribbean Islands just as Marco Polo was the first European to journey to China. (a) is incorrect because the first non-indigenous person to land in North America was Leif Erikson. (c) is incorrect because Cortez was the first European to land in Central America. (d) is incorrect because Cook was the first European to land in the Pacific Islands.

19. **(c)**    (c) is correct because 1861 marked the emancipation of Russian serfs just as 1865 marked the emancipation of American slaves. (a) is incorrect because the French Revolution occurred in 1789. (b) is incorrect because the American purchase of Alaska occurred in 1867. (d) is incorrect because the Eighteenth Amendment was passed in 1920.

20. **(a)**    (a) is correct because Lincoln died in 1865 just as Washington died in 1799. (b) is incorrect because Buchanan died in 1868. (c) is incorrect because McKinley died in 1901. (d) is incorrect because Arthur died in 1886.

21. **(d)**    (d) is correct because parallels are another name for lines of latitude as meridians are another name for lines of longitude. (a) is incorrect because line is a general term and could apply to either longitude or latitude. (b) is incorrect because equator refers to a specific line of latitude. (c) is incorrect because degrees are a measurement of longitude and latitude.

22. **(a)**    (a) is correct because just as Leibniz was a rationalist, Locke was an empiricist. (b) is incorrect because atomism refers to the belief that all matter is composed of atoms. (c) is incorrect because an idealist believes the external world is a creation of the mind. (d) is incorrect because phenomenology refers to a method of inquiry in which one closely inspects one's own thought processes.

23. **(d)**    (d) is correct because just as a bird expert is an ornithologist, a fish expert is an ichthyologist. (a) is incorrect because a cancer expert is called an oncologist. (b) is incorrect because a numismatist is a currency expert. (c) is incorrect because a metalurgist is an expert in metals.

24. **(b)**    (b) is correct because just as Gustave Eiffel designed the Eiffel Tower, Frank Lloyd Wright designed the Guggenheim Museum. (a) is incorrect because while the museum bears his name, he was not the designer of the building. (c) is incorrect; Walter Gropius was the leader and designer of the Bauhaus School. (d) is incorrect because Egon Schiele is an artist, not an architect.

25. **(c)**    (c) is correct because one standard pound is equal to 16 oz. just as one troy pound is equal to 12 oz. All other measurements, (a), (b), and (d), are irrelevant.

26. **(c)**    (c) is correct because as a chronometer measures time, an anemometer measures wind speed. (a) is incorrect because a scale measures weight. (b) is incorrect because a barometer measures atmospheric pressure. (d) is incorrect because an odometer measures distance.

27. **(b)**    (b) is the correct answer. All of the others, (a), (c), and (d), are irrelevant.

28. **(d)**    (d) is the correct answer because English has 460 million speakers worldwide and Spanish has approximately 357 million speakers globally. Choices (a), (b), and (c) are irrelevant.

29. **(c)**     (c) is correct because as farming is a primary economic activity, manufacturing is a secondary economic activity. (a) is incorrect because service activity is a tertiary economic activity. (b) is incorrect because information and research involves a quarternary economic activity. (d) is incorrect because mining is a primary economic activity.

30. **(a)**     (a) is correct because Donatello was known for his bronze sculpture as Dürer was known for his copper engravings. (b), (c), and (d) are incorrect because Dürer did not work in these media.

31. **(d)**     (d) is correct because Buonarroti is the little used last name of Michelangelo as Van Rijn is the less known last name of Rembrandt. (a) is incorrect because Donatello was the name of an Italian sculptor. (b) is incorrect because Edvard Munch was a twentieth century Norwegian expressionist painter. (c) is incorrect because Roy Lichtenstein was a twentieth century American pop artist.

32. **(c)**     (c) is correct because a group of turkeys is called a rafter just as a group of lions is called a pride. (a) is incorrect because gaggle refers to a group of geese. (b) is incorrect because a flock is a generic term for a group of birds. (d) is incorrect because herd refers to a group of cattle.

33. **(c)**     (c) is correct because business is a collective term for ferrets as swarm is a collective term for bees. (a) is incorrect because bears gather in sleuths. (b) is incorrect because a group of eagles is called a convocation. (d) is incorrect because a collective term for elks is gang.

34. **(b)**     (b) is correct because Terpsichore was the Muse of dance as Erato was the Muse of love. (a) is incorrect because Urania was the Muse of astronomy. (c) is incorrect because Euterpe was the Muse of music. (d) is incorrect because Calliope was the Muse of poetry.

35. **(a)**     (a) is correct because Lakota is the name of a tribe in a confederation of tribes called the Sioux nation as the Mohawk tribe is a member of the Iroquois confederation. Choices (b), (c), and (d) are not part of the Iroquois confederation.

36. **(c)**     (c) is correct because *Wealth of Nations* is Smith's most famous work, as *Common Sense* is Thomas Paine's most famous work. (a) is incorrect because *Civil Disobedience* was penned by Henry David Thoreau. (b) is incorrect because *Origin of Species* was written by Charles Darwin. (d) is wrong because *Poor Richard's Almanac* was written by Benjamin Franklin.

37. **(d)**     (d) is the correct answer because a newton is a unit of force just as hertz is a unit of frequency. (a) is incorrect because a joule is a unit of energy. (b) is incorrect because a tesla is a unit of magnetic flux density. (c) is incorrect because a watt is a unit of power.

38. **(a)**     (a) is correct because cotton is given for the second anniversary gift as paper is given for the first. (b) is incorrect because leather is given for the third anniversary. (c) is incorrect because linen is given for the fourth. (d) is incorrect because crystal is given for the fifteenth.

39. **(b)**     (b) is correct because temporal and occipital are lobes (sections) of the brain as the ventricle and auricle are chambers of the heart. (a) is incorrect because the pylorus is the lower section of the stomach. (c) is incorrect because thoracic is the section of vertebrae between the neck and the abdomen. (d) is incorrect because a nevus is a birthmark.

40. **(c)**     (c) is correct because the skin is the largest of the organs, just as the femur is the largest of the bones of the skeleton. (a), (b), and (d) are incorrect because these are not the largest of the body's organs.

41. **(c)**     (c) is the correct response because just as a barometer measures atmospheric pressure, a galvanometer measures electrical currents. (a) is incorrect because an anemometer measures wind speed. (b) is incorrect because a bolometer measures small amounts of radiant energy. (d) is incorrect because a densitometer measures the thickness or darkness of film.

42. **(c)**     (c) is correct because John Fitch invented the first American steamboat as Alexander Bell invented the telephone. (a) is incorrect because Humphrey Davy invented the miner's lamp. (b) is incorrect because John Deere invented the steel plowshare. (d) is incorrect because Robert Fulton was erroneously credited with inventing the first steamboat. He actually improved upon Fitch's model.

43. **(b)**     (b) is correct because marble and limestone are both sedimentary rocks, just as amethyst and opal are both forms of quartz. (a) is incorrect because loam is a type of soil. (c) is incorrect because lava is molten rock. (d) is incorrect because obsidian is a glass that results from molten rock.

44. **(d)**     (d) is the correct response because soap is basic while lemons are acidic; acids and bases are two forms of chemical composition classification. (a) is incorrect because vinegar is acetic acid. (b) is incorrect be-

cause aspirin is acetylsalicylic acid. (c) is incorrect because batteries are usually composed of sulfuric acid.

45. **(b)**   (b) is correct because a negatively charged ion is called an anion, just as a positively charged ion is called a cation. (a) is incorrect because a neutron is an uncharged particle. (c) is incorrect because a proton is a positively charged particle that exists in the atomic nucleus. (d) is incorrect because an electron is a negatively charged particle that orbits the atomic nucleus.

46. **(d)**   (d) is correct because just as 0° latitude is also known as the equator, 23.5° north latitude is called the tropic of Cancer. (a) is incorrect because the prime meridian is 0° longitude. (b) is incorrect because the tropic of Capricorn lies at 23.5° south latitude. (c) is incorrect because the middle latitudes refers to the area between the tropics and their respective polar circles.

47. **(a)**   (a) is the correct response because a sphygmomanometer is an instrument used by a doctor (to measure blood pressure) just as a compass is an instrument used by a navigator. (b), (c), and (d) are incorrect because these occupations would have no use for this instrument.

48. **(a)**   (a) is correct because a cartographer (a map expert) is a more specific type of geographer, just as an arachnologist (a spider expert) is a more specific type of entomologist (insect expert). (b) is incorrect because a geologist studies rocks and minerals. (c) is incorrect because an archaeologist studies past civilizations and the history of humankind. (d) is incorrect because a botanist studies plants.

49. **(b)**   (b) is correct because the *Spirit of St. Louis* is the plane in which Charles Lindbergh made his first trans-Atlantic flight, as the *Santa-Maria* is Pinedo's trans-Atlantic plane. (a) Richard Byrd is incorrect because his plane was the *America*. (c) Chamberlain's plane was the *Columbia*. (d) Reed's plane was the *Lame Duck*.

50. **(d)**   (d) is correct because Ghana was formerly called the Gold Coast as most of Northern Africa was called the Barbary Coast. (a) is incorrect because Zimbabwe was formerly known as Rhodesia. (b) is incorrect because Chad is part of the Central African Republic. (c) is incorrect because South Africa was formerly called the Union of South Africa by the Boers who colonized it.

51. **(c)**  (c) is correct because glands are the speciality of an endocrinologist as the skin is the area of specialization for the dermatologist. (a) is incorrect because a specialist dealing with teeth is an orthodontist. (b) is incorrect because a specialist dealing with eyes is an ophthalmologist. (d) is incorrect because a specialist dealing with intestines is a gastroenterologist.

52. **(a)**  (a) is correct because Conrad was born in Berdichev just as Shakespeare was born in Stratford-on-Avon. (b) is incorrect because Tolstoy was born in Yasnaya Polyana, Russia. (c) is incorrect because Vladimir Nabokov was born in St. Petersburg, Russia. (d) is incorrect because Solzhenitsyn was born in Kislovodsk, Russia.

53. **(c)**  (c) is correct because Augustus was the first emperor following the decline of Julius' Republic. (a), (b), and (d) are incorrect because technically none of these forms of government existed during Rome's Golden Age.

54. **(b)**  (b) is correct because a coronation is the ceremony during which a monarch receives a crown just as an inauguration is the induction ceremony for a president. (a), (c), and (d) are incorrect because all of the induction ceremonies are religiously based, not political.

55. **(b)**  (b) is correct because a saxophone belongs to the family of instruments known as woodwinds just as the violin belongs to the family of instruments known as the stringed instruments. (a) is incorrect because brass instruments do not use a reed, as does the saxophone. (c) is incorrect because percussion instruments, such as drums, are struck to produce sounds. (d) is incorrect because horn is a general term for any breath-propelled instruments.

56. **(a)**  (a) is correct because there are 14 lines in a sonnet and three in a haiku. (b), (c), and (d) are irrelevant.

57. **(b)**  (b) is the correct answer because Meursault is the last name of the main character in Albert Camus' famous novel *The Stranger*. (a) is incorrect because Gregor is the first name of Kafka's main character Samsa, in the novel *The Metamorphosis*. (c) is incorrect because it is the title of Camus' famous novel, not the character. (d) is incorrect because Franz is Kafka's first name.

58. **(c)**    (c) is the correct answer because Aphrodite is the Roman name for the Greek goddess Venus and Zeus is the Roman name for the Greek god Jupiter. (a) is incorrect because Apollo is a Roman, not Greek, god. (b) is incorrect because Hecate is the goddess of witchcraft. (d) is incorrect because Mercury is the Greek name for Hermes.

59. **(d)**    (d) is correct because just as Michelangelo and Leonardo were both Renaissance artists, Monet and Renoir were both impressionist paint-ers. (a) is incorrect because Dali was a surrealist, not an impressionist. (b) is incorrect because Goya was a nineteenth century artist known for his bleak outlook and imagery. (c) is incorrect because Cassatt was an impressionist.

60. **(a)**    (a) is correct because D.H. Lawrence was the author of *Lady Chatterly's Lover*, whose main character was Lady Chatterly, and Ma-dame Bovary was the main character of Gustave Flaubert's novel of the same name. (b) is incorrect because V.S. Naipaul was a post-colonial author and not the author of *Lady Chatterly's Lover*. (c) is incorrect be-cause, although E.M. Forester was a contemporary of Lawrence's, he did not write *Lady Chatterly's Lover*. (d) is incorrect because Wyndham Lewis, also a contemporary of Lawrence's, did not write the novel either.

61. **(c)**    (c) is the correct answer because Clytaemnestra and Agam-memnon were husband and wife as were Eleanor and Franklin Roosevelt. (a) is incorrect because *Lysistrata* is a work by Aristophanes. (b) is incor-rect because *Antigone* was a drama written by Sophocles. (d) is incorrect because Caligula was a Roman emperor, not a fictional character.

62. **(c)**    (c) is correct because Tiberius succeeded Augustus as emperor of Rome as John Major succeeded Margaret Thatcher as prime minister of England. (a) is incorrect because Claudius was the third Roman emperor after Augustus. (b) is incorrect because Julius was emperor before Augustus. (d) is incorrect because Nero was the fourth emperor following Augustus.

63. **(b)**    (b) is correct because K2 is the second tallest mountain to Everest as Africa is the second largest continent to Asia. (a) is incorrect because Australia, part of Oceania, is not the second largest continent; it is the smallest. (c) is incorrect because Antarctica is the fifth largest conti-nent. (d) is incorrect because South America is the fourth largest conti-nent.

64. **(a)**    (a) is correct because George Eliot was the pen name used by Mary Ann Evans, as Mark Twain was the pseudonym used by Samuel

Clemens. (b) is incorrect because Isak Dennisen's real name is Karen Blixon. (c) is incorrect because Virginia Woolf wrote under her own name. (d) is incorrect because George Sand was the pseudonym for Amandine-Aurore-Lucie Dupin.

65. **(c)**     (c) is the correct answer because *Lust for Life* was the biographical movie of Vincent Van Gogh as *Barfly* was the life story of the poet Charles Bukowski. (a) is incorrect because Robert Frost was not the subject of the movie *Barfly*. (b) is incorrect because Salvador Dali was not the subject of the movie *Barfly*. (d) is incorrect because Jack Kerouac was not the subject of the movie *Barfly*.

66. **(a)**     (a) is correct because Byron was part of the Romantic movement in England, and Melville was part of the parallel transcendental movement in the U.S. (b) is incorrect because Salinger was a contemporary American novelist. (c) is incorrect because Eliot was an early twentieth century Christian poet. (d) is incorrect because Shelley was another Romantic poet.

67. **(a)**     (a) is correct because democracy refers to a political system governed through the citizenry. In a theocracy, the church is the government. (b) is incorrect because state rule is characteristic of a totalitarian government. (c) is incorrect because populace is analogous to citizenry. (d) is incorrect because a monarchy is ruled by a royal family.

68. **(a)**     (a) is correct because cervine is the adjective pertaining to the characteristics of a deer. (b) is incorrect because reptilian is the adjective for any classification of reptile. (c) is incorrect because fowl is the noun referring to any of the various birds of the order of Galliformes. (d) is incorrect because a mule cannot be classified as having cervine qualities because it is a hybrid of an ass and a horse.

69. **(b)**     (b) is correct because sharp and flat are opposites as positive and negative are. (a) is incorrect because tone is a general term referring to the pitch, quality, or duration of a sound. (c) is incorrect because bass refers to the lowest musical register of a tone. (d) is incorrect because treble refers to a high pitch.

70. **(d)**     (d) is the correct answer because Asoka converted to Buddhism allowing it to spread throughout India. (a) is incorrect because Taoism is a philosophy based on the teachings of Lao Tsu. (b) is incorrect because Jainism was founded by Vardhamana Maravira in 600 B.C.E. (c) is incorrect because Hinduism already existed in India at the time of Asoka's conversion.

71. **(b)**     (b) is the correct answer because the ulna is the corollary to the radius in the arm as the fibula is the correlative bone to the tibia in the leg. (a) is incorrect because sternum is the center bone of the rib cage. (c) is incorrect because the femur, the longest bone in the body, is found in the thigh, not the arm. (d) is incorrect because the mandibular is the jawbone.

72. **(d)**     (d) is correct because xeno- is the prefix for people. (a) is incorrect because geno- is the prefix for sex. (b) is incorrect because hydro- is the prefix for water. (c) is incorrect because mastigo- is the prefix for flogging.

73. **(c)**     (c) is correct because Thomas Jefferson and Benjamin Franklin were political contemporaries in the New World, as were Jean Paul Marat and the Marquis de Sade during the French Revolution. (a) is incorrect because Robespierre was a French Revolutionary. (b) is incorrect because Thoreau was a transcendentalist poet. (d) is incorrect because Henry Hudson was a New World explorer.

74. **(a)**     (a) is correct because $\pi r^2$ is the formula for the area of a circle and $2\pi r$ is the formula for circumference. (b) is incorrect because width is also known as the diameter of a circle. (c) is incorrect because it refers to a three dimensional object. (d) is incorrect because it also refers to a three-dimensional object.

75. **(c)**     (c) is correct because a calorie is a unit of heat as an acre is a unit of measurement for area. (a) is incorrect because pressure is measured in p.s.i. (pounds per square inch). (b) is incorrect because the volume of an object refers to its internal capacity. (d) is incorrect because force is measured in foot-pounds.

76. **(a)**     (a) is the correct answer because John Sununu was Chief of Staff during George Bush's presidency as Leon Panetta was Chief of Staff during Bill Clinton's first term. (b) is incorrect because John Sununu was not Ronald Reagan's Chief of Staff, Edwin Meese was. (c) is incorrect because Edwin Meese was not a president. (d) is incorrect because John Sununu was not Gerald Ford's Chief of Staff.

77. **(c)**     (c) is correct because the periodic abbreviation for iron is Fe. (a) is incorrect because the periodic abbreviation for magnesium is Mg. (b) is incorrect because the periodic abbreviation for fermium is Fm. (d) is incorrect because the periodic abbreviation for zinc is Zn.

78. **(a)**    (a) is correct because Gropius established the school known as Bauhaus and Plato created the Academy. (b) is incorrect because the Citadel is a United States military institute, not established by Gropius. (c) is incorrect because Cambridge is an English university also not established by Gropius. (d) is incorrect because Montessori, a school of pedagogical method, was not established by Gropius, but by the woman whose name it bears.

79. **(c)**    (c) is correct because Goddard invented the liquid fueled rocket as Babbage invented the computer. (a) is incorrect because Xerox is a trade name for a photo static copier. (b) is incorrect because the fountain pen was invented by Lewis Waterman. (d) is incorrect because the electric typewriter was invented by Thomas A. Edison.

80. **(a)**    (a) is correct because the Nile is the largest river in Africa as the Yangtze is the largest in China. (b) and (c) are incorrect because the Hwang Ho is another name for the Yellow River, which is the second largest river in China. (d) is incorrect because Ashikaga was a Shogun, not a river.

81. **(c)**    (c) is correct because Turner and Prescott were Old Western historians and contemporaries like the ancient Roman historians Livy and Polio. (a) is incorrect because Patricia Limerick is a contemporary historian, considered among the New Western historians. (b) is incorrect because influenza is a disease, not a historian. (d) is incorrect because Moffit is a contemporary New Jersey historian and anthropologist.

82. **(d)**    (d) is correct because an indigenous tribe, known as the Yanomami, reside in the Brazilian rain forests. (a) is incorrect because although Argentina is a South American country, it is not home to the Yanomami tribe. (b) is incorrect because the Yanomami do not live in Egypt. (c) is incorrect because the Yanomami do not live in Micronesia.

83. **(c)**    (c) is correct because Planck is considered the father of quantum physics as Euclid is considered the father of geometry. (a) is incorrect because Goddard is known to be the founding theorist of rocketry. (b) is incorrect because Newton is considered the father of the study of physics. (d) is incorrect because Pascal invented the discipline known as calculus.

84. **(a)**    (a) Pluto is the Roman equivalent of Hades, the Greek god of the underworld, just as Vulcan is the Roman equivalent of the Hephaestus, the Greek god of fire and craftspersonship. (b) is incorrect because Frigg

is the Norse goddess of marriage. (c) is incorrect because Loki is the Norse god of mischief. (d) is incorrect because Isis is the Egyptian queen of the gods.

85. **(d)** (d) is correct because Monticello was established by Thomas Jefferson, as Falling Water was established by Frank Lloyd Wright. (a) is incorrect because John Adams had nothing to do with Monticello. (b) is incorrect because although Benjamin Franklin was a contemporary of Jefferson, he resided in Philadelphia, not Virginia, home to Monticello. (c) is incorrect because Andrew Jackson did not have any association with Monticello.

86. **(b)** (b) is correct because the Prado museum is located in Madrid, Spain. (a) is incorrect because Rome, although full of museums, does not house the Prado. (c) is incorrect because the Prado is not located in Sante Fe, New Mexico. (d) is incorrect because the Prado is not located in Prague, in the Czech Republic.

87. **(d)** (d) is correct because Voltaire is considered the leading French Enlightenment theorist, similar to his American Enlightenment counterpart, Benjamin Franklin. (a) is incorrect because Goethe was a German author. (b) is incorrect because Baudelaire was a French symbolist poet. (c) is incorrect because Corbiseur was an architect.

88. **(c)** (c) is correct because Joseph Conrad was born in Ukraine as Mark Twain was born in the United States. (a) is incorrect because Conrad was not born in Scotland. (b) is incorrect because Conrad was not born in England. (d) is incorrect because Conrad was not born in Ireland.

89. **(b)** (b) is correct because a collector of butterflies is known as a lepidopterist, whereas a collector of stamps is known as a philatelist. (a) is incorrect because a connoisseur of minerals and gems is a lapidist. (c) is incorrect because a numismatist collects coins and (d) is incorrect because a collector of clocks is called a chronometist.

90. **(b)** (b) is correct because Andrew Johnson was Abe Lincoln's vice president as George Bush was Ronald Reagan's. (a) is incorrect because Adams was never vice president. (c) is incorrect because Hayes was never vice president. (d) is incorrect because Jackson was never vice president.

91. **(a)** (a) is correct because Spanish is the main language of Peru as Hindi is of India. (b), (c), and (d) are incorrect because although these

languages are spoken throughout the world none of them are the official language of Peru.

92. **(c)**    (c) is correct because Italy's basic monetary unit is the lira, as the rupee is the basic monetary unit of India. (a) is incorrect because Egypt's monetary unit is based on the Egyptian pound. (b) is incorrect because the drachma is Greece's basic monetary unit. (d) is incorrect because Spain uses the peseta as its basic monetary unit.

93. **(c)**    (c) is correct because bibliophiles have an interest in books as Anglophiles have an interest in England. (a) is incorrect because a bible is a type of book a bibliophile may collect. (b) is incorrect because a theologian would study or have a love of religion. (d) is incorrect because audiophiles have an interest in music.

94. **(d)**    (d) is correct because bears gather in sleuths as geese fly in gaggles. (a) and (b) are incorrect because both zebra and horses gather in herds. (c) is incorrect because the collective term for worms is a clew.

95. **(a)**    (a) is correct because men are feared by androphobes as women are feared by gynophobes. (b) is incorrect because homophobia is the fear of homosexuals. (c) is incorrect because spermaphobia is the fear of germs. (d) is incorrect because zoophobia is a fear of animals.

96. **(d)**    (d) is correct because concave and convex are opposite lens shapes, as they curve in and out, respectively. Reflect and absorb are opposite reactions of light on a surface. (a) is incorrect because light that is bent is said to be refracted. (b) is incorrect because scattered refers to a haphazard arrangement of light. (c) is incorrect because converge refers to light rays coming together.

97. **(b)**    (b) is correct because Zaire is the new name of the region formerly known as the Belgian Congo as Ceylon is the former name of Sri Lanka. (a) is incorrect because Zimbabwe is a country in Africa. (c) is incorrect because Ghana is a North African country. (d) is incorrect because Uruguay is a South American country.

98. **(d)**    (d) is correct because succulent, filled with water, is the opposite of arid, void of water. Melodious is full harmony, whereas cacophonous refers to discordant sound. (a) is incorrect because dry is a synonym for arid. (b) is incorrect because petulant refers to something or someone ill-tempered. (c) is incorrect because sweet refers to having a sugary taste.

99. **(c)**   (c) is the correct response because 4 is the cube root of 64 just as 2 is the cube root of 8. All other responses are incorrect.

100. **(d)**   (d) is the correct response because just as birds are kept in an aviary, another name for an ant farm is a formicary. (a) is incorrect because fish are kept in an aquarium. (b) and (c) are incorrect because insects and reptiles are kept in a terrarium.

# MAT – Practice Test 2 Answer Sheet

1. ⓐ ⓑ ⓒ ⓓ
2. ⓐ ⓑ ⓒ ⓓ
3. ⓐ ⓑ ⓒ ⓓ
4. ⓐ ⓑ ⓒ ⓓ
5. ⓐ ⓑ ⓒ ⓓ
6. ⓐ ⓑ ⓒ ⓓ
7. ⓐ ⓑ ⓒ ⓓ
8. ⓐ ⓑ ⓒ ⓓ
9. ⓐ ⓑ ⓒ ⓓ
10. ⓐ ⓑ ⓒ ⓓ
11. ⓐ ⓑ ⓒ ⓓ
12. ⓐ ⓑ ⓒ ⓓ
13. ⓐ ⓑ ⓒ ⓓ
14. ⓐ ⓑ ⓒ ⓓ
15. ⓐ ⓑ ⓒ ⓓ
16. ⓐ ⓑ ⓒ ⓓ
17. ⓐ ⓑ ⓒ ⓓ
18. ⓐ ⓑ ⓒ ⓓ
19. ⓐ ⓑ ⓒ ⓓ
20. ⓐ ⓑ ⓒ ⓓ
21. ⓐ ⓑ ⓒ ⓓ
22. ⓐ ⓑ ⓒ ⓓ
23. ⓐ ⓑ ⓒ ⓓ
24. ⓐ ⓑ ⓒ ⓓ
25. ⓐ ⓑ ⓒ ⓓ
26. ⓐ ⓑ ⓒ ⓓ
27. ⓐ ⓑ ⓒ ⓓ
28. ⓐ ⓑ ⓒ ⓓ
29. ⓐ ⓑ ⓒ ⓓ
30. ⓐ ⓑ ⓒ ⓓ
31. ⓐ ⓑ ⓒ ⓓ
32. ⓐ ⓑ ⓒ ⓓ
33. ⓐ ⓑ ⓒ ⓓ
34. ⓐ ⓑ ⓒ ⓓ

35. ⓐ ⓑ ⓒ ⓓ
36. ⓐ ⓑ ⓒ ⓓ
37. ⓐ ⓑ ⓒ ⓓ
38. ⓐ ⓑ ⓒ ⓓ
39. ⓐ ⓑ ⓒ ⓓ
40. ⓐ ⓑ ⓒ ⓓ
41. ⓐ ⓑ ⓒ ⓓ
42. ⓐ ⓑ ⓒ ⓓ
43. ⓐ ⓑ ⓒ ⓓ
44. ⓐ ⓑ ⓒ ⓓ
45. ⓐ ⓑ ⓒ ⓓ
46. ⓐ ⓑ ⓒ ⓓ
47. ⓐ ⓑ ⓒ ⓓ
48. ⓐ ⓑ ⓒ ⓓ
49. ⓐ ⓑ ⓒ ⓓ
50. ⓐ ⓑ ⓒ ⓓ
51. ⓐ ⓑ ⓒ ⓓ
52. ⓐ ⓑ ⓒ ⓓ
53. ⓐ ⓑ ⓒ ⓓ
54. ⓐ ⓑ ⓒ ⓓ
55. ⓐ ⓑ ⓒ ⓓ
56. ⓐ ⓑ ⓒ ⓓ
57. ⓐ ⓑ ⓒ ⓓ
58. ⓐ ⓑ ⓒ ⓓ
59. ⓐ ⓑ ⓒ ⓓ
60. ⓐ ⓑ ⓒ ⓓ
61. ⓐ ⓑ ⓒ ⓓ
62. ⓐ ⓑ ⓒ ⓓ
63. ⓐ ⓑ ⓒ ⓓ
64. ⓐ ⓑ ⓒ ⓓ
65. ⓐ ⓑ ⓒ ⓓ
66. ⓐ ⓑ ⓒ ⓓ
67. ⓐ ⓑ ⓒ ⓓ
68. ⓐ ⓑ ⓒ ⓓ

69. ⓐ ⓑ ⓒ ⓓ
70. ⓐ ⓑ ⓒ ⓓ
71. ⓐ ⓑ ⓒ ⓓ
72. ⓐ ⓑ ⓒ ⓓ
73. ⓐ ⓑ ⓒ ⓓ
74. ⓐ ⓑ ⓒ ⓓ
75. ⓐ ⓑ ⓒ ⓓ
76. ⓐ ⓑ ⓒ ⓓ
77. ⓐ ⓑ ⓒ ⓓ
78. ⓐ ⓑ ⓒ ⓓ
79. ⓐ ⓑ ⓒ ⓓ
80. ⓐ ⓑ ⓒ ⓓ
81. ⓐ ⓑ ⓒ ⓓ
82. ⓐ ⓑ ⓒ ⓓ
83. ⓐ ⓑ ⓒ ⓓ
84. ⓐ ⓑ ⓒ ⓓ
85. ⓐ ⓑ ⓒ ⓓ
86. ⓐ ⓑ ⓒ ⓓ
87. ⓐ ⓑ ⓒ ⓓ
88. ⓐ ⓑ ⓒ ⓓ
89. ⓐ ⓑ ⓒ ⓓ
90. ⓐ ⓑ ⓒ ⓓ
91. ⓐ ⓑ ⓒ ⓓ
92. ⓐ ⓑ ⓒ ⓓ
93. ⓐ ⓑ ⓒ ⓓ
94. ⓐ ⓑ ⓒ ⓓ
95. ⓐ ⓑ ⓒ ⓓ
96. ⓐ ⓑ ⓒ ⓓ
97. ⓐ ⓑ ⓒ ⓓ
98. ⓐ ⓑ ⓒ ⓓ
99. ⓐ ⓑ ⓒ ⓓ
100. ⓐ ⓑ ⓒ ⓓ

# MILLER ANALOGIES

# PRACTICE TEST 2

**TIME:**  50 Minutes
100 Analogies

**DIRECTIONS**: Read each of the following analogies carefully, and choose the BEST answer to each item. Fill in your responses in the answer sheets provided.

1.  PARTHENON : (a. Greece b. Athens c. Paris d. Dresden) :: SISTINE CHAPEL : ROME

2.  $H_2O$ : WATER :: $CO_2$ : (a. carbon dioxide  b. carbon monoxide c. ammonia d. salt)

3.  HENRY DAVID THOREAU : *CIVIL DISOBEDIENCE* :: RALPH WALDO EMERSON : (a. *Self-Reliance* b. *The Tell-Tale Heart* c. *Walden* d. *Leaves of Grass*)

4.  AGGRAVATE : EXACERBATE :: MITIGATE : (a. legislate b. assuage c. abrachiate d. dissociate)

5.  H : HYDROGEN :: Fe : (a. iron b. fluorine c. nickel d. sodium)

6.  (a. Plantae b. Protista c. Chiroptera d. Fungi) : MUSHROOM :: ANIMALIA : MOUSE

7.  FRANK LLOYD WRIGHT : (a. author b. sculptor c. architect d. choreographer) :: MICHELANGELO : PAINTER

8.  HANDEL : *MESSIAH* :: ORFF : (a. *Carmina Burana* b. *Pomp and Circumstance* c. *The Nutcracker Suite* d. *The Rite of Spring*)

9.  BARBARIC : (a. civilized b. savage c. content d. enraged) :: DIVINE : SACRED

10. PRESIDENT : DEMOCRACY :: (a. dictator b. emperor
    c. Parliament d. king) : MONARCHY

11. (a. cylinder b. circle c. triangle d. oval) : SQUARE :: $\pi r^2$ : L × H

12. MULTIPLICATION : DIVISION :: INTEGRATION : (a. substitu-
    tion b. function  c. equation d. derivation)

13. OCTAGON : (a. dodecahedron b. pentagon c. decagon d. polygon) ::
    8 : 12

14. 3, 3 : 9, 9 :: −4, −4 : (a. 16, 16 b. −16, −16 c. 8, 8 d. −8, −8)

15. sin 90 degrees : 1 :: (a. cos 90 degrees b. tan 90 degrees c. cos 180
    degrees d. tan 45 degrees) : 0

16. CRESCENDO : LOUDER :: (a. pianissimo b. fortissimo c. forte
    d. diminuendo) : SOFTER

17. LEONARDO DA VINCI : RENAISSANCE :: REMBRANDT :
    (a. baroque b. classical c. romantic d. impressionist)

18. ADAGIO : (a. largo b. allegretto c. presto d. mezzo-piano :: VIVACE
    : ALLEGRO

19. BEETHOVEN : *EROICA* :: MOZART : (a. *Hebrides Overture*
    b. *Rigoletto* c. *Don Giovanni* d. *Nocturne*)

20. TEMPO : SPEED :: BEAT : (a. metronome b. rhythm c. percussion
    d. meter)

21. *THE GRAPES OF WRATH* : (a. Steinbeck b. Dos Passos c. Hesse
    d. Heller) :: *FOR WHOM THE BELL TOLLS* : HEMINGWAY

22. HISTORY : RICHARD III :: (a. comedy b. romance c. tragedy
    d. fantasy) : ROMEO AND JULIET

23. MARX : COMMUNISM :: MUSSOLINI : (a. nazism b. nationalism
    c. fascism d. socialism)

24. RATIOCINATE : LOGICAL :: (a. deaminate b. fulminate
    c. sophistic d. monarchistic) : IRRATIONAL

25. MAHABHARATA : INDIAN :: GILGAMESH : (a. French
    b. English c. Sumerian d. Roman)

26. PLATO : *REPUBLIC* :: (a. More b. Socrates c. Coleridge d. Huxley)
    : *UTOPIA*

27. HENRY VIII : (a. 1400s b. 1500s c. 1600s d. 1700s) :: MOZART :
    1700s

28. NIGHT : NOCTURNAL :: (a. evening b. morning c. day d. noon) :
    DIURNAL

29. AMERICA'S CUP : (a. soccer b. steeplechase c. yachting d. gymnas-
    tics) :: STANLEY CUP : HOCKEY

30. RIGHT TO KEEP AND BEAR ARMS : SECOND AMENDMENT
    :: RIGHT TO JURY TRIAL : (a. Fourth Amendment b. Fifth
    Amendment c. Sixth Amendment d. Seventh Amendment)

31. NOBEL PEACE PRIZE : MARTIN LUTHER KING, JR. ::
    (a. Nobel Prize in Physics b. Nobel Prize in Chemistry c. Nobel Prize
    in Medicine d. Nobel Prize in Literature) : IRENE JOILET-CURIE

32. NEIL ARMSTRONG : LUNAR LANDING :: CHUCK YEAGER :
    (a. first to break the speed of sound b. first to break the speed of light
    c. first American in space d. first in orbit)

33. IDAHO : ID :: MONTANA : (a. MN b. MO c. MS d. MT)

34. WASHINGTON : UNITED STATES :: (a. Berlin b. Munich
    c. Vienna d. Hamburg) : GERMANY

35. MOSCOW : RUSSIA :: (a. Perth b. Melbourne c. Sydney
    d. Canberra) : AUSTRALIA

36. ABOLITION OF SLAVERY : THIRTEENTH AMENDMENT ::
    WOMEN'S SUFFRAGE : (a. Eighteenth Amendment b. Nineteenth
    Amendment c. Twentieth Amendment d. Thirty-first Amendment)

37. (a. Roosevelt b. Coolidge c. Taft d. Ford) : TRUMAN :: WILSON : HARDING

38. QUANTUM THEORY : (a. Galileo b. Newton c. Planck d. Ramsay) :: RELATIVITY : EINSTEIN

39. WALT WHITMAN : *SONG OF MYSELF* :: NATHANIEL HAWTHORNE : (a. *Rappaccini's Daughter* b. *The Raven* c. *Gulliver's Travels* d. *Billy Budd*)

40. CASSIUS : (a. Polonius b. Laertes c. Brutus d. MacDuff) :: ANTO-NIO : OLIVIA

41. GERSHWIN : *RHAPSODY IN BLUE* :: BERNSTEIN : (a. *Adagio for Strings* b. *Porgy and Bess* c. *The Devil and Daniel Webster* d. *West Side Story*)

42. SOPHOCLES : *OEDIPUS REX* :: EURIPIDES : (a. *Prometheus Bound* b. *Lysistrata* c. *Medea* d. *Antigone*)

43. (a. Anton Chekhov b. Victor Hugo c. Oscar Wilde d. Henrik Ibsen) : *THE THREE SISTERS* :: GEORGE BERNARD SHAW : *SAINT JOAN*

44. KAFKA : *METAMORPHOSIS* :: (a. Coleridge b. Wordsworth c. Eliot d. Stoppard) : *THE WASTE LAND*

45. (a. Aesculapius b. Apollo c. Nike d. Selene) : MEDICINE :: CHAOS : VOID

46. (a. Tyche b. Thanatos c. Nyx d. Athena) : DEATH :: EROS : LOVE

47. MARS : WAR :: (a. Psyche b. Salacia c. Somnus d. Venus) : LOVE

48. CHROM : (a. motion b. color c. disease d. pain) :: DERM : SKIN

49. (a. anti b. aero c. acro d. arch) : TOP :: ANDRO : MAN

50. ETHNO : RACE :: (a. cardio b. crypto c. chrono d. choreo) : DANCE

51. (a. pronoun b. preposition, c. adjective d. article) : NOUN :: AD-VERB : VERB

52. GERMAN SURRENDER : V-E DAY :: JAPANESE SURRENDER : (a. V-J Day b. Bastille Day c. Veteran's Day d. Pearl Harbor Day)

53. LIE : LAY :: LAY : (a. laid b. laying c. lying d. lain)

54. WORK : *W=fd* :: VELOCITY : (a. *v=d/t* b. *V=fw* c. *Wt=mg* d. *R=V/I*)

55. (a. yellow b. red c. green d. indigo) : ORANGE :: BLUE : VIOLET

56. GINSBERG : *HOWL* :: (a. Burroughs b. Kesey c. Kerouac d. DiPrima) : *ON THE ROAD*

57. SYRIA : ASIA :: (a. Panama b. Colombia c. Venezuela d. Ecuador) : NORTH AMERICA

58. HEMI : (a. close b. under c. half d. outside) :: ANTE : BEFORE

59. 1/2 : 50% :: 2/5 : (a. 30% b. 35% c. 40% d. 45%)

60. PHENOTYPE : (a. molecular structure b. physical appearance c. heredity d. natural selection) :: GENOTYPE : GENETIC COMPO-SITION

61. ELECTRON : NEGATIVE :: NEUTRON : (a. positive b. variable c. proton d. none)

62. C : CELSIUS :: (a. F b. f c. fh d. Fh) : FAHRENHEIT

63. OZ : OUNCE :: (a. tsp b. tbsp c. tasp d. pt) : TABLESPOON

64. 32 DEGREES FAHRENHEIT : 0 DEGREES CELSIUS :: (a. 100 degrees Fahrenheit b. 125 degrees Fahrenheit c. 212 degrees Fahrenheit d. 225 degrees Fahrenheit) : 100 DEGREES CELSIUS

65. BASEBALL : 9 :: FOOTBALL : (a. 9 b. 10 c. 11 d. 12)

66. VITAMIN A : CAROTENE :: (a. thiamine b. riboflavin c. niacin d. ascorbic acid) : VITAMIN C

67. FULMINATE : (a. cajole b. denounce c. exemplify d. placate) :: COMMEND : PRAISE

68. UNIX : (a. programming language b. computer system c. operating system d. peripheral) :: FORTRAN : LANGUAGE

69. ROSENCRANTZ : (a. Horatio b. Regan c. Gloucester d. Sebastian) :: DUNCAN : MALCOLM

70. DANTE : *INFERNO* :: (a. Byron b. Milton c. Wordsworth d. Shelley) : *PARADISE LOST*

71. HELLER : *CATCH-22* :: (a. Updike b. Pynchon c. Irving d. Kerouac) : *GRAVITY'S RAINBOW*

72. 8 : (a. 2 b. 4 c. 6 d. 8 ) :: DIAMETER : RADIUS

73. $2^3$ : $3^3$ :: 8 : (a. 18 b. 24 c. 27 d. 36)

74. CAT : KITTEN :: KANGAROO : (a. wallaby b. joey c. cub d. marsupial)

75. EAGLE : (a. feline b. equine c. bovine d. aquiline) :: DOG : CANINE

76. ANTELOPE : HERBIVORE :: OWL : (a. carnivore b. omnivore c. avian d. nocturnal)

77. KENNEDY : JOHNSON :: EISENHOWER : (a. Nixon b. Ford c. Kissinger d. Humphrey)

78. TOKYO : JAPAN :: (a. Tripoli b. Baghdad c. Aden d. Riyadh) : IRAQ

79. (a. Dallas b. Houston c. Fort Worth d. Austin) : TEXAS :: DENVER : COLORADO

80. SALT LAKE CITY : UTAH :: (a. Birmingham b. Huntsville c. Montgomery d. Tuscaloosa) : ALABAMA

81. BECOME : (a. became b. becoming c. becomed d. become) :: SHRINK : SHRANK

82. AURAL : ORAL :: EAR : (a. eyes b. nose c. mouth d. hand)

83. *FLYER* : WRIGHT BROTHERS :: (a. *Beagle* b. Galapagos
    c. Explorer d. *Calypso*) : DARWIN

84. SLOOP : 1 :: BARQUE : (a. 1 b. 2 c. 4 d. 7)

85. ACROPHOBIA : (a. blood b. heights c. food d. death) :: HYDRO-
    PHOBIA : WATER

86. REGICIDE : (a. king b. president c. friend d. child) :: PATRICIDE :
    FATHER

87. (a. feet b. yards c. inches d. meters) : MILE :: 1,760 : 1

88. (a. registration b. license c. patent d. statute) : INVENTION ::
    COPYRIGHT : NOVEL

89. HUMERUS : ARM :: (a. tarsus b. sternum c. clavicle d. femur) : LEG

90. FRONTAL LOBE : (a. touch b. speech c. memory d. hearing) ::
    OCCIPITAL LOBE : VISION

91. (a. teleologist b. theologist c. thanatologist d. zoologist) : NATURE ::
    ICTHYOLOGIST : FISH

92. *BEOWULF* : GRENDEL :: *HAMLET* : (a. Ophelia b. Polonius
    c. Gertrude d. Claudius)

93. CHROMOSOME : (a. gene b. RNA c. DNA d. enzyme) :: CELL :
    NUCLEUS

94. ORWELL : *1984* :: (a. Thoreau b. Emerson c. Burgess d. Huxley) :
    *BRAVE NEW WORLD*

95. (a. Coleridge b. Ibsen c. Tolstoy d. Wordsworth) : *KUBLA KHAN* ::
    YEATS : *SAILING TO BYZANTIUM*

96. SARTRE : (a. *A Streetcar Named Desire* b. *Our Town* c. *The Pur-
    loined Letter* d. *No Exit*) :: JOYCE : *ULYSSES*

97.   BIBLE : CHRISTIANITY :: (a. Bhagavad-Gita  b. New Testament
      c. Koran  d. Talmud) : ISLAM

98.   (a. *caveat emptor*  b. *avant-garde*  c. *primus inter pares*  d. *tabula rasa*)
      : LET THE BUYER BEWARE :: *COGITO ERGO SUM* : I THINK,
      THEREFORE I AM

99.   ANDROUS : MAN :: DENDRON : (a. movement  b. blood  c. skin
      d. tree)

100.  I THINK, THEREFORE I AM : RENE DESCARTES :: THERE IS
      ONLY ONE GOOD, KNOWLEDGE, AND ONE EVIL, IGNO-
      RANCE : (a. Plato  b. Socrates  c. Machiavelli  d. Nietzsche)

# Practice Test 2

## ANSWER KEY

| | | | |
|---|---|---|---|
| 1. (b) | 26. (a) | 51. (c) | 76. (a) |
| 2. (a) | 27. (b) | 52. (a) | 77. (a) |
| 3. (a) | 28. (c) | 53. (a) | 78. (b) |
| 4. (b) | 29. (c) | 54. (a) | 79. (d) |
| 5. (a) | 30. (d) | 55. (b) | 80. (c) |
| 6. (d) | 31. (b) | 56. (c) | 81. (a) |
| 7. (c) | 32. (a) | 57. (a) | 82. (c) |
| 8. (a) | 33. (d) | 58. (c) | 83. (a) |
| 9. (b) | 34. (a) | 59. (c) | 84. (c) |
| 10. (d) | 35. (d) | 60. (b) | 85. (b) |
| 11. (b) | 36. (b) | 61. (d) | 86. (a) |
| 12. (d) | 37. (a) | 62. (a) | 87. (b) |
| 13. (a) | 38. (c) | 63. (b) | 88. (c) |
| 14. (a) | 39. (a) | 64. (c) | 89. (d) |
| 15. (a) | 40. (c) | 65. (c) | 90. (b) |
| 16. (d) | 41. (d) | 66. (d) | 91. (a) |
| 17. (a) | 42. (c) | 67. (b) | 92. (d) |
| 18. (a) | 43. (a) | 68. (c) | 93. (a) |
| 19. (c) | 44. (c) | 69. (a) | 94. (d) |
| 20. (b) | 45. (a) | 70. (b) | 95. (a) |
| 21. (a) | 46. (b) | 71. (b) | 96. (d) |
| 22. (c) | 47. (d) | 72. (b) | 97. (c) |
| 23. (c) | 48. (b) | 73. (c) | 98. (a) |
| 24. (c) | 49. (c) | 74. (b) | 99. (d) |
| 25. (c) | 50. (d) | 75. (d) | 100. (b) |

# DETAILED EXPLANATIONS
# OF ANSWERS

1.  **(b)**    (b) is correct because the Parthenon is in Athens as the Sistine Chapel is in Rome. All other choices are irrelevant.

2.  **(a)**    (a) is correct because $H_2O$ is the chemical symbol for water just as $CO_2$ is the chemical symbol for carbon dioxide. Carbon monoxide (b) is CO, ammonia (c) is $NH_3$, and salt (d) is NaCl.

3.  **(a)**    (a) is correct because Henry David Thoreau wrote *Civil Disobedience* just as Ralph Waldo Emerson wrote *Self-Reliance*. (b) is incorrect because Edgar Allen Poe wrote *The Tell-Tale Heart*. (c) is wrong because Henry David Thoreau wrote *Walden*, and (d) is incorrect because Walt Whitman wrote *Leaves of Grass*.

4.  **(b)**    (b) is the correct response because aggravate and exacerbate are synonyms meaning to worsen, just as assuage is a synonym for mitigate which means to lessen or make milder. (a) is incorrect because legislate means to create laws. An abrachiate (c) is an animal without gills, and dissociate (d) means to separate.

5.  **(a)**    (a) is correct because H is the chemical symbol for hydrogen just as Fe is the chemical symbol for iron. (b) is incorrect because flourine is F; (c) is wrong because nickel is Ni; and (d) is incorrect because sodium is Na.

6.  **(d)**    (d) is the correct response because a mushroom belongs to the kingdom Fungi as a mouse belongs to the kingdom Animalia. Plantae (a) refers to green plants, Protista (b) refers to acellular or unicellular organisms, and Chiroptera (c) refers to bats.

7.  **(c)**    (c) is correct because Frank Lloyd Wright was an architect just as Michelangelo was a painter.

8.  **(a)**    (a) is the correct answer because Handel composed the *Messiah* as Orff composed *Carmina Burana*. (b) is incorrect because Elgar composed *Pomp and Circumstance*; (c) is incorrect because Tchaikovsky composed *The Nutcracker Suite*; and (d) is wrong because Stravinsky composed *The Rite of Spring*.

9. **(b)** (b) is the correct response because barbaric is a synonym for savage just as divine is a synonym for sacred. (a) is not the correct choice because civilized means refined. (c) is incorrect because content means relaxed, and (d) is incorrect because enraged means angry.

10. **(d)** (d) is the correct choice because a president is the leader of a democracy in the same way that a king is the leader of a monarchy. (a) is incorrect because a dictator is a tyrannical ruler. An emperor (b) rules an empire, and Parliament (c) is the national legislature in England.

11. **(b)** (b) is correct because the area of a circle is given by $\pi r^2$ just as the area of a square is given by $L \times H$.

12. **(d)** (d) is the correct response because multiplication is the mathematical opposite of division just as integration is the mathematical opposite of derivation.

13. **(a)** (a) is the correct choice because an octagon has 8 sides and a dodecahedron has 12 sides. A pentagon (b) has 5 sides, a decagon (c) has 10 sides, and a polygon (d) is a closed figure of 3 or more sides.

14. **(a)** (a) is the correct response because coordinate point 9, 9 is the square of coordinate point 3, 3 just as coordinate point 16, 16 is the square of coordinate point –4, –4. All other answer choices are irrelevant.

15. **(a)** (a) is correct because the sin of 90 degrees is 1 as the cos 90 degrees is 0. All other answer choices are irrelevant.

16. **(d)** (d) is the correct response because crescendo means to become louder while diminuendo means to become softer. Pianissimo (a) means very soft or quiet, and fortissimo (b) and forte (c) both mean very loud.

17. **(a)** (a) is correct because Leonardo da Vinci was a Renaissance painter as Rembrandt was a baroque painter. (b), (c), and (d) are incorrect because Rembrandt did not paint in these styles.

18. **(a)** (a) is the correct answer because largo is of a slower tempo than adagio, as allegro is of a slower tempo than vivace. In order, from slowest to fastest tempo, the terms are: largo, grave, adagio, andante, moderato, allegretto, allegro, vivace, presto, and prestissimo.

19. **(c)**    (c) is the correct response because Beethoven wrote *Eroica* also called Symphony No. 3, just as Mozart wrote *Don Giovanni*. (a), (b), and (d) are incorrect because Mozart did not compose these works.

20. **(b)**    (b) is correct because tempo is a musical term referring to speed as beat is a musical term referring to rhythm. A metronome (a) is a machine used for keeping rhythm; percussion (c) refers generally to the percussion section of an orchestra; and meter (d) refers to rhythm as it relates to poetry.

21. **(a)**    (a) is the correct response because Steinbeck wrote *The Grapes of Wrath* and Hemingway wrote *For Whom the Bell Tolls*. (b) is incorrect because Dos Passos' most famous work is *Manhattan Transfer*. (c) is incorrect because Hesse's most famous work is *Siddhartha*, and (d) is incorrect because Joseph Heller's most famous work is *Catch 22*.

22. **(c)**    (c) is the correct choice because William Shakespeare's play, *Richard III,* is a history just as Shakespeare's play *Romeo and Juliet* is a tragedy. Generally, Shakespeare's plays are divided into four catgories: the comedies, the histories, the romances, and the tragedies.

23. **(c)**    (c) is the correct response because Marx founded modern communism just as Mussolini founded modern fascism. Nationalism (b) refers to extreme support of one's own country. Hitler founded Nazism (a), and Socialism (d) is an economic system used throughout the world.

24. **(c)**    (c) is the correct response because to ratiocinate is to think logically just as sophistic thinking is irrational. Deaminate (a) is to remove an amino group from an organic compound; fulminate (b) is to denounce; and monarchistic (d) refers to belief in a monarchy.

25. **(c)**    (c) Mahabharata is an Indian epic just as Gilgamesh is a Sumerian epic. All other choices are irrelevant.

26. **(a)**    (a) is the correct response because Plato wrote the *Republic* just as Thomas More wrote *Utopia*. (b) is incorrect because Socrates produced no written works, but his philosophy is understood through the writings of Plato. Coleridge (c) is incorrect because he was a Romantic poet and literary critic, famous for long form poems such as *Christabel* and *Rime of the Ancient Mariner*. (d) is incorrect because Aldous Huxley's most famous work is *Brave New World*.

27. **(b)**    (b) is the right answer because King Henry VIII lived during the 1500s just as Mozart lived during the 1700s.

28. **(c)**    (c) is the correct response because nocturnal refers to an animal active mainly at night as diurnal refers to an animal active mainly during the day.

29. **(c)**    (c) is the correct response because the America's Cup is the championship prize for yachting just as the Stanley Cup is the championship prize for hockey. (a) is incorrect because the World Cup is the championship prize for soccer. (b) is incorrect because a steeplechase is an equestrian event. (d) is incorrect because gymnastics is a competitive event.

30. **(d)**    (d) is the correct response because the Second Amendment is the right to keep and bear arms just as the Seventh Amendment is the right to a jury trial. The Fourth Amendment (a) guarantees against unlawful search and seizure, and the Fifth Amendment (b) allows defendants to refuse to testify against themselves. The Sixth Amendment (c) guarantees a speedy trial.

31. **(b)**    (b) is correct because Martin Luther King, Jr. won the Nobel Peace Prize just as Irene Joliet-Curie won the Nobel Prize in Chemistry. (a), (c), and (d) are incorrect because Irene Joliet-Curie did not win these prizes.

32. **(a)**    (a) is the correct response because Neil Armstrong was the first American walk on the moon just as Chuck Yeager was the first American to break the speed of sound. (b) is incorrect because breaking the speed of light remains an impossibility. (c) is incorrect because the first American in space was Alan Shepard. (d) is incorrect because the first person in orbit was Yuri Gagarin.

33. **(d)**    (d) is correct because the postal abbreviation for Idaho is ID just as the postal abbreviation for Montana is MT. MN (a) is Minnesota, MO (b) is Missouri, and MS (c) is Mississippi.

34. **(a)**    (a) is the correct response because Washington is the capital of the United States just as Berlin is the capital of Germany. (b) and (d) are incorrect because neither Munich nor Hamburg is a capital city. (c) is incorrect because Vienna is in another country.

35. **(d)**   (d) Moscow is the capital of Russia as Canberra is the capital of Australia. Perth, Melbourne, and Sydney are all major cities in Australia, but none is the nation's capital.

36. **(b)**   (b) The Thirteenth Amendment abolished slavery just as the Nineteenth Amendment gave women the right to vote. The Eighteenth Amendment (a) prohibited the use, manufacture, and sale of alcohol. The Twentieth Amendment (c) changed the date of inauguration. (d) is incorrect because there are 26 amendments to the Constitution.

37. **(a)**   (a) is correct because Roosevelt was president before Truman just as Wilson was president before Harding. (b) is incorrect because Coolidge was the 30th president, preceding Hoover. (c) is incorrect because Taft was the 27th president, preceding Wilson. (d) is incorrect because Ford was the 38th president, preceding Carter.

38. **(c)**   (c) is correct because Planck discovered quantum theory as Einstein discovered the theory of relativity. (a) is incorrect because Galileo discovered the rules of planetary motion. (b) is incorrect because Newton described what has come to be called Newtonian physics, compared with Planck's quantum physics. (d) is incorrect because William Ramsay discovered helium.

39. **(a)**   (a) is the correct response because Walt Whitman wrote *Song of Myself* just as Nathaniel Hawthorne wrote *Rappaccini's Daughter*. Herman Melville wrote *Billy Budd* (d), Jonathan Swift wrote *Gulliver's Travels* (c), and Edgar Allen Poe wrote *The Raven* (b).

40. **(c)**   (c) is correct because Cassius and Brutus appear in Shakespeare's play *Julius Caesar* just as Antonio and Olivia appear in Shakespeare's play *Twelfth Night*. (a) and (b) are incorrect because Polonius and Laertes both appear in *Hamlet*, and (d) is incorrect because Macduff appears in *Macbeth*.

41. **(d)**   (d) is incorrect because Gershwin wrote *Rhapsody in Blue* as Bernstein wrote *West Side Story*. Barber wrote *Adagio for Strings* (a), Gershwin wrote *Porgy and Bess* (b), and Moore wrote *The Devil and Daniel Webster* (c).

42. **(c)**   (c) is correct because Sophocles wrote *Oedipus Rex* and Euripides wrote *Medea*. Aeschylus wrote *Prometheus Bound* (a), Aristophanes wrote *Lysistrata* (b), and Sophocles wrote *Antigone* (d).

43. **(a)**   (a) is the correct choice because Anton Chekhov wrote *The Three Sisters* and George Bernard Shaw wrote *Saint Joan*. Victor Hugo (b) wrote *Les Miserables*, Oscar Wilde (c) wrote *The Importance of Being Earnest*, and Henrik Ibsen (d) wrote *A Doll's House*.

44. **(c)**   (c) is the correct response because Kafka wrote the *Metamorphosis* and T. S. Eliot wrote *The Waste Land*. (a) is incorrect because Coleridge wrote *Lyrical Ballads*. (b) is incorrect because Wordsworth wrote *Poems Chiefly of Early and Late Years*, and (d) is incorrect because Stoppard wrote *Rosencrantz and Guildenstern Are Dead*.

45. **(a)**   (a) is correct because Aesculapius is the Greek god of medicine just as Chaos is the Greek god of the void. Apollo (b) is the god of the sun, Nike (c) is the goddess of victory, and Selene (d) is the goddess of the moon.

46. **(b)**   (b) is the correct choice because Thanatos is the Greek god of death and Eros is the Greek god of love. Tyche (a) is the goddess of fortune, Nyx (c) is the goddess of night, and Athena (d) is the goddess of wisdom.

47. **(d)**   (d) is the correct response because Mars is the Roman god of war just as Venus is the Roman goddess of love. Psyche (a) is the goddess of the soul, Salacia (b) is the goddess of the oceans, and Somnus (c) is the god of sleep.

48. **(b)**   (b) is the right answer because -chrom is a suffix meaning color and -derm is a suffix meaning skin. Kinesis means motion (a), pathos is the term for disease (c), and algia means pain (d).

49. **(c)**   (c) is the correct answer because acro- is a prefix meaning top just as andro is a prefix meaning man. Anti- (a) is the prefix meaning against, aero- (b) means air, and arch- (d) means chief.

50. **(d)**   (d) is the correct response because ethno is a prefix referring to race or ethnicity just as choreo is a prefix referring to dance. Cardio (a) means relating to the heart, crypto (b) means hidden, and chrono (c) means time.

51. **(c)**   (c) is the correct answer because an adjective modifies a noun in the same way that an adverb modifies a verb. A pronoun (a) substitutes

for a noun, a preposition (b) defines the relationship of a noun to a verb, and an article (d) (a, an, or the) signals the presence of a noun.

52. **(a)**    (a) is correct because V-E Day, May 8, 1945, is the day the Germans surrendered to the Allied forces in World War II just as V-J Day, August 15, 1945, is the day the Japanese surrendered. (b) is incorrect because Bastille Day refers to the storming of a French prison by the proletariat of that nation, signaling the beginning of the French Revolution. Veteran's Day (c) is an American holiday remembering the war dead. Pearl Harbor Day (d) commemorates those who died in the Japanese attack on Pearl Harbor on December 7, 1941.

53. **(a)**    (a) is the correct response because lay is the past tense of the verb lie in the same way that laid is the past tense of the verb lay. Laying (b) is the present participle of lay, lying (c) is the present participle of lie, and lain (d) is the past participle of lie.

54. **(a)**    (a) is correct because $W=fd$ is the formula for determining work just as velocity is determined by the formula $v=d/t$. All other formulae are irrelevant.

55. **(b)**    (b) is the right choice because red has a longer wavelength than orange just as blue has a longer wavelength than violet. In order from longest to shortest the colors in the visible spectrum are: red, orange, yellow, green, blue, indigo, violet.

56. **(c)**    (c) is correct because Allen Ginsberg wrote the poem *Howl* and Jack Kerouac wrote the novel *On the Road*. William Burroughs's (a) most famous work is *Naked Lunch*. Ken Kesey's (b) most famous work is *One Flew Over the Cuckoo's Nest,* and Diane DiPrima's most famous work is *Memoirs of a Beatnik*.

57. **(a)**    (a) is correct because the country Syria is a part of the Asian continent just as Panama is a part of the North American continent. Colombia (b), Venezuela (c), and Ecuador (d) are all part of the South American continent.

58. **(c)**    (c) is the correct response because the prefix hemi- means half just as the prefix ante- means before. The prefix para- means close (a), hypo- means under (b), and exo- means outside (d).

59. **(c)**    (c) is correct because the fraction 1/2 expressed as a percentage

is 50 percent, the same way that the fraction 2/5 expressed as a percentage is 40 percent. All other fractions are irrelevant.

60. **(b)**    (b) is correct because an organism's phenotype describes its physical appearance just as its genotype describes its genetic composition. Molecular structure (a) is irrelevant because it is not confined to living things. Heredity (c) refers to the passage of genes from an organism to its offspring. Natural selection (d) refers to the extinction of certain species because they are less equipped to survive in a given environment than a competing species.

61. **(d)**    (d) is the correct choice because an electron is negatively charged in the same way that a neutron has no charge. A proton is positively charged so (a) and (c) are incorrect. Variable (b) is not relevant to this question.

62. **(a)**    (a) is correct because C is the abbreviation for Celsius; F is the abbreviation for Fahrenheit. All other abbreviations are fictitious.

63. **(b)**    (b) is correct because the abbreviation for ounce is oz; and the abbreviation for tablespoon is tbsp. The abbreviation for teaspoon is tsp, for pint is pt, for pound is lb, and for quart is qt.

64. **(c)**    (c) is correct because the freezing point for water is 0 degrees Celsius or 32 degrees Fahrenheit; the boiling point for water is 100 degrees Celsius or 212 degrees Fahrenheit. All other temperatures are irrelevant.

65. **(c)**    (c) A baseball team fields 9 players simultaneously just as a football team fields 11 players simultaneously. All other numbers are incorrect.

66. **(d)**    (d) is correct because another name for vitamin A is carotene and another name for vitamin C is ascorbic acid. Thiamine (a) is vitamin B1, riboflavin (b) is vitamin B2, and niacin (c) is also known as nicotinic acid.

67. **(b)**    (b) is the correct answer because fulminate means to denounce just as commend means to praise. Cajole (a) means to coax, exemplify (c) means to make an example of, and placate (d) means assuage.

68. **(c)**    (c) is correct because UNIX is a computer operating system just as FORTRAN is a computer programming language. (a) and (b) are

general terms and do not refer to a specific language or system. Peripheral (d) refers to a device that works with a computer, but is not integral to the functioning of the computer, such as a printer.

69. **(a)**   (a) is the right choice because Rosencrantz and Horatio are characters in Shakespeare's *Hamlet* just as Malcolm and Duncan are characters in Shakespeare's *Macbeth*. Regan (b) and Gloucester (c) appear in the play *King Lear*, and Sebastian (d) appears in *Twelfth Night*.

70. **(b)**   (b) is correct because Dante wrote *Inferno* and Milton wrote *Paradise Lost*. (a), (c), and (d) were all Romantic poets.

71. **(b)**   (b) is the correct choice because Joseph Heller wrote *Catch-22* and Thomas Pynchon wrote *Gravity's Rainbow*. John Updike (a) wrote *The Witches of Eastwick*, Washington Irving (c) wrote *The History of New York*, and Jack Kerouac (d) wrote *Dharma Bums*.

72. **(b)**   (b) is correct because if the diameter of a circle is 8, then its radius will be 4. All other choices are irrelevant.

73. **(c)**   (c) is the right answer because $2^3$ is 8; $3^3$ is 27. All other choices are irrelevant.

74. **(b)**   (b) is correct because a kitten is a baby cat and a joey is a baby kangaroo. A wallaby (a) is another animal. A cub (c) is a generic term for an animal that has not reached maturity. A marsupial (d) is the classification into which the kangaroo falls.

75. **(d)**   (d) is correct because something with eagle-like features is aquiline just as something with dog-like features is canine. Feline (a) refers to cat-like, equine (b) refers to horse-like, and bovine (c) refers to cow-like.

76. **(a)**   (a) is the correct response because an antelope is an herbivore (plant eater) just as an owl is a carnivore (meat eater). Omnivore (b) refers to an animal (such as a human) that eats both meat and plants. Avian (c) is a general term for a bird. Nocturnal (d) refers to an animal that is active primarily at night.

77. **(a)**   (a) is the correct response because Johnson was Kennedy's vice president just as Nixon was Eisenhower's vice president. Ford (b)

was Nixon's vice president, and became president when Nixon resigned. Kissinger (c) was never president or vice president. Humphrey (d) was Lyndon Johnson's vice president.

78. **(b)**   (b) is the correct response because Tokyo is the capital of Japan just as Baghdad is the capital of Iraq. Tripoli (a) is the capital of Libya, Aden (c) is the capital of Yemen, and Riyadh (d) is the capital of Saudi Arabia.

79. **(d)**   (d) is the correct response because Austin is the capital of Texas just as Denver is the capital of Colorado. All others are major cities in Texas, but not the capital.

80. **(c)**   (c) is the correct response because Salt Lake City is the capital of Utah just as Montgomery is the capital of Alabama. All others are major cities in Alabama, but not the capital.

81. **(a)**   (a) is correct because the past tense of the verb become is became just as the past tense of the verb shrink is shrank. All other choices are incorrect.

82. **(c)**   (c) is correct because just as aural relates to the ear; oral relates to the mouth. Optical relates to the eyes (a), nasal refers to the nose (b), and manual refers to the hand (d).

83. **(a)**   (a) is the correct choice because *Flyer* was the name of the Wright brothers' first airplane and *Beagle* was the name of Charles Darwin's ship. Galapagos (b) refers to the island group where Darwin did his research. Explorer (c) is a general term. The *Calypso* (d) is the name of the ship captained by the late Jacques Yves Cousteau.

84. **(c)**   (c) is the correct response because a sloop is a sailing ship with a single mast and a barque is a sailing ship with 3-5 masts. All other choices are irrelevant.

85. **(b)**   (b) is correct because acrophobia is a fear of heights and hydrophobia is a fear of water. Hemophobia is a fear of blood (a), sitophobia is a fear of food (c), and necrophobia is a fear of death (d).

86. **(a)**   (a) is correct because killing a king is called regicide just as killing one's father is called patricide.

87. **(b)**   (b) is the correct response because there are 1,760 yards in a mile. There are 5,280 feet (a) in a mile, there are 63,360 inches (c) in a mile, and roughly 1,500 meters (d) in a mile.

88. **(c)**   (c) is the correct response because just as a patent protects an invention, a copyright protects a written work. Registration (a) and license (b) are general terms that are not specific to protection of ownership. A statute (d) refers to a law.

89. **(d)**   (d) is correct because the humerus is a bone in the arm just as the femur is a bone in the leg. The tarsus (a) is the part of the foot between the metatarsus and the leg. The sternum (b) is commonly referred to as the breastbone. The clavicle (c) is commonly called the collarbone.

90. **(b)**   (b) is the correct response because the frontal lobe of the brain is responsible for speech just as the occipital lobe is responsible for vision. Touch (a) is a function of the parietal lobe, memory (c) and hearing (d) are functions of the temporal lobe.

91. **(a)**   (a) is correct because a teleologist studies nature as an icthyologist studies fish. (b) is incorrect because a theologist studies religion. (c) is incorrect because a thanatologist studies death, and (d) is incorrect because a zoologist studies animals.

92. **(d)**   (d) is the correct response because Grendel is the primary antagonist in *Beowulf* just as Claudius is the primary antagonist in *Hamlet*. While Ophelia (a), Gertrude (c), and Polonius (b) are characters in *Hamlet*, they are not the primary antagonists.

93. **(a)**   (a) is the correct response because a gene is a constituent part of a chromosome as a nucleus is a constituent part of a cell. RNA (b) and DNA (c) are compounds that carry information, and an enzyme (d) is a chemical that performs a specific function, so these are incorrect.

94. **(d)**   (d) is the correct response because George Orwell wrote *1984* based on Stalin's USSR as Aldous Huxley wrote *Brave New World* based on Roosevelt's USA. (a), (b), and (c) were all writers and social critics, however, they are not relevant to this question.

95. **(a)**   (a) is correct because Coleridge wrote *Kubla Khan* just as Yeats wrote *Sailing to Byzantium*. Ibsen (b) is best known for *A Doll's*

*House* and *Ghosts*, while Tolstoy (c) is best known for *War and Peace*. Wordsworth (d) is best known for his Romantic poetry.

96. **(d)**    (d) is correct because Sartre wrote *No Exit* and Joyce wrote *Ulysses*. *A Streetcar Named Desire* (a) was written by Tennessee Williams, *Our Town* (b) was written by Thornton Wilder, and *The Purloined Letter* (c) was written by Edgar Allen Poe.

97. **(c)**    (c) is correct because the Bible is the primary holy book of the Christian faith just as the Koran is the primary holy book of Islam. The Bhagavad-Gita (a) is a Hindu holy book, the New Testament (b) refers to a portion of the Bible, and the Talmud (d) is the book of Jewish law.

98. **(a)**    (a) is the correct response because *caveat emptor* means let the buyer beware just as *cogito ergo sum* means I think, therefore I am.

99. **(d)**    (d) is the correct answer because androus is a suffix meaning man and dendron is a suffix meaning tree. Kinesis means movement (a), emia means blood (b), and derm means skin (c).

100. **(b)**    (b) Descartes said, "I think, therefore I am," just as Socrates said, "There is only one good, knowledge, and one evil, ignorance." All other choices are incorrect because these quotes are not attributable to these philosophers.

# MAT – Practice Test 3 Answer Sheet

1. ⓐ ⓑ ⓒ ⓓ
2. ⓐ ⓑ ⓒ ⓓ
3. ⓐ ⓑ ⓒ ⓓ
4. ⓐ ⓑ ⓒ ⓓ
5. ⓐ ⓑ ⓒ ⓓ
6. ⓐ ⓑ ⓒ ⓓ
7. ⓐ ⓑ ⓒ ⓓ
8. ⓐ ⓑ ⓒ ⓓ
9. ⓐ ⓑ ⓒ ⓓ
10. ⓐ ⓑ ⓒ ⓓ
11. ⓐ ⓑ ⓒ ⓓ
12. ⓐ ⓑ ⓒ ⓓ
13. ⓐ ⓑ ⓒ ⓓ
14. ⓐ ⓑ ⓒ ⓓ
15. ⓐ ⓑ ⓒ ⓓ
16. ⓐ ⓑ ⓒ ⓓ
17. ⓐ ⓑ ⓒ ⓓ
18. ⓐ ⓑ ⓒ ⓓ
19. ⓐ ⓑ ⓒ ⓓ
20. ⓐ ⓑ ⓒ ⓓ
21. ⓐ ⓑ ⓒ ⓓ
22. ⓐ ⓑ ⓒ ⓓ
23. ⓐ ⓑ ⓒ ⓓ
24. ⓐ ⓑ ⓒ ⓓ
25. ⓐ ⓑ ⓒ ⓓ
26. ⓐ ⓑ ⓒ ⓓ
27. ⓐ ⓑ ⓒ ⓓ
28. ⓐ ⓑ ⓒ ⓓ
29. ⓐ ⓑ ⓒ ⓓ
30. ⓐ ⓑ ⓒ ⓓ
31. ⓐ ⓑ ⓒ ⓓ
32. ⓐ ⓑ ⓒ ⓓ
33. ⓐ ⓑ ⓒ ⓓ
34. ⓐ ⓑ ⓒ ⓓ

35. ⓐ ⓑ ⓒ ⓓ
36. ⓐ ⓑ ⓒ ⓓ
37. ⓐ ⓑ ⓒ ⓓ
38. ⓐ ⓑ ⓒ ⓓ
39. ⓐ ⓑ ⓒ ⓓ
40. ⓐ ⓑ ⓒ ⓓ
41. ⓐ ⓑ ⓒ ⓓ
42. ⓐ ⓑ ⓒ ⓓ
43. ⓐ ⓑ ⓒ ⓓ
44. ⓐ ⓑ ⓒ ⓓ
45. ⓐ ⓑ ⓒ ⓓ
46. ⓐ ⓑ ⓒ ⓓ
47. ⓐ ⓑ ⓒ ⓓ
48. ⓐ ⓑ ⓒ ⓓ
49. ⓐ ⓑ ⓒ ⓓ
50. ⓐ ⓑ ⓒ ⓓ
51. ⓐ ⓑ ⓒ ⓓ
52. ⓐ ⓑ ⓒ ⓓ
53. ⓐ ⓑ ⓒ ⓓ
54. ⓐ ⓑ ⓒ ⓓ
55. ⓐ ⓑ ⓒ ⓓ
56. ⓐ ⓑ ⓒ ⓓ
57. ⓐ ⓑ ⓒ ⓓ
58. ⓐ ⓑ ⓒ ⓓ
59. ⓐ ⓑ ⓒ ⓓ
60. ⓐ ⓑ ⓒ ⓓ
61. ⓐ ⓑ ⓒ ⓓ
62. ⓐ ⓑ ⓒ ⓓ
63. ⓐ ⓑ ⓒ ⓓ
64. ⓐ ⓑ ⓒ ⓓ
65. ⓐ ⓑ ⓒ ⓓ
66. ⓐ ⓑ ⓒ ⓓ
67. ⓐ ⓑ ⓒ ⓓ
68. ⓐ ⓑ ⓒ ⓓ

69. ⓐ ⓑ ⓒ ⓓ
70. ⓐ ⓑ ⓒ ⓓ
71. ⓐ ⓑ ⓒ ⓓ
72. ⓐ ⓑ ⓒ ⓓ
73. ⓐ ⓑ ⓒ ⓓ
74. ⓐ ⓑ ⓒ ⓓ
75. ⓐ ⓑ ⓒ ⓓ
76. ⓐ ⓑ ⓒ ⓓ
77. ⓐ ⓑ ⓒ ⓓ
78. ⓐ ⓑ ⓒ ⓓ
79. ⓐ ⓑ ⓒ ⓓ
80. ⓐ ⓑ ⓒ ⓓ
81. ⓐ ⓑ ⓒ ⓓ
82. ⓐ ⓑ ⓒ ⓓ
83. ⓐ ⓑ ⓒ ⓓ
84. ⓐ ⓑ ⓒ ⓓ
85. ⓐ ⓑ ⓒ ⓓ
86. ⓐ ⓑ ⓒ ⓓ
87. ⓐ ⓑ ⓒ ⓓ
88. ⓐ ⓑ ⓒ ⓓ
89. ⓐ ⓑ ⓒ ⓓ
90. ⓐ ⓑ ⓒ ⓓ
91. ⓐ ⓑ ⓒ ⓓ
92. ⓐ ⓑ ⓒ ⓓ
93. ⓐ ⓑ ⓒ ⓓ
94. ⓐ ⓑ ⓒ ⓓ
95. ⓐ ⓑ ⓒ ⓓ
96. ⓐ ⓑ ⓒ ⓓ
97. ⓐ ⓑ ⓒ ⓓ
98. ⓐ ⓑ ⓒ ⓓ
99. ⓐ ⓑ ⓒ ⓓ
100. ⓐ ⓑ ⓒ ⓓ

# MILLER ANALOGIES

# PRACTICE TEST 3

**TIME:** 50 Minutes
100 Analogies

---

**DIRECTIONS**: Read each of the following analogies carefully, and choose the BEST answer to each item. Fill in your responses in the answer sheets provided.

---

1. CONSUMPTION : TUBERCULOSIS :: (a. the pox b. the clap c. the black death d. the flu) : BUBONIC PLAGUE

2. LEAGUE OF NATIONS : WILSON :: UNITED NATIONS :
   (a. Truman b. Roosevelt c. Eisenhower d. Kennedy)

3. PHILIP : VALOIS :: HENRY : (a. Windsor b. Saxe-Coburg c. Tudor d. Hanover)

4. JAMES VI OF SCOTLAND : JAMES I OF GREAT BRITAIN ::
   EDWARD VIII : (a. Edward I b. Elizabeth II c. Duke of Kent
   d. Duke of Windsor)

5. LINCOLN : JOHN WILKES BOOTH :: McKINLEY : (a. John Hinkley b. James Earl Ray c. Leon Czolgosz d. Charles Guiteau)

6. NICHOLAS II : RUSSIA :: (a. Louis XVI b. Louis XVIII c. Louis XIX d. Henri III) : FRANCE

7. CATHERINE THE GREAT : LATVIA :: NAPOLEAN : (a. France b. Elba c. Corsica d. Waterloo)

8. PRAETORIAN GUARD : ROME :: SCOTS GUARD : (a. Great Britain b. Scotland c. Germany d. France)

9. WASHINGTON : ADAMS :: NIXON : (a. Carter b. Ford c. Reagan d. Johnson)

10. HUNDRED YEARS WAR : 113 YEARS :: THIRTY YEAR WAR : (a. 60 years b. 30 years c. 34 years d. 52 years)

11. PLUTO : TOMBAUGH :: LUCY : (a. Schultz b. Johanson c. Leakey d. Linus)

12. COUSTEAU : *CALYPSO* :: DARWIN : (a. Galapagos b. *Origin of Species* c. *Beagle* d. *Turtle*)

13. FRANKLIN ROOSEVELT : ELEANOR :: JAMES MADISON : (a. Martha b. Mary c. "Lady Bird" d. Dolly)

14. LUDWIG : NYMPHENBURG :: ARTHUR : (a. Camelot b. Versailles c. Guinevere d. Joyeus Gard)

15. U.S. SENATE : CONGRESS :: HOUSE OF COMMONS : (a. House of Lords b. Parliament c. Storting d. Cabinet)

16. TAUNG CHILD : DART :: LAOLTI FOOTPRINTS : (a. Richard Leakey b. Louis Leakey c. Mary Leakey d. Louise Leakey)

17. MAORI : TATTOOS :: CELTIC : (a. wode b. mead c. dirt d. saffron)

18. YURI GAGARIN : *VOSTOK I* :: NEIL ARMSTRONG : (a. *Apollo 8* b. *Apollo 11* c. *Apollo 17* d. *Gemini 3*)

19. APPELLATION : SOBRIQUET :: LOUIS XIV : (a. The Cruel b. The Sun King c. The Just d. The Confessor)

20. ALARIC : VISIGOTH :: (a. Caesar b. Clovis c. Attila d. Hadrian) : HUN

21. EARTH : MOON :: MARS : (a. Europa b. Oberon c. Phobos d. Nereid)

22. PYRAMIDS : EGYPT :: (a. Colossus b. Great Library c. Hanging Gardens d. Taj Mahal) : BABYLON

23. EUCLID : GEOMETRY :: HIPPOCRATES : (a. drama b. medicine c. sculpture d. astronomy)

24. BLACK MONDAY : 1987 :: (a. Fat Tuesday b. Black Friday
    c. Black Tuesday d. Red Monday) : 1929

25. S.B. ANTHONY : DOLLAR :: (a. A. Lincoln b. F. Roosevelt c. R.
    Nixon d. G. Washington) : DIME

26. HOLY GRAIL : LANCELOT :: GOLDEN FLEECE : (a. Ulysses
    b. Orestes c. Jason d. Paris)

27. BELL : TELEPHONE :: GALILEO : (a. wind tunnel b. zipper
    c. lightning rod d. water thermometer)

28. NORSE : OLYMPUS :: GREEK : (a. Oden b. Thor c. Asgard
    d. Loki)

29. AGENT ORANGE : VIETNAM :: MUSTARD GAS : (a. Civil War
    b. War of 1812 c. World War I d. World War II)

30. FREQUENCY MODULATION : FM :: (a. attitude modulation
    b. amplitude modulation c. amplified modulation d. animated modu-
    lation) : AM

31. DIAMOND : CUBIC ZIRCONIUM :: GOLD : (a. quartz b. silver
    c. alloy d. pyrite)

32. EEG : (a. blood b. bone c. eye d. brain) :: EKG : HEART

33. MARQUIS : MARCHIONESS :: (a. duke b. earl c. knight d. lord) :
    COUNTESS

34. ASTHMA : LUNGS :: LEUKEMIA : (a. blood b. gall bladder c. liver
    d. immune system)

35. EVERGLADES : FLORIDA :: GRAND CANYON : (a. Colorado
    b. Arizona c. Utah d. Nevada)

36. MOUNT EVEREST : HIMALAYAS :: (a. Athos b. Montserrat
    c. Mount McKinley d. Matterhorn) : ALPS

37. HIGHLANDS : SCOTLAND :: BLACK FOREST : (a. France
    b. Belgium c. Germany d. Austria)

38. BOER WAR : SOUTH AFRICA :: CRIMEAN WAR : (a. Greece
    b. Russia c. Turkey d. Sweden)

39. HAVANA : CUBA :: (a. Kingston b. Montego Bay c. Ochos Rios
    d. Negril) : JAMAICA

40. PERSIA : IRAN :: PHRYGIA : (a. Egypt b. Turkey c. Spain d. India)

41. ALEUTIAN ISLANDS : ALASKA :: AUCKLAND ISLANDS :
    (a. Brazil b. China c. Argentina d. New Zealand)

42. LIVINGSTONE : AFRICA :: (a. Hudson b. Ponce de Léon
    c. La Salle d. Cabot) : LOUISIANA

43. LAKE OF LUCERNE : SWITZERLAND :: LAKE VICTORIA :
    (a. Great Britain b. Canada c. Australia d. Kenya)

44. BLACK FRIARS : DOMINICANS :: (a. Methodists b. Scientologists
    c. Jesuits d. Jehovah) : SOCIETY OF JESUS

45. SAPPHIRE : CORUNDUM :: AMETHYST: (a. graphite b. quartz
    c. feldspar d. garnet)

46. DESCARTES : SOLIPSISM :: (a. Xenophanes b. Zeno c. Pyrrho
    d. Epicurus) : STOICISM

47. BOXING DAY : DECEMBER 26 :: EARTH DAY : (a. April 19
    b. May 19 c. April 22 d. May 22)

48. PORSCHE : VOLKSWAGON :: FORD : (a. Oldsmobile b. Model T
    c. Cadillac d. Du Pont)

49. GRAM : MASS :: (a. cubit b. watt c. volume d. degree) : POWER

50. REVOLVER : COLT :: (a. cannon b. machine gun c. crossbow
    d. musket) : GATLING

51. JAPAN : YEN :: PORTUGAL : (a. peseta b. cruzeiro c. escudo
    d. rand)

52. AUSTRIA : GERMAN :: (a. France b. Sweden c. Norway
    d. Greenland) : DANISH

53. RIGEL : ORION :: (a. Sirus b. Capella c. Sol d. Polaris) : LITTLE
    DIPPER

54. AFRICA : KILIMANJARO :: NORTH AMERICA : (a. Mt.
    McKinley b. Mt. Helena c. Mt. Everest d. Boston Mountains)

55. ASIA : DEAD SEA :: NORTH AMERICA : (a. Grand Canyon
    b. Lake Michigan c. Death Valley d. Caribbean Sea)

56. AURORA BOREALIS : NORTHERN LIGHTS :: (a. Aurora Polaris
    b. Aurora Luminescence c. Aurora Australis d. Solar Winds) :
    SOUTHERN LIGHTS

57. PAPYRUS : EGPYT :: (a. stone tablets b. marble tablets c. clay
    tablets d. rice paper) : BABYLONIA

58. NOAH : JUDEO-CHRISTIAN :: (a. Gilgamesh b. Jason c. Deucalion
    d. Plato) : GREEK

59. TURPENTINE : PINE :: (a. soap b. ink c. rattan d. dye) : PALM

60. VICTORIA : BRITISH COLUMBIA :: (a. Toronto b. Montreal
    c. Hamilton d. Ottawa) : ONTARIO

61. UNIVERSITY OF ARIZONA : (a. Phoenix b. Flagstaff
    c. Prescott d. Tucson) :: FORDHAM : NEW YORK CITY

62. THE SNOW QUEEN : ANDERSEN :: UNCLE REMUS : (a. Grimm
    b. Faust c. Harris d. Disney)

63. LIGHT : SOUND :: (a. 186,000 feet per second b. 186,000 miles per
    second c. 1,860 miles per second d. 1,680 miles per second) : 1,088
    FEET PER SECOND

64. BIO : LIFE :: HEMI : (a. half b. earth c. split d. world)

65. LIVY : HISTORY :: (a. Pindar b. Zeno c. Horace d. Sappho) :
POETRY

66. WASHINGTON : MT. VERNON :: (a. Arthur b. Grant c. Roosevelt
d. Cleveland) : HYDE PARK

67. *WALL STREET JOURNAL* : NEW YORK :: (a. *Sun Times*
b. *Examiner* c. *Star* d. *Inquirer*) : PHILADELPHIA

68. PUERTO RICO : RICH PORT :: NEVADA : (a. flat land b. cold
night c. snow clad d. new start)

69. HELIUM : SUN :: NEON : (a. new b. light c. bright d. extreme)

70. LUXEMBOURG : CONSTITUTIONAL MONARCHY :: ICE-
LAND : (a. traditional monarchy b. constitutional monarchy
c. independent commonwealth d. republic)

71. HYDROGEN : 1 :: CARBON : (a. 6 b. 8 c. 9 d. 12)

72. EMMY : TELEVISION :: (a. Nobel b. Tony c. Pulitzer d. Fermi) :
JOURNALISM

73. (a. Throgs Neck b. Brooklyn c. George Washington d. Verrazano
Narrows) : NEW YORK :: GOLDEN GATE : SAN FRANCISCO

74. PULLET : HEN :: ELVER : (a. wild fowl b. eel c. zebra d. hare)

75. EGYPT : PHILIPPINES :: POUND : (a. yen b. peso c. nuevo sol
d. dinar)

76. JUPITER : PLANET :: (a. Io b. Moon c. Europa d. Ganymede) :
SATELLITE

77. ESTROGEN : OVARIES :: GASTRIN : (a. stomach glands
b. adrenal medulla c. thyroid d. pancreas)

78. MARGARET THATCHER : ELIZABETH II :: (a. Stanley Baldwin
b. William Pitt, the younger c. Herbert Asquith d. Benjamin Disraeli)
: VICTORIA

79. BRADLEY : HARTFORD :: (a. Gatwick b. Logan c. Dulles d. Midway) : WASHINGTON, D.C.

80. ROMAN CATHOLIC : POPE :: EPISCOPALIAN : (a. bishop b. archbishop c. cardinal d. apostle)

81. *HOMO HABILIS* : 2,000,000 :: NEANDERTHAL : (a. 10,000 b. 15,000 c. 75,000 d. 200,000)

82. NEST : VIPERS :: (a. gaggle b. band c. gross d. pack) : GORILLAS

83. CORAL SNAKE : BLACK WIDOW SPIDER :: GARDEN SNAKE : (a. harvest spider b. latrodectus geometricus c. brown recluse d. grey widow)

84. QUEENSLAND : AUSTRALIA :: (a. Texas b. Washington, DC c. Boston d. San Francisco) : UNITED STATES

85. KORAN : ISLAM :: BHAGAVAD-GITA : (a. Buddhism b. Confucianism c. Baha'i d. Hinduism)

86. ULNA : ARM :: (a. tarsals b. humerus c. mandible d. tibia) : LEG

87. DOG : CANIDAE :: (a. frog b. squirrel c. cat d. lizard) : RANIDAE

88. GAEA : TERRA :: HESTIA : (a. Juno b. Saturn c. Eros d. Vestia)

89. K : KAPPA :: (a. Z b. Q c. D d. L) : KOPPA

90. ARABIC : ROMAN :: 600 : (a. MD b. CC c. DC d. MX)

91. LEDA : HELEN :: (a. Metis b. Diona c. Themis d. Io) : APHRODITE

92. MACRO : LARGE :: HOMO : (a. small b. same c. male d. similar)

93. CZAR : RUSSIA :: KHAN : (a. Mongolia b. Egypt c. Turkey d. China)

94. BALL : MUSKET :: (a. wire b. nut c. bolt d. wood) : CROSSBOW

95. SITAR : STRING :: DOUMBEK : (a. keys b. pedals c. stick d. skin)

96. JOAN OF ARC : BURNING :: ROBESPIERRE : (a. hanging
    b. starvation c. guillotine d. firing squad)

97. FISSION : SPLITTING :: FUSION : (a. cooling b. heating
    c. combining d. melting)

98. SHIVA : KALI :: ODEN : (a. Frey b. Frigg c. Loki d. Thor)

99. SALVATION ARMY : WILLIAM BOOTH :: (a. Girl Scouts b. Boy
    Scouts c. Sierra Club d. Red Cross) : JEAN HENRI DURANT

100. AMNESIA : MEMORY :: (a. astigmatism b. tinnitus c. rhinitis
    d. othematoma) : VISION

# Practice Test 3

## ANSWER KEY

| | | | |
|---|---|---|---|
| 1. (c) | 26. (c) | 51. (c) | 76. (d) |
| 2. (b) | 27. (d) | 52. (d) | 77. (a) |
| 3. (c) | 28. (c) | 53. (d) | 78. (d) |
| 4. (d) | 29. (c) | 54. (a) | 79. (c) |
| 5. (c) | 30. (b) | 55. (c) | 80. (b) |
| 6. (a) | 31. (d) | 56. (c) | 81. (c) |
| 7. (c) | 32. (d) | 57. (c) | 82. (b) |
| 8. (d) | 33. (b) | 58. (c) | 83. (a) |
| 9. (b) | 34. (a) | 59. (c) | 84. (a) |
| 10. (b) | 35. (b) | 60. (a) | 85. (d) |
| 11. (b) | 36. (d) | 61. (d) | 86. (d) |
| 12. (c) | 37. (c) | 62. (c) | 87. (a) |
| 13. (d) | 38. (b) | 63. (b) | 88. (d) |
| 14. (a) | 39. (a) | 64. (a) | 89. (b) |
| 15. (b) | 40. (b) | 65. (c) | 90. (c) |
| 16. (c) | 41. (d) | 66. (c) | 91. (b) |
| 17. (a) | 42. (c) | 67. (d) | 92. (b) |
| 18. (b) | 43. (d) | 68. (c) | 93. (a) |
| 19. (b) | 44. (c) | 69. (a) | 94. (c) |
| 20. (c) | 45. (b) | 70. (d) | 95. (d) |
| 21. (c) | 46. (b) | 71. (a) | 96. (c) |
| 22. (c) | 47. (c) | 72. (c) | 97. (c) |
| 23. (b) | 48. (b) | 73. (d) | 98. (b) |
| 24. (c) | 49. (b) | 74. (b) | 99. (d) |
| 25. (b) | 50. (b) | 75. (b) | 100. (a) |

# DETAILED EXPLANATIONS OF ANSWERS

1.  **(c)**   (c) is correct because the black death is the common name for the bubonic plague as consumption is for tuberculosis. (a) is incorrect because the pox is the common name for either small pox or syphilis. (b) is incorrect because it is the common name for venereal disease. (d) is incorrect because the flu is the common name for influenza.

2.  **(b)**   (b) is correct because the United Nations was formed during Roosevelt's presidency as the League of Nations was under Wilson. (a), (c), and (d) are incorrect because the UN was not founded under these presidencies.

3.  **(c)**   (c) is correct because Henry was the founder of the House of Tudor as Philip was the founder of the House of Valois. (a) is incorrect because George V founded Windsor. (b) is incorrect because Edward VII founded Saxe-Coburg. (d) is incorrect because George I founded Hanover.

4.  **(d)**   (d) is correct because Edward VIII became the Duke of Windsor, after he abdicated, as James VI of Scotland became James I of Great Britain after Elizabeth I died. (a), (b), and (c) are wrong, as Edward did not take those titles.

5.  **(c)**   (c) is correct because Leon Czolgosz shot William McKinley as Booth shot Lincoln. (a) is incorrect because Hinkley shot Reagan. (b) is incorrect because Ray shot King. (d) is incorrect because Guiteau shot Garfield.

6.  **(a)**   (a) is correct because Louis XVI was the last king of France as Nicholas II was the last czar of Russia. (b), (c), and (d) are incorrect because these rulers were not the last king of France.

7.  **(c)**   (c) is correct because Napoleon was born in Corsica as Catherine was born in Latvia. (a) is incorrect because Napoleon ruled France. (b) is incorrect because he was exiled to Elba. (d) is incorrect because he was defeated at Waterloo.

8.  **(d)**   (d) is correct because the Scots guard was the personal guard of the kings of France as the Praetorian guard was the personal guard of the Roman emperors. (a), (b), and (c) are incorrect because the Scots Guard was not their personal guard.

9.  **(b)**    (b) is correct because Nixon was followed by Ford in office, as Washington was followed by Adams. (a) is incorrect because Carter followed Ford. (c) is incorrect because Reagan followed Carter. (d) is incorrect because Johnson followed Kennedy.

10. **(b)**    (b) is correct because the Thirty Years War lasted 30 years, as the Hundred Years War lasted 113. (a), (c), and (d) are irrelevant.

11. **(b)**    (b) is correct because Lucy (*Australopithecus afarensis*) was discovered by Johanson and Taieb as Pluto was discovered by Tombaugh. (a) and (d) are incorrect because they refer to the comic strip "Peanuts." (c) is incorrect because Louis Leakey discovered *homo Habilis*.

12. **(c)**    (c) is correct, Darwin's ship was the *Beagle* as Cousteau's was the *Calypso*. (a) is incorrect because the Galapagos were the islands to which he was traveling. (b) is incorrect because it is the title of his book. (d) is irrelevant.

13. **(d)**    (d) is correct because Dolly was Madison's wife as Eleanor was Roosevelt's. (a) is incorrect because Martha was Washington's wife. (b) is incorrect because Mary was Lincoln's wife. (c) is incorrect because Lady Bird was Johnson's wife.

14. **(a)**    (a) is correct because Camelot was Arthur's castle, as Nymphenburg was Ludwig's. (b) is incorrect because it was the palace of the kings of France. (c) is incorrect because it is the name of Arthur's wife. (d) is incorrect because it is Lancelot's castle.

15. **(b)**    (b) is correct because the House of Commons is one of the two houses of Parliament as the Senate is one of the two houses of Congress. (a) is incorrect because it is a house of Parliament (c) is incorrect because Storting is Norway's Parliament. (d) is incorrect because it refers to the appointed inner circle of the American president.

16. **(c)**    (c) is correct because Mary Leakey found the Laolti footprints as Dart found the Taung child. (a) is incorrect because Richard Leakey made many important finds in East Africa. The Laolti footprints, however, were not among them. (b) is incorrect because Louis Leakey unearthed Zinjanthropus. (d) is incorrect because Louise Leakey is a fictitious name.

17. **(a)**    (a) is correct because the Celts would decorate their bodies with wode as the Maori would with tattoos. (b) is incorrect because it is a

beverage. (c) is incorrect because the Celts did not decorate their bodies with dirt. (d) is incorrect because saffron is a spice.

18. **(b)**   (b) is correct because Armstrong was captain of the *Apollo 11* spacecraft as Gagarin was captain of *Vostok I*. (a), (c), and (d) are incorrect because Neil Armstrong did not command these missions. However, *Apollo 8* (a) was the first mission to accomplish a manned lunar orbit.

19. **(b)**   (b) is correct because the sobriquet of Louis XIV was the Sun King. (a), (c), and (d) are irrelevant because Louis XIV did not take these titles.

20. **(c)**   (c) is correct because Attila was the ruler of the Huns as Alaric was the ruler of the Visigoths. (a) is incorrect because Caesar was the ruler of the Romans. (b) is incorrect because Clovis was the ruler of the Franks. (d) is incorrect because Hadrian was a ruler of Rome.

21. **(c)**   (c) is correct because Phobos is a satellite of Mars as the Moon is a satellite of Earth. (a) is incorrect because Europa is a moon of Jupiter. (b) is incorrect because Oberon is a moon of Uranus. (d) is incorrect because Nereid is a moon of Neptune.

22. **(c)**   (c) is correct because the wonder of the world that was located in Babylon was the Hanging Gardens as the pyramids were in Egypt. (a) and (b) are incorrect because even though they are wonders of the world they were not in Babylon. (d) is incorrect because it is not a wonder of the world nor in Babylon.

23. **(b)**   (b) is correct because Hippocrates was the founder of modern medicine as Euclid was the founder of geometry. (a), (c), and (d) are irrelevant because Hippocrates was not the founder of these disciplines.

24. **(c)**   (c) is correct because Black Tuesday was the day that the stock market crashed in 1929 as Black Monday was the day the market fell in 1987. (a) is incorrect because Fat Tuesday is the day before Ash Wednesday. (b) and (d) are irrelevant.

25. **(b)**   (b) is correct because Roosevelt is on the front of a dime as Anthony is on the front of the dollar coin. (a) is incorrect because Lincoln is on the penny. (c) is incorrect because Nixon is not on a coin. (d) is incorrect because Washington is on the quarter.

26. **(c)**   (c) is correct because Jason's quest was the golden fleece as Lancelot's was the Holy Grail. (a) is incorrect because Ulysses's quest was to get home. (b) is incorrect because Orestes was the son of Agammemnon. (d) is incorrect because Paris was the ruler of Troy.

27. **(d)**   (d) is correct because Galileo invented the water thermometer as Bell invented the telephone. (a) is incorrect because Eiffel invented the wind tunnel. (b) is incorrect because Judson invented the zipper. (c) is incorrect because Franklin invented the lightning rod.

28. **(c)**   (c) is correct because Asgard was the home of the Norse gods as Olympus was the home of the Greek gods. (a), (b), and (d) are incorrect because they are the proper names of Norse gods.

29. **(c)**   (c) is correct because mustard gas was used during World War I as agent orange was used during the Vietnam conflict. (a), (b), and (d) are incorrect because these chemical weapons were not introduced during these conflicts.

30. **(b)**   (b) is correct because AM stands for amplitude modulation as FM stands for frequency modulation. (a), (c), and (d) are incorrect.

31. **(d)**   (d) is correct because pyrite resembles gold as the cubic zirconium looks like a diamond. (a) is incorrect because quartz is a silicon mineral formation. (b) is incorrect because silver is an element. (c) is incorrect because an alloy is formed by mixing metals.

32. **(d)**   (d) is correct because an EEG is a test for the brain as EKG is a test for the heart. (a), (b), and (c) are incorrect because an EEG does not measure their activity.

33. **(b)**   (b) is correct because the feminine form of earl is countess as the feminine form of marquis is marchioness. (a) is incorrect because duchess is the feminine form of duke. (c) is incorrect because lady is the feminine form of knight. (d) is incorrect because lady is the feminine form of lord.

34. **(a)**   (a) is correct because leukemia directly affects the blood as asthma directly affects the lungs. (b), (c), and (d) are incorrect because leukemia does not directly affect these areas.

35. **(b)** (b) is correct because the Grand Canyon National Park is in Arizona as the Everglades National Park is in Florida. (a), (c), and (d) are incorrect because the Grand Canyon is not in these states.

36. **(d)** (d) is correct because the Matterhorn is in the Alps as Mt. Everest is located in the Himalayas. (a) is incorrect because Athos is located in Greece. (b) is incorrect because Monserrat is located in Spain. (c) is incorrect because Mt. McKinley is located in the U.S.

37. **(c)** (c) is correct because the Black Forest is an area of Germany as the Highlands is an area of Scotland. (a), (b), and (d) are incorrect because the Black Forest is not found in these nations.

38. **(b)** (b) is correct because the Crimean War was fought in Russia as the Boer was fought in South Africa. (a), (c), and (d) are incorrect because the Crimean War was not fought in these places.

39. **(a)** (a) is correct because Kingston is the capital of Jamaica as Havana is the capital of Cuba. (b), (c), and (d) are incorrect because, although they are cities in Jamaica, they are not the capitals.

40. **(b)** (b) is correct because ancient Phrygia is in modern Turkey as ancient Persia is in modern Iran. (a), (c), and (d) are incorrect because Phrygia was not included within their boundaries.

41. **(d)** (d) is correct because the Auckland Islands are off the coast of New Zealand as the Aleutian Islands are off the coast of Alaska. (a) is incorrect because Fernando de Nororna Islands are located off the coast of Brazil. (b) is incorrect because Taiwan is located off the coast of China. (c) is incorrect because the Falkland Islands are located off the coast of Argentina.

42. **(c)** (c) is correct because La Salle was known for his exploration of the Louisiana area as Livingstone was known for his exploration of Africa. (a) is incorrect because Hudson was known for exploring the Atlantic northeast. (b) is incorrect because Ponce de Léon was known for exploring the Florida area. (d) is incorrect because Cabot was known for exploring the coast of South America.

43. **(d)** (d) is correct because Lake Victoria is located in Kenya as the Lake of Lucerne is located in Switzerland. (a) is incorrect because, although Victoria rules Great Britain, there is no Lake Victoria. (b) is incor-

rect because Victoria Island is located in Canada. (c) is incorrect because the state of Victoria is located in Australia.

44. **(c)**   (c) is correct because the Jesuits is another name for the Society of Jesus as the Black Friars was another name for the Dominicans. (a) is incorrect because Methodism is a sect of Protestantism. (b) is incorrect because Scientologists are those who follow the teachings of author L. Ron Hubbard. (d) is incorrect because this is one of the names humanity has given to its spiritual focus.

45. **(b)**   (b) is correct because amethyst is a variety of quartz as sapphire is a variety of corundum. (a) is incorrect because graphite is a form of carbon. (c) and (d) are incorrect because, although they are minerals, amethyst is not included among their varieties.

46. **(b)**   (b) is the correct answer because Zeno founded the school of stoicism as Descartes founded the school of solipsism. (a) is incorrect because Xenophanes founded the Eleatic school. (c) is incorrect because Pyrrho introduced skepticism. (d) is incorrect because Epicurus introduced hedonism.

47. **(c)**   (c) is correct because Earth Day is on April 22 as Boxing Day is on December 26. (a), (b), and (d) are incorrect because Earth Day is not observed on these days.

48. **(b)**   (b) is correct because Henry Ford designed the Model T as Ferdinand Porsche designed the Volkswagen. (a), (c), and (d) are incorrect because Oldsmobile and Cadillac are made by General Motors in which the Du Pont family members and associates have owned large blocks of stock.

49. **(b)**   (b) is correct because watt is a unit of power as gram is a unit of mass. (a) is incorrect because cubit is a unit of length. (c) is incorrect because volume is a unit of capacity. (d) is incorrect because degree is a unit of temperature.

50. **(b)**   (b) is correct because Gatling invented the machine gun as Colt invented the revolver. (a) is incorrect because the cannon was developed by Schwartz. (c) and (d) are incorrect because their inventors are unknown.

51. **(c)**   (c) is correct because the escudo is the currency of Portugal as the yen is the currency of Japan. (a) is incorrect because the peseta is the

currency of Spain. (b) is incorrect because the cruzeiro is the currency of Brazil. (d) is incorrect because the rand is the currency of South Africa.

52. **(d)**   (d) is correct because the official language of Greenland is Danish as the official language of Austria is German. (a) is incorrect because the official language of France is French. (b) is incorrect because the official language of Sweden is Swedish. (c) is incorrect because the official language of Norway is Norwegian.

53. **(d)**   (d) is correct because Polaris is the brightest star in the Little Dipper as Rigel is the brightest star in Orion. (a) is incorrect because Sirus is located in Canis Major. (b) is incorrect because Capella is located in Auriga. (c) is incorrect because Sol is our sun.

54. **(a)**   (a) is correct because Mt. McKinley is the highest point in North America as Kilimanjaro is the highest point in Africa. (b) and (d) are incorrect because, although in North America, they are not the highest points. (c) is incorrect because Mt. Everest is in Asia.

55. **(c)**   (c) is correct because Death Valley is the lowest point in North America as the Dead Sea is the lowest point in Asia. (a), (b), and (d) are incorrect because, although in North America, they are not the lowest points.

56. **(c)**   (c) is correct because Aurora Australis is another name for the southern lights as Aurora Borealis is another name for the northern lights. (a) is incorrect because it is the name for both southern and northern lights. (b) is incorrect because Aurora Luminesence is a general term, referring to either the northern or southern lights. (d) is incorrect because it refers to a stream of charged particles emanating from the upper atmosphere of the sun.

57. **(c)**   (c) is correct because clay tablets were used for writing in Babylonia as papyrus was in Egypt. (a), (b), and (d) are incorrect because these materials were not used in this capacity in Babylonia.

58. **(c)**   (c) is correct because Deucalion was the hero of the great flood myth in Greek mythology as Noah was in Judeo-Christian. (a) is incorrect because Gilgamesh is the protagonist of an ancient Sumerian epic of the same name. (b) is incorrect because Jason is a figure in Greek mythology. (d) is incorrect because Plato was an ancient Greek philosopher.

59. **(c)**  (c) is correct because rattan comes from the palm tree as turpentine comes from the pine tree. (a) is incorrect because soap, once made from animal products, is now synthetically produced. (b) is incorrect because ink, at its simplest, is a pigment suspended in a liquid. (d) is incorrect because dye generally refers to a pigment used to color fabrics.

60. **(a)**  (a) is correct because Toronto is the capital of Ontario as Victoria is the capital of British Columbia. (b), (c), and (d) are all incorrect because, although all are cities in Canada, they are not the capital of Ontario.

61. **(d)**  (d) is correct because the University of Arizona is located in Tucson as Fordham is located in New York City. (a), (b), and (c) are incorrect because, although all are cities in Arizona, the university is not located there.

62. **(c)**  (c) is correct because Harris created Uncle Remus as Andersen created the Snow Queen. (a) and (d) are incorrect because, although they created many fictional characters, they did not create Uncle Remus. (b) is incorrect because Faust was a character in a novel by Goethe.

63. **(b)**  (b) is correct because light travels at 186,000 miles per second in a vacuum as sound travels 1,088 feet per second in a vacuum. (a), (c), and (d) are irrelevant.

64. **(a)**  (a) is correct because hemi is Greek for half as bio is Greek for like. (b), (c), and (d) are incorrect because they are not the Greek word for half.

65. **(c)**  (c) is correct because Horace was a Latin poet as Livy was a Latin historian. (a) is incorrect because Pindar was a Greek poet. (b) is incorrect because Zeno was a Greek philosopher. (d) is incorrect because Sappho was a Greek poet.

66. **(c)**  (c) is correct because F. Roosevelt was buried at Hyde Park as Washington was buried at Mt. Vernon. (a) is incorrect because Arthur was buried in Albany. (b) is incorrect because Grant was buried in New York City. (d) is incorrect because Cleveland was buried in Princeton.

67. **(d)**  (d) is correct because the *Inquirer* is based in Philadelphia as the *Wall Street Journal* is based in New York. (a) is incorrect because the *Sun Times* is based in Chicago. (b) is incorrect because the *Examiner* is

based in San Francisco. (c) is incorrect because the *Star* is a national tabloid.

68. **(c)**    (c) is correct because the name Nevada comes from the Spanish for snow-clad as Puerto Rico comes from the Spanish for rich port. (a), (b), and (d) do not refer to this Western state.

69. **(a)**    (a) is correct because neon comes from the Greek word for new as helium comes from the Greek word for sun. (b), (c), and (d) are irrelevant.

70. **(d)**    (d) is correct because Iceland's form of government is a republic as Luxembourg's is a constitutional monarchy. (a), (b), and (c) are incorrect because, although all are forms of government, none applies to Iceland.

71. **(a)**    (a) is correct because carbon's atomic number is 6 as hydrogen's atomic number is 1. (b) is incorrect because oxygen is atomic number 8. (c) is incorrect because fluorine is atomic number 9. (d) is incorrect because magnesium is atomic number 12.

72. **(c)**    (c) is correct because a Pulitzer is given as an award in the field of journalism as the Emmy is given in the field of television. (a) is incorrect because the Nobel Prize is awarded in the fields of physics, chemistry, medicine, literature, peace, and economic science. (b) is incorrect because the Tony is awarded in the field of Broadway theater. (d) is incorrect because the Fermi is awarded for achievement in atomic energy.

73. **(d)**    (d) is correct because the Verrazano Narrows is the longest suspension bridge in New York, as the Golden Gate is the longest suspension bridge in San Francisco. (a), (b), and (c) are all incorrect because, although they are all suspension bridges in New York, they are not the longest.

74. **(b)**    (b) is correct because elver is the name for a young eel as pullet is the name for a young hen. (a) is incorrect because the name for a young wild fowl is a flapper. (c) is incorrect because the name for a young zebra is a foal. (d) is incorrect because the name for a young hare is a leveret.

75. **(b)**    (b) is correct because the peso is the currency of the Philippines as the pound is the currency of Egypt. (a) is incorrect because the yen is the currency of Japan. (c) is incorrect because the nuevo sol is the

currency of Peru. (d) is incorrect because the dinar is the currency of Algeria.

76. **(d)**    (d) is correct because Ganymede is the largest satellite in our solar system as Jupiter is the largest planet. (a), (b), and (c) are incorrect because, although all are satellites, they are not the largest.

77. **(a)**    (a) is correct because gastrin is a hormone produced by the stomach glands as estrogen is a hormone produced by the ovaries. (b) is incorrect because the adrenal medulla produces the hormone adrenaline. (c) is incorrect because the thyroid produces the hormones thyroxin and calcitonin. (d) is incorrect because the pancreas produces the hormone glucagon.

78. **(d)**    (d) is correct because Disraeli was prime minister under Victoria, as Thatcher was under Elizabeth II. (a) is incorrect because Baldwin was under George V. (b) is incorrect because Pitt, the younger was under George III. (c) is incorrect because Asquith was under George V.

79. **(c)**    (c) is correct because Dulles Airport is located in Washington, DC as Bradley Airport is located in Hartford, CT. (a) is incorrect because Gatwick is located in London. (b) is incorrect because Logan is located in Boston. (d) is incorrect because Midway is located in Chicago.

80. **(b)**    (b) is correct because the Archbishop of Canterbury is the head of the Episcopalian faith as the Pope is the head of the Roman Catholic faith. (a), (c), and (d) are incorrect because they are all lower church offices.

81. **(c)**    (c) is correct because Neanderthal man existed circa 75,000, as Homo Hablis existed circa. 2,000,000. (a), (b), and (d) are insignificant.

82. **(b)**    (b) is correct because band is the collective noun for gorillas as nest is the collective noun for vipers. (a) is incorrect because it refers to geese. (c) is incorrect because it refers to oxen. (d) is incorrect because it refers to hounds.

83. **(a)**    (a) is correct because the harvest spider, like the garden snake, is harmless to humans, as the black widow spider and the coral snake are dangerous to humans. (b), (c), and (d) are all incorrect because they are spiders dangerous to humans.

84. **(a)**    (a) is correct because Texas is a state in the United States as Queensland is a state in Australia. (b), (c), and (d) are all incorrect because they are cities.

85. **(d)**    (d) is correct because the Bhagavad-Gita is a work of Hinduism as the Koran is a work of Islam. (a) is incorrect because Tripitika is a work of Buddhism. (b) is incorrect because Analects is a work of Confucianism. (c) is incorrect because Bayán is a work of Baha'i.

86. **(d)**    (d) is correct because the tibia is a bone in the leg as the ulna is an arm bone. (a) is incorrect because the tarsals bones are in the foot. (b) is incorrect because the humorus is a bone in the arm. (c) is incorrect because the mandible bone is in the head.

87. **(a)**    (a) is correct because the family name for frog is ranidae as the family name for dog is canidae. (b) is incorrect because the squirrel is in the sciurdae family. (c) is incorrect because the cat is in the felide family. (d) is incorrect because the lizard is in the squamata family.

88. **(d)**    (d) is correct because Vestia is the Roman name for Hestia as Terra is the Roman name for Gaea. (a) is incorrect because Juno is the Roman name for Hera. (b) is incorrect because Saturn is the Roman name for Cronos. (c) is incorrect because Eros is the Roman name for Cupid.

89. **(b)**    (b) is correct because Q is the Roman letter for the Greek koppa as K is the Roman equivalent for the Greek kappa. (a) is incorrect because Z is Roman for zeta. (c) is incorrect because D is Roman for delta. (d) is incorrect because L is Roman for lambda.

90. **(c)**    (c) is correct because Arabic numeral 600 is equivalent to Roman numeral DC. (a) is incorrect because the Arabic value of the Roman numeral MD is 1,500. (b) is incorrect because the Arabic equivalent of CC is 200. (d) is incorrect because MX equals 1,010.

91. **(b)**    (b) is correct because Diona was the mother of Aphrodite as Leda was the mother of Helen. (a) is incorrect because Metis was the mother of Athena. (c) is incorrect because Themis was the mother of the Fates. (d) is incorrect because Io was the mother of Epaphus.

92. **(b)**    (b) is correct because homo is Greek for same as macro is Greek for large. (a) is incorrect because the Greek word for small is micro (c) is incorrect because the Greek word for male is andro. (d) is incorrect because homeo is Greek for similar.

93. **(a)**    (a) is correct because a khan was a ruler in Mongolia as a czar was a ruler in Russia. (b) is incorrect because a pharaoh ruled in Egypt. (c) is incorrect because a sultan ruled in Turkey. (d) is incorrect because an emperor ruled in China.

94. **(c)**    (c) is correct because a bolt is shot from a crossbow as a ball is shot from a musket. (a), (b), and (d) are incorrect because these objects were not fired from a crossbow.

95. **(d)**    (d) is correct because sound is produced from the skin of the doumbek as it is produced from the string on a sitar. (a) and (b) are incorrect because they refer to a keyboard instrument, such as a piano, or an organ. (c) is incorrect because this is a general term, musically referring to a percussion implement.

96. **(c)**    (c) is correct because Robespierre was executed by guillotine as Joan of Arc was executed by burning. (a), (b), and (d) are incorrect because, although all are forms of execution, none apply here.

97. **(c)**    (c) is correct because fusion creates energy by combining the nuclei as fission creates energy by splitting a nucleus. (a), (b), and (d) are incorrect because while these terms are used in the creation of nuclear energy, they do not specifically refer to fusion.

98. **(b)**    (b) is correct because Frigg was the goddess consort of Oden in Norse mythology as Kali was to Shiva in Hindu mythology. (a) is incorrect because Frey was the god of prosperity. (b) is incorrect because Loki was the god of evil. (d) is incorrect because Thor was the god of thunder.

99. **(d)**    (d) is correct because Durant was the founder of the Red Cross as Booth was the founder of the Salvation Army. (a) is incorrect because Juliette Low founded the Girl Scouts. (b) is incorrect because Sir Robert Powell founded the Boy Scouts. (c) is incorrect because John Muir founded the Sierra Club.

100. **(a)**    (a) is correct because vision is effected by astigmatism as memory is effected by amnesia. (b) is incorrect because tinnitus effects the hearing. (c) is incorrect because rhinitis effects the sense of smell. (d) is incorrect because othematoma, cauliflower ear, effects the hearing.

# MAT – Practice Test 4 Answer Sheet

1. ⓐ ⓑ ⓒ ⓓ
2. ⓐ ⓑ ⓒ ⓓ
3. ⓐ ⓑ ⓒ ⓓ
4. ⓐ ⓑ ⓒ ⓓ
5. ⓐ ⓑ ⓒ ⓓ
6. ⓐ ⓑ ⓒ ⓓ
7. ⓐ ⓑ ⓒ ⓓ
8. ⓐ ⓑ ⓒ ⓓ
9. ⓐ ⓑ ⓒ ⓓ
10. ⓐ ⓑ ⓒ ⓓ
11. ⓐ ⓑ ⓒ ⓓ
12. ⓐ ⓑ ⓒ ⓓ
13. ⓐ ⓑ ⓒ ⓓ
14. ⓐ ⓑ ⓒ ⓓ
15. ⓐ ⓑ ⓒ ⓓ
16. ⓐ ⓑ ⓒ ⓓ
17. ⓐ ⓑ ⓒ ⓓ
18. ⓐ ⓑ ⓒ ⓓ
19. ⓐ ⓑ ⓒ ⓓ
20. ⓐ ⓑ ⓒ ⓓ
21. ⓐ ⓑ ⓒ ⓓ
22. ⓐ ⓑ ⓒ ⓓ
23. ⓐ ⓑ ⓒ ⓓ
24. ⓐ ⓑ ⓒ ⓓ
25. ⓐ ⓑ ⓒ ⓓ
26. ⓐ ⓑ ⓒ ⓓ
27. ⓐ ⓑ ⓒ ⓓ
28. ⓐ ⓑ ⓒ ⓓ
29. ⓐ ⓑ ⓒ ⓓ
30. ⓐ ⓑ ⓒ ⓓ
31. ⓐ ⓑ ⓒ ⓓ
32. ⓐ ⓑ ⓒ ⓓ
33. ⓐ ⓑ ⓒ ⓓ
34. ⓐ ⓑ ⓒ ⓓ

35. ⓐ ⓑ ⓒ ⓓ
36. ⓐ ⓑ ⓒ ⓓ
37. ⓐ ⓑ ⓒ ⓓ
38. ⓐ ⓑ ⓒ ⓓ
39. ⓐ ⓑ ⓒ ⓓ
40. ⓐ ⓑ ⓒ ⓓ
41. ⓐ ⓑ ⓒ ⓓ
42. ⓐ ⓑ ⓒ ⓓ
43. ⓐ ⓑ ⓒ ⓓ
44. ⓐ ⓑ ⓒ ⓓ
45. ⓐ ⓑ ⓒ ⓓ
46. ⓐ ⓑ ⓒ ⓓ
47. ⓐ ⓑ ⓒ ⓓ
48. ⓐ ⓑ ⓒ ⓓ
49. ⓐ ⓑ ⓒ ⓓ
50. ⓐ ⓑ ⓒ ⓓ
51. ⓐ ⓑ ⓒ ⓓ
52. ⓐ ⓑ ⓒ ⓓ
53. ⓐ ⓑ ⓒ ⓓ
54. ⓐ ⓑ ⓒ ⓓ
55. ⓐ ⓑ ⓒ ⓓ
56. ⓐ ⓑ ⓒ ⓓ
57. ⓐ ⓑ ⓒ ⓓ
58. ⓐ ⓑ ⓒ ⓓ
59. ⓐ ⓑ ⓒ ⓓ
60. ⓐ ⓑ ⓒ ⓓ
61. ⓐ ⓑ ⓒ ⓓ
62. ⓐ ⓑ ⓒ ⓓ
63. ⓐ ⓑ ⓒ ⓓ
64. ⓐ ⓑ ⓒ ⓓ
65. ⓐ ⓑ ⓒ ⓓ
66. ⓐ ⓑ ⓒ ⓓ
67. ⓐ ⓑ ⓒ ⓓ
68. ⓐ ⓑ ⓒ ⓓ

69. ⓐ ⓑ ⓒ ⓓ
70. ⓐ ⓑ ⓒ ⓓ
71. ⓐ ⓑ ⓒ ⓓ
72. ⓐ ⓑ ⓒ ⓓ
73. ⓐ ⓑ ⓒ ⓓ
74. ⓐ ⓑ ⓒ ⓓ
75. ⓐ ⓑ ⓒ ⓓ
76. ⓐ ⓑ ⓒ ⓓ
77. ⓐ ⓑ ⓒ ⓓ
78. ⓐ ⓑ ⓒ ⓓ
79. ⓐ ⓑ ⓒ ⓓ
80. ⓐ ⓑ ⓒ ⓓ
81. ⓐ ⓑ ⓒ ⓓ
82. ⓐ ⓑ ⓒ ⓓ
83. ⓐ ⓑ ⓒ ⓓ
84. ⓐ ⓑ ⓒ ⓓ
85. ⓐ ⓑ ⓒ ⓓ
86. ⓐ ⓑ ⓒ ⓓ
87. ⓐ ⓑ ⓒ ⓓ
88. ⓐ ⓑ ⓒ ⓓ
89. ⓐ ⓑ ⓒ ⓓ
90. ⓐ ⓑ ⓒ ⓓ
91. ⓐ ⓑ ⓒ ⓓ
92. ⓐ ⓑ ⓒ ⓓ
93. ⓐ ⓑ ⓒ ⓓ
94. ⓐ ⓑ ⓒ ⓓ
95. ⓐ ⓑ ⓒ ⓓ
96. ⓐ ⓑ ⓒ ⓓ
97. ⓐ ⓑ ⓒ ⓓ
98. ⓐ ⓑ ⓒ ⓓ
99. ⓐ ⓑ ⓒ ⓓ
100. ⓐ ⓑ ⓒ ⓓ

# MILLER ANALOGIES

# PRACTICE TEST 4

**TIME:** 50 Minutes
100 Analogies

---

**DIRECTIONS**: Read each of the following analogies carefully, and choose the BEST answer to each item. Fill in your responses in the answer sheets provided.

---

1. CHARLES I : CROMWELL :: NICHOLAS II : (a. Rasputin b. Trotsky c. Stalin d. Lenin)

2. TRIANGLE : LEG :: CIRCLE : (a. radius b. side c. diameter d. arc)

3. CARBOXYLIC ACID PLUS ALCOHOL : (a. metal b. ester c. phenol d. amine) :: ACID PLUS BASE : SALT

4. POTATO : PEA :: (a. tomato b. cucumber c. beet d. corn) : BEAN

5. TANGENT : COTANGENT :: COSINE : (a. sine b. cosecant c. secant d. hypotenuse)

6. SODIUM : POTASSIUM :: ARGON : (a. calcium b. magnesium c. chlorine d. krypton)

7. TRANSPIRE : (a. occur b. pass c. weaken d. puncture) :: BREACH : BREAK

8. UNION : OR :: INTERSECTION : (a. both b. none c. all d. and)

9. (a. crest b. amplitude c. refraction d. edge) : TROUGH :: HIGH : LOW

10. PARE : APPLE :: (a. husk b. trim c. pollinate d. hybrid) : CORN

11. $x : x^2 + 3x :: xy :$ (a. $x^2 + 3y$ b. $x^2y + 3xy$ c. $x^2y^2 + 3y$ d. $x^2y^2 + 3xy$)

12. COLLUVIUM : SEDIMENTS :: GEOMETRIC MINERALS :
    (a. salts b. crystals c. tetrahedra d. mica)

13. INDUCTION : (a. suppression b. regulation c. promotion
    d. repression) :: LACTOSE OPERON : ARGININE OPERON

14. PRODUCT : FACTOR :: SUM : (a. integer b. quotient c. proctor
    d. addend)

15. (a. tranquilizer b. soporific c. stimulant d. analgesic) : SOMNOLENT
    :: ANXIOLYTIC : CALM

16. DONOR : (a. conjugation b. recipient c. HFR d. induction) :: $F^+$ : $F^-$

17. CORUSCATE : DIAMOND :: (a. shine b. soft c. flat d. refined) :
    GOLD

18. 8 : 2 :: 125 : (a. 15.65 b. 25 c. 5 d. 12.55)

19. GRADUATE CYLINDER : MILLILITER :: (a. pipette b. ounce
    c. scale d. analytical balance) : MILLIGRAM

20. SLED : RUNNER :: WAGON : (a. slat b. handle c. wheel
    d. wagoneer)

21. APERITIF : DRINK :: (a. chocolate b. dessert c. hors d'oeuvre
    d. soup) : FOOD

22. BREW : BEER :: (a. season b. leaf c. steep d. simmer) : TEA

23. ROCKSLIDE : HILL :: (a. fall b. flow c. creep d. slump) : CURVE

24. VIRGIL : *AENEID* :: (a. Chaucer b. Shakespeare c. Johnson
    d. Homer) : *ILIAD*

25. (a. acid rain b. distilled water c. baking soda d. litmus paper) :
    NEUTRAL :: VINEGAR : ALKALINE

26. 7 : 49 :: 11 : (a. 121 b. 144 c. 81 d. 13)

27. RANID : (a. fox b. frog c. rabbit d. grasshopper) :: CANID : WOLF

28. EDENTATE : TEETH :: ALBINO : (a. white b. fragile c. pigment d. small)

29. GENE : CHROMOSOME :: (a. bird b. feather c. flight d. bone) : WING

30. ABSORBED : SCATTERED :: SPECTROPHOTOMETER : (a. turbidity b. nephelometer c. voltmeter d. light)

31. BLINDERS : (a. partial b. central c. peripheral d. occasional) :: BLINDFOLD : TOTAL

32. IONIC : COLUMN :: GAMBREL : (a. ceiling b. mantel c. entry d. roof)

33. (a. lens b. microscope c. opera glasses d. telescope) : BINOCULARS :: SPINET : PIANO

34. $g : g^2 + 3g - 2 :: 3 :$ (a. 16 b. 2 c. –2 d. 10)

35. REYNARD : VIXEN :: (a. stallion b. doe c. steer d. jennet) : COW

36. PATTERN : GARMENT :: (a. DNA b. intellect c. hormones d. environment) : HEREDITY

37. pH : HYDROGEN ION :: (a. galvanometer b. current c. pH meter d. cuvette) : ELECTRONS

38. (a. Chaucer b. Ralph Waldo Emerson c. Joseph Heller d. James Joyce) : LOUISA MAY ALCOTT :: TRUMAN CAPOTE : PEARL S. BUCK

39. (a. Nathaniel Hawthorne b. Mark Twain c. Charles Dickens d. Ernest Hemingway) : MISSISSIPPI :: HENRY JAMES : NEW YORK

40. AMOEBA : (a. membranes b. gills c. cilia d. pseudopod) ::
    OCTOPUS : TENTACLE

41. NEOLOGISM : (a. book b. word c. property d. equation) ::
    INNOVATION : CONCEPT

42. DENSE : DISPERSE :: (a. release b. dilute c. erode d. inflict) :
    EXPAND

43. IMPROMPTU : MEMORIZED :: SPONTANEOUS : (a. impetuous
    b. static c. calculated d. glib)

44. IMPERVIOUS : AGITATED :: (a. enlightened b. depressive
    c. perturbed d. pretentious) : IGNORANT

45. JOHN KENNEDY : LYNDON BAINES JOHNSON :: GEORGE
    WASHINGTON : (a. John Adams b. Benjamin Harrison c. Andrew
    Jackson d. Benjamin Franklin)

46. BENEVOLENT : MALIGNANT :: COOPERATIVE : (a. deleterious
    b. resistant c. evasive d. eager)

47. 60° : sin 60° :: 30° : (a. $\sqrt{3/2}$ b. 1/2 c. 1 d. 2 / $\sqrt{3}$)

48. RIVER : ESTUARY :: (a. sand b. cove c. ocean d. land) : SHORE

49. PASSE PARTOUT : (a. code b. lock c. safe d. master key) ::
    NOUVEAU RICHE : NEWLY WEALTHY

50. (a. Patagonia b. Fierro c. Bolivar d. San Martin) :
    REVOLUTIONARY :: BORGES : AUTHOR

51. (a. absorbance b. adsorption c. reflection d. scattering) :
    TRANSMITTANCE :: INTAKE : OUTPUT

52. (a. grotesque b. imperfect c. pseudo d. exiguous) : COUNTERFEIT ::
    INCHOATE : SHAPELESS

53. WASP : HYMENOPTERA :: (a. dogs b. bears c. humans d. cats) :
    PRIMATES

54. SEDULOUS : (a. retreating b. habitual c. careless d. bored) ::
PREEMPTORY : YIELDING

55. VALETUDINARIAN : (a. hypochondriac b. doctor c. hospital
d. psychiatrist) :: VICTIM : PARANOIC

56. MORTAR : (a. fire b. pestle c. brick d. cement) :: ANVIL :
HAMMER

57. GESTATION : (a. birth b. elimination c. conclusion d. resorption) ::
LACTATION : WEANING

58. Given

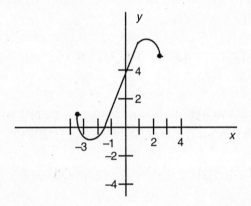

(3, 8) : MAXIMUM :: (−2, −1) : (a. inflection point b. minimum
c. slope d. intersection)

59. (a. bacteria b. coliforms c. hepatitis virus d. rickettsia) : EOSIN
METHYLENE BLUE AGAR :: YEASTS : SABOURAUD'S AGAR

60. BLOOD : COAGULATE :: GRAVY : (a. rarefy b. congeal c. deepen
d. separate)

61. (a. Dali b. Cezanne c. Matisse d. Picasso) : CUBISM ::
LICHTENSTEIN : POP ART

62. RETROGRADE : ROTATION :: (a. object b. reverse c. circular
d. method) : MOTION

63. COCAINE : STIMULANT :: (a. amphetamines b. ritalin
c. barbiturates d. LSD) : DEPRESSANT

64. (a. shark b. whale c. flounder d. guppy) : FISH :: PLATYPUS : BIRD

65. STREP THROAT : BACTERIA :: (a. Rocky Mountain spotted fever b. chickenpox c. amoebic dysentery d. tuberculosis) : VIRUS

66. COMPLEX NUMBER : REAL NUMBER :: RATIONAL NUMBER : (a. irrational number b. imaginary number c. integer d. real number)

67. TRIVIAL : (a. minutia b. enigma c. levity d. palavar) :: CATHOLIC : UNIVERSALITY

68. VACILLATE : (a. switch b. divide c. endure d. waver) :: FLUCTUATE : MOVE

69. BLACKSMITH : FORGE :: PAINTER : (a. studio b. canvas c. brush d. mix)

70. (a. Skinner b. Freud c. Piaget d. Pavlov) : INTELLECTUAL DEVELOPMENT :: ERICKSON : EGO IDENTITY

71. VULGAR : CRUDE :: BIASED : (a. prejudiced b. charming c. rough d. just)

72. ANTI-PYROGENIC : ACETAMINOPHEN :: ANTI-INFLAMMATORY : (a. salicylates b. phenacetin c. caffeine d. codeine)

73. FERN : (a. seed b. leaf c. spore d. fruit) :: OAK : ACORN

74. ALBINISM : (a. albumin b. serotonin c. carotene d. melanin) :: MALNUTRITION : CALORIES

75. (a. –COOH b. –OH c. $R - \underset{\underset{O}{\|}}{C} - OR$ d. $-\underset{\underset{O}{\|}}{C} - N -$) : ALCOHOL ::

    –NH$_2$ : AMINO

76. NaCl : ROCK SALT :: SiO$_2$ : (a. crystals b. ice c. calcareous rock d. quartz)

77. MERCURIAL : (a. erratic b. metaphorical c. meretricious d. penal) ::
    PENNYLESS : IMPOVERISHED

78. MERCER : (a. music b. animals c. textiles d. soldiers) ::
    RESTAURATEUR : FOOD

79. LIGATURE : (a. closing b. cutting c. binding d. arguing) :: HOOK :
    FISHING

80. BAROQUE : CLASSICAL :: (a. Renaissance b. Romanesque
    c. Medieval d. Classical) : ROMANTIC

81. PEREGRINATION : (a. flight b. walk c. flee d. wings) :: CRUISE :
    SAIL

82. MERGANSER : (a. penguin b. horse c. duck d. dog) :: GERNSEY :
    COW

83. BUDDHA : (a. China b. India c. Japan d. Cambodia) :: JESUS :
    ISRAEL

84. TACHYCARDIA : FAST :: (a. angina b. sphygmomanometer
    c. bradycardia d. cardiac arrhythmia) : SLOW

85. MORTARBOARD : COMMENCEMENT :: CROWN :
    (a. indoctrination b. ordination c. induction d. coronation)

86. TRANSMOGRIFY : LANGUAGE :: (a. form b. color c. size d. time)
    : TRANSLATE

87. AGNOSTIC : ATHEIST :: (a. question b. decision c. doubt
    d. definition) : STATEMENT

88. BARRIER : LINE :: ATOLL : (a. square b. triangle c. circle d. spiral)

89. FLEET : (a. quick b. ship c. ocean d. lugubrious) :: PENSIVE :
    THOUGHTFUL

90. BRACKISH : (a. murky b. unclean c. salty d. wet) :: FLAXEN :
    YELLOW

91. LEONINE : LION :: (a. cervine b. equine c. porcine d. bovine) : DEER

92. GRANT : (a. 15 b. 17 c. 22 d. 18) :: REAGAN: 40

93. HUBRIS : PRIDE :: (a. starvation b. satiation c. satisfaction d. nutrition) : HUNGER

94. COCCI : ROUND :: (a. bacilli b. spirochete c. mycoplasma d. spheroplast) : ROD

95. TRAVAIL : WORK :: (a. return b. pillage c. borrow d. kill) : STEAL

96. (a. blood b. milk c. table d. alcohol) : LACTOSE :: FRUIT : FRUCTOSE

97. UPBRAID : REPROACH :: (a. miniscule b. large c. enormous d. lower) : SMALL

98. ENDEMIC : (a. neighborhood b. planet c. region d. building) :: PANDEMIC : COUNTRY

99. FORGIVE : (a. pacify b. exculpate c. contumeliate d. ruminate) :: FATAL : LETHAL

100. MORIBUND : (a. morbid b. dying c. laughing d. hungry) :: GERIATRIC : OLD

# Practice Test 4

## ANSWER KEY

| | | | |
|---|---|---|---|
| 1. (d) | 26. (a) | 51. (a) | 76. (d) |
| 2. (d) | 27. (b) | 52. (c) | 77. (a) |
| 3. (b) | 28. (c) | 53. (c) | 78. (c) |
| 4. (c) | 29. (b) | 54. (c) | 79. (c) |
| 5. (c) | 30. (b) | 55. (a) | 80. (d) |
| 6. (d) | 31. (c) | 56. (b) | 81. (b) |
| 7. (b) | 32. (d) | 57. (a) | 82. (c) |
| 8. (d) | 33. (c) | 58. (b) | 83. (b) |
| 9. (a) | 34. (a) | 59. (b) | 84. (c) |
| 10. (a) | 35. (c) | 60. (b) | 85. (d) |
| 11. (d) | 36. (a) | 61. (d) | 86. (a) |
| 12. (b) | 37. (b) | 62. (b) | 87. (a) |
| 13. (d) | 38. (b) | 63. (c) | 88. (c) |
| 14. (d) | 39. (b) | 64. (b) | 89. (a) |
| 15. (b) | 40. (d) | 65. (b) | 90. (c) |
| 16. (b) | 41. (b) | 66. (c) | 91. (a) |
| 17. (a) | 42. (c) | 67. (a) | 92. (d) |
| 18. (c) | 43. (c) | 68. (d) | 93. (a) |
| 19. (d) | 44. (a) | 69. (a) | 94. (a) |
| 20. (c) | 45. (a) | 70. (c) | 95. (b) |
| 21. (c) | 46. (b) | 71. (a) | 96. (b) |
| 22. (c) | 47. (b) | 72. (a) | 97. (a) |
| 23. (d) | 48. (d) | 73. (c) | 98. (c) |
| 24. (d) | 49. (d) | 74. (d) | 99. (b) |
| 25. (b) | 50. (d) | 75. (b) | 100. (b) |

# DETAILED EXPLANATIONS
# OF ANSWERS

1.  **(d)**   (d) is correct because Charles I was an English ruler executed at the start of a revolution which resulted in non-royal leadership by Cromwell. Nicholas II was a Russian ruler executed at the start of a revolution which resulted in non-royal leadership by Lenin. Rasputin (a) preceded the revolution and was never an acknowledged leader. Trotsky (b) never had leadership of the Soviet Union and Stalin (c) was a leader after Lenin.

2.  **(d)**   The leg is part of the triangle, likewise, an arc (d) is part of a circle. The radius (a) and diameter (c) are parts of the circle, but they do not enclose the circle like the arcs do. A side (b) is a line which is part of a triangle, not a circle.

3.  **(b)**   Ester is correct because when a carboxylic acid plus alcohol react, an ester results. When an acid and a base react, a salt results. A metal (a) is usually an element of two or more elements together, phenol (c) is an aromatic hydrocarbon, and an amine (d) will involve a nitrogen atom, so none of these fits the analogy of what results when any carboxylic acid is added to an alcohol.

4.  **(c)**   (c) is correct because a potato and a beet are both root vegetables. A pea and a bean are both pod vegetables. Tomato (a) and cucumber (b) are both fruits. Corn (d) is neither a root nor a pod vegetable.

5.  **(c)**   The cotangent is the complementary trigonometric function to tangent. Thus, the complementary function of cosine is secant (c). Sine (a) and cosecant (b) comprise the other pair of functions. The hypotenuse (d) is the longest leg of a right triangle. While the hypotenuse is used in calculating trigonometric functions, it is not one.

6.  **(d)**   Krypton is correct because sodium and potassium are found on the Periodic Table in Group IA, with sodium in Period 3 and potassium in Period 4. Argon and krypton are found in Group VIII, argon in Period 3 and krypton in Period 4. Calcium (a), magnesium (b), and chlorine (c) do not fit in a category with argon and therefore do not fit the analogy.

7.  **(b)**   (b) is correct because to transpire is to pass through a surface

just as to breach is to break through a surface. Occur (a) does not specifically refer to breaking or passing through a surface. A substance that transpires does not necessarily weaken (c) or puncture (d) the surface.

8. **(d)** The union of sets includes all the elements of the sets. In contrast, the intersection of sets includes only the elements which are common to all the sets, i.e., the elements in one set and (d) in all other sets. Choices (a) both and (c) all are equivalent to the union, for cases of only two sets. Finally, none (b) would be the null set.

9. **(a)** Crest is correct because the high part of a wave is the crest, while the low part is the trough. Amplitude (b) is one half of the distance between the crest and the trough. Refraction (c) is the change in direction of certain waves, while the edge (d) is the outer area. None of these three terms can be used to complete the analogy.

10. **(a)** (a) is correct because to pare an apple is to remove its outer covering, just as to husk corn is to remove its outer covering. Trim (b) refers to cutting but not specifically to the removal of an outer covering. Pollinate (c) and hybrid (d) refer to breeding.

11. **(d)** In this analogy, the term $x$ is squared and added to 3 multiplied by $x$ ($x^2 + 3x$). Thus, the term $xy$ should also be squared and added to 3 multiplied by $x^2y^2$, or $x^2y^2 + 3xy$.

12. **(b)** Crystals is correct because colluvium is a collective term for sediments deposited by mass movement. Crystal is a collective term for all geometric minerals. Not all salts (a) have a geometric pattern to their structure. Tetrahedra (c), although geometric, may not be minerals. Mica (d) does not have a regular geometric pattern.

13. **(d)** Repression is correct because the lactose operon works by induction, meaning that it functions only when the substrate lactose is present. The arginine operon works by repression, meaning that its function is repressed when too much arginine is present. The processes of suppression (a), regulation (b), and promotion (c) all impact on enzymatic gene regulation, but do not refer to the actual type of operon, and therefore do not complete the analogy.

14. **(d)** (d) is correct because in math a product is the result of multiplying two or more factors, just as a sum is the result of adding two or more addends. Integers (a) are not exclusively numbers to be added and

a quotient (b) is the result of division. Proctor (c) is incorrect because this refers to someone who oversees the administration of an exam.

15. **(b)**    (b) is correct because a soporific makes one somnolent or sleepy. An anxiolytic makes one calm. A tranquilizer (a) makes one calm but not necessarily sleepy. Stimulant (c) is incorrect because this has just the opposite effect. Analgesic (d) is incorrect because this refers to a pain reliever.

16. **(b)**    Recipient is correct because in the conjugation process, bacterial donor cells are referred to as $F^+$, while recipient cells are referred to as $F^-$. The process is conjugation (a), but this term does not complete the analogy. HFR (c) are high frequency recombination cells, but these cells donate. Induction (d) is a term which refers to the making of an enzyme only when its substrate is present.

17. **(a)**    (a) is correct because to coruscate is to sparkle as a diamond does. To shine is to be bright (but not sparkling) as gold is. Gold is soft (b) compared to a diamond but that isn't a visual attribute as both coruscate and sparkle are. (c) and (d) are incorrect because while they are physical attributes, they do not refer to their visual interaction with light.

18. **(c)**    The cube root of 8 is 2; likewise, the cube root of 125 is 5.

19. **(d)**    Analytical balance is correct because a graduated cylinder is a device used for measuring liquids in the unit known as the milliliter. The analogy is therefore completed by the device which measures things in the mass unit known as the milligram. The pipette (a) is a measuring device but measures in milliliters. The ounce (b) is a unit of measure, not a measuring device. The scale (c) technically measures weight, rather than mass. Thus, the analytical balance is the device which measures mass in the unit known as the milligram.

20. **(c)**    (c) is correct because a sled moves on runners. A wagon moves on wheels. (a), (b), and (d) are incorrect because while they refer to the operation or parts of a wagon, they are not integral to its movement.

21. **(c)**    (c) is correct because an aperitif is by definition a drink served as an appetizer just as an hors d'oeuvre is by definition a food served as an appetizer. Chocolate (a) is a dessert (b), not an appetizer. Soup (d) may be served as an appetizer but is not exclusively an appetizer by definition.

22. **(c)**  (c) is correct because you brew beer to prepare it as you steep tea to prepare it. You don't simmer (d) tea leaves (b)—you boil the water, then pour it over the leaves in a separate container. While it is optional to season (a) the tea or the beer, it is not a part of the creation of those beverages.

23. **(d)**  Slump is correct because a rockslide occurs because of a down slope movement of rocks on a hill. A slump is the sliding of rocks and other materials along a curve, usually due to erosion at the base of the curve. Flows (b) occur when materials have a semiliquid behavior, and do not have to be on curves. A fall (a) occurs from a high place such as a cliff and does not have to involve a curve. None of these words are related to the word curve and cannot be used to complete the analogy.

24. **(d)**  (d) is the correct response. Virgil wrote the *Aeneid*. (d) Homer wrote the *Iliad*. (a) Chaucer, (b) Shakespeare, and (c) Johnson are all incorrect because they are not authors of the *Iliad*.

25. **(b)**  (b) is the correct answer. Vinegar is an acidic substance. Therefore, we are looking for a word that is a neutral substance. (b) distilled water is neutral. (a) is incorrect because acid rain is acidic. (c) is incorrect because baking soda is alkaline. (d) is wrong because litmus paper is used to test the pH of substances.

26. **(a)**  Here, 49 is the square of 7. Therefore, the correct answer should be the square of 11, which is 121, (a). 144 (b) is the square of 12; 81 (c) is the square of 9. 13 (d) is the next prime number in the series, 7, 11, 13, …

27. **(b)**  (b) is correct because ranids are a family of animals consisting of types of frogs just as canids are a family of animals consisting of types of wolves and other doglike animals. The fox (a), rabbit (c), and grasshopper (d) are not even in the amphibian class as frogs are, so they couldn't be in the same family and are therefore incorrect.

28. **(c)**  (c) is correct because an edentate animal lacks teeth just as an albino animal lacks pigment. (a) is incorrect because an albino animal does not lack white. (b) and (d) are incorrect because there is nothing to suggest that an albino animal would be fragile or small.

29. **(b)**  (b) is correct because many genes make up a chromosome. Many feathers make up a wing. (a) is incorrect because many birds do not

comprise a wing. (c) is incorrect because flight is the function of the wing. Only a couple of bones (d) are needed for a wing and they are not the principal part of a wing.

30. **(b)**    Nephelometer is correct because absorbed light is measured by a spectrophotometer, whereas scattered light is measured by a nepheometer. Turbidity (a) is the amount of light that is lost due to scattering, but it is not a measuring tool, and therefore does not complete the analogy. A voltmeter (c) is a measuring instrument, but it does not measure absorbed or scattered light. Although absorbed and scattered refer to light (d), the analogy cannot be completed with this term, since it is the device for measuring scattered light that is being sought.

31. **(c)**    (c) is correct because blinders block peripheral vision. A blindfold blocks total vision. Blinders specifically block peripheral vision so partial (a), central (b), and occasional (d) are not precise enough.

32. **(d)**    (d) is correct because ionic is a style of column just as gambrel is a style of roof. Gambrel is a term used only for a roof. Ceiling (a), mantel (b), and entry (c) are general architectural terms to which gambrel does not refer, and are therefore incorrect.

33. **(c)**    (c) is correct because opera glasses are a compact low-powered type of binoculars. A spinet is a compact low-powered (in quantity and quality of sound) type of piano. A lens (a) is incorrect because it does not refer to the quality of the instrument that uses it. Microscope (b) and telescope (d) are general types of instruments that are not inherently low-powered.

34. **(a)**    This analogy defines $g$ as a function of $g^2 + 3g - 2$. When 3 is substituted for $g$, then $3^2 + 3 \times 3 - 2 = 16$.

35. **(c)**    (c) is the correct answer. A reynard is a male fox and a vixen is a female fox. Steer is the male and cow is the female version of an ox. (a) Stallion is the the word for a male horse. (b) Doe is the female version and buck is the male version of deer. (d) Jennet is a female donkey.

36. **(a)**    (a) is the correct response. A pattern is used as a blueprint for creating a garment. (a) DNA is the blueprint for heredity. (b) Intellect relates to your intelligence and is not a blueprint for heredity. (c) Hormones are a product of living cells that circulate and have an influence

on other cells. (d) Environment is the outside influences on a person and does not have a direct effect on heredity.

37. **(b)**   (b) is correct because pH is a measure of hydrogen ion concentration, while current is a measure of flow of electrons. The galvanometer (a) and the pH meter (c) are the instruments which are used to make the measurements and therefore do not complete the analogy to what is actually measured. The cuvette (d) is a tube which holds solutions to be measured and therefore does not complete the analogy to what is actually being measured.

38. **(b)**   (b) is the correct answer. Truman Capote and Pearl S. Buck were contemporaries. They both contributed to twentieth century literature. (b) Ralph Waldo Emerson and Louisa May Alcott were writers in the nineteenth century. (a) Chaucer wrote in the thirteenth century. (c) Joseph Heller is a twentieth century author. (d) James Joyce is also a twentieth century author.

39. **(b)**   (b) is the correct answer. Henry James was an author who wrote about New York in his novels. Mark Twain was an author who wrote about the Mississippi in his books. (a) Nathaniel Hawthorne wrote about colonial New England. (c) Charles Dickens wrote about old England. (d) Ernest Hemingway wrote about the relationship between humans and their environment.

40. **(d)**   (d) is the correct response. An octopus moves through the water using its tentacles. An amoeba moves by extending a (d) pseudopod. (a) Membranes are plant or animal tissues. (b) Gills are fish organs used to obtain water. (c) Cilia are hairlike appendages found in some plants or animals.

41. **(b)**   (b) is correct because a neologism is a new word, just as an innovation is a new concept. Neologism refers specifically to words so all other answer choices are incorrect.

42. **(c)**   (c) is correct because dense means many things in one place, and disperse means few things in one place, just as if something is eroding, it is becoming smaller, rather than expanding. (a) is incorrect because to release something is to let it go. (b) is incorrect because to dilute something is to make it less concentrated. (d) is incorrect because to inflict means to cause harm.

43. **(c)**   (c) is correct because an impromptu performance is one that is not rehearsed or memorized, just as something that is spontaneous is not calculated. (a) is incorrect because something that is impetuous is impulsive, and therefore a synonym. (b) is incorrect because static implies a lack of action, and action is implied in the analogy. (d) is incorrect because someone who is glib is thought to be insincere.

44. **(a)**   (a) is the correct answer. A person who is impervious (not capable of being affected or disturbed) cannot be agitated (excited, disturbed). A person who is (a) enlightened (instructed, informed) is not ignorant. (b) is incorrect because the relationship between the given words does not exist between a person who is depressive (sad) and ignorant. A depressive person may be ignorant. (c) perturbed (upset) and (d) pretentious are wrong because a perturbed or pretentious person may be ignorant.

45. **(a)**   (a) is the correct response. John Kennedy was president and Lyndon Baines Johnson was his vice president. George Washington was president and (a) John Adams was his vice president. (b) Benjamin Harrison was the 23rd president. (c) Andrew Jackson was the 7th president. (d) Benjamin Franklin never held elected office.

46. **(b)**   (b) is correct because benevolent and malignant are antonyms, as are cooperative and resistant. (a) is incorrect because deliterious means harmful in a subtle way. (c) is incorrect because evasive means vague. (d) is incorrect because eager is a synonym of cooperative.

47. **(b)**   (b) is correct because this analogy is a direct computation of the sign of the angle. Thus $30° = 1/2$. The $\cos 30° = 2/\sqrt{3}$ (d), and thus is incorrect.

48. **(d)**   (d) is correct because the place where a river and an ocean meet is called an estuary. The place where land and ocean meet is called a shore. A shore is not always sand (a), and a cove (b) is just one type of place where land and ocean (c) meet.

49. **(d)**   (d) is correct because a passe partout is something that allows passage through any obstacle, like a master key through any lock, just as someone who is said to be nouveau riche is disparaged because they have only recently become wealthy. (a), (b), and (c) are incorrect because they are the opposite of a passe partout.

50. **(d)**   (d) is correct because Jose de San Martin is a revolutionary

from Argentina. Jorge Luis Borges is an author from Argentina. Patagonia (a) is a region. Fierro (b) was a gaucho – not a revolutionary – and Bolivar (c) was from Venezuela.

51. **(a)** Absorbance is correct because intake is the taking of something internally, while output is the opposite. The analogy therefore is to be completed by the opposite of transmittance which is absorbance. Adsorption (b) implies the attachment of something to a surface, rather than the taking of something into the internal. Reflection (c) and scattering (d) are terms which refer to the action of light when it strikes a particle in liquid, but neither term is opposite to absorbance.

52. **(c)** (c) is the correct answer. The relationship between the given words is that the words are synonyms of each other. If something is inchoate (incomplete), then it is shapeless (has no shape) because it is not finished. Something that is (c) pseudo (sham, showing a superficial resemblance) is counterfeit (not real, copied). (a) grotesque (bizarre) is wrong because if something is grotesque, it doesn't have to be counterfeit. (b) is incorrect because if something is imperfect it may or may not be counterfeit. The words are not necessarily synonyms. (d) is wrong because if something is exiguous (scanty in amount) it is not counterfeit.

53. **(c)** Humans is correct because the wasp belongs to the order Hymenoptera, while humans belong to the order Primates. Dogs (a), bears (b), and cats (d) belong to the order Carnivora, and therefore these choices cannot be used to complete the analogy.

54. **(c)** (c) is correct because sedulous behavior is careful—the opposite of careless (c), just as preemptory behavior is urgent and doesn't permit contradiction—the opposite of yielding. (a) is incorrect because retreating is not necessarily related to the word careful. (b) is incorrect because habitual refers to something done out of habit. (d) is incorrect because it refers to a feeling of ennui.

55. **(a)** (a) is correct because a valetudinarian is someone who is in poor health and is overly concerned about their ailments, as compared to a hypochondriac, who is overly concerned about imaginary ailments. This is analogous to someone who is the victim of an actual offense, as compared with someone who imagines that offenses are being plotted against them. (b), (c), and (d) are incorrect because while any of these people might need or want the services of those listed in the answer choices, they do not complete the analogy.

56. **(b)**   (b) is correct because a mortar supports material that is being ground up by a pestle. An anvil supports material shaped with a hammer. Fire (a) is incorrect because it is used in conjunction with a hammer and anvil, not a mortar. A different type of mortar is used with a brick (c), but they don't reshape a third item. Cement (d) is incorrect because it is a building material, rather than a method of shaping that material.

57. **(a)**   (a) is correct because completed gestation ends with birth just as completed lactation ends with weaning. Elimination and conclusion, (b) and (c) respectively, are general terms. Resorption (d) does not refer exclusively to gestation and occurs when gestation cannot be completed.

58. **(b)**   The graph shows many points. The point $(3, 8)$ is the maximum of this curve. The minimum point (b) is $(-2, -1)$. The inflection point (a) is $(0, 4)$. The intersection (d) of the $y$-axis is the point $(0, 4)$ (in this case the same as the inflection point). The intersection with the $x$-axis are the points $(-1, 0)$ and $(-3, 0)$. The slope (c) is not defined as a point but a change in the rise of the curve.

59. **(b)**   Coliforms is correct because eosine methylene blue agar is used to isolate coliforms from other bacterial species, especially in the testing of water for purity. Sabouraud's agar is used to isolate yeasts from bacterial species which might be growing with the yeasts. Bacteria (a) does not complete the analogy, since very few bacteria will grow on eosin methylene blue agar. Rickettsia (d) does not complete the analogy, since these are very fastidious organisms and require special conditions for growth. Hepatitis virus (c) is problematic in contaminated water supplies, and the presence of coliform agents in water is indicative that hepatitis virus could also be present, but this virus will not grow on eosin methylene blue agar and therefore this term does not complete the analogy.

60. **(b)**   (b) is correct because the term used for the thickening of blood after it leaves the veins or arteries is coagulate. The term used for the thickening of gravy after it leaves the gravy boat is congeal. To rarefy (a) is to thin out and gravy does not deepen (c) or separate (d) after pouring.

61. **(d)**   (d) is the correct answer. Lichtenstein is a painter known for his works in pop art. (d) Picasso is the painter who is famous for Cubism. (a) Dali is known for surrealism. (b) Cezanne is know for impressionism. (c) Matisse is known for abstract painting.

62. **(b)**    (b) is correct because a retrograde type of rotation is a reverse type of motion. Object (a) is incorrect because it refers to that which is in motion, not to the motion itself. Circular (c) motion is not necessarily reverse. Method (d) is a general term not referring specifically to motion.

63. **(c)**    Barbiturates is correct because cocaine is a stimulant, while barbiturates are considered to be members of the depressant drugs. Amphetamines (a) and ritalin (b) are considered to be stimulants, not depressants. LSD (d) is also not a depressant, but rather a psychedelic drug. None of these fit the analogy.

64. **(b)**    (b) is correct because a whale resembles a fish but is a mammal. A platypus resembles a bird (has a bill) but is a mammal. Other answer choices (a), (c), and (d) are fish.

65. **(b)**    Chicken pox is correct because strep throat is caused by a bacteria while chicken pox is caused by a virus. Rocky Mountain spotted fever (a) is caused by a rickettsial bacteria, amoebic dysentery (c) is caused by a protozoal parasite, and tuberculosis (d) is caused by a bacteria. These three answers cannot be used to complete the analogy.

66. **(c)**    A real number is part of the set of complex numbers, which includes all numbers. The set of rational numbers includes natural numbers, counting numbers, and integers (c). Rational numbers and irrational numbers (a) comprise the set of real numbers. Real numbers (d) and imaginary numbers (b) comprise the set of complex numbers.

67. **(a)**    (a) is the correct answer. The relationship between the given words could be stated as: If something is catholic (general) it has universality (it can be applied anywhere). If something is trivial (unimportant), then it deals with minutia (a minor detail). (b) enigma (riddles, puzzles) is wrong because if something is frivolous, it may or may not have universality. (d) is incorrect because palavar (word, speech) may or may not be trivial.

68. **(d)**    (d) is correct because to vacillate means to waver between two courses of action in an indecisive manner, just as fluctuate means to move from one area to another. (a) is incorrect because to switch means to be decisive. (b) and (c) are incorrect because they are unrelated to the other terms.

69. **(a)**    (a) is correct because a blacksmith's place of work is a forge

just as a painter's place of work is a studio. A forge is also the type of equipment a blacksmith works on but a painter's canvas (b) is not analogous to that type of forge, as a canvas is part of the finished product. Brush (c) is a tool used by a painter in the same way that a hammer would be by a blacksmith. Mix (d) is a general term that could apply to many crafts.

70. **(c)**  (c) is the correct response. Erickson was a psychologist known for his study of ego identity. (c) Piaget was a psychologist known for his study of intellectual development. (a) Skinner was a behavioral psychologist. (b) Freud was a psychiatrist who studied the unconscious mind. (d) Pavlov was a psychologist who studied operant conditioning in dogs.

71. **(a)**  (a) is correct because vulgar and crude are synonyms, just as biased and prejudiced are synonyms. (b) is incorrect because charming is a positive quality, whereas biased is not. (c) is incorrect because although rough is a synonym for vulgar and crude, it is not a synonym for biased. (d) is incorrect because just implies impartiality, which is an antonym of biased.

72. **(a)**  Salicylates is correct because a specific anti-pyrogenic agent is acetaminophen, while a specific anti-inflammatory agent is the family referred to as salicylates. Phenacetin (b), caffeine (c), and codeine (d) do not have anti-inflammatory attributes, and do not complete the analogy.

73. **(c)**  (c) is correct because a fern reproduces by releasing spores. An oak reproduces by dropping acorns. A fern doesn't have seeds (a) or fruit (d).

74. **(d)**  (d) is the correct answer. Malnutrition is caused by a lack of calories in the body. Albinism (lack of pigmentation) is caused by a lack of (d) melanin. (a) Albumin is the white substance found in an egg and has no relationship to albinism. (b) Serotonin is wrong. (c) Carotene is found in vegetables and provides vitamin A. It has no relation to albinism.

75. **(b)**  –OH is correct because the –OH group is the functional alcohol group, while the –$NH_2$ is the functional amino group. –COOH (a) is a functional carboxylic acid. R—C—OR (c) is the functional ester. —C—N— (d) is a functional amide. None of the other answers can be used as an amino group.

76. **(d)** Quartz is correct because the common name for sodium chloride (NaCl) is rock salt, while the common name for silicon dioxide ($SiO_2$) is quartz. $SiO_2$ is a crystal (a), but this is a generic term and does not complete the analogy. Ice (b) is a form of crystal which does not depend on $SiO_2$ for its formation. Calcareous rock (c) is made of calcium and not $SiO_2$.

77. **(a)** (a) is correct because mercurial refers to erratic behavior, just as someone who is pennyless is said to be impoverished. (b) is incorrect because something that is metaphorical stands for something other than itself. (c) is incorrect because something that is meretricious is attractive in a vulgar way. (d) is incorrect because something that is penal involves punishment for a crime.

78. **(c)** (c) is correct because a mercer is a dealer in textiles, just as a restaurateur sells food. All other answer choices are irrelevant.

79. **(c)** (c) is correct because a ligature is a tool used for binding just as a hook is a tool used for fishing. All other answer choices are irrelevant because a ligature is not used to perform these tasks.

80. **(d)** (d) is correct because in music, the Baroque period immediately precedes the Classical period just as the Classical period immediately precedes the Romantic period. The Renaissance (a) and Medieval (c) periods precede the Baroque, and Romanesque (b) is an architecture term referring to a period around the 1000s.

81. **(b)** (b) is correct because a peregrination is a trip by foot as is a walk. A cruise is a travel by boat as is a sail. Peregrination is not specifically fleeing (c), and while wings (d) could be considered an aid in travel, they do not refer to the journey itself.

82. **(c)** (c) is correct because a merganser is a type of duck (having a long, narrow bill for fishing) just as a gernsey is a type of cow. There are many varieties of each of the other answer choices, however, merganser is not among them.

83. **(b)** (b) is correct because Buddha was born in India just as Jesus was born in Israel. Buddhism is more common in some of the other countries such as China (a), Japan (c), and Cambodia (d), but Christianity, the religion based on Jesus's teachings, is also more common in countries other than his birth country.

84. **(c)**    Bradycardia is correct because tachycardia is an increase in heart rate above the normal rate, so it may be described as fast. Bradycardia is a decrease in heart rate and may be described as slow. Angina (a) is a pain in the chest due to inadequate blood supply to the heart muscle, but is not necessarily related to the rhythm of the heart rate. The sphygmomanometer (b) is an instrument used to measure blood pressure and is not descriptive of heart rate. Cardiac arrhythmia (d) is a term which can refer to any change in heart rate—increase or decrease, and therefore does not fit the analogy.

85. **(d)**    (d) is correct because a mortarboard is worn on one's head at commencement or graduation, just as a crown is placed on one's head during a coronation. (a) is incorrect because this refers to the installation of an idea into one's mind. (b) is incorrect because this applies to the clergy. (c) is incorrect because this applies to the armed forces.

86. **(a)**    (a) is correct because to transmogrify means to change form just as to translate means to change language. (b) and (c) can be said to be a change in form, but are too specific to complete the analogy. (d) is incorrect because time cannot be changed by external means.

87. **(a)**    (a) is correct because an agnostic questions the existence of god, just as the atheist decides that there is no god. (b) is incorrect because the agnostic has not made a clear cut decision, other than the decision to be an agnostic. (c) is incorrect because doubt does not have parity with the analogy. (d) is incorrect because definition implies a decision.

88. **(c)**    Circle is correct because a barrier reef is formed in a line. An atoll is a circle shaped reef surrounding a lagoon. A square (a) and a triangle (b) are not the correct shapes for an atoll. A spiral (d) is also not the shape of an atoll.

89. **(a)**    (a) is correct because something that is fleet (e.g., fleet-footed) is said to be quick and graceful, just as a pensive person is a thoughtful person. (b) is incorrect because a ship is a part of a different sort of fleet, or group of ships, that sails upon the ocean (c). Something that is lugubrious (d) is gloomy.

90. **(c)**    (c) is correct because brackish water is salty and briny, just as something that is flaxen is yellow in color. (a) and (b) are incorrect because brackish water is not inherently dark or unclean. (d) is incorrect because all water is wet, and this term is therefore too general.

91. **(a)**   (a) is correct because leonine means having the characteristics of a lion, just as cervine means having the characteristics of a deer. (b) is incorrect because equine refers to horses. (c) is incorrect because porcine refers to pigs. (d) is incorrect because bovine refers to cows.

92. **(d)**   (d) is correct because Grant was the 18th president just as Reagan was the 40th. All other answer choices are irrelevant.

93. **(a)**   (a) is correct because hubris is an excessive form of pride, just as starvation is an excessive form of hunger. (b), (c), and (d) are incorrect because they are the opposite of hunger.

94. **(a)**   Bacilli is correct because cocci are bacteria which have a round shape, while bacilli are bacteria which have a rod shape. Spirochetes (b) are spiral bacteria. Mycoplasma (c) and spheroplasts (d) do not have cell walls and therefore their shapes always appear round.

95. **(b)**   (b) is correct because travail means unpleasant, tiresome work, just as pillage is a severe form of steal. (a) is incorrect because it is an opposite of steal. (c) is incorrect because the word implies returning. (d) is incorrect because this is not a form of stealing.

96. **(b)**   Milk is correct because the major sugar component found in fruit is fructose, while the major sugar component of milk is lactose. Alcohol (d), of itself, does not contain lactose. The sugar referred to as table (c) sugar is sucrose, and the sugar referred to as blood (a) sugar is glucose, and neither of these fit the analogy of where lactose is found.

97. **(a)**   (a) is correct because to upbraid means to reproach severely, just as something that is miniscule is very small. (b) and (c) are incorrect because they are opposites of miniscule. (d) is incorrect because it is unrelated.

98. **(c)**   (c) is correct because something that is endemic affects a single region, however, is serious enough to be considered problematic, just as a pandemic is something that effects an entire country. (a) and (d) are incorrect because they are too small to foster something that could be considered endemic. (b) is incorrect because a planet is too large to be considered an endemic.

99. **(b)**   (b) is correct because to exculpate means to forgive, just as both fatal and lethal mean to cause death. (a) is incorrect because to pacify

means to calm. (c) is incorrect because to contumeliate means to annoy. (d) is incorrect because to ruminate means to muse on a particular idea or thought.

100. **(b)**    (b) is correct because to be moribund means to be dying just as to be geriatric means to be old. (a) is incorrect because morbid means in an unhealthy mental state. (c) is incorrect because while one could be laughing while moribund, this is unlikely. (d) is incorrect because someone in a dying state is rarely hungry, unless their hunger is the cause of their state, in which case this term is too specific.

# MAT – Practice Test 5 Answer Sheet

| | | |
|---|---|---|
| 1. ⓐ ⓑ ⓒ ⓓ | 35. ⓐ ⓑ ⓒ ⓓ | 69. ⓐ ⓑ ⓒ ⓓ |
| 2. ⓐ ⓑ ⓒ ⓓ | 36. ⓐ ⓑ ⓒ ⓓ | 70. ⓐ ⓑ ⓒ ⓓ |
| 3. ⓐ ⓑ ⓒ ⓓ | 37. ⓐ ⓑ ⓒ ⓓ | 71. ⓐ ⓑ ⓒ ⓓ |
| 4. ⓐ ⓑ ⓒ ⓓ | 38. ⓐ ⓑ ⓒ ⓓ | 72. ⓐ ⓑ ⓒ ⓓ |
| 5. ⓐ ⓑ ⓒ ⓓ | 39. ⓐ ⓑ ⓒ ⓓ | 73. ⓐ ⓑ ⓒ ⓓ |
| 6. ⓐ ⓑ ⓒ ⓓ | 40. ⓐ ⓑ ⓒ ⓓ | 74. ⓐ ⓑ ⓒ ⓓ |
| 7. ⓐ ⓑ ⓒ ⓓ | 41. ⓐ ⓑ ⓒ ⓓ | 75. ⓐ ⓑ ⓒ ⓓ |
| 8. ⓐ ⓑ ⓒ ⓓ | 42. ⓐ ⓑ ⓒ ⓓ | 76. ⓐ ⓑ ⓒ ⓓ |
| 9. ⓐ ⓑ ⓒ ⓓ | 43. ⓐ ⓑ ⓒ ⓓ | 77. ⓐ ⓑ ⓒ ⓓ |
| 10. ⓐ ⓑ ⓒ ⓓ | 44. ⓐ ⓑ ⓒ ⓓ | 78. ⓐ ⓑ ⓒ ⓓ |
| 11. ⓐ ⓑ ⓒ ⓓ | 45. ⓐ ⓑ ⓒ ⓓ | 79. ⓐ ⓑ ⓒ ⓓ |
| 12. ⓐ ⓑ ⓒ ⓓ | 46. ⓐ ⓑ ⓒ ⓓ | 80. ⓐ ⓑ ⓒ ⓓ |
| 13. ⓐ ⓑ ⓒ ⓓ | 47. ⓐ ⓑ ⓒ ⓓ | 81. ⓐ ⓑ ⓒ ⓓ |
| 14. ⓐ ⓑ ⓒ ⓓ | 48. ⓐ ⓑ ⓒ ⓓ | 82. ⓐ ⓑ ⓒ ⓓ |
| 15. ⓐ ⓑ ⓒ ⓓ | 49. ⓐ ⓑ ⓒ ⓓ | 83. ⓐ ⓑ ⓒ ⓓ |
| 16. ⓐ ⓑ ⓒ ⓓ | 50. ⓐ ⓑ ⓒ ⓓ | 84. ⓐ ⓑ ⓒ ⓓ |
| 17. ⓐ ⓑ ⓒ ⓓ | 51. ⓐ ⓑ ⓒ ⓓ | 85. ⓐ ⓑ ⓒ ⓓ |
| 18. ⓐ ⓑ ⓒ ⓓ | 52. ⓐ ⓑ ⓒ ⓓ | 86. ⓐ ⓑ ⓒ ⓓ |
| 19. ⓐ ⓑ ⓒ ⓓ | 53. ⓐ ⓑ ⓒ ⓓ | 87. ⓐ ⓑ ⓒ ⓓ |
| 20. ⓐ ⓑ ⓒ ⓓ | 54. ⓐ ⓑ ⓒ ⓓ | 88. ⓐ ⓑ ⓒ ⓓ |
| 21. ⓐ ⓑ ⓒ ⓓ | 55. ⓐ ⓑ ⓒ ⓓ | 89. ⓐ ⓑ ⓒ ⓓ |
| 22. ⓐ ⓑ ⓒ ⓓ | 56. ⓐ ⓑ ⓒ ⓓ | 90. ⓐ ⓑ ⓒ ⓓ |
| 23. ⓐ ⓑ ⓒ ⓓ | 57. ⓐ ⓑ ⓒ ⓓ | 91. ⓐ ⓑ ⓒ ⓓ |
| 24. ⓐ ⓑ ⓒ ⓓ | 58. ⓐ ⓑ ⓒ ⓓ | 92. ⓐ ⓑ ⓒ ⓓ |
| 25. ⓐ ⓑ ⓒ ⓓ | 59. ⓐ ⓑ ⓒ ⓓ | 93. ⓐ ⓑ ⓒ ⓓ |
| 26. ⓐ ⓑ ⓒ ⓓ | 60. ⓐ ⓑ ⓒ ⓓ | 94. ⓐ ⓑ ⓒ ⓓ |
| 27. ⓐ ⓑ ⓒ ⓓ | 61. ⓐ ⓑ ⓒ ⓓ | 95. ⓐ ⓑ ⓒ ⓓ |
| 28. ⓐ ⓑ ⓒ ⓓ | 62. ⓐ ⓑ ⓒ ⓓ | 96. ⓐ ⓑ ⓒ ⓓ |
| 29. ⓐ ⓑ ⓒ ⓓ | 63. ⓐ ⓑ ⓒ ⓓ | 97. ⓐ ⓑ ⓒ ⓓ |
| 30. ⓐ ⓑ ⓒ ⓓ | 64. ⓐ ⓑ ⓒ ⓓ | 98. ⓐ ⓑ ⓒ ⓓ |
| 31. ⓐ ⓑ ⓒ ⓓ | 65. ⓐ ⓑ ⓒ ⓓ | 99. ⓐ ⓑ ⓒ ⓓ |
| 32. ⓐ ⓑ ⓒ ⓓ | 66. ⓐ ⓑ ⓒ ⓓ | 100. ⓐ ⓑ ⓒ ⓓ |
| 33. ⓐ ⓑ ⓒ ⓓ | 67. ⓐ ⓑ ⓒ ⓓ | |
| 34. ⓐ ⓑ ⓒ ⓓ | 68. ⓐ ⓑ ⓒ ⓓ | |

# MILLER ANALOGIES

# PRACTICE TEST 5

**TIME:**     50 Minutes
            100 Analogies

> **DIRECTIONS**: Read each of the following analogies carefully, and choose the BEST answer to each item. Fill in your responses in the answer sheets provided.

1.  BISHOP : MITER :: KING (a. throne b. scepter c. crown d. seal)

2.  DYNAMICS : TEMPO :: PIANO : (a. lento b. measure c. legato d. sforzando)

3.  MARY ANN EVANS : GEORGE ELIOT :: AUTHOR : (a. publisher b. editor c. character d. pseudonym)

4.  PROPOSE : SUGGESTION :: (a. propound b. query c. issue d. imply) : FIAT

5.  (a. 212 b. 451 c. 150 d. 32) : FAHRENHEIT :: 100 : CELSIUS

6.  ATTORNEY : DISBAR :: (a. nobleman b. professor c. prima donna d. priest) : UNFROCK

7.  HARPSICHORD : (a. viola b. harp c. cello d. violin) :: PIANO : HAMMERED DULCIMER

8.  LINE : FOOT :: (a. square b. distance c. cube d. weight) : CORD

9.  (a. granivorous b. frugivorous c. herbivorous d. omnivorous) : CARNIVOROUS :: CANARY : HAWK

10. L : (a. LL b. D c. XL d. C) :: X : XX

11. (a. works b. stem c. time d. crystal) : WATCH :: CRANKSHAFT : CAR

12. AENEAS : VIRGIL :: (a. Hercules b. Penelope c. Odysseus d. Dido) : HOMER

13. PUMICE : (a. lava b. porous c. volcano d. molten) :: AMBER : RESIN

14. CHAPTER : NOVEL :: (a. rhyme b. meter c. anthology d. stanza) : POEM

15. TROCHEE : IAMB :: TUESDAY : (a. Monday b. delay c. Wednesday d. day)

16. E.G. : N.B. :: FOR EXAMPLE : (a. and others b. by that fact c. note well d. and so forth)

17. (a. circumference b. diameter c. radius d. pi) : CIRCLE :: PERIMETER : SQUARE

18. GEORGIA O' KEEFFE : ANSEL ADAMS :: (a. choreography b. architecture c. sculpture d. painting) : PHOTOGRAPHY

19. (a. bread b. horseshoe c. boot d. furniture) : BLACKSMITH :: SHOE : COBBLER

20. (a. tadpole b. toad c. newt d. amphibian) : FROG :: NYMPH : DRAGONFLY

21. 12 : 144 :: (a. 2 b. 9 c. 6 d. 12) : 36

22. 6.4587 : 6 :: 10.28943 : (a. 28 b. 10 c. 9 d. 1)

23. GLUCOSE : STARCH :: (a. tricarboxylic acid b. carbonic acid c. amino acid d. triglyceride) : PROTEIN

24. ORATOR : LINGUIST :: (a. speech b. French c. language d. eloquence) : FLUENCY

25. CURRICULUM : CURRICULA :: ALUMNUS : (a. alumni b. alma mater c. senior d. alumna)

26. PHOTOSYNTHESIS : CHLOROPHYLL :: DIGESTION : (a. animal b. enzyme c. food d. energy)

27. MERCURY : Hg :: GOLD : (a. W b. Pb c. Au d. O)

28. NYLON : POLYAMIDE :: (a. twill b. cotton c. wool d. dacron) : POLYESTER

29. NUMERATOR : (a. quotient b. denominator c. product d. hypotenuse) :: OVER : UNDER

30. POLIOMYELITIS : SALK :: SMALLPOX : (a. Blackwell b. Fleming c. Jenner d. Langerhans)

31. NUCLEUS : (a. proton b. electron c. atom d. neutron) :: PLANET : SATELLITE

32. (a. 4 b. 10 c. 5 d. 1) : 16 :: WASHINGTON : LINCOLN

33. (a. horse b. griffin c. minotaur d. wolf) : FISH :: CENTAUR : MERMAID

34. Given

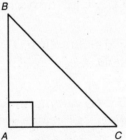

$AB : AC :: BC :$ (a. $AC^2$ b. $\sqrt{(AB^2 + AC^2)}$ c. $AB^2$ d. $AB + AC$)

35. $(x, y) : \sqrt{xy^2} + 2x^2y - 4y :: (4, y) :$ (a. $2\sqrt{y}$ b. $6y$ c. $14\sqrt{y}$ d. $30y$)

36. 10 : (a. Downing St. b. Broadway c. Baker St. d. 5th Avenue) :: 1600 : PENNSYLVANIA AVENUE

37. CONDUCTOR : (a. baton b. orchestra c. Bernstein d. composer) :: TEACHER : CLASS

38. HUMERUS : PHALANGES :: ARM : (a. elbow b. radius c. toes d. tibia)

39. SWITZERLAND : (a. Ceylon b. Nepal c. Madagascar d. Portugal) ::
    ALPS : HIMALAYAS

40. (a. Elizabethan b. Edwardian c. eighteenth century d. Jacobian) :
    VICTORIAN :: SIXTEENTH CENTURY : NINETEENTH
    CENTURY

41. (a. epistemology b. existentialism c. ontology d. hermeneutics) :
    POSITIVISIM :: KIERKEGAARD : COMTE

42. PSYCHE : MIND :: EGO : (a. self b. the unconscious c. id d. mental)

43. (a. angel b. human c. animal d. misanthropist) :
    ANTHROPOMORPHIZE :: DEMON : DEMONIZE

44. TURNER : (a. England b. Germany c. Holland d. Brittany) :: VAN
    GOGH : HOLLAND

45. WOLVES : (a. pup b. canine c. pack d. prey) :: SEALS : POD

46. CITY : (a. architect b. advocate c. mayor d. journalist) ::
    WASHINGTON, D.C. : L'ENFANT

47. MESOZOIC : ERA :: (a. Jurassic b. Tertiary c. Pennsylvanian
    d. Paleozoic) : PERIOD

48. HABITAT : PLACE :: (a. carrying capacity b. competition c. niche
    d. predation) : ROLE

49. DENSITY : NUMBER :: (a. dispersion b. habitat c. cohort
    d. patches) : DISTRIBUTION PATTERN

50. ATHENS : OSLO :: GREECE : (a. Norway b. Crete c. Aegean
    d. Czech Republic)

51. $4 + 5 : (4 + 5)^5 - (4 - 5)^2 :: a + b :$ (a. $(a + b)^5 - (a + b)^2$ b. $(a + b)^4 -$
    $a^2 - 2ab - b^2$) c. $(a + b)^3$ d. $(a + b)^5 - a^2 + 2ab - b^2$)

52. VISUAL : AURAL :: MAGNIFYING GLASS : (a. telephone
    b. microscope c. hearing aid d. binoculars)

53. WAGNER : OPERA :: STRAUSS : (a. jazz b. Gregorian c. tarantella d. waltz)

54. ALGERIA : DINAR :: (a. Turkey b. Poland c. Israel d. Kuwait) : ZLOTY

55. (a. order b. addition c. quantity d. multiplication) : GROUPING :: COMMUTATIVE : ASSOCIATIVE

56. 2 : (a. circle b. circumference c. distance d. diameter) :: 1 : RADIUS

57. SHREW : (a. turtle b. antelope c. grasshopper d. swallow) :: RODENT : RUMINANT

58. (a. auxin b. cytokinin c. phytolexins d. glucose) : PHOTOTROPISM :: GIBBERELLIN : GROWTH

59. INCH : FOOT :: CENTIMETER : (a. millimeter b. meter c. liter d. gram)

60. Given graphs A and B:

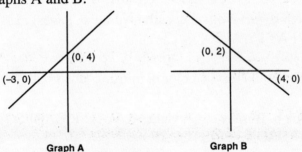

Graph A  Graph B

GRAPH A : (0, 4) :: GRAPH B : (a. (–3, 0) b. (2, 0) c. (4, 0) d. (0, 2))

61. (a. visible b. fluorescent c. ultraviolet d. quanta) : INFRARED :: SHORT : LONG

62. A : T :: C : (a. Y b. D c. M d. G)

63. BASIC : (a. saline b. acidic c. alkaline d. complex) :: BLUE : RED

64. (a. jetsam b. wharf c. land d. building) : DEFENESTRATE :: SHIP : JETTISON

65. FUZZY : (a. texture b. touch c. furry d. tactile) :: PUNGENT : OLFACTORY

66. (a. orange b. red c. purple d. brown) : BLUE :: RED : GREEN

67. OCCUPY : VACANT :: (a. tenant b. fumigate c. undertake d. cultivate) : FALLOW

68. DIAGONAL : RECTANGLE :: CHORD : (a. triangle b. circle c. hexagon d. rhombus)

69. METER : YARD :: (a. liter b. inch c. pint d. milliliter) : QUART

70. WHEREFORE : WHERE :: (a. location b. question c. person d. therefore) : PLACE

71. RODIN : BRONZE :: STIEGLITZ : (a. oil b. stone c. tin d. film)

72. SISYPHEAN : HERCULEAN :: ENDLESS : (a. labor b. difficult c. ongoing d. perpetual)

73. (a. protein b. metabolism c. carbohydrate d. sugar) : LIPID :: AMINO ACID : FATTY ACID

74. BLACK : WHITE :: (a. color b. mirror c. absorb d. red) : REFLECT

75. (a. DeFoe b. Burney c. Cervantes d. Poe) : PICARESQUE :: RICHARDSON : EPISTOLARY

76. (a. food b. quantity c. nutrition d. cuisine) : GOURMAND :: QUALITY : GOURMET

77. Jane, Mary, and Todd all have money to go to the candy store. Jane buys chocolate drops and pays with only dimes. Mary buys a lollipop, and she only has pennies. Todd has a dollar bill but does not buy anything.

    MARY : PENNIES :: TODD : (a. dollar b. dimes c. chocolate drops d. lollipop)

78. MONOCOT : (a. one b. two c. three d. four) :: DICOT: FIVE

79. HUMAN BODY : 37° :: ROOM : (98.6° b. 32° c. 25° d. 0°)

80. HANDEL : MOZART :: (a. romantic b. operatic c. baroque
    d. modern) : CLASSICAL

81. FRUCTOSE : LACTOSE :: (a. cream b. fruit c. skim d. cereal) :
    MILK

82. BAY OF BENGAL : ARABIAN SEA :: EAST : (a. south b. north
    c. China d. west)

83. HOROWITZ : PIANO :: MA : (a. harp b. piccolo c. cello d. baritone)

84. REVOLUTIONARY : CIVIL :: (a. Bull Run b. Bunker Hill c. Alamo
    d. Wounded Knee) : GETTYSBURG

85. OLIGARCH : CHORISTER :: MONARCH : (a. conductor b. soloist
    c. section d. leader)

86. (a. thermostat b. kilowatt c. thermometer d. calorie) : HEAT ::
    NANOMETER : LENGTH

87. Given (k, m), then g = 2, if k < 0, m < 0
    $\qquad\qquad\qquad$ = 1, if k < 0, m = 0
    $\qquad\qquad\qquad$ = 3, if k < 0, m > 0
    $\qquad\qquad\qquad$ = 4, if k > 0

    (−1, 2) : 3 :: (4, −1) : (a. 1 b. 3 c. 4 d. 2)

88. BIZET : *CARMEN* :: MOZART : (a. *Eine Kleine Nachtmusik* b. *The
    Barber of Seville* c. *Don Giovanni* d. *Cherubino*)

89. NOCTURNAL : DIURNAL :: (a. lizard b. mammal c. bat
    d. hibernation) : SQUIRREL

90. SUCH IS LIFE : *C'EST LA VIE* :: (a. good day b. behold c. pen name
    d. such is war) : *NOM DE PLUME*

91. 2001 : 365 :: 2004 : (a. 52 b. 366 c. 1901 d. 3)

92. RIGHT : (a. correct b. ambidextrous c. dexter d. righteous) :: LEFT : SINISTER

93. MEXICO : CORTES :: (a. Argentina b. Bolivia c. El Salvador d. Peru) : PIZZARO

94. XYLEM : ROOTS :: (a. arteries b. veins c. phloem d. leaves) : HEART

95. TELESCOPE : BINOCULARS :: MONOCLE : (a. screen b. spectacles c. focus d. microscope)

96. KEY : TURNKEY :: (a. corkscrew b. drill c. spatula d. jackhammer) : SOMMELIER

97. PLANE : PERPENDICULAR :: FLOOR : (a. ceiling b. gable c. wall d. cellar)

98. 1215 : MAGNA CARTA :: 1789 : (a. Declaration of Independence b. *Common Sense* c. Twelfth Amendment d. U.S. Constitution)

99. 56 : EVEN :: (a. 12 b. 17 c. 150 d. 65) : PRIME

100. Given

| $x$ | $y$ | $z$ |
| --- | --- | --- |
| 4 | 10 | 22 |
| 2 | 15 | 33 |
| 2 | 20 | 44 |
| 4 | 25 | 55 |

$(x = 2, y = 15) : 33 :: (x = 4, z = 55) : $ (a. 44 b. 55 c. 25 d. 10)

# Practice Test 5

## ANSWER KEY

| | | | | | | | |
|---|---|---|---|---|---|---|---|
| 1. | (c) | 26. | (b) | 51. | (d) | 76. | (b) |
| 2. | (a) | 27. | (c) | 52. | (c) | 77. | (a) |
| 3. | (d) | 28. | (d) | 53. | (d) | 78. | (c) |
| 4. | (c) | 29. | (b) | 54. | (b) | 79. | (c) |
| 5. | (a) | 30. | (c) | 55. | (a) | 80. | (c) |
| 6. | (d) | 31. | (b) | 56. | (d) | 81. | (b) |
| 7. | (b) | 32. | (d) | 57. | (b) | 82. | (d) |
| 8. | (c) | 33. | (a) | 58. | (a) | 83. | (c) |
| 9. | (a) | 34. | (b) | 59. | (b) | 84. | (b) |
| 10. | (d) | 35. | (d) | 60. | (d) | 85. | (a) |
| 11. | (b) | 36. | (a) | 61. | (c) | 86. | (d) |
| 12. | (c) | 37. | (b) | 62. | (d) | 87. | (c) |
| 13. | (a) | 38. | (c) | 63. | (b) | 88. | (c) |
| 14. | (d) | 39. | (b) | 64. | (d) | 89. | (c) |
| 15. | (b) | 40. | (a) | 65. | (d) | 90. | (c) |
| 16. | (c) | 41. | (b) | 66. | (a) | 91. | (b) |
| 17. | (a) | 42. | (a) | 67. | (d) | 92. | (c) |
| 18. | (d) | 43. | (b) | 68. | (b) | 93. | (d) |
| 19. | (b) | 44. | (c) | 69. | (a) | 94. | (a) |
| 20. | (a) | 45. | (c) | 70. | (c) | 95. | (b) |
| 21. | (c) | 46. | (a) | 71. | (d) | 96. | (a) |
| 22. | (b) | 47. | (c) | 72. | (b) | 97. | (c) |
| 23. | (c) | 48. | (c) | 73. | (a) | 98. | (d) |
| 24. | (d) | 49. | (a) | 74. | (c) | 99. | (b) |
| 25. | (a) | 50. | (a) | 75. | (c) | 100. | (c) |

# DETAILED EXPLANATIONS
# OF ANSWERS

1.  **(c)**    (c) is correct because a bishop's headdress is a miter, just as a king's headdress is a crown. All other choices (a), (b), and (d) are incorrect because while they are symbols of royalty, they are not headdresses.

2.  **(a)**    (a) is correct because piano (meaning soft) describes the dynamics (volume) of a musical passage. Lento (slow) describes the tempo at which the piece is played. (b) is incorrect because a measure is a division in the written musical score. (c) is incorrect because legato refers to a manner of playing music that is smooth and connected. (d) is incorrect because sforzando refers to a forceful manner of playing, with strong stresses and accents.

3.  **(d)**    (d) is correct because Mary Ann Evans was an author, and George Eliot was her pseudonym. (a) and (b) are incorrect because they refer to the publishing process of a book, and (c) refers to the writing process.

4.  **(c)**    (c) is correct because one proposes a suggestion just as one issues a fiat, or command. (a) is incorrect because to propound means to display. (b) is incorrect because to query means to ask a question. (d) is incorrect because to imply means to say something without conveying it directly.

5.  **(a)**    (a) is correct because 212 is the temperature at which water boils on the Fahrenheit scale, just as 100 is the temperature at which water boils on the Celsius scale. All other answer choices are irrelevant.

6.  **(d)**    (d) is correct because attorneys who are banned from their profession are said to be disbarred, while priests who are banned from their profession are said to be unfrocked. (a) is incorrect because a nobleman derives power from an inherited line. (b) is incorrect because a professor would be fired from a teaching position. (c) is incorrect because a prima donna refers to the current most talented ballerina in a dance company, who would lose that title to a more talented dancer.

7.  **(b)**    (b) is correct because pianos and hammered dulcimers are instruments whose strings are struck. Harpsichords and harps are

instruments with strings that are plucked. All other answers are generally played with a bow.

8. **(c)** (c) is correct because a foot is a unit of linear measurement just as a cord is a unit of cubic measurement. (a) is incorrect because it is a geometric figure. (b) is incorrect because it refers to that which is measured rather than a unit of measure. (d) is incorrect because weight is another criteria for measuring a three-dimensional object.

9. **(a)** (a) is correct because a canary is a granivorous, or seed-eating bird, just as a hawk is a carnivorous bird. (b) is incorrect because a frugivorous bird is one that eats fruit. (c) is incorrect because an herbivorous animal would exclusively eat plants. (d) is incorrect because an omnivorous creature would eat both meat and plants.

10. **(d)** (d) is correct because C (the Roman numeral representing 100) is twice L (the Roman numeral representing 50). (a) is incorrect because the form of Roman numerals dictates that there should be as little repetition as possible. (b) is incorrect because D is the Roman numeral representing 500. (c) is incorrect because XL represents the Arabic numeral 40.

11. **(b)** (b) is correct because in a car, the crankshaft transmits the motion generated by the engine, just as the stem transmits the motion of winding the watch. (a) is incorrect because the works measure time, but do not directly transmit motion produced by winding. (c) is incorrect because time is what the watch measures. (d) is incorrect because the crystal merely protects the face of the watch.

12. **(c)** (c) is correct because Aeneas is the hero of Virgil's epic work, *The Aeneid*, just as Odysseus is the hero of Homer's epic *The Odyssey*. (a) is incorrect because Hercules is a hero of Greek mythology. (b) and (d) are incorrect because Penelope and Dido are minor characters in *The Odyssey*.

13. **(a)** (a) is correct because amber is a solid substance composed of hardened resin, just as pumice is a solid substance composed of hardened lava. (b) is incorrect because porous (meaning not water tight) may be a characteristic of rock, but not a rock itself. (c) is incorrect because a volcano is the source of igneous rocks, not the rocks themselves. (d) is incorrect because molten refers to the liquid state of rock.

14. **(d)** (d) is correct because just as a chapter is a section of a novel, a stanza is a section of a poem. (a) and (b) are incorrect because rhyme and

meter may be characteristics of a poem, but neither is a section of one. (c) An anthology refers to a collection of works with a related theme. A poem may be part of an anthology, but an anthology cannot be a section of a poem.

15. **(b)** (b) is correct because the word Tuesday is an example of a trochee—a pair of syllables with the accent on the first syllable, just as the word delay is an example of an iamb—a pair of syllables with the accent on the second syllable. All other choices are trochaic.

16. **(c)** (c) is correct because *e.g.* is an abbreviation for the Latin phrase *exempla gratia*, meaning for example just as *n.b.* is an abbreviation for the Latin phrase *nota bene*, meaning note well.

17. **(a)** (a) is correct because the perimeter of a square is the measure of a square's outer edge, just as the circumference of a circle is the measure of the circle's outer edge. The diameter of a circle (b) and the radius (c) are measurements within a circle, and are therefore incorrect. (d) is incorrect because pi, or $\pi$, is a number used to calculate the measurements of geometric shapes, roughly equal to 3.14159.

18. **(d)** (d) is correct because Ansel Adams was a photographer, just as Georgia O'Keeffe was a painter. These artists did not participate in these other disciplines, (a), (b), and (c), and they are therefore incorrect.

19. **(b)** (b) is correct because a cobbler (or shoemaker) produces shoes, while a blacksmith produces horseshoes. A blacksmith does not produce any of the other items, so (a), (c), and (d) are incorrect.

20. **(a)** (a) is correct because an immature dragonfly is a nymph, just as an immature frog is a tadpole. (b) is incorrect because a toad is a mature type of amphibian. (c) is incorrect because a newt is another type of amphibian. (d) is incorrect because amphibian is a general term.

21. **(c)** (c) is correct because 12 squared is 144 just as 6 squared is 36. All other answer choices are irrelevant.

22. **(b)** (b) is correct because the number 6.4587 is truncated to the integer 6. Therefore, 10.28943 when truncated becomes 10.

23. **(c)** (c) is correct because a monosaccharide is a unit of which the starch molecule is made. Amino acids are the units of which a protein is

made. Triglycerides (d) are the units of which fatty acids are made, but they are not related to the protein. Tricarboxylic acid (a) and carbonic acid (b) are usually not considered to be structural units.

24. **(d)** (d) is correct because a successful linguist has the quality of fluency (in languages), just as a successful orator has the gift of eloquence (in public speaking). (a) is incorrect because speech is too general a term. (b) is incorrect because French is too specific a term. (c) is incorrect because language refers to the talent of both a linguist and an orator.

25. **(a)** (a) is correct because curricula is the plural of curriculum, just as alumni is the plural of alumnus. (b) is incorrect because this refers to the school one attended. (c) is incorrect because this refers to a rank or position in that school. (d) is incorrect because alumna is the female form of alumnus.

26. **(b)** (b) is correct because chlorophyll is the chemical necessary for plants to create food from sunlight and carbon dioxide (i.e., photosynthesis), just as an enzyme is necessary for digestion in animals. (a) is incorrect because an animal is the creature that carries out the process of digestion. (c) is incorrect because food is the raw material for digestion. (d) is incorrect because energy is the product of digestion.

27. **(c)** (c) is correct because Hg is the chemical symbol for mercury, just as Au is the symbol for gold. (a) is incorrect because W is the symbol for tungsten, (b) is incorrect because Pb is the symbol for lead, and (d) is incorrect because O is the symbol for oxygen.

28. **(d)** (d) is correct because nylon is a type of polyamide and Dacron is a type of polyester. Both nylon and dacron are fabrics and therefore the choices of twill (a), cotton (b), and wool (c), appear appropriate at first, however, they are not types of polyester.

29. **(b)** (b) is correct because just as over is on top of under, so too is the numerator on top of the denominator. The quotient (a) is the answer to a division problem and therefore does not have a position under the numerator. The product (c) is the answer to a multiplication problem, and the hypotenuse (d) is the side of a right triangle which is across from the right angle. None of the other three terms show the over and under analogy.

30. **(c)** (c) is correct because Jonas Salk discovered the vaccine for

poliomyelitis just as Edward Jenner discovered a vaccine for smallpox. (a) is incorrect because Elizabeth Blackwell was the first woman in the United States to receive a medical degree. (b) is incorrect because Fleming shared the Nobel Prize for the development of penicillin. (d) is incorrect because Langerhans was a German anatomist.

31. **(b)**    (b) is correct because a satellite revolves around a planet just as electrons revolve around the nucleus of an atom. (a) and (d) are incorrect because these particles comprise the nucleus. (c) is incorrect because this term is too general to complete the analogy.

32. **(d)**    (d) is correct because Abraham Lincoln was the sixteenth president, just as George Washington was the first. (a) is incorrect because the fourth president was Madison, the ninth (b) was Harrison, and the fifth (c) was Monroe.

33. **(a)**    (a) is correct because a mermaid is a mythical creature said to be part woman, part fish, just as a centaur was a creature said to be part man, part horse. (b) is incorrect because a griffin was said to be part eagle and part lion. (c) is incorrect because a minotaur was said to be part man and part bull. (d) is incorrect because the mythical creature associated with a wolf was a werewolf, said to be part wolf and part human.

34. **(b)**    The triangle is a 45–45–90 right triangle. In this type of triangle the lengths of the sides opposite the 45° angles are equal in length, therefore $AB = AC$ and the analogy is one of equality. Also by the Pythagorean Theorem, in a right triangle the hypotenuse squared is equal to the sum of the individual legs squared: $BC^2 = AB^2 + AC^2$. In order to find the length of side $BC$, you must take the square root of the sum of the equation. Therefore, the answer is $\sqrt{(AB^2 + AC^2)}$.

35. **(d)**    This analogy is in the form of a function, the pair $(x, y)$ is transformed into $\sqrt{xy^2} + 2x^2y - 4y$. When $(4, y)$ is substituted into the expression:

$$\sqrt{4y^2} + 2(4)^2y - 4y =$$

$$2y + 2*16y - 4y =$$

$$2y + 32y - 4y = 30y$$

36. **(a)**    (a) is correct because 10 Downing St. is the address of the British Prime Minister just as 1600 Pennsylvania Ave. is the address of the

President of the United States. (b) is incorrect because Broadway is associated with New York's musical theaters. (c) is incorrect because Baker St. is associated with fictional sleuth Sherlock Holmes. (d) is incorrect because Fifth Avenue in New York is associated with the American fashion industry.

37. **(b)**  (b) is correct because a conductor leads an orchestra in the same way that a teacher leads a class. (a) is incorrect because it is the object that a conductor uses. (c) is incorrect because Bernstein is the name of a famous American conductor. (d) is incorrect because a composer writes the music that orchestras and individual musicians perform.

38. **(c)**  (c) is correct because the humerus is a bone of the upper arm just as phalanges are the bones of the toes and fingers. (a) is incorrect because elbow refers to a joint, not a bone. (b) is incorrect because the radius, along with the ulna, is a bone in the lower arm. (d) is incorrect because the tibia is a bone in the lower leg.

39. **(b)**  (b) is correct because the Alps are a mountain range in Switzerland just as the Himalayas are in Nepal. All other choices are irrelevant.

40. **(a)**  (a) is correct because the Victorian Age occurred in the ninteenth century as the Elizabethan Age occurred in the sixteenth century. The Jacobean Age (d) occurred in the seventeenth century, and Edwardian (b) occurred in the twentieth century.

41. **(b)**  (b) is correct because Auguste Comte originated positivism, a system of thought based on a hierarchy of the sciences, just as Sören Kierkegaard originated existentialism, a system of thought based on individual experience, freedom of choice, and responsibility for one's actions. (a) is incorrect because epistemology refers to the study of knowledge and its acquisition. (c) is incorrect because ontology refers to the debate surrounding the existence of god. (d) is incorrect because hermeneutics refers to the study of the principles of interpretation.

42. **(a)**  (a) is correct because in the field of psychology, psyche is a synonym for mind, just as ego is a synonym for the self. (b) is incorrect because the unconscious is a part of the mind that one is rarely aware of but that has a strong influence on behavior. (c) is incorrect because id refers to the instinctual part of the mind. (d) is incorrect because mental is a general term that refers to the overall processes described by the other answer choices.

43. **(b)**   (b) is correct because demonizing something means to characterize it as evil, just as to anthropomorphize something is to give human characteristics to an animal, plant, material object, etc. (a) is incorrect because an angel is a mythical creature said to be semi-divine. (c) is incorrect because an animal is a general term referring to something without total human characteristics. (d) is incorrect because a misanthrope is someone who hates humans.

44. **(a)**   (a) is correct because Van Gogh is a painter from Holland just as Turner is a painter from England. All other answer choices are irrelevant.

45. **(c)**   (c) is correct because a group of seals is called a pod just as a group of wolves is called a pack. (a) is incorrect because a pup is an immature wolf or dog, or seal. (b) is incorrect because canine is a general term referring to the characteristics of a dog or wolf. (d) is incorrect because prey refers to a living creature eaten by another living creature.

46. **(a)**   (a) is correct because the city of Washington, D.C., was designed by architect Pierre L'Enfant. (b) is incorrect because an advocate is someone who supports an idea or campaign. (c) is incorrect because a mayor is an elected official who functions as a city administrator. (d) is incorrect because a journalist reports the news of a city.

47. **(c)**   Pennsylvanian is correct because Mesozoic is an era defined on the Geological Time Scale, while Pennsylvanian is a period as defined on the Geological Time Scale. Jurassic (a) and Tertiary (b) are periods as defined on the Geological Time Scale. Paleozoic (d) is an era, not a period and therefore does not complete the analogy.

48. **(c)**   Niche is correct because the habitat of an organism is the place where it lives, while its niche is its role. Carrying capacity (a) refers to the number of individuals which an environment can support, and has nothing to do with the role of the individual. Competition (b) occurs between two individuals who need the same resources, but is not concerned with the role of the individual. Predation (d) is when one individual exploits another, usually as a food source, and this term does not relate to the role of the individual.

49. **(a)**   Dispersion is correct because population density is the number of individuals per unit area, while dispersion is the distribution pattern of a population. Habitat defines where a population lives, not how it is

distributed. Cohort (c) refers to a group of individuals who are together, not to the distribution of the group. Patches (d) refer to local areas of habitat, not to distribution patterns. Therefore, none of these words can complete the analogy.

50. **(a)**    (a) is correct because Athens is the capital city of Greece just as Oslo is the capital city of Norway. (b) is incorrect because Crete is an island in the Greek archipelago. (c) is incorrect because Aegean is the sea surrounding many of the Greek islands. (d) is incorrect because Czech Republic is a nation whose capital is Prague.

51. **(d)**    The expression $(4 + 5)$ is transformed into the expression $(4 + 5)^5 - (4 + 5)^2$. Therefore, the expression $a + b$ then becomes $(a + b)^5 - (a - b)^2 = (a + b)^5 - a^2 + 2ab - b^2$.

52. **(c)**    (c) is correct because a magnifying glass magnifies visual images just as a hearing aid amplifies aural sounds. (a) is incorrect because a telephone transmits, rather than magnifies sound. (b) and (d) are incorrect because a microscope and binoculars magnify visual images.

53. **(d)**    (d) is correct because Wagner was a composer known for his operas just as Strauss was known for his waltzes. (a) is incorrect because jazz is an American musical form derived from ragtime and blues. (b) is incorrect because Gregorian refers to a mode of monastic chanting. (c) is incorrect because the tarantella is a dance.

54. **(b)**    (b) is correct because the dinar is the basic unit of currency in Algeria, just as the zloty is the basic currency in Poland. (a) is incorrect because the basic unit of currency in Turkey is the Turkish lira. (c) is incorrect because the monetary unit of Israel is the shekel. (d) is incorrect because the monetary unit in Kuwait is the Kuwaiti dinar.

55. **(a)**    (a) is correct because in multiplication and addition, the associative principle states that grouping does not affect the computation of a group of numbers, just as the commutative property states that order does not affect the computation of a group of numbers. (b) and (d) are incorrect because addition and multiplication are implicit in the principles. (c) is incorrect because quantity is a general term.

56. **(d)**    (d) is correct because the diameter of a circle is twice the radius of a circle. That is, the proportion of diameter to radius is 2 to 1. (a) is incorrect because a circle is the general figure to which diameter and

radius refer. (b) is incorrect because the circumference of a circle refers to the measure of its outer edge. (c) is incorrect because distance is a term referring to linear measure.

57. **(b)**    (b) is correct because a shrew is a rodent just as an antelope is a member of the order of ruminants. (a) is incorrect because a turtle is of the order testudinata. (c) is incorrect because a grasshopper is of the order orthopterous. (d) is incorrect because a swallow is of the family hirundinidae.

58. **(a)**    Auxin is correct because gibberellin is a type of plant hormone which influences plant growth. Phototropism is influenced by the plant hormone auxin. Cytokinins (b) are responsible for binding transfer RNAs to ribosomes, phytolexins (c) are naturally occurring antibiotics produced by some plants to protect themselves, and glucose (d) is the food which plants make for energy. None of these plant chemicals influence phototropism, and none are hormones. They therefore cannot be used to complete the analogy.

59. **(b)**    An inch is smaller than a foot; 12 inches are in a foot. A centimeter is smaller than a meter; ten centimeters are in a meter. A millimeter (a) is smaller than the centimeter, not larger. The choices (c) liter and (d) gram are not units of length and therefore cannot be compared to the other units of length.

60. **(d)**    The point (0, 4) in Graph A is the $y$-intercept. The $y$-intercept in Graph B is (0, 2) or choice (d). Choice (a), (–3, 0) is the $x$-intercept of Graph A. Choice (b) is not an intercept of either graph; while choice (c) is the $x$-intercept of Graph B.

61. **(c)**    Ultraviolet is correct because ultraviolet light has a short wavelength, whereas infrared has a long wavelength. The word wavelength does not complete the analogy which is a comparison of short to long. Visible (a) light falls in a medium wavelength range and therefore does not complete the analogy. Fluorescent light begins in UV wavelength ranges but then the electrons are excited to emit light in the visible ranges. Fluorescent (b) does not therefore complete the short: long analogy.

62. **(d)**    G is correct because A, the abbreviation for adenine, always pairs in DNA with T, which is the abbreviation for thymine. C, which is the letter for cytosine, always pairs with G for guanine. Y (a), D (b), and

M (c) are not involved in DNA base pairing and therefore do not complete the analogy.

63. **(b)**   (b) is correct because litmus paper is blue when exposed to bases and red when it is exposed to acids. (a) is incorrect because saline is a solution of salt and water. (c) is incorrect alkaline is another name for a basic solution. (d) Complex is incorrect because it does not refer to the litmus paper, but rather to the substance the paper measures.

64. **(d)**   (d) is correct because to defenestrate something is to toss it from a building, just as to jettison something is to toss it from a ship. (a) is incorrect because jetsam refers to the debris left by a shipwreck that sinks, compared with flotsam, which floats. (b) is incorrect because a wharf is a pier in a port. (c) is incorrect because land refers to that which is not sea.

65. **(d)**   (d) is correct because a pungent scent is detected through the sense of smell, or the olfactory sense, just as something that feels fuzzy is detected through the tactile sense, or sense of touch. (a) is incorrect because texture is a general term which fuzzy might describe. (b) is incorrect because touch does not complete the analogy because it is not comparable to the form olfactory. (c) is incorrect because furry is a synonym for fuzzy.

66. **(a)**   (a) is correct because red and green are opposite colors; that is, each contains the primary color or colors not included in the other, just as blue and orange are likewise opposite colors. All other answer choices are irrelevant.

67. **(d)**   (d) is correct because a space that is not being occupied is vacant, just as a field which is not being cultivated is fallow. (a) is incorrect because tenant refers to someone occupying a building by renting rather than by owning. (b) is incorrect because fumigate refers to a process of treating a building with pesticides. (c) is incorrect because undertake means to begin a task.

68. **(b)**   A diagonal connects two vertices of a rectangle and divides the rectangle into two pieces. A chord connects two points on a circle (by definition) and divides the circle into two pieces. Chords are not found in triangles (a), hexagons (c), or rhombi (d).

69. **(a)**   Liter is correct because a meter is the metric unit which is slightly larger than a yard. A liter is the metric unit which is slightly larger

than a quart. An inch (b) is not a metric unit and it is a measure of length rather than a liquid. It also does not show the larger to smaller analogy. A pint (c) is a unit of liquid measure, but a pint is smaller than a quart and it is also not a metric unit. A milliliter is a metric unit (d) of liquid measure, but it does not show the larger to smaller part of the analogy.

70. **(c)**    (c) is correct because "where" is used to inquire about a place, just as "wherefore" is used to inquire about a person. (a) is incorrect because a location would be a response to a "where" question. (b) is incorrect because question is too general a term to complete the analogy. (d) is incorrect because therefore is an adverb.

71. **(d)**    (d) is correct because Rodin was a sculptor whose primary artistic medium was bronze, just as Stieglitz' (a photographer) primary medium was film. All other answer choices are irrelevant.

72. **(b)**    (b) is correct because a Sisyphean task is one that is endless, just as a Herculean task is one which is very difficult. (a) is incorrect because both figures refer to labor. (c) and (d) are incorrect because both of these terms could be used to describe a Sisyphean task.

73. **(a)**    (a) is correct because lipids are composed of fatty acids, just as proteins are composed of amino acids. (b) is incorrect because this refers to the rate at which the body processes food. (c) is incorrect because a carbohydrate is a compound of carbon, hydrogen, and oxygen. (d) is incorrect because sugar is another name for sucrose.

74. **(c)**    (c) is correct because objects that appear white reflect all the colors of the spectrum, just as objects which appear black absorb all the colors of the spectrum. (a) is incorrect because color is a general term that does not comment on absorption or reflection. (b) is incorrect because a mirror reflects an image, rather than a specific color. (d) is incorrect because red is a specific color.

75. **(c)**    (c) is correct because just as Richardson wrote in an epistolary style (a story conveyed through letters), Cervantes wrote in a picaresque style (in which the characters actions are conveyed episodically). All other answer choices used a variety of styles.

76. **(b)**    (b) is correct because a gourmet desires quality in food, just as a gourmand desires quantity. (a) is incorrect because food is a general term that applies to either. (c) is incorrect because nutrition may or may

not be a factor in the desires of either. (d) is incorrect because cuisine is another general term.

77. **(a)**    The analogy associates Mary with her type of money, in this case, pennies. Thus, Todd should also be associated with money, and the paragraph stated that he had a dollar bill (a). Jane had the dimes (b), not Todd. The remaining choices, (c) chocolate drops and (d) lollipop, were the candies that Jane and Mary purchased, and would not apply to Todd.

78. **(c)**    Three is correct because the angiosperm plants which are classified as dicot generally have flower parts in multiples of five, while monocot type of plants has flower parts in multiples of three. Other flower part arrangements do not exist, with the exception of a few dicots which have flower parts in multiples of four (d), but the analogy asks for the arrangement corresponding to monocots, so four will not complete the analogy. One (a) is the number of seed leaves which a monocot has, but this does not fit the analogy since dicot would then have to be paired with the word two (b).

79. **(c)**    25° is correct because human body temperature is 37° on the Celsius scale. Room temperature on the Celsius scale is 25°. The Fahrenheit scale records human body temperature as 98.6° (a), therefore this choice would not complete the analogy. The Fahrenheit Scale records freezing temperature as 32° (b), while the Celsius Scale records it as 0° (d). Therefore these two choices also do not complete the analogy.

80. **(c)**    (c) is correct because Mozart was a composer in the classical style, just as Handel composed in the baroque style. All other answer choices are irrelevant.

81. **(b)**    (b) is correct because lactose is sugar found in milk, just as fructose is sugar found in fruit. (a) and (c) are incorrect because they describe different types of milk. (d) is incorrect because this is a general term for a variety of grains.

82. **(d)**    (d) is correct because the Bay of Bengal is a body of water directly east of India, just as the Arabian Sea is just west of India. All other answer choices are irrelevant.

83. **(c)**    (c) is correct because Vladimir Horowitz is a classical pianist, just as Yo-Yo Ma is a classical cellist. All other answer choices are irrelevant.

84. **(b)**    (b) is correct because the Battle of Gettysburg was a major battle in the Civil War, just as the Battle of Bunker Hill was a major battle in the Revolutionary War. (a) is incorrect because Bull Run was a battle in the Civil War. (c) is incorrect because the Alamo was an American fort. (d) is incorrect because the Battle of Wounded Knee was a conflict between American and Native American forces.

85. **(a)**    (a) is correct because an oligarch is one who rules a country as a member of a relatively small ruling group, just as a chorister is a member of a relatively small musical group. This is compared with a monarch, who alone guides a country, just as a conductor alone guides an orchestra. (b) is incorrect because a soloist would be analogous to a noble, someone who stands out, but is under the authority of the conductor. (c) and (d) are incorrect because section and leader are non-specific terms.

86. **(d)**    (d) is correct because a calorie is a unit of heat, just as a nanometer is a unit of length. (a) is incorrect because a thermostat is used to regulate heat. (b) is incorrect because a kilowatt is a measure of energy. (c) is incorrect because a thermometer is used to measure heat.

87. **(c)**    The given relationship defines the values of $g$, with respect to the values of $k$ and $m$. For $(-1, 2)$, $k < 0$, and $m > 0$, then by the definition, $g = 3$. For $(4, 1)$, $k > 0$, and the value of $g = 4$, regardless of the value of $m$.

88. **(c)**    (c) is correct because just as Bizet composed the opera *Carmen*, so Mozart composed the opera *Don Giovanni*. Mozart also composed *Eine Kleine Nachtmusik*, however this was not an opera.

89. **(c)**    (c) is correct because a squirrel is a diurnal mammal, one that is active during the day, just as most bats are nocturnal mammals, and are active during the night. (a) is incorrect because a lizard is a diurnal reptile. (b) is incorrect because it is too general. (d) is incorrect because it refers to seasonal sleep/activity patterns, rather than to daily ones.

90. **(c)**    (c) is correct because "C'est la vie" is a French expression meaning "such is life," just as "Nom de plume" is a French expression meaning pen name. (a) is incorrect because French for good day is "bon jour." (b) is incorrect because French for behold is "viola." (d) is incorrect because French for such is war is "c'est la guerre."

91. **(b)**    (b) is correct because 2001, which is not divisible by four, will have 365 days, just as 2004 will be a leap year, and therefore will have 366 days. All other choices are irrelevant.

92. **(c)**    (c) is correct because sinister refers to something left-leaning, just as dexter refers to anything right-leaning. (a) is incorrect because there is nothing correct or incorrect about being on the left or right. (b) is incorrect because ambidextrous refers to someone with equal fluidity with the left or right hand. (d) is incorrect because it is unrelated to the analogy.

93. **(d)**    (d) is correct because Hernando Cortes was a Spanish explorer who conquered Mexico, just as Pizzaro was the Spanish explorer who conquered Peru. All other choices are irrelevant.

94. **(a)**    (a) is correct because xylem is the tissue of a plant which conducts sap away from the roots, while arteries are the tissues of animals which conduct blood away from the heart. Veins (b) are the animal tissues which conduct blood toward the heart, while phloem (c) is the plant tissue which conducts sap toward the roots. Therefore, neither of these can be used to complete the analogy which is dependent on the concept of conduction "away from." Leaves (d) are not primarily involved with fluid conduction.

95. **(b)**    (b) is correct because a telescope is a magnifier for one eye and binoculars are a pair of magnifiers for both eyes, just as a monocle is a magnifier for one eye, and spectacles are magnifiers for both eyes. (a) is incorrect because a screen is something upon which an image is projected. (c) is incorrect because focus refers to the clarity of an image. (d) is incorrect because a microscope may be either for one or two eyes.

96. **(a)**    (a) is correct because a key is the tool of a turnkey (warden), just as a corkscrew is the tool of a sommelier, or wine steward. All other choices are incorrect since a sommelier would have no use for these tools.

97. **(c)**    (c) is correct because a floor is a plane, or flat surface, to which a wall is perpendicular. (a) is incorrect because a ceiling is also a plane to which a wall is perpendicular. (b) is incorrect because a gable refers to an arch over a doorway. (d) is incorrect because a cellar is a part of a building that is below ground level.

98. **(d)**    (d) is correct because the Magna Carta was signed in 1215 just as the U.S. Constitution was signed in 1789. (a) is incorrect because the Declaration of Independence was signed in 1776. (b) is incorrect because *Common Sense* was a pamphlet written by Thomas Paine. (c) is incorrect because the Twelfth Amendment was not added in 1789.

99. **(b)** (b) is correct because 56 is an even number, meaning it is divisible by two, just as 17 is a prime number, meaning it is divisible by only itself and one. All other answer choices are irrelevant.

100. **(c)** The table provides the relationships between the variables $x$, $y$, and $z$. For $x = 2$ and $y = 15$, the $z$ value is 33. Then for $x = 4$ and $z = 55$, the $y$ value is 25 (c). Choice (d) is incorrect because while $x = 4$, $z = 22$, not 55. Choices (a) and (b) are $z$ values and not $y$ values.

# MAT – Practice Test 6 Answer Sheet

1. ⓐ ⓑ ⓒ ⓓ
2. ⓐ ⓑ ⓒ ⓓ
3. ⓐ ⓑ ⓒ ⓓ
4. ⓐ ⓑ ⓒ ⓓ
5. ⓐ ⓑ ⓒ ⓓ
6. ⓐ ⓑ ⓒ ⓓ
7. ⓐ ⓑ ⓒ ⓓ
8. ⓐ ⓑ ⓒ ⓓ
9. ⓐ ⓑ ⓒ ⓓ
10. ⓐ ⓑ ⓒ ⓓ
11. ⓐ ⓑ ⓒ ⓓ
12. ⓐ ⓑ ⓒ ⓓ
13. ⓐ ⓑ ⓒ ⓓ
14. ⓐ ⓑ ⓒ ⓓ
15. ⓐ ⓑ ⓒ ⓓ
16. ⓐ ⓑ ⓒ ⓓ
17. ⓐ ⓑ ⓒ ⓓ
18. ⓐ ⓑ ⓒ ⓓ
19. ⓐ ⓑ ⓒ ⓓ
20. ⓐ ⓑ ⓒ ⓓ
21. ⓐ ⓑ ⓒ ⓓ
22. ⓐ ⓑ ⓒ ⓓ
23. ⓐ ⓑ ⓒ ⓓ
24. ⓐ ⓑ ⓒ ⓓ
25. ⓐ ⓑ ⓒ ⓓ
26. ⓐ ⓑ ⓒ ⓓ
27. ⓐ ⓑ ⓒ ⓓ
28. ⓐ ⓑ ⓒ ⓓ
29. ⓐ ⓑ ⓒ ⓓ
30. ⓐ ⓑ ⓒ ⓓ
31. ⓐ ⓑ ⓒ ⓓ
32. ⓐ ⓑ ⓒ ⓓ
33. ⓐ ⓑ ⓒ ⓓ
34. ⓐ ⓑ ⓒ ⓓ

35. ⓐ ⓑ ⓒ ⓓ
36. ⓐ ⓑ ⓒ ⓓ
37. ⓐ ⓑ ⓒ ⓓ
38. ⓐ ⓑ ⓒ ⓓ
39. ⓐ ⓑ ⓒ ⓓ
40. ⓐ ⓑ ⓒ ⓓ
41. ⓐ ⓑ ⓒ ⓓ
42. ⓐ ⓑ ⓒ ⓓ
43. ⓐ ⓑ ⓒ ⓓ
44. ⓐ ⓑ ⓒ ⓓ
45. ⓐ ⓑ ⓒ ⓓ
46. ⓐ ⓑ ⓒ ⓓ
47. ⓐ ⓑ ⓒ ⓓ
48. ⓐ ⓑ ⓒ ⓓ
49. ⓐ ⓑ ⓒ ⓓ
50. ⓐ ⓑ ⓒ ⓓ
51. ⓐ ⓑ ⓒ ⓓ
52. ⓐ ⓑ ⓒ ⓓ
53. ⓐ ⓑ ⓒ ⓓ
54. ⓐ ⓑ ⓒ ⓓ
55. ⓐ ⓑ ⓒ ⓓ
56. ⓐ ⓑ ⓒ ⓓ
57. ⓐ ⓑ ⓒ ⓓ
58. ⓐ ⓑ ⓒ ⓓ
59. ⓐ ⓑ ⓒ ⓓ
60. ⓐ ⓑ ⓒ ⓓ
61. ⓐ ⓑ ⓒ ⓓ
62. ⓐ ⓑ ⓒ ⓓ
63. ⓐ ⓑ ⓒ ⓓ
64. ⓐ ⓑ ⓒ ⓓ
65. ⓐ ⓑ ⓒ ⓓ
66. ⓐ ⓑ ⓒ ⓓ
67. ⓐ ⓑ ⓒ ⓓ
68. ⓐ ⓑ ⓒ ⓓ

69. ⓐ ⓑ ⓒ ⓓ
70. ⓐ ⓑ ⓒ ⓓ
71. ⓐ ⓑ ⓒ ⓓ
72. ⓐ ⓑ ⓒ ⓓ
73. ⓐ ⓑ ⓒ ⓓ
74. ⓐ ⓑ ⓒ ⓓ
75. ⓐ ⓑ ⓒ ⓓ
76. ⓐ ⓑ ⓒ ⓓ
77. ⓐ ⓑ ⓒ ⓓ
78. ⓐ ⓑ ⓒ ⓓ
79. ⓐ ⓑ ⓒ ⓓ
80. ⓐ ⓑ ⓒ ⓓ
81. ⓐ ⓑ ⓒ ⓓ
82. ⓐ ⓑ ⓒ ⓓ
83. ⓐ ⓑ ⓒ ⓓ
84. ⓐ ⓑ ⓒ ⓓ
85. ⓐ ⓑ ⓒ ⓓ
86. ⓐ ⓑ ⓒ ⓓ
87. ⓐ ⓑ ⓒ ⓓ
88. ⓐ ⓑ ⓒ ⓓ
89. ⓐ ⓑ ⓒ ⓓ
90. ⓐ ⓑ ⓒ ⓓ
91. ⓐ ⓑ ⓒ ⓓ
92. ⓐ ⓑ ⓒ ⓓ
93. ⓐ ⓑ ⓒ ⓓ
94. ⓐ ⓑ ⓒ ⓓ
95. ⓐ ⓑ ⓒ ⓓ
96. ⓐ ⓑ ⓒ ⓓ
97. ⓐ ⓑ ⓒ ⓓ
98. ⓐ ⓑ ⓒ ⓓ
99. ⓐ ⓑ ⓒ ⓓ
100. ⓐ ⓑ ⓒ ⓓ

# MILLER ANALOGIES

# PRACTICE TEST 6

**TIME:**    50 Minutes
          100 Analogies

**DIRECTIONS**: Read each of the following analogies carefully, and choose the BEST answer to each item. Fill in your responses in the answer sheets provided.

1.  GRABEN : (a. faults b. lakes c. rivers d. cliffs) :: VALLEY : MOUNTAINS

2.  HALCYON : (a. informal b. cautious c. tranquil d. peripheral) :: PALPABLE : MANIFEST

3.  VII : XXI :: IX : (a. VI b. XXI c. XXVII d. XXIX)

4.  FROND : FERN :: THREAD : (a. sewing b. cotton c. fiber d. needle)

5.  46 : CHROMOSOMES :: 206 : (a. muscles b. nerves c. bones d. teeth)

6.  PEGASUS : HORSE :: ORION : (a. hunter b. bear c. bull d. dog)

7.  (a. kindle b. garnish c. squander d. enumerate) : LIST :: RECLAIM : SALVAGE

8.  COMPRESSED AIR : (a. shaft b. pneumatic c. diesel d. gas) :: LIQUID : TURBINE

9.  ORNITHOLOGY : BIRDS :: (a. mycology b. cytology c. oncology d. biology) : FUNGI

10. (a. atom b. electron c. charge d. ferrous) : ELEMENT :: COMPOUND : MOLECULE

161

11. MARY ANN EVANS : (a. Willa Cather b. Silas Marner c. Emily Brontë d. George Eliot) :: SAMUEL CLEMENS : MARK TWAIN

12. 0.00036 : 3.6E–4 :: 1234.56 : (a. 1.23456E+3 b. 1.23456E+2 c. 123.456E+3 d. 1.23456E–3)

13. HIMALAYAS : (a. Australia b. North America c. South America d. Asia) :: ALPS : EUROPE

14. FACADE : PERSONALITY :: (a. lumber b. resin c. veneer d. leaf) : WOOD

15. HUMMINGBIRD : OSTRICH :: MERCURY : (a. Jupiter b. Earth c. Mars d. Venus)

16. LEWIS CARROLL : (a. Moby Dick b. Alice c. Hester Prynne d. Yossarian) :: CERVANTES : DON QUIXOTE

17. GLUCOSE : (a. vinegar b. honey c. vegetables d. poultry) :: ASCORBIC ACID : LEMON

18. SURGERY : (a. intelligence b. personality c. appearance d. emotions) :: CONDITIONING : BEHAVIOR

19. (a. adaptation b. restraint c. perception d. intelligence) : SURVIVAL :: CREATIVITY : GENIUS

20. (a. $\sqrt{250}$ b. $\sqrt{500}$ c. $\sqrt{625}$ d. $\sqrt{1000}$ ) : 25 :: $\sqrt{100}$ : 10

21. DIMMER SWITCH : (a. shaft b. light c. elevator d. light bulb) :: THERMOSTAT : HEAT

22. (a. Civil War b. Desert Storm c. World War I d. Korean War) : TRUMAN :: WORLD WAR II : FRANKLIN ROOSEVELT

23. (a. names b. mixtures c. molecules d. elements) : FAMILIES :: FOOD : GROUPS

24. GOOSE : GOSLING :: (a. mallard b. swan c. owl d. osprey) : CYGNET

25. EQUATOR : NORTH POLE :: ZERO : (a. 90 b. 145 c. 180 d. 270)

26. ALGAE : (a. fungi b. molds c. agar d. protozoa) :: PENICILLIUM : ANTIBIOTIC

27. CONTRAVENE : HARMONIZE :: FUGUE : (a. opine b. demur c. vigilant d. intercede)

28. JAPAN : ISLANDS :: (a. Australia b. Italy c. France d. Switzerland) : PENINSULA

29. (a. bacteria b. radium c. nitrous oxide d. rabies) : PASTEUR :: TUBERCULOSIS : KOCH

30. VIRGIL : DANTE :: (a. Marley b. Dickens c. Cratchit d. ghosts) : SCROOGE

31. THYROID : (a. enzyme b. ligament c. joint d. gland) :: HEART : MUSCLE

32. MENDEL : GENETICS :: DARWIN : (a. evolution b. blood groups c. culture d. relative dating)

33. TEXTURE : SURFACE :: (a. size b. mass c. shape d. contents) : VOLUME

34. ECONOMICS : INCOME :: (a. geography b. genetics c. earth d. cultural anthropology) : POLITICS

35. Children in a classroom are assigned to different desks. The third grade girls are given blue seats while the third grade boys are given green seats. The second grade girls are seated in purple seats and the second grade boys in red seats. The first graders all have yellow seats.

    THIRD GRADE BOYS : GREEN :: FIRST GRADE GIRLS : (a. yellow b. purple c. red d. blue)

36. (a. trial by jury b. religious freedom c. income taxes d. 18-year-old vote) : I :: SLAVERY ABOLISHED : XIII

37. CUNEIFORM : HIEROGLYPHICS :: (a. phonics b. stylus c. drawing d. alphabet) : PICTOGRAM

38. (a. space travel b. color printing c. insurance d. human anatomy) : PROBABILITY THEORY :: BLOOD CIRCULATION : HUMAN PHYSIOLOGY

39. (a. population b. computer c. statistics d. validity) : SAMPLES :: DECK : CARDS

40. FUEL : POLLUTION :: WATER : (a. erosion b. energy c. congestion d. agriculture)

41. RNA : (a. one b. three c. five d. seven) :: DNA : SIX

42. (a. new moon b. crescent c. first quarter d. gibbous) : 30 :: FULL MOON : 15

43. FASCISM : DICTATORSHIP :: LAISSEZ-FAIRE : (a. free market economy b. historical development c. legal education d. scientific classification)

44. FRANCIS DRAKE : CALIFORNIA COAST :: (a. Hernando de Soto b. Hernando Cortes c. Ponce de Leon d. Jacques Cartier) : FLORIDA

45. HARTFORD : (a. Nebraska b. Connecticut c. Illinois d. New Jersey) :: AUSTIN : TEXAS

46. OPERCULUM : GILLS :: (a. pupil b. retina c. eyelid d. iris) : EYE

47. EMMA LAZARUS : (a. Liberty Bell b. America c. Red Cross d. Statue of Liberty) :: FRANCIS SCOTT KEY : NATIONAL ANTHEM

48. (a. verdant b. specious c. venerable d. nascent) : EXTINCT :: BLOOM : DEGENERATE

49. IGNEOUS : CRUST :: (a. granite b. cobalt c. ozone d. basalt) : OCEAN

50. Given the graphs

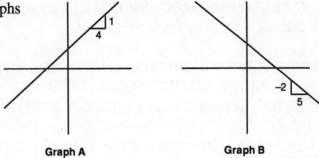

**Graph A**    **Graph B**

GRAPH B : –2/5 :: GRAPH A : (a. –5/2 b. 5 c. 2/5 d. 1/4)

51. ARGOS : JASON :: (a. *Pequod* b. *Bounty* c. *Nautilus* d. *Enterprise*) : BLIGH

52. *THE DIVINE COMEDY* : (a. essay b. abstract c. sonnet d. narrative) :: *EVANGELINE* : POEM

53. CADMIUM : CORROSION :: (a. ions b. metal c. lead d. science) : RADIATION

54. MONROE DOCTRINE : 1823 :: (a. Missouri Compromise b. Bill of Rights c. Louisiana Purchase d. Panama Canal) : 1803

55. SARTRE : EXISTENTIALIST :: (a. Orwell b. Joyce c. Kipling d. Sandburg) : SATIRIST

56. HENRY CLAY : (a. The Wizard of Menlo Park b. Iron Chancellor c. The Great Compromiser d. Old Hickory) :: LA GUARDIA : THE LITTLE FLOWER

57. HYPOTHERMIA : BODY HEAT :: (a. humiliation b. controversy c. regret d. spirit) : STATURE

58. (a. cabal b. exigency c. omen d. priority) : SECRET :: UNIVERSITY : ACADEMIC

59. DIAGNOSIS : (a. remission b. controversy c. interpretation d. pronunciation) :: TRAVESTY : MISREPRESENTATION

60. DISEASE : TOXINS :: BANKRUPTCY : (a. money b. economics c. debts d. inflation)

61. CREEP : SLOW :: AVALANCHE : (a. snow b. water c. rapid d. debris)

62. DEER : HERD :: RABBIT : (a. colony b. flock c. pack d. litter)

63. (a. orator b. senator c. topic d. filibuster) : SPEECH :: NARRATIVE : EVENT

64. DIATOMS : CHLOROPHYLL :: BACTERIA : (a. cytoplasm b. cellulose c. nucleus d. carbon dioxide)

65. (a. the Doppler effect b. comets c. x-rays d. aurora) : RADIATION :: THE BLUE SHIFT : LIGHT

66. Given perpendicular lines with slopes $m_1$ and $m_2$ then

    $m_1 : -1/m_2 :: m_1 = 5 : m_2 =$ (a. 1/5 b. 1/2 c. $-1/5$ d. $-1/2$)

67. IMPECUNIOSITY: DEPRESSION :: (a. sorrow b. love c. passion d. anger) : JOY

68. COLLABORATION: (a. collusion b. notoriety c. cabal d. soloing) : FAME : INFAMY

69. OSMIUM : SILVER :: (a. steel b. oak c. balsa d. granite) : PINE

70. AESTHETICS: (a. literature b. philosophy c. psychology d. science) :: AGRONOMY: AGRICULTURE

71. NEBULA: (a. morning star b. protostar c. cloud d. crab) :: CONSTELLATION : URSA MINOR

72. CELESTIAL : (a. earthly b. visceral c. infernal d. divine) :: LOFTY : NETHER

73. BASEBALL PLAYER : DIAMOND :: (a. spelunker b. archaeologist c. researcher d. scientist) : CAVES

74. 10.2598 : 2598 :: 21.3926 : (a. 21 b. 0.3926 c. 3926 d. 39.26)

75. ROCKIES : NORTH :: (a. Appalachian b. Andes c. Alps d. Zagros) :
    SOUTH

76. BANAL : TRITE :: (a. ephemeral b. divine c. permanent d. unreal) :
    TEMPORARY

77. CONTRITE : (a. punctual b. dogmatic c. penitent d. pessimistic) :
    CONCISE : SUCCINCT

78. (a. endoplasmic reticulum b. mitochondrion c. ribosome
    d. chromosome) : CELL :: ACTIVE GALACTIC NUCLEUS :
    GALAXY

79. GAGGLE : GEESE :: (a. crew b. rafter c. class d. drift ) : SWANS

80. (a. ligament b. muscle c. arm d. pauldron) : SHOULDER :: SKULL :
    BRAIN

81. PERIOD : ERA :: DISCONFORMITY : (a. conformity
    b. unconformity c. eon d. epoch)

82. CETACEA : WHALES :: FALCONIFORMES : (a. aves b. birds
    c. robin d. eagle)

83. PHILANTHROPIST : HUMANITARIAN :: (a. art b. money
    c. education d. medicine) : TIME

84. INTEGER : 5 :: PRIME NUMBER : (a. 1 b. 9 c. 3 d. 6)

85. THIEF : (a. implusive b. furtive c. irrational d. destitute) ::
    DELINQUENT : INTRACTABLE

86. SPECTROPHOTOMETRY: ABSORPTION OF LIGHT ::
    (a. coulometry b. potentiometry c. chromatography
    d. electrophoresis) :: CURRENT

87. MESOZOIC : REPTILES :: CENOZOIC : (a. mammals
    b. amphibians c. era d. succession)

88. SAUNTER : WALK :: (a. fortissimo b. fosse c. adagio d. arpeggio ) :
    ANDANTE

89. Given arbitrary angles A and B

    COMPLEMENTARY : A + B = 90° :: SUPPLEMENTARY : (a. A − B = 90° b. A + B = 90° c. A − B = 180° d. A + B = 180°)

90. $f + g / g - f : g + f / f - g :: a + b - 3 / 2a - 5b :$ (a. $b + a - 3 / 2b - 5a$ b. $b + a - 3 / 2a - 5b$ c. $a + b - 3 / a + b$ d. $b + a / a - b$)

91. (a. rod b. stylus c. mold d. kiln) : CLAY :: CHISEL : STONE

92. ISOAMYL ACETATE : BANANA :: (a. methyl salicylate b. ethyl butyrate c. benzyl acetate d. methyl anthranilate : WINTERGREEN

93. AREA : REAA :: TOYS : (a. YOTS b. TOZS c. TOYT d. TOY)

94. ARM : (a. tricep b. metacarpal c. tibia d. radius) :: LEG : FEMUR

95. WRITER : DRAFTS :: (a. notes b. studies c. sketches d. methods) : ARTIST

96. MINISTER : BIBLE :: (a. plumb b. furnace c. book d. delimiter) : CARPENTER

97. A coin is tossed 10 times.

    TAILS : 6 :: HEADS : (a. 5 b. 6 c. 10 d. 4)

98. GEOCHRONOLOGY : ISOTOPES :: BIOGENOUS DEPOSIT DATING : (a. rocks b. succession c. foraminiferal ooze d. magnetic minerals)

99. PORRINGER : BOWL :: (a. base b. meat c. platter d. dinner) : PLATE

100. FARROW : SOW :: (a. graze b. calf c. ruminate d. bull) : COW

# Practice Test 6

## ANSWER KEY

| | | | |
|---|---|---|---|
| 1. (a) | 26. (c) | 51. (b) | 76. (a) |
| 2. (c) | 27. (c) | 52. (d) | 77. (c) |
| 3. (c) | 28. (b) | 53. (c) | 78. (b) |
| 4. (c) | 29. (d) | 54. (c) | 79. (d) |
| 5. (c) | 30. (d) | 55. (a) | 80. (d) |
| 6. (a) | 31. (d) | 56. (c) | 81. (b) |
| 7. (d) | 32. (a) | 57. (a) | 82. (d) |
| 8. (b) | 33. (b) | 58. (a) | 83. (b) |
| 9. (a) | 34. (d) | 59. (c) | 84. (c) |
| 10. (a) | 35. (a) | 60. (c) | 85. (b) |
| 11. (d) | 36. (b) | 61. (c) | 86. (a) |
| 12. (a) | 37. (d) | 62. (a) | 87. (a) |
| 13. (d) | 38. (c) | 63. (d) | 88. (c) |
| 14. (c) | 39. (a) | 64. (a) | 89. (d) |
| 15. (a) | 40. (a) | 65. (a) | 90. (a) |
| 16. (b) | 41. (c) | 66. (c) | 91. (b) |
| 17. (b) | 42. (a) | 67. (b) | 92. (a) |
| 18. (c) | 43. (a) | 68. (a) | 93. (a) |
| 19. (a) | 44. (c) | 69. (b) | 94. (d) |
| 20. (c) | 45. (b) | 70. (b) | 95. (c) |
| 21. (b) | 46. (c) | 71. (d) | 96. (a) |
| 22. (d) | 47. (d) | 72. (c) | 97. (d) |
| 23. (d) | 48. (d) | 73. (a) | 98. (c) |
| 24. (b) | 49. (d) | 74. (c) | 99. (c) |
| 25. (a) | 50. (d) | 75. (b) | 100. (b) |

# DETAILED EXPLANATIONS
# OF ANSWERS

1. **(a)** (a) is correct because a graben is a portion of the earth's crust that is surrounded on at least two sides by faults, just as a valley is surrounded by mountains. (b), (c), and (d) are incorrect because a graben is not formed by these structures.

2. **(c)** (c) is the correct response. If something is palpable (capable of being touched, tangible), then it is manifest (obvious). If something is halcyon (calm, peaceful), then it is tranquil (calm). (a) Informal (casual) has no relationship to halcyon. (b) Cautious (careful) is not a synonym of halcyon. (d) Peripheral (covering a border area) has no relation to halcyon.

3. **(c)** (c) is the correct answer. VII = 7, XXI = 21. What number is VII (7) multiplied by to get XXI (21)? The answer is 3. Therefore, IX (9) multiplied by 3 would give you (c) XXVII = 27. (a) VI = 6, (b) XXI = 21, and (d) XXIX = 29 are incorrect.

4. **(c)** (c) is the correct answer. A fern is made up of fronds (leaves). A (c) fiber is made up of strands of thread. (a) Thread is used in sewing, but sewing does not make up thread. (b) Cotton is a fabric. You can buy cotton thread, but the cotton is not a composite of the thread. (d) Needle is an instrument used with thread.

5. **(c)** (c) is the correct response. There are 46 chromosomes in each cell. There are 206 (c) bones in the human body. (a) muscles and (b) nerves are incorrect. (d) There are 32 permanent teeth in the human body.

6. **(a)** (a) is correct. Pegasus is the name of the constellation that represents a horse. Orion is the constellation that represents a (a) hunter. (b) Bear is Ursa Major. (c) Bull is Taurus. (d) Canus Major is a dog.

7. **(d)** (d) is the correct response. When you reclaim (claim back) something, you salvage it (rescue it from ruin). When you (d) enumerate something, you list it. (a) Kindle means to start a fire or stir emotions. (b) Garnish means to decorate something. (c) Squander means to spend lavishly.

8. **(b)** (b) is correct. Power coming from the release of liquid under pressure is used in turbine engines. Power coming from compressed air is used to drive (b) pneumatic devices. (a) Shaft is a component of a machine. (c) Diesel is the type of fuel used for engines. (d) Gas is used to operate some machines, but is not associated with compressed air.

9. **(a)** (a) is correct. Ornithology is the study of birds. (a) Mycology is the study of fungi. (b) Cytology is a branch of biology for the study of cells. (c) Oncology is the branch of medicine dealing with cancer. (d) Biology is the study of life processes.

10. **(a)** (a) is the right answer. The smallest part of a compound is a molecule. The smallest part of an atom (a) is the element. (b) An electron is a negatively charged particle and is not the smallest part of an element. A (c) charge tells you whether the particle is positive or negative. (d) Ferrous relates to an iron type of metal.

11. **(d)** (d) is correct. Samuel Clemens is the real name of the author who called himself Mark Twain. Mary Ann Evans is the real name of the author who called herself (d) George Eliot. (a) Willa Cather is the author of *My Antonia*. (b) *Silas Marner* is a book written by George Eliot. (c) Emily Brontë is the author of *Wuthering Heights*.

12. **(a)** The analogy rewrites the decimal number in scientific notation. Therefore, 1234.56 written in scientific notation is 1.23456E+3.

13. **(d)** (d) is the correct response. The Alps are a mountain range in Europe. The Himalayas are a mountain range in (d) Asia. The Himalayas are not found in (a) Australia, (b) North America, or (c) South America.

14. **(c)** (c) is correct. A facade (appearance that doesn't reflect the whole person) is only the outside appearance of a personality. A (c) veneer is the thin layer on the outside of wood. (a) lumber is logs cut into usable wood and does not have the same relationship as the given words. (b) Resin is a substance obtained from the sap of some trees. (d) A leaf is a stem of foliage and has no relationship to wood.

15. **(a)** (a) is the right answer. A hummingbird is the smallest type of bird. An ostrich is the largest bird. Mercury is the smallest planet, and Jupiter (a) is the largest planet. (b) Earth, (c) Mars, and (d) Venus are not as large as Jupiter.

16. **(b)**    (b) is the correct answer. Cervantes created a character named Don Quixote. Lewis Carroll created a character named (b) Alice. (a) Moby Dick was a whale in a book written by Melville. (c) Hester Prynne was a character in the *Scarlet Letter* written by Hawthorne. (d) Yossarian was a character in *Catch 22* written by Heller.

17. **(b)**    (b) is the correct response. Ascorbic acid is a natural substance found in lemon. (b) Glucose is a natural substance found in honey. (a) Glucose is not found in vinegar. (c) Vegetables may or may not contain glucose. (d) Poultry does not contain glucose.

18. **(c)**    (c) is correct. Conditioning (bringing about a response to a specific stimulus) alters behavior. Surgery alters (c) appearance. For the most part, surgery is not a means of altering (a) intelligence, (b) personality, or (d) emotions.

19. **(a)**    (a) is the correct response. Creativity is a necessary quality relating to genius. (a) Adaption is a necessary quality for survival. (b) Restraint (confinement or reserve) has nothing to do with survival. (c) Perception (insight) is a positive quality, but is not necessarily related to survival. (d) Intelligence is helpful but surely not required for survival.

20. **(c)**    (c) is the correct response. The square root of 100 is 10. The square root of 625 is 25. (a) The square root of 250 is not 25. (b) The square root of 500 is not 25. (d) The square root of 1,000 is not 25.

21. **(b)**    (b) is the correct answer. A thermostat regulates heat as a dimmer switch regulates light. (a) A shaft is part of an automobile and it doesn't regulate speed. (c) An elevator is a machine which raises or lowers people or freight. (d) A lightbulb is not directly related to a dimmer switch.

22. **(d)**    (d) is the correct answer. World War II occurred under Franklin Roosevelt's administration. The Korean War occurred under Truman's administration. (a) The Civil War was associated with Lincoln. (b) Desert Storm occurred under Bush's administration. (c) World War I was under Wilson's administration.

23. **(d)**    (d) is correct. Food can be classified into groups. (d) Elements can be classified into families. (a) Names doesn't have the same relationship as the given words. (b) Mixtures cannot be classified into

families. (c) Molecules (smallest particles of matter) cannot be classified into families.

24. **(b)**   (b) is the correct answer. A goose is a mature gosling, or gosling is the name of a young goose. A cygnet is the name for a young swan. (a) Mallard is a type of duck. Ducklings are baby ducks. (c) An owl is a bird and owlet is the word for an immature owl. (d) An osprey is a large hawk.

25. **(a)**   (a) is the correct response. The equator is at a latitude of zero degrees. The north pole is at a latitude of 90 degrees. The north pole is not at a latitude of (b) 145 degrees, (c) 180 degrees, or (d) 270 degrees.

26. **(c)**   Agar is made from algae, while some antibiotics are made from penicillium. Agar is not made from fungi (a), molds (b), or protozoa (c), and these terms do not therefore fit the analogy.

27. **(c)**   (c) is the correct response. Contravene (go against someone's wishes) is the antonym of harmonize (agree). Fugue is a disturbed state of mind where a person unconsciously goes through an experience and has no recollection afterwards. (c) Vigilant means to be highly aware of your surroundings. (a) Opine means to have an opinion. (b) Demur means to object or protest. (d) Intercede means to intervene on someone's behalf.

28. **(b)**   (b) is the correct response. Japan is a country composed of islands. (b) Italy is a country which is a peninsula. (a) Australia is a continent. (c) France is a country located in Europe. (d) Switzerland is on the European continent.

29. **(d)**   (d) is the correct response. Koch, a German scientist, was famous for discovering a cure for tuberculosis. Pasteur was famous for discovering a vaccine for rabies. (a) Leeuwenhoek was famous for pioneering microscopy. Curie was famous for the discovery of (b) radium. (c) Priestley was famous for discovering nitrous oxide.

30. **(d)**   (d) is correct because Virgil was Dante's guide in the first two books of *The Divine Comedy* just as ghosts were Scrooge's guides in *A Christmas Carol*. Marley (a) is incorrect because while he was Scrooge's first visitor, he did not accompany him on his journey. Dickens (b) is the author of *A Christmas Carol*. Cratchit (c) is incorrect because he was Scrooge's assistant.

31. **(d)**   (d) is the correct answer. The heart is a muscle. The thyroid is a (d) gland. (a) An enzyme is a complex protein produced by living cells that induce or accelerate chemical reactions. (b) Ligaments are tissues that hold bones together. (c) Joint is the point of contact between bones.

32. **(a)**   (a) is the correct response. Mendel studied genetics. Darwin studied the process of (a) evolution. (b) Blood groups, (c) culture, and (d) relative dating were not studied by Darwin.

33. **(b)**   (b) is the correct response. Texture relates to the nature of a material's surface. (b) Mass (quantity of matter that a material possesses) relates to the volume (space occupied as measured by cubic units) of a material. (a) Size is not related to volume as in the given words. (c) Shape has no relation to volume. (d) Contents tell you what is available.

34. **(d)**   (d) is correct. Economics is the science of production, distribution, and consumption of goods and services. (d) Cultural anthropology deals with patterns of social and cultural phenomena and includes the study of politics. (a) Geography is the study of the Earth's surface. (b) Genetics is the study of heredity and doesn't include politics. (c) Earth science is the study of the present features and past evolution of the Earth.

35. **(a)**   The paragraph gives the relationships between the school children and their seat color. The analogy for third grade boys directly relates their seat color to them, third grade boys to green. Since all the first graders are in yellow seats, the sex of the first graders is not considered in the seat assignments. The first grade girls and boys all sit in yellow seats. The purple seats (b) are for the second grade girls, and the red (c) seats are for the second grade boys. The blue (d) seats are reserved for the third grade girls.

36. **(b)**   (b) is the correct response. Slavery was abolished with the XIII (Thirteenth) Amendment to the U.S. Constitution. The First Amendment (b) I established, among other things, the right to religious freedom. (a) The right to trial by jury was established by the VII (Seventh) Amendment, which is part of the Bill of Rights. (c) Income taxes were authorized by the XVI (Sixteenth) Amendment. (d) The voting age was lowered to 18 by the XXVI (Twenty-sixth) Amendment.

37. **(d)**   (d) is the correct answer. Cuneiform is the Sumerian writing system and hieroglyphics is the Egyptian writing system. A pictogram is a writing system used in China and Japan and the (d) alphabet is a letter version of a writing system. (a) Phonics is the use of a letter-sound relationship in language. (b) Stylus is a writing instrument. (c) Drawing is

a version of writing, but is not a formal writing system.

38. **(c)**   (c) is the correct response. Blood circulation is explained by the study of human physiology. (c) Insurance is based on the study of probability theory. (a) Space travel has no relation to probability theory. (b) Color printing has no relation to probability theory. (d) Human anatomy cannot be explained by probability theory.

39. **(a)**   (a) is correct. When a dealer shuffles a deck of cards, he/she ensures that the cards from the whole deck are randomly distributed. When an experimenter wants to test a theory or find out information, he/she will use a sample (small number of cases) from the total population that are randomly distributed. (b) Computer is a machine and has no relation to the analogy. (c) Statistics is the science of gathering and interpreting data. (d) Validity is that the experiment is based on logical soundness.

40. **(a)**   (a) is correct. Fuel burning is a major source of air pollution. Water is the major source of soil erosion. Water is not the major source of (b) energy. Water is not the source of (c) congestion. Water is not the source of (d) agriculture. Water is a necessary ingredient in agriculture.

41. **(c)**   Five is correct because DNA contains the six-carbon sugar deoxyribose, whereas RNA contains the five-carbon sugar ribose. The numbers one, three, and seven have no related significance to RNA for this analogy.

42. **(a)**   (a) is the correct response. The full moon shows up 15 days in the cycle of the moon's orbit. The new moon occurs after 30 days in the moon's orbit. (b) The crescent moon occurs after 26 1/4 days. (c) The first quarter occurs after 7 1/2 days. (d) The gibbous moon occurs after 11 1/4 days and after 18 3/4 days.

43. **(a)**   (a) is the right answer. Fascism is a political movement that stands for a centralized autocratic government headed by a dictatorial leader. Fascism is associated with dictatorship. Laissez-faire is associated with a free market economy. (b) Historical development has no relation to laissez-faire. (d) Scientific classification has no relation to laissez-faire.

44. **(c)**   (c) is the correct answer. Francis Drake was an explorer of the California coast. (c) Ponce de Leon explored Florida. (a) Hernando de Soto explored the Mississippi River near Memphis. (b) Hernando Cortes

explored Mexico. (d) Jacques Cartier explored the Gulf of St. Lawrence in Canada.

45. **(b)** (b) is the right answer. Austin is the capital of Texas. Hartford is the capital of (b) Connecticut. Lincoln is the capital of (a) Nebraska. Springfield is the capital of (c) Illinois. Trenton is the capital of (d) New Jersey.

46. **(c)** Eyelid is correct because the operculum is a covering which protects the gills, while the eyelid is a covering which protects the eye. The pupil (a), retina (b), and iris (d) are parts of the eye itself, and therefore could not complete the analogy, which is dependent on an independent structure.

47. **(d)** (d) is the correct answer. Francis Scott Key was famous for writing the poem that later became the *National Anthem*. Emma Lazarus was known for her poem "Colossus" on the (d) Statue of Liberty. (a) The Liberty Bell is in Independence Hall and was created to commemorate the 50th anniversary of the Commonwealth of Pennsylvania. (b) *America* was written by Rev. Samuel Francis Smith. (c) Red Cross is associated with Clara Barton.

48. **(d)** (d) is the correct answer. The opposite of bloom (to be in health) is to degenerate (to fall apart). The opposite of extinct (no longer exists) is to be (d) nascent (beginning to develop). (a) Verdant (green with growing plants) is not the opposite of extinct. (b) Specious (seeming to be genuine) has no relation to extinct. (c) Venerable (treated with respect) also has no relation to extinct.

49. **(d)** (d) is the correct response. Igneous rock is found primarily in the Earth's crust. (d) Basalt rock is found on the ocean floors. (a) Granite is not usually found in the ocean. (b) Cobalt is not found primarily in the ocean. (c) Ozone is found primarily in the atmosphere.

50. **(d)** In graph B the slope of the line is change in $y$ divided by the change in $x$, or $-2/5$. The slope on the line in graph A can be computed the same way. The change in $y$ is 1, and the change in $x$ is 4; therefore the slope is 1/4.

51. **(b)** (b) is the correct answer. The *Argos* is the ship that Jason captained. The *Bounty* (b) is the ship that Bligh (*Mutiny on the Bounty*) captained. (a) The *Pequod* was Captain Ahab's ship from *Moby-Dick*. (c) The *Nautilus* was central to Verne's *20,000 Leagues Under the Sea*. (d)

The *Enterprise* was Captain Kirk's ship from the *Star Trek* television serial.

52. **(d)**   (d) is the correct response. *Evangeline* is a poem written by Longfellow. *The Divine Comedy* is a descriptive narrative of an imaginary journey through the various levels of hell written by Dante. (a) An essay is a composition. (b) An abstract is a summary of a piece of work. (c) A sonnet is a type of poem.

53. **(c)**   (c) is the correct response. Cadmium is used to plate metals and alloys to protect them from corrosion. (c) Lead is used to protect people and things from radiation. (a) Ions are electrically charged particles and don't protect from radiation. (b) Metal is an opaque, ductile, or lustrous substance, and is a chemical element. The term is too general to be a protection from radiation. (d) Science is not related to radiation as a protective device.

54. **(c)**   (c) is the correct answer. The date of the Monroe Doctrine was 1823. The date of the (c) Louisiana Purchase was 1803. The date of the (a) Missouri Compromise was 1820. The date of the (b) Bill of Rights was 1791. The Panama Canal (d) was built in 1914.

55. **(a)**   (a) is the correct answer. Sartre was an author who wrote books that dealt with existentialism. (a) Orwell was an author who wrote *Animal Farm*, this made him a satirist. (b) Joyce was known for his stream of consciousness writing style. (c) Kipling wrote about the British in India. (d) Sandburg was a poet who wrote about Chicago and the Midwest.

56. **(c)**   (c) is the right answer. Fiorello La Guardia was a former mayor of New York who was known as the Little Flower. Henry Clay was known as (c) the Great Compromiser. Thomas Alva Edison was known as (a) The Wizard of Menlo Park. Bismarck was known as the (b) Iron Chancellor. Andrew Jackson was known as (d) Old Hickory.

57. **(a)**   (a) is the correct response. Hypothermia is the loss of body heat from exposure to cold. (a) Humiliation (injury to self-respect) is the loss of stature. (b) Controversy has no relation to stature. (c) Regret is what you would feel after you lose stature. (d) Spirit is not related to stature as the given words.

58. **(a)**   (a) is correct. A university is an academic society. A (a) cabal is a secret society. An (b) exigency is an urgent need or requirement and has no relation to secret. An (c) omen is an event believed to be a sign or

warning of a future occurrence and has no relation to secret. A (d) priority (something that takes precedence) has no relation to secret.

59. **(c)**    (c) is the right answer. A travesty is a synonym for misrepresentation. A diagnosis and (c) interpretation are synonyms. When a doctor makes a diagnosis, he/she interprets your symptoms. (a) Remission (release or abatement) is not a synonym of diagnosis. (b) Controversy (opposing views) and diagnosis are not synonyms. (d) Pronunciation (say or speak correctly) is not related to diagnosis.

60. **(c)**    (c) is the correct answer. Disease is caused by toxins in your body. Bankruptcy is caused by (c) debts (owing money to someone else). (a) Money doesn't cause bankruptcy by itself. The lack of money causes you to be bankrupt. (b) Economics doesn't cause bankruptcy. (d) Inflation (the abnormal increase in the volume of money and credit resulting in a substantial and continuing rise in the general price level) doesn't directly cause bankruptcy.

61. **(c)**    Rapid is correct because a creep is a specific type of flow, an extremely slow, down-slope movement, while an avalanche is a rapid mass-movement process. Snow (a) and debris (d) are two types of avalanches, but do not form the speed dependent analogy. Water (b) may flow slowly or rapidly, but is not a specific type of flow.

62. **(a)**    (a) is the correct answer. A group of deer is called a herd. A group of rabbit(s) is called a (a) colony. (b) A flock is a group of ducks. (c) A pack is a group of wolves or coyotes. (d) A litter is a group of cats.

63. **(d)**    (d) is the right answer. A narrative is an extended telling of an event. A (d) filibuster is an extensive speech. (a) An orator is a person who gives a speech. A (b) senator is a person who gives a speech. If she gives an extended speech that inhibits voting, she is known to be engaged in filibustering. (c) A topic is what a person gives a speech on.

64. **(a)**    (a) is the right answer. One celled plants called diatoms contain chlorophyll. Bacteria contains (a) cytoplasm. (b) Cellulose is a plant material and bacteria are not plants. (c) A Nucleus is the center of the cell and doesn't have the same relationship with the given words. (d) Carbon dioxide is a byproduct of respiration.

65. **(a)**    The Doppler effect is correct because the Doppler effect is a change in the wavelength of radiation caused by a change in the position of the source and the observer. The blue shift is a change in the

wavelength of light which is also caused by a change in the position of the source and the observer. Comets (b) are small icy bodies which orbit the sun, but there are no apparent wavelength changes as they orbit. X-rays (c) are a form of radiation, but the analogy is the change in wavelength which is observed due to the relationship of the source to the observer; therefore x-rays in and of themselves do not complete the analogy. An aurora (d) is a display of lights but the apparent changes which take place are not due to the relative positions of the source and observer, but rather are due to a guiding magnetic field.

66. **(c)**   Perpendicular lines have slopes which are negative reciprocals of each other. This is also stated in the analogy as $m_1 : 1/m_2$. Therefore if $m_1 = 5$, the slope of $m_2$ must be $-1/5$, choice (c).

67. **(b)**   (b) is correct because impecuniosity, or poverty, can produce feelings of depression in much the same way that love can produce feelings of joy. (a) and (d) are incorrect because these are opposites of joy. (c) is incorrect because passion may be aroused by both positive and negative emotions.

68. **(a)**   (a) is correct because collusion refers to a form of collaboration in which the participants have dubious intentions, just as infamy refers to fame for negative things. (b) Notoriety is a general term for fame. (c) is incorrect because a cabal is a group of people doing something harmful; however, it is of a different form and does not complete the analogy. (d) Soloing is also an opposite of collaboration however, it is a general opposite, and not the specific opposite needed to complete the analogy.

69. **(b)**   (b) is correct because osmium is a stronger metal than silver, just as oak is stronger than pine. (a) and (d) are incorrect because although they are stronger than pine, they are wholly different materials. (c) is incorrect because this type of wood is softer than pine.

70. **(b)**   (b) is correct. Agronomy is a branch of agriculture dealing with raising crops and the care of soil. Aesthetics is a branch of philosophy (b) dealing with the nature and appreciation of beauty. (a) Literature is the study of written works. (c) Psychology is the study of human behavior. (d) Science is the study of the laws of the universe.

71. **(d)**   Crab is correct because the crab is the name of a specific nebula while Ursa Minoris is the name of a specific constellation. The morning star (a) changes throughout the year and therefore does not complete the analogy of a specific name. A protostar (b) is the precursor to

a star and therefore does not complete the analogy for a specific name. A nebula is a (c) cloud of gas and dust, but this does not complete the analogy of a specific name.

72. **(c)** (c) is correct because celestial is the direct opposite of infernal in the same way that lofty is the direct opposite of nether. (a) and (b) are incorrect because while they are temporal opposites, they are not direct opposites. (d) is incorrect because divine and celestial are synonyms.

73. **(a)** (a) is correct because a spelunker explores caves *specifically* just as a baseball player needs specifically to play on a diamond. All other answer choices are related to the general idea framed by the question, but none of them provides the precise parallel that is required.

74. **(c)** The analogy relates the number 10.2598 to its decimal part, 2598. Then the decimal part of 21.3926 is 3926.

75. **(b)** Andes is correct because the Rockies are mountains which are found in North America, while the Andes are mountains which are found in South America. The Appalachian (a) mountains are found in North America, so this answer does not complete the analogy. The Alps (c) and the Zagros (d) are mountain ranges found in the Northern Hemisphere, so they also will not complete the analogy.

76. **(a)** (a) is correct because both banal and trite mean commonplace, just as ephemeral and temporary both mean short-lived. (b) is incorrect because something that is divine is thought to be permanent (c), which is the opposite of temporary. (d) is incorrect because something that is temporary must have been real, if only for a short time.

77. **(c)** (c) is correct because both contrite and penitent mean to be remorseful, just as concise and succinct both mean brief. (a) is incorrect because punctual means to be on time, (b) is incorrect because dogmatic means stubborn, and (d) pessimistic is incorrect because this refers to someone who takes a negative perspective on a given situation.

78. **(b)** Mitochondrion is correct because the active glactic nucleus is the central energy source of a galaxy while the mitochondrion is the energy source of the cell. The endoplasmic reticulum (a), ribosomes (c), and chromosomes (d) are not responsible for energy production, nor are they central to the cell.

79. **(d)** (d) is correct because a group of geese is called a gaggle, just as a group of swans is called a drift. Crew (a) and class (c) are general

terms for a gathering, and a rafter (b) refers to a group of turkeys.

80. **(d)**   (d) is correct because a pauldron is a piece of armor that protects the shoulder, just as the skull protects the brain. (a) and (b) are parts of the shoulder, but are not concerned with its protection. (c) is incorrect because this is the larger appendage of which the shoulder is a part.

81. **(b)**   Uniformity is correct because a period is subdivision of an era while disconformity is a subdivision of unconformity which is a break in the geological time record. While eon (c) and epoch (d) are related to era and therefore appear to be appropriate responses, they do not complete the analogy which is based on a part to whole relationship. (a) conformity would be the opposite of unconformity and would therefore not complete the part to whole relationship.

82. **(d)**   Eagle is correct because Cetacea is the order to which whales belong and eagles belong to the order falconiformes. Aves (a) is the class rather than the order to which all birds (b) belong, so neither aves nor birds complete the analogy. Robins (c) belong to a different order.

83. **(b)**   (b) is correct because just as a philanthropist donates money to a given cause, a humanitarian donates time. (a) is incorrect because while a philanthropist may donate valuable art to help a cause, this is too specific to complete the analogy. (c) is incorrect because while a philanthropist might donate money to a school, he or she is not directly donating education, just as giving money to a hospital is not directly giving medicine (d).

84. **(c)**   The number 5 is an example of an integer. To complete the analogy, an example of a prime number is needed. A prime number is a number greater than 1 (therefore choice (a), 1, is incorrect) whose only factors are itself and 1. Choice (b) has factors of 1, 3, and 9 and thus is not prime. Likewise, choice (d) has factors 1, 2, and 3. The only prime number choice is (c).

85. **(b)**   (b) is correct because just as a delinquent must be intractable, or difficult to control, so a thief must be furtive and sly. (a) and (c) are incorrect because there is nothing to suggest that a given thief is either impulsive or irrational. A thief may be destitute (d), however, in the case of a successful thief this may not be the case.

86. **(a)**   Coulometry is correct because spectrophotometry is the measurement of the absorption of light, while coulometry is a measurement of current. Potentiometry (b) measures the potential of an electrode compared to another electrode; it does not measure current. Chromatography (c) separates dissolved solutes into two phases, and it is therefore not a measurement technique. While it involves the movement of charged particles in response to an electrical current, it is not a measurement of current (d) and therefore does not complete the analogy of the measurement technique to the thing measured.

87. **(a)**   Mammals is correct because the Mesozoic era was dominated by reptiles while the Cenozoic era was dominated by mammals, but not by amphibians (b). While the Mesozoic is an era, (c) this choice does not complete the analogy. Succession (d) refers to a progression of life forms and not to the one which dominates an era.

88. **(c)**   (c) is correct because adagio is slower in tempo than andante as a saunter is a leisurely walk. Fortissimo (a) and arpeggio (d) are musical terms but do not fit the analogy. Fosse may sound like a musical term but it refers to a ditch, especially a moat.

89. **(d)**   The analogy is a direct definition of complementary angles; complementary angles are two angles whose sum is equal to 90°, such as two angles comprising a right angle, or the two smaller angles in a right triangle. By definition, supplementary angles are those whose sum is 180°. Thus, for A and B to be supplementary, A + B = 180°.

90. **(a)**   In the expression $f + g / g - f$, $f$ and $g$ are switched to yield $g + f / f - g$. Therefore in the expression, $a + b - 3 / 2a - 5b$, when $a$ and $b$ are switched, the expression becomes: $b + a - 3 / 2b - 5a$.

91. **(b)**   (b) is correct because a stylus is used to cut into clay just as a chisel is used to cut into stone. (a) is incorrect because a rod is a general term for a long cylindrical object. (c) is incorrect because a mold is used to shape clay into a preset form. (d) is incorrect because a kiln is an oven used to harden, or "fire" clay.

92. **(a)**   Methyl salicyate is correct because isoamylacetate provides the characteristic flavor and taste of banana, while methyl salicylate  provides the characteristic flavor and taste of wintergreen. Ethyl butyrate (b) is the characteristic flavor of pineapple, benzyl acetate (c) is the characteristic

flavor of peach, and methyl anthranilate (d) is the characteristic flavor of grape. None of these choices completes the analogy of the chemical to the characteristic flavor.

93. **(a)**   The letters in *area* have been rearranged to form *reaa*. Likewise, the letters in *toys* should be rearranged. Choice (a) rearranges them to form *yots*. The other choices do not include all of the letters in *toys*.

94. **(d)**   (d) is correct because the radius is a bone in the upper arm just as the femur is a bone in the upper leg. (a) is incorrect because the tricep is the muscle at the rear of the upper arm. (b) is incorrect because the metacarpals are the bones of the hand. (c) is incorrect because this is a bone in the lower leg.

95. **(c)**   (c) is correct because just as a writer may produce many drafts before a finished product, an artist may produce many sketches before a final product is produced. An artist may take notes (a), or study (b) before painting; however, this does not take the same form as the finished product. An artist may also try different methods (d), but once again, this may not resemble the final product.

96. **(a)**   (a) is correct because just as a minister uses a Bible in his or her work, so does a carpenter use a plumb in his or her work. (b) is incorrect because the phase of housebuilding in which a carpenter is involved would not include a furnace. (c) is incorrect because while a carpenter may refer to a book, it is not something that he/she always needs. (d) is incorrect because a delimiter is a character that marks the beginning or end of a group of data on magnetic tape.

97. **(d)**   When a coin is tossed, only two outcomes are possible, heads or tails. Since the number of tails is given as 6, then the number of heads must be equal to the total tosses minus the number of tails, or $10 - 6 = 4$.

98. **(c)**   Foraminiferal ooze is correct because geochronology is the science of dating which depends on the nuclear breakdown of isotopes. Biogenous deposit dating is the science of dating which depends on foraminiferal ooze. Rocks (a) are useful for dating but something within the rocks is used to identify the date of the rock formation. Succession (b) is used for dating, but biogenous deposit dating is dependent on the presence of foraminifera, not on the succession of species within sediments. Magnetic minerals (d) are used for magnetic reversal dating, but not for biogenous deposit dating and therefore this answer does not complete the analogy.

99. **(c)**   (c) is correct because a porringer is a type of bowl just as a platter is a type of plate. (a) is incorrect because base is a general term that can refer to anything upon which another thing rests. (b) is incorrect because while meat may be placed in either a porringer or a platter, it is not a type of plate. (d) is incorrect because while both of these objects would be useful at dinner, the term does not define a type of plate or a type of bowl.

100. **(b)**   (b) is correct because just as a sow gives birth to a farrow (or young pig), so does a cow give birth to a calf. (a) is incorrect because this refers to the feeding of a cow. (c) is incorrect because this is a type of animal, e.g., an antelope. (d) is incorrect because this is the name for a male cow.

# MAT – Practice Test 7 Answer Sheet

| | | |
|---|---|---|
| 1. ⓐ ⓑ ⓒ ⓓ | 35. ⓐ ⓑ ⓒ ⓓ | 69. ⓐ ⓑ ⓒ ⓓ |
| 2. ⓐ ⓑ ⓒ ⓓ | 36. ⓐ ⓑ ⓒ ⓓ | 70. ⓐ ⓑ ⓒ ⓓ |
| 3. ⓐ ⓑ ⓒ ⓓ | 37. ⓐ ⓑ ⓒ ⓓ | 71. ⓐ ⓑ ⓒ ⓓ |
| 4. ⓐ ⓑ ⓒ ⓓ | 38. ⓐ ⓑ ⓒ ⓓ | 72. ⓐ ⓑ ⓒ ⓓ |
| 5. ⓐ ⓑ ⓒ ⓓ | 39. ⓐ ⓑ ⓒ ⓓ | 73. ⓐ ⓑ ⓒ ⓓ |
| 6. ⓐ ⓑ ⓒ ⓓ | 40. ⓐ ⓑ ⓒ ⓓ | 74. ⓐ ⓑ ⓒ ⓓ |
| 7. ⓐ ⓑ ⓒ ⓓ | 41. ⓐ ⓑ ⓒ ⓓ | 75. ⓐ ⓑ ⓒ ⓓ |
| 8. ⓐ ⓑ ⓒ ⓓ | 42. ⓐ ⓑ ⓒ ⓓ | 76. ⓐ ⓑ ⓒ ⓓ |
| 9. ⓐ ⓑ ⓒ ⓓ | 43. ⓐ ⓑ ⓒ ⓓ | 77. ⓐ ⓑ ⓒ ⓓ |
| 10. ⓐ ⓑ ⓒ ⓓ | 44. ⓐ ⓑ ⓒ ⓓ | 78. ⓐ ⓑ ⓒ ⓓ |
| 11. ⓐ ⓑ ⓒ ⓓ | 45. ⓐ ⓑ ⓒ ⓓ | 79. ⓐ ⓑ ⓒ ⓓ |
| 12. ⓐ ⓑ ⓒ ⓓ | 46. ⓐ ⓑ ⓒ ⓓ | 80. ⓐ ⓑ ⓒ ⓓ |
| 13. ⓐ ⓑ ⓒ ⓓ | 47. ⓐ ⓑ ⓒ ⓓ | 81. ⓐ ⓑ ⓒ ⓓ |
| 14. ⓐ ⓑ ⓒ ⓓ | 48. ⓐ ⓑ ⓒ ⓓ | 82. ⓐ ⓑ ⓒ ⓓ |
| 15. ⓐ ⓑ ⓒ ⓓ | 49. ⓐ ⓑ ⓒ ⓓ | 83. ⓐ ⓑ ⓒ ⓓ |
| 16. ⓐ ⓑ ⓒ ⓓ | 50. ⓐ ⓑ ⓒ ⓓ | 84. ⓐ ⓑ ⓒ ⓓ |
| 17. ⓐ ⓑ ⓒ ⓓ | 51. ⓐ ⓑ ⓒ ⓓ | 85. ⓐ ⓑ ⓒ ⓓ |
| 18. ⓐ ⓑ ⓒ ⓓ | 52. ⓐ ⓑ ⓒ ⓓ | 86. ⓐ ⓑ ⓒ ⓓ |
| 19. ⓐ ⓑ ⓒ ⓓ | 53. ⓐ ⓑ ⓒ ⓓ | 87. ⓐ ⓑ ⓒ ⓓ |
| 20. ⓐ ⓑ ⓒ ⓓ | 54. ⓐ ⓑ ⓒ ⓓ | 88. ⓐ ⓑ ⓒ ⓓ |
| 21. ⓐ ⓑ ⓒ ⓓ | 55. ⓐ ⓑ ⓒ ⓓ | 89. ⓐ ⓑ ⓒ ⓓ |
| 22. ⓐ ⓑ ⓒ ⓓ | 56. ⓐ ⓑ ⓒ ⓓ | 90. ⓐ ⓑ ⓒ ⓓ |
| 23. ⓐ ⓑ ⓒ ⓓ | 57. ⓐ ⓑ ⓒ ⓓ | 91. ⓐ ⓑ ⓒ ⓓ |
| 24. ⓐ ⓑ ⓒ ⓓ | 58. ⓐ ⓑ ⓒ ⓓ | 92. ⓐ ⓑ ⓒ ⓓ |
| 25. ⓐ ⓑ ⓒ ⓓ | 59. ⓐ ⓑ ⓒ ⓓ | 93. ⓐ ⓑ ⓒ ⓓ |
| 26. ⓐ ⓑ ⓒ ⓓ | 60. ⓐ ⓑ ⓒ ⓓ | 94. ⓐ ⓑ ⓒ ⓓ |
| 27. ⓐ ⓑ ⓒ ⓓ | 61. ⓐ ⓑ ⓒ ⓓ | 95. ⓐ ⓑ ⓒ ⓓ |
| 28. ⓐ ⓑ ⓒ ⓓ | 62. ⓐ ⓑ ⓒ ⓓ | 96. ⓐ ⓑ ⓒ ⓓ |
| 29. ⓐ ⓑ ⓒ ⓓ | 63. ⓐ ⓑ ⓒ ⓓ | 97. ⓐ ⓑ ⓒ ⓓ |
| 30. ⓐ ⓑ ⓒ ⓓ | 64. ⓐ ⓑ ⓒ ⓓ | 98. ⓐ ⓑ ⓒ ⓓ |
| 31. ⓐ ⓑ ⓒ ⓓ | 65. ⓐ ⓑ ⓒ ⓓ | 99. ⓐ ⓑ ⓒ ⓓ |
| 32. ⓐ ⓑ ⓒ ⓓ | 66. ⓐ ⓑ ⓒ ⓓ | 100. ⓐ ⓑ ⓒ ⓓ |
| 33. ⓐ ⓑ ⓒ ⓓ | 67. ⓐ ⓑ ⓒ ⓓ | |
| 34. ⓐ ⓑ ⓒ ⓓ | 68. ⓐ ⓑ ⓒ ⓓ | |

# MILLER ANALOGIES

# PRACTICE TEST 7

**TIME:** 50 Minutes
100 Analogies

**DIRECTIONS**: Read each of the following analogies carefully, and choose the BEST answer to each item. Fill in your responses in the answer sheets provided.

1. BLUEPRINT : BUILDING :: SCORE : (a. contest b. exam c. symphony d. segment)

2. FINGER : KNUCKLE :: (a. joint b. ulna c. bone d. elbow) : ARM

3. RIDDLE : (a. question b. enigma c. problem d. query) :: MAZE : LABYRINTH

4. (a. red b. blue c. yellow d. green) : ENVY :: RED : RAGE

5. CRAVEN : (a. cowardly b. beautiful c. divided d. powerful) :: COLLOQUIAL : CASUAL

6. CHLOROPHYLL : GREEN :: HEMOGLOBIN : (a. bilirubin b. biliverdin c. red d. malachite green)

7. ESCHATOLOGY : (a. finality b. judgment c. death d. religion) :: EMPIRICISM : OBSERVATIONS

8. MARXISM : MARX :: GOLDEN MEAN : (a. Socrates b. Plato c. Aristotle d. Aristophanes)

9. SLOPE : LINE :: CURVATURE : (a. circle b. arc c. radius d. diameter)

10. BLASTULA : (a. heart b. novel c. embryo d. plant) :: ACORN : OAK

11. CALYX : (a. cup b. bowl c. rod d. sphere) :: BOX : SQUARE

12. HYPOCHONDRIAC : HEALTH :: (a. philanthropist b. miser c. millionaire d. philosopher) : MONEY

13. HALCYON : (a. martial b. hero c. tranquilizer d. passionate) :: PEACEFUL : WARLIKE

14. (a. celsius b. fahrenheit c. inch d. centimeter) : TEMPERATURE :: METER : LENGTH

15. PASSED : ELATION :: (a. present b. failed c. current d. rejection) : DEJECTION

16. HUGHES : ENKEPHALIN :: MENDEL : (a. genetics b. cloning c. x-rays d. hormones)

17. BRITTEN : *BILLY BUDD* :: VERDI : (a. *Aida* b. *Carmen* c. *La Straniera* d. *Norma*)

18. EMILY BRONTË : (a. Olivia Vernon b. Acton Bell c. Ellis Bell d. Alexandria Zenobia) :: STEPHEN KING : RICHARD BACHMAN

19. CAESURA : (a. stop b. poem c. stanza d. pause) :: CONCLUSION : END

20. LINE : LENGTH :: PLANE : (a. volume b. length c. width d. area)

21. ONOMATOPOEIA : BUZZ :: (a. road b. race car c. speedway d. meter) : PALINDROME

22. PHILOLOGIST : (a. thought b. conjecture c. language d. insects) :: ORNITHOLOGIST : BIRDS

23. REBUTTAL : SPEECH :: (a. applause b. commentary c. review d. renewal) : PERFORMANCE

24. *BEAU GESTE* : NOBLE GESTURE : (a. *magnum opus* b. *mea culpa* c. *alma mater* d. *memento mori*) : FOSTERING MOTHER

25. ROMAN : STATUES :: BYZANTINE : (a. painting b. mosaic
    c. iconography d. sculpture)

26. (a. pulsar b. polaris c. zenith d. equinox) : NADIR :: NORTH :
    SOUTH

27. $f + g + h : f + g + h / 2 :: a + b :$ (a. $a + b + c$ b. $a + b / 2$ c. $a + b + c / 2$, d. $a - b / 2$)

28. PAMPHLET : TEXTBOOK :: (a. view b. scope c. area d. aspect) :
    PANORAMA

29. BOAST : PRAISE :: ATONE : (a. commend b. compliment c. amend
    d. detract)

30. MISER : THRIFT :: (a. hedonist b. sadist c. socialist d. atheist) :
    PLEASURE

31. THICK : THIN :: AA LAVA : (a. tephra b. tubes c. pahoehoe
    d. pillows)

32. CEREBELLUM : BRAIN :: (a. veins b. arteries c. ventricles d. aorta)
    : HEART

33. COSMOGONY : (a. folktales b. creations c. mythology
    d. cosmology) :: BILDUNGSROMAN : COMING OF AGE

34. 2 : 8 :: 5 : (a. 25 b. 10 c. 125 d. 40)

35. OSSEUS : (a. teeth b. bones c. skull d. ribs) :: VISCERAL : BODY

36. ACID : 4 :: ALKALI : (a . 6 b. 0 c. 5 d. 8)

37. ANION : NEGATIVE :: (a. ion b. neutron c. cation d. proton) :
    POSITIVE

38. ANODE : POSITIVE :: (a. diode b. cathode c. LED d. transistor) :
    NEGATIVE

39. FORTRAN : (a. math b. graphics c. spreadsheets d. information processing) :: COBOL : BUSINESS

40. SOFTWARE : COMPUTER :: (a. textbooks b. chalk c. blackboard d. school) : TEACHER

41. SERENDIPITOUS : PLANNED :: INDEFATIGABLE : (a. slow b. industrious c. lazy d. sickly)

42. BOILING POINT : 100° :: FREEZING POINT : (a. celsius b. 212° c. 0° d. 32°)

43. $2x + y : 4x^2 + 4xy + y^2$ :: $a - b$ : (a. $a^2 - b^2$ b. $a^2 + b^2$ c. $a^2 - 2ab + b^2$ d. $2a^2 - 2b$)

44. POSTULATE : CLAIM :: (a. grieve b. cavil c. pike d. cabal) : CARP

45. MESTRAL : VELCRO :: (a. Bic b. Edison c. Biro d. Tupper) : BALLPOINT PEN

46. MILE : 5,280 :: ACRE : (a. $10,240^2$ b. $56,017^2$ c. $29,411^2$ d. $43,560^2$)

47. ODD NUMBER : 5 :: EVEN NUMBER : (a. 7 b. 2 c. 9 d. 1)

48. CORONA : SUN :: (a. stratosphere b. troposphere c. chromosphere d. thermosphere) : EARTH

49. CAPO : (a. coda b. denouement c. cadenza d. aria) :: BEGINNING : END

50. CENTENNIAL : 100 YEARS :: (a. sesquicentennial b. septennial c. sexennial d. decennial) : 7 YEARS

51. DIONYSUS : BACCHUS :: NOX : (a. Aurora b. Tyche c. Selene d. Nyx)

52. ALIAS : IDENTITY :: (a. name b. illusion c. idea d. appearance) : PERCEPTION

53. SANTAYANA : JAMES :: (a. Plato b. Aristotle c. Plotinus
    d. Arelius) : SOCRATES

54. AESTHETICS : BEAUTY :: PHENOMENALISM : (a. knowledge
    b. ethics c. appearances d. justice)

55. USURY : (a. money b. interest c. tax d. payment) :: VOLUBLE :
    FLUENT

56. LABOR : (a. field b. gestation c. yoke d. vex) :: URBANE : SUAVE

57. PARABLE : MORAL :: SATIRE : (a. ridicule b. irony c. myth
    d. disagreement)

58. ZERO-POINT ENERGY : MOTION :: ABSOLUTE ZERO :
    (a. force b. temperature c. speed d. joules)

59. Given triangles ABC ≈ DEF

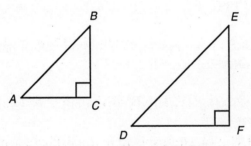

$\overline{AB}$ : $\overline{DE}$ :: $\overline{BC}$ : (a. $\overline{DF}$ b. $\overline{AC}$ c. $\overline{DE}$ d. $\overline{EF}$)

60. HYPERBOLE : (a. curve b. exaggeration c. method d. fable) ::
    OXYMORON : CONTRADICTION

61. NICOTINE : TOBACCO :: (a. DDT b. NTE c. THC d. FAA) :
    MARIJUANA

62. RETARD : ADVANCE :: (a. postpone b. educate c. assist
    d. reschedule) : PROCEED

63. JOULE : ENERGY :: (a. newton b. pounds c. meter d. mass) :
    FORCE

64. GARRULOUS : (a. taciturn b. dour c. talkative d. bucolic) :: OFFEND : AGGRAVATE

65. PLAGIARIZE : STEAL :: (a. festoon b. baroque c. accessorize d. refurbish) : DECORATE

66. ORDER : DISORDER :: (a. melifluous b. harmony c. euphony d. polyphony) : CACOPHONY

67. TYPO : SPELLING :: ANACHRONISM : (a. location b. method c. costume d. time)

68. VINEGAR : ACETIC ACID :: (a. carbonic acid b. baking soda c. sodium bicarbonate d. carbon tetrachloride) : SODA WATER

69. MOTIF : REFRAIN :: (a. novel b. song c. subplot d. prologue ) : POEM

70. BIT : BYTE :: 1 : (a. 6 b. 16 c. 10 d. 8)

71. FORBEARANCE : (a. imposition b. impatience c. patience d. misery) :: KNAVERY : TRICKERY

72. PEDESTRIAN : MUNDANE :: (a. petulant b. pedantic c. vivacious d. wry) : INSOLENT

73. HUMAN : BRAIN :: (a. program b. CPU c. microprocessor d. memory) : COMPUTER

74. JOLLY ROGER : (a. unions b. pirates c. missionaries d. seamen) :: MAPLE LEAF : CANADA

75. LANGUR : (a. shark b. llama c. monkey d. tiger ) :: BOTTLENOSE : DOLPHIN

76. PARTISAN : TRAITOR :: (a. deluge b. pond c. famine d. storm) : DROUGHT

77. (a. potassium b. copper c. magnesium d. lithium) : RED :: SODIUM : YELLOW

78. 1/3 : 0.333 :: 9/8 : (a. 1.125 b. 125.0 × 10⁻² c. 1 1/8 d. 0.777)

79. ESSENTIAL : SUPERFLUOUS :: SCURRILOUS : (a. vulgar
    b. refined c. impetuous d. contumelious)

80. MEATUS : (a. body b. river c. canal d. ocean) :: STRAIT : WATER

81. ACEPHALOUS : (a. limb b. heart. c. head d. spouse) ::
    UNOPPOSED : RIVAL

82. FABACEOUS : (a. plant b. seed c. shrub d. bean) :: AQUILINE :
    EAGLE

83. MECCA : ISLAM :: (a. Medina b. Amristar c. Nepal d. Ganges) :
    HINDUISM

84. (a. conjunctiva b. tympanic membrane c. vestibulocochlear nerve
    d. cochlea) : SOUND :: RETINA : LIGHT

85. ALGEBRA : EQUATION :: GEOMETRY : (a. element b. proof
    c. set d. statistic)

86. TIZANO VECELLIO : TITIAN :: DOMENIKOS
    THEOTOKOPOULOS : (a. Domenik b. El Greco c. Theo d. Poulous)

87. WARHOL : POP ART :: (a. Picasso b. Pollack c. Mondrian
    d. Matisse) : CUBISM

88. TIFFANY : GLASS :: CHRISTO JAVACHEF : (a. islands
    b. sculpture c. found objects d. painting)

89. MYOPIC : NEARSIGHTED :: HABERDASHER : (a. soldier
    b. clothier c. educator d. editor)

90. LAPIDARY : DIAMONDS :: COOPER : (a. jewelry b. beer c. casks
    d. cheese)

91. TALMUD : JUDAISM :: (a. Tao Te Ching b. Koran c. Veda
    d. Sutra) : HINDUISM

92. ASSOCIATIONS : (a. celestial sphere b. cosmic rays c. binary stars d. cardinal points) :: SCATTERED : BOUND

93. WRIGHT : AIRPLANE :: (a. Garnerin b. Zeppelin c. Montgolfier d. Selfridge) : HOT AIR BALLOON

94. NORSE : JUDEO-CHRISTIAN :: (a. Bragi b. Balder c. Buri d. Ask) : ADAM

95. OEDIPUS : (a. Clytaemnestra b. Jocasta c. Antigone d. Cassandra) :: CLAUDIUS : GERTRUDE

96. DARWIN : EVOLUTION :: BOHR : (a. atomic structure b. x-ray diffraction c. dynamite d. electrons)

97. Given that *B // C*,

    $\angle 1 : \angle 2 :: \angle 4 :$ (a. 2 b. 3 c. 1 d. 6)

98. STEVENSON : EISENHOWER :: (a. Wilke b. Dewey c. Landon d. Davis) : COOLIDGE

99. FIFTEENTH AMENDMENT : VOTING RIGHTS :: NINETEENTH AMENDMENT : (a. prohibition b. cruel and unusual punishment c. voting rights d. succession)

100. EPICENE : (a. prehistoric b. artificial c. androgynous d. stubborn) :: ENTENTE : AGREEMENT

# Practice Test 7

## ANSWER KEY

| | | | |
|---|---|---|---|
| 1. (c) | 26. (c) | 51. (d) | 76. (a) |
| 2. (d) | 27. (b) | 52. (b) | 77. (d) |
| 3. (b) | 28. (d) | 53. (a) | 78. (a) |
| 4. (d) | 29. (c) | 54. (c) | 79. (b) |
| 5. (a) | 30. (a) | 55. (b) | 80. (a) |
| 6. (c) | 31. (c) | 56. (c) | 81. (c) |
| 7. (a) | 32. (d) | 57. (d) | 82. (d) |
| 8. (c) | 33. (b) | 58. (b) | 83. (d) |
| 9. (b) | 34. (c) | 59. (d) | 84. (d) |
| 10. (c) | 35. (b) | 60. (b) | 85. (b) |
| 11. (a) | 36. (d) | 61. (c) | 86. (b) |
| 12. (b) | 37. (c) | 62. (a) | 87. (a) |
| 13. (a) | 38. (b) | 63. (a) | 88. (a) |
| 14. (a) | 39. (a) | 64. (c) | 89. (b) |
| 15. (b) | 40. (a) | 65. (c) | 90. (c) |
| 16. (a) | 41. (c) | 66. (c) | 91. (c) |
| 17. (a) | 42. (c) | 67. (d) | 92. (c) |
| 18. (c) | 43. (c) | 68. (a) | 93. (c) |
| 19. (d) | 44. (b) | 69. (a) | 94. (d) |
| 20. (d) | 45. (c) | 70. (d) | 95. (b) |
| 21. (b) | 46. (d) | 71. (c) | 96. (a) |
| 22. (c) | 47. (b) | 72. (a) | 97. (b) |
| 23. (a) | 48. (d) | 73. (b) | 98. (d) |
| 24. (c) | 49. (a) | 74. (b) | 99. (c) |
| 25. (c) | 50. (b) | 75. (c) | 100. (c) |

# DETAILED EXPLANATIONS OF ANSWERS

1. **(c)**   (c) is correct because a blueprint is a written plan for a building just as a score is a written plan for a symphony. (a) and (b) are incorrect because while a score can be issued in a contest or an exam, this is an alternate definition. (d) is incorrect because a score represents an entire work, not just a segment.

2. **(d)**   (d) is correct because the joint of a finger is called the knuckle and the joint of the arm is called the elbow. (a) and (c) are incorrect because they are too general to complete the analogy. (b) is incorrect because this refers to one of the bones of the lower arm.

3. **(b)**   (b) is correct because enigma is a synonym of riddle just as maze is a synonym for labyrinth. (a), (c), and (d) are partial synonyms; however, they do not express the subtlety of a riddle, and are therefore incorrect.

4. **(d)**   (d) is correct because green is the color associated with envy just as red is the color associated with rage. (a) is incorrect because, as we have seen, red is associated with rage. (b) is incorrect because blue is associated with sadness. (c) is incorrect because yellow is associated with cowardice.

5. **(a)**   (a) is correct because craven and cowardly are synonyms just as colloquial and casual are synonyms. (b), (c), and (d) are unrelated.

6. **(c)**   (c) is correct because chlorophyll is the chemical found in plants which is green, while the heme pigment in hemoglobin is red. Bilirubin (a), biliverdin (b), and malachite green (d) are all pigments, but none of them contain the red color of hemoglobin, so none of them can complete the analogy.

7. **(a)**   (a) is correct because eschatology concerns itself with all final things just as empiricism concerns itself with observable reality. (b), (c), and (d) may be concerns of the eschatologist, but only inasmuch as they represent and concern themselves with finality.

8.  **(c)**   (c) is correct because Aristotle is the thinker who advocated the golden mean, a philosophy of moderation, just as Karl Marx advocated the idea that came to be known as Marxism.

9.  **(b)**   The slope is a property of a line. Likewise, the curvature is a property of an arc (b). Radius (c) and diameter (d) are parts of a circle (a). While a circle does have curvature, it is a closed object, while an arc, like a line, is open.

10. **(c)**   (c) is correct because a blastula is an early stage of an embryo just as an acorn is an early stage of an oak. (a) is incorrect because while the heart emerges from the blastula, this is too specific. (b) is incorrect because an early stage of a novel is a rough draft. (d) is incorrect because an early stage of a plant is a seedling.

11. **(a)**   (a) is correct because a calyx is a cup-shaped portion of a plant or animal organ, just as a box is generally rectangular in shape. (b), (c), and (d) are incorrect because a calyx does not suggest this shape.

12. **(b)**   (b) is correct because just as a hypochondriac is overly concerned about his or her health, a miser is overly concerned about his or her money. (a) is incorrect because a philanthropist readily parts with his or her money. (c) is incorrect because there is nothing inherent in the term millionaire to show that he or she is overly concerned about money. (d) is incorrect because a philosopher would be concerned with money in the context of its philosophical implications.

13. **(a)**   (a) is correct because halcyon means peaceful and martial means warlike. (b) is incorrect because there is no inherent connotation in the word hero to mean either peaceful or warlike. (c) is incorrect because tranquilizer is a noun, rather than an adjective, and has a peaceful connotation. (d) passionate is incorrect because passion can be either peaceful or warlike.

14. **(a)**   Celsius is correct because celsius is the metric unit for temperature while meter is the metric unit for length. Centimeter (d) is a division within the unit of meter and therefore does not complete the analogy. Fahrenheit (b) is a unit for measuring temperature, but it is not a metric unit. Inch (c) is an English unit for measuring length and therefore does not complete the analogy.

15. **(b)**   (b) is correct because passing a test of some kind creates a feeling of elation, while failing creates a feeling of dejection. (a) and (c)

are incorrect because they are unrelated. (d) is incorrect because while rejection would cause dejection, it is not parallel with passed, and therefore does not complete the analogy.

16. **(a)**    (a) is correct because just as John Hughes discovered the brain chemical enkephalin, Mendel pioneered the science of genetics. (b) is incorrect because gene cloning was pioneered by the National Institutes of Health. (c) is incorrect because x-rays were discovered by Konrad and von Roentgen. (d) is incorrect because hormones were discovered by Bayliss and Starling.

17. **(a)**    (a) is correct because *Billy Budd* is an opera written by Britten, just as *Aida* is an opera written by Verdi. (b) is incorrect because *Carmen* was written by Bizet. (c) and (d) are incorrect because these operas were written by Bellini.

18. **(c)**    (c) is correct because this was Emily Brontë's pseudonym, just as Bachman was King's pseudonym. The remaining answer choices were pen names of Anne Brontë.

19. **(d)**    (d) is correct because in poetry, a caesura is a pause, just as a conclusion marks the end of a piece of writing. (a) is incorrect because a stop is more specific than a pause. (b) and (c) are incorrect because they are general terms for a work and its sections.

20. **(d)**    The measurement of a line (one dimension) is its length. The measurement of a plane (two dimensions) is the area. Volume (a) is a measurement in three dimensions. Width (c) is also a measurement of a line (in one dimension).

21. **(b)**    (b) is correct because an onomatopoeia is a word whose sound suggests its meaning, like buzz. This is analogous to a palindrome which is a word, phrase, sentence fragment, or sentence spelled the same backward and forward; for example—race car. All other answer choices are incorrect because they are not palindromes.

22. **(c)**    (c) is correct because a philologist studies language just as an ornithologist studies birds. (a) is incorrect because someone who studies thought and thought systems would be a philosopher, a psychologist, or an epistemologist. (b) is incorrect because it is unrelated to the other segments of the analogy. (d) is incorrect because an entomologist studies insects.

23. **(a)**   (a) is correct because applause usually follows a performance, just as a rebuttal usually follows a speech. (b), (c), and (d) may all occur after a performance, but not immediately.

24. **(c)**   (c) is correct because the literal translation of *alma mater* is fostering mother, just as the literal translation of *beau geste* is a noble gesture. (a) is incorrect because *magnum opus* means major work. (b) is incorrect because *mea culpa* means my fault. (d) is incorrect because *memento mori* means reminder of death.

25. **(c)**   (c) is correct because Byzantine art is characterized by its use of iconography in its religious themes, just as Roman art used statues. All other answer choices were known and used by the Byzantines, however not to the elevated status of iconography.

26. **(c)**   Zenith is correct because the North is the direction toward the top of most maps, while the South is the opposite or downward direction. The zenith is the overhead direction in the sky while standing on Earth, while the nadir is the underfoot direction or directly opposite the zenith. Pulsar (a) and equinox (d) are not directional terms, nor are they opposite from the term nadir. Polaris (b) is the name given to the North Star, but it does not fit into the analogy since it is the name of a specific star and is not a term used specifically to imply direction.

27. **(b)**   In this analogy, the expression, $f + g + h$, is simply divided by 2. Then $a + b$ should also be divided by 2, giving $a + b / 2$, choice (b).

28. **(d)**   (d) is correct because a pamphlet gives one a small amount of information, while a textbook gives one a great deal of information. This is analogous to an aspect giving one a small view of an area, and a panorama giving one a broad view of an area. (a), (b), and (c) are incorrect because they are too general to complete the analogy.

29. **(c)**   (c) is correct because to boast is to praise oneself, just as to atone is to make amends to oneself. (a) and (b) are incorrect because commend and compliment are synonyms meaning to praise. (d) is incorrect because to detract is an antonym of praise.

30. **(a)**   (a) is correct because a hedonist is primarily concerned with his or her own pleasure, just as a miser is concerned with his or her own thrift. (b) is incorrect because a sadist is identified with cruelty. (c) is incorrect because a socialist is concerned with an economic system. (d) is incorrect because an atheist is one who believes that there is no god.

31. **(c)**   Pahoehoe is correct because thick can imply a very viscous fluid, while thin implies a fluid which is free flowing. AA lava is the name given to very viscous or thick lava, while the Hawaiian word pahoehoe is used worldwide to describe highly fluid or thin lava. Tephra (a), tubes (b), and pillows (d) are words which refer to lava, but they do not describe the fluidity of the lava and therefore cannot complete the analogy.

32. **(d)**   (d) is correct because the cerebellum is a part of the brain, just as the aorta is a part of the heart. (a) and (b) are part of the circulatory system, but not a direct part of the heart. (c) is not the best answer, because ventricles refer to two chambers of the heart, and therefore does not complete the analogy.

33. **(b)**   (b) is correct because a cosmogony is a story of creation, such as Genesis, and a bildungsroman is a coming of age story, such as Joyce's *Portrait of the Artist as a Young Man*. (a) and (c) are too general, since folktales and mythologies may be concerned with creation, but they are not limited to that. (d) is incorrect because cosmology is the systematic study of the universe.

34. **(c)**   The relationship in this analogy is that the second number is the first number cubed. Thus, 5 cubed is 125 (c). (a) is not the correct answer since 25 is 5 squared. (b) 10 and (d) 40 are only multiples of 5.

35. **(b)**   (b) is correct because osseus means relating to the bones just as visceral means relating to the body. (a), (c), and (d) are too specific to complete the analogy.

36. **(d)**   (d) is correct because, on the pH scale, anything below 7 is an acid, and therefore anything above 7 is a base (alkali). The other choices are below 7 and are, therefore, acids.

37. **(c)**   (c) is correct because an anion is an ion with a negative charge, just as a cation is an ion with a positive charge. (a) is incorrect because it is too general. (b) is incorrect because a neutron is a particle without a charge. (d) is incorrect because a proton has a positive charge, but is not an ion.

38. **(b)**   (b) is correct because electrical currents flow from an anode (+) to a cathode (−). (a), (c), and (d) are incorrect because these are general terms that do not correspond to a specific negative or positive charge.

39. **(a)**    (a) is correct because FORTRAN is a computer language geared toward math, just as COBOL is a computer language geared toward business. (b) is incorrect because FORTRAN is not designed to be a graphic-intensive language. (c) and (d) are incorrect because they refer to general applications of computer programs rather than languages.

40. **(a)**    (a) is correct because a computer uses software as a source for instructions just as a teacher uses a textbook as a source for instructions. (b) and (c) are incorrect because these would correspond to a computer's hardware. (d) is incorrect because this would refer to the building in which the computer is housed.

41. **(c)**    (c) is correct because something that is serendipitous is spontaneous rather than planned, just as someone who is indefatigable is industrious (b) rather than lazy. (a) and (d) are incorrect because neither of these terms implies laziness.

42. **(c)**    0° is correct because the boiling point of water is 100° on the Celsius scale, while the freezing point of water is 0° on the Celsius scale. The temperature of 212° (b) is the Fahrenheit temperature for boiling water and therefore does not relate to the freezing point. Celsius (a) is the name of the temperature scale which has the boiling point at 100° and does not complete the analogy for the corresponding freezing point. The temperature of 32° (d) is the freezing point of water, but it is on the Fahrenheit scale and therefore does not complete the analogy.

43. **(c)**    The second expression, $4x^2 + 4xy + y^2$, is the square of the first expression, $2x + y$. Hence, the expression $a - b$, squared is $a^2 - 2ab + b^2$, (c).

44. **(b)**    (b) is correct because postulate and claim have similar meanings (to state a position), just as cavil and carp have similar meanings. (a) is incorrect because to grieve means to feel sadness over a loss. (c) is incorrect because a pike is a pointed stick. (d) is incorrect because a cabal is a group gathered to cause harm.

45. **(c)**    (c) is correct because just as Mestral invented velcro, so did the Biro brothers invent the ballpoint pen. (a) is incorrect because this is a brand name of a ballpoint pen, not its inventor. (b) is incorrect because although Edison invented a great many things, the ballpoint pen was not among them. (d) is incorrect because Earl Tupper invented Tupperware®.

46. **(d)** (d) is correct because a mile is 5,280 feet, just as an acre is 43,560 square feet. All other answer choices are irrelevant.

47. **(b)** The number 5 is an example of an odd number. Therefore, an example of an even number is needed to complete the analogy. The only even number amongst the choices is 2 (b). The other choices: 7 (a), 9 (c), and 1 (d) are all odd.

48. **(d)** Thermosphere is correct because the thermosphere is the outermost shell of the atmosphere of the Earth. The corona is the outermost layer of the atmosphere of the sun. The stratosphere (a) and the troposphere (b) are a part of the Earth's atmosphere, but they do not complete the analogy because they are not the outermost layer. The chromosphere (c) does not complete the analogy because it is a part of the atmosphere of the sun.

49. **(a)** (a) is correct because the capo is the beginning of a musical piece and the coda is the end. (b) is incorrect because denouement refers to the action in a novel following the conclusion. (c) is incorrect because a cadenza is an ornamental passage near the end of a piece of music. (d) is incorrect because an aria is an extended vocal solo in an opera.

50. **(b)** (b) is correct because centennial refers to a period of 100 years just as septennial refers to a period of seven years. (a) is incorrect because sesquicentennial refers to a period of 150 years. (c) is incorrect because sexennial refers to a period of six years. (d) is incorrect because decennial refers to a period of ten years.

51. **(d)** (d) is correct because Dionysus is the Greek god of wine, and Bacchus is his Roman counterpart, just as Nox is the Greek goddess of night and Nyx is her Roman counterpart. (a) is incorrect because Aurora is the Greek goddess of the dawn. (b) is incorrect because Tyche is the goddess of fortune or fate. (c) is incorrect because Selene is the Greek goddess of the moon.

52. **(b)** (b) is correct because an alias is a false identity, just as an illusion is a false perception. (a) is incorrect because name corresponds to alias rather than perception. (c) and (d) are incorrect because an idea and appearance do not imply falsehood.

53. **(a)** (a) is correct because Santayana was a student of William James as Plato was a student of Socrates. (b) is incorrect because Aristotle

was a student of Plato. (c) is incorrect because Plotinus was an Egyptian and founder of Neoplatonism. (d) is incorrect because Marcus Arelius was a Roman emperor and Stoic.

54. **(c)** (c) is correct because just as aesthetics are concerned with beauty, so phenomenalism is concerned with the notion that all that can be known are appearances, and that man cannot know the true nature of reality. (a) is incorrect because the study of knowledge is called epistemology. (b) and (d) are general terms, the nature of which has inspired many branches of philosophy.

55. **(b)** (b) is correct because usury is another term for interest on a loan, just as voluble is another word for fluent. (a) and (d) are incorrect because they are general financial terms that do not exclusively apply to interest. (c) is incorrect because tax refers to money taken by the government to be used in the interest of the governed.

56. **(c)** (c) is correct because yoke is synonymous with labor, just as urbane is synonymous with suave. (a) is incorrect because a field may be an area of labor, but not labor itself. (b) is incorrect because while labor can be said to be the culmination of gestation, it is not the process itself. (d) Vex means to annoy and is therefore incorrect.

57. **(d)** (d) is correct because a parable illustrates a moral just as a satire illustrates a disagreement with a given condition. (a) is incorrect because while a satire may ridicule its subject, this is a method rather than an illustration. (b) is incorrect because a satire may contain irony; this is not inherent in the form. (c) is incorrect because a myth is a story told to explain something that is not understood.

58. **(b)** Temperature is correct because zero-point energy is the point at which all motion stops. Absolute zero is the zero energy point on the Kelvin temperature scale. Force (a), speed (c), and joules (d) are not related to the zero point of motion and therefore do not complete the analogy.

59. **(d)** These triangles are similar, thus corresponding sides are similar. Therefore, the ratio of $\overline{AB}:\overline{DE}$ is equivalent to the ratios $\overline{BC}:\overline{DE}$ (d) and $AC:DF$.

60. **(b)** (b) is correct because hyperbole refers to exaggeration for effect just as an oxymoron (such as home office) uses contradiction for

effect. (a) is incorrect because a curve refers to the mathematical construct of hyperbola. (c) is incorrect because it is too general. (d) is incorrect because a fable is a story that illustrates a moral.

61. **(c)** (c) is correct because nicotine is the active drug in tobacco just as THC is the active drug in marijuana. (a) is incorrect because DDT was a pesticide removed from the market because of its carcinogenic properties. (b) is incorrect because NTE is an acronym for the National Teachers Examination. (d) is incorrect because the FAA is the Federal Aviation Administration.

62. **(a)** (a) is correct because retard and advance are antonyms, just as postpone and proceed are antonyms. (b) and (c) are incorrect because in this context, both would mean to aid or advance. (d) is incorrect because to reschedule does not inherently imply a delay.

63. **(a)** Newton is correct because the joule is the SI unit for the measurement of energy. The Newton is the SI unit for the measurement of force. Pounds (b) are also used as a measure of force, but the pound is not the acceptable SI unit. Meter (c) is the SI unit for the measurement of length. Mass (d) is not a unit of measure and therefore could not complete the analogy.

64. **(c)** (c) is correct because garrulous is synonymous with talkative, just as offend and aggravate are synonymous. (a) and (b) are incorrect because they both mean quiet and severe. (d) is incorrect because bucolic means rustic.

65. **(c)** (c) is correct because to plagiarize something is, in effect, to steal it, just as to festoon is to decorate with flowers, ribbons, etc. (a) and (b) are incorrect because they refer a specific style of decoration. (d) is incorrect because to refurbish something is to completely redesign it.

66. **(c)** (c) is correct because order and disorder are antonyms, just as euphony (meaning harmonious sounds) and cacophony (meaning discordant sounds) are antonyms. (a) and (b) are incorrect because although their meanings are appropriate, they do not follow the form of the analogy. (d) is incorrect because polyphony means many voices.

67. **(d)** (d) is correct because a typo is an error in spelling, just as an anachronism is a chronological impossibility. An example of an anachronism would be Shakespeare's inclusion of a clock in the play *Julius Caesar*. (a) and (c) are incorrect because although an anachronism

could be exposed in the areas of location and costume, it is not restricted to these areas. (b) is incorrect because method is a general term that does not completely apply.

68. **(a)**    (a) is correct because acetic acid is the main ingredient in the food vinegar, but it is very dilute. Carbonic acid is likewise the main ingredient in the food soda water, and it is also very dilute. Baking soda (b) is made of a carbonate, but it is not a diluted chemical. Sodium bicarbonate (c) is the chemical found in baking soda, but it is not the diluted chemical for soda water. Carbon tetrachloride (d), is a very toxic chemical and is therefore not a food. None of the other three terms fit this analogy.

69. **(a)**    (a) is correct because a motif is a recurring theme in a novel, just as a refrain is a recurring portion of a poem. (b) is incorrect because although songs have refrains, this section of the analogy is concerned with the motif. (c) is incorrect because a subplot is a secondary story within a larger story. (d) is incorrect because a prologue is an introductory speech or monologue.

70. **(d)**    (d) is correct because when a computer processes information, it does so in bytes, each byte containing 8 bits, or binary digits.

71. **(c)**    (c) is correct because forbearance and patience are synonyms just as knavery and trickery are synonyms. (a) is incorrect because an imposition refers to an unwelcome request. (b) is incorrect because this is an antonym of the correct answer. (d) is incorrect because misery means extreme sadness.

72. **(a)**    (a) is correct because pedestrian and mundane have similar meanings (mediocre or commonplace), just as petulant and insolent have similar meanings (peevish). (b) is incorrect because its meaning is similar to pedestrian. (c) is incorrect because vivacious means full of life. (d) is incorrect because wry means cynical.

73. **(b)**    (b) is correct because in a human, the brain is the center of information processing, just as the CPU, or central processing unit, is in a computer. (a) is incorrect because a program is a set of instructions along which the computer operates. (c) is incorrect because the microprocessor is too specific to complete the analogy. It would be analogous to a specific portion of the brain. (d) is incorrect because memory is too general.

74. **(b)**   (b) is correct because the legendary pirate flag was adorned with a skull and crossbones, or Jolly Roger, just as the flag of Canada is adorned with a maple leaf. All other answer choices are incorrect because these groups did not have an independent flag.

75. **(c)**   (c) is correct because a langur is a specific type of monkey (found in Asia) just as a bottlenose is a specific type of dolphin. (a), (b), and (d) are incorrect because none of the animals have a subtype called a langur.

76. **(a)**   (a) is correct because a partisan is loyal to their party, and a traitor is disloyal to their party, just as a deluge is too much water in a given area, and a drought is not enough water in a given area. (b) is incorrect because a pond is not the direct opposite of a drought. (c) is incorrect because a famine refers to a lack of food or water in an area, and is therefore an indirect synonym of drought. (d) is incorrect because a drought is a severe shortage of water, and the word storm does not imply the severe conditions that deluge does.

77. **(d)**   (d) is the correct answer. When placed in a flame, certain elements produce specific colors. Lithium produces a red flame, while sodium produces a yellow flame. Potassium (a) produces a violet flame, copper (b) produces a green flame, and magnesium (c) produces a white flame, so only lithium fits the analogy.

78. **(a)**   The relationship is the decimal form of a fraction. The fraction (9/8) is written in decimal form as 1.125 (a). Choice (b) is given in scientific notation, not in decimal form. Choice (c) is in fraction format. While 0.777 (d) is in decimal form, it is not equivalent to 9/8.

79. **(b)**   (b) is correct because essential (meaning necessary) and superfluous (meaning unnecessary) are antonyms, just as scurrilous (meaning vulgar) and refined are antonyms. (a) is incorrect because this is a synonym of scurrilous. (c) is incorrect because impetuous means impulsive. (d) is incorrect because contumelious means incessantly annoying.

80. **(a)**   (a) is correct because a meatus is a natural passage in the body, just as a strait is a natural passage through bodies of water. (b) and (d) are incorrect because these are natural bodies of water. (c) is incorrect because a canal is a humanmade passage between two bodies of water.

81. **(c)**   (c) is correct because to be acephalous means to be without a head, just as to be unopposed means to be without a rival. (a) and (b) are incorrect because acephalous does not refer to these organs. (d) is incorrect because to be without a spouse is to be single.

82. **(d)**   (d) is correct because fabaceous refers to the qualities of a bean, just as aquiline refers to the characteristics of an eagle. (a), (b), and (c) are incorrect because they are too general to sufficiently complete the analogy.

83. **(d)**   (d) is correct because Mecca is the holy city of the Islamic faith, just as the Ganges River is the holy place of Hinduism. (a) is incorrect because Medina is a holy city to Islam, not Hinduism. (b) is incorrect because Amristar is a holy city to the Sikhs. (c) is incorrect because Nepal is in Tibet.

84. **(d)**   Cochlea is correct because the cochlea is the organ of hearing, while the retina is a membrane connected by the optic nerve to the brain, making sight possible. The tympanic membrane (b) and the vestibulocochlear nerve (c) are found within the ear. But they are not the actual organ of hearing. The conjunctiva (a), which is not a sense organ, is found within the eye and therefore cannot be used to complete the analogy.

85. **(b)**   The study of algebra involves solving equations, and the study of geometry involves proofs of relations between lines, angles, and others. Elements (a) are parts of sets and not found in geometry. Sets (c) are found in number theory, and statistics (d) is a separate field of study.

86. **(b)**   (b) is correct because the painter commonly known as Titian was, in fact, named Tizano Vecellio, just as the painter commonly known as El Greco was in fact named Domenikos Theotokopoulos. All other answer choices are ficticious.

87. **(a)**   (a) is correct because as Warhol was considered the pioneer of Pop Art, so Picasso was considered the pioneer of Cubism. (b) is incorrect because Pollack was an Abstract Expressionist. (c) is incorrect because Mondrian the master of the De Stijl movement. (d) is incorrect because Matisse was an Expressionist.

88. **(a)**   (a) is correct because just as Tiffany is famous for his stained glass, Javachef is famous for surrounding the islands of Biscayne Bay with

pink fabric. (b), (c), and (d) are incorrect because Javachef did not work in these media.

89. **(b)**    (b) is correct because myopic refers to a condition commonly called nearsightedness, and a haberdasher refers to a men's clothier. All other answer choices are irrelevant.

90. **(c)**    (c) is correct because a lapidary is someone who crafts precious stones, just as a cooper is someone who makes barrels and casks. All other choices are irrelevant.

91. **(c)**    (c) is correct because the Veda are the holy writings of Hinduism, just as the Talmud is a holy book of the Jewish faith. (a) is incorrect because the Tao Te Ching contains the tenets of Taoism. (b) is incorrect because the Koran is the holy book of Islam. (d) is incorrect because a sutra is a Buddhist commentary.

92. **(c)**    Binary stars is correct because scattered objects are not held together by any force, whereas bound objects are held together by a common force. This analogy shows an opposite characteristic. Associations are scattered stars which are not bound by gravity, whereas binary stars are bound together through their orbiting of a common center of mass. This is a difficult analogy and requires the previous knowledge of the definition of association which at first glance seems to imply some type of a bond. Celestial sphere (a), cosmic rays (b), and cardinal points (d), while they are all terms applicable to astronomy, do not complete the opposite analogy and do not suggest an interrelationship with scattered versus bound.

93. **(c)**    (c) is correct because just as the Wright brothers engineered the first airplane flight, so did the Montgolfier brothers engineer the first hot air balloon flight. (a) is incorrect because Garnerin was credited with the first parachute jump. (b) is incorrect because Zeppelin was credited with the first rigid-frame airship flight. (d) is incorrect because Selfridge is noted as the first airplane fatality.

94. **(d)**    (d) is correct because Adam is the first man in the Judeo-Christian faith, just as Ask was the first man in Norse mythology. (a) is incorrect because Bragi is the Norse god of poetry. (b) is incorrect because Balder is the Norse god of light. (c) is incorrect because Buri is the progenitor of the gods in Norse mythology.

95. **(b)** (b) is correct because Oedipus and Jocasta entered into a forbidden marriage (mother to son) in Sophocles' Theban plays, just as Claudius and Gertrude entered into a forbidden marriage (brother-in-law to sister-in-law) in Shakespeare's *Hamlet*. (a) is incorrect because Clytaemnestra was the wife of Agammemnon. (c) is incorrect because Antigone was the daughter of Oedipus. (d) is incorrect because Cassandra was a prophet in Greek mythology.

96. **(a)** (a) is correct because Charles Darwin was the first to establish a concrete theory of evolution just as Niels Bohr was the first to establish an acceptable concrete model of atomic structure. (b) is incorrect because x-ray diffraction was discovered by Max von Laue. (c) is incorrect because dynamite was first created by Alfred Nobel. (d) is incorrect because electrons were first described by Joseph Thompson.

97. **(b)** Angles 1 and 2 are vertical angles and thus are equal. Angles 4 and 5 are vertical angles, but 5 is not offered as a choice. Then what other angle is equal to 4? The lines B and C are parallel, thus angles 3 and 5 are equal. Then angles 4 and 5 and 3 (b) are all equal.

98. **(d)** (d) is correct because John W. Davis unsuccessfully ran against Calvin Coolidge for the presidency of the United States just as Adlai Stevenson unsuccessfully ran against Dwight Eisenhower. (a), (b), and (c) are incorrect because all these candidates unsuccessfully ran against Franklin Roosevelt.

99. **(c)** (c) is correct because the Fifteenth Amendment gave voting rights to men of all races, just as the Nineteenth Amendment gave voting rights to women. (a) is incorrect because prohibition was set in the Eighteenth Amendment. (b) is incorrect because cruel and unusual punishment was prohibited in the Eighth Amendment. (d) is incorrect because the order of presidential succession was spelled out in the Twenty-fifth Amendment.

100. **(c)** (c) is correct because epicene and androgynous mean having both male and female characteristics, just as entente and agreement both mean an understanding reached between parties. (a), (b), and (d) are unrelated to the meaning of these terms.

# MAT – Practice Test 8 Answer Sheet

| | | |
|---|---|---|
| 1. ⓐ ⓑ ⓒ ⓓ | 35. ⓐ ⓑ ⓒ ⓓ | 69. ⓐ ⓑ ⓒ ⓓ |
| 2. ⓐ ⓑ ⓒ ⓓ | 36. ⓐ ⓑ ⓒ ⓓ | 70. ⓐ ⓑ ⓒ ⓓ |
| 3. ⓐ ⓑ ⓒ ⓓ | 37. ⓐ ⓑ ⓒ ⓓ | 71. ⓐ ⓑ ⓒ ⓓ |
| 4. ⓐ ⓑ ⓒ ⓓ | 38. ⓐ ⓑ ⓒ ⓓ | 72. ⓐ ⓑ ⓒ ⓓ |
| 5. ⓐ ⓑ ⓒ ⓓ | 39. ⓐ ⓑ ⓒ ⓓ | 73. ⓐ ⓑ ⓒ ⓓ |
| 6. ⓐ ⓑ ⓒ ⓓ | 40. ⓐ ⓑ ⓒ ⓓ | 74. ⓐ ⓑ ⓒ ⓓ |
| 7. ⓐ ⓑ ⓒ ⓓ | 41. ⓐ ⓑ ⓒ ⓓ | 75. ⓐ ⓑ ⓒ ⓓ |
| 8. ⓐ ⓑ ⓒ ⓓ | 42. ⓐ ⓑ ⓒ ⓓ | 76. ⓐ ⓑ ⓒ ⓓ |
| 9. ⓐ ⓑ ⓒ ⓓ | 43. ⓐ ⓑ ⓒ ⓓ | 77. ⓐ ⓑ ⓒ ⓓ |
| 10. ⓐ ⓑ ⓒ ⓓ | 44. ⓐ ⓑ ⓒ ⓓ | 78. ⓐ ⓑ ⓒ ⓓ |
| 11. ⓐ ⓑ ⓒ ⓓ | 45. ⓐ ⓑ ⓒ ⓓ | 79. ⓐ ⓑ ⓒ ⓓ |
| 12. ⓐ ⓑ ⓒ ⓓ | 46. ⓐ ⓑ ⓒ ⓓ | 80. ⓐ ⓑ ⓒ ⓓ |
| 13. ⓐ ⓑ ⓒ ⓓ | 47. ⓐ ⓑ ⓒ ⓓ | 81. ⓐ ⓑ ⓒ ⓓ |
| 14. ⓐ ⓑ ⓒ ⓓ | 48. ⓐ ⓑ ⓒ ⓓ | 82. ⓐ ⓑ ⓒ ⓓ |
| 15. ⓐ ⓑ ⓒ ⓓ | 49. ⓐ ⓑ ⓒ ⓓ | 83. ⓐ ⓑ ⓒ ⓓ |
| 16. ⓐ ⓑ ⓒ ⓓ | 50. ⓐ ⓑ ⓒ ⓓ | 84. ⓐ ⓑ ⓒ ⓓ |
| 17. ⓐ ⓑ ⓒ ⓓ | 51. ⓐ ⓑ ⓒ ⓓ | 85. ⓐ ⓑ ⓒ ⓓ |
| 18. ⓐ ⓑ ⓒ ⓓ | 52. ⓐ ⓑ ⓒ ⓓ | 86. ⓐ ⓑ ⓒ ⓓ |
| 19. ⓐ ⓑ ⓒ ⓓ | 53. ⓐ ⓑ ⓒ ⓓ | 87. ⓐ ⓑ ⓒ ⓓ |
| 20. ⓐ ⓑ ⓒ ⓓ | 54. ⓐ ⓑ ⓒ ⓓ | 88. ⓐ ⓑ ⓒ ⓓ |
| 21. ⓐ ⓑ ⓒ ⓓ | 55. ⓐ ⓑ ⓒ ⓓ | 89. ⓐ ⓑ ⓒ ⓓ |
| 22. ⓐ ⓑ ⓒ ⓓ | 56. ⓐ ⓑ ⓒ ⓓ | 90. ⓐ ⓑ ⓒ ⓓ |
| 23. ⓐ ⓑ ⓒ ⓓ | 57. ⓐ ⓑ ⓒ ⓓ | 91. ⓐ ⓑ ⓒ ⓓ |
| 24. ⓐ ⓑ ⓒ ⓓ | 58. ⓐ ⓑ ⓒ ⓓ | 92. ⓐ ⓑ ⓒ ⓓ |
| 25. ⓐ ⓑ ⓒ ⓓ | 59. ⓐ ⓑ ⓒ ⓓ | 93. ⓐ ⓑ ⓒ ⓓ |
| 26. ⓐ ⓑ ⓒ ⓓ | 60. ⓐ ⓑ ⓒ ⓓ | 94. ⓐ ⓑ ⓒ ⓓ |
| 27. ⓐ ⓑ ⓒ ⓓ | 61. ⓐ ⓑ ⓒ ⓓ | 95. ⓐ ⓑ ⓒ ⓓ |
| 28. ⓐ ⓑ ⓒ ⓓ | 62. ⓐ ⓑ ⓒ ⓓ | 96. ⓐ ⓑ ⓒ ⓓ |
| 29. ⓐ ⓑ ⓒ ⓓ | 63. ⓐ ⓑ ⓒ ⓓ | 97. ⓐ ⓑ ⓒ ⓓ |
| 30. ⓐ ⓑ ⓒ ⓓ | 64. ⓐ ⓑ ⓒ ⓓ | 98. ⓐ ⓑ ⓒ ⓓ |
| 31. ⓐ ⓑ ⓒ ⓓ | 65. ⓐ ⓑ ⓒ ⓓ | 99. ⓐ ⓑ ⓒ ⓓ |
| 32. ⓐ ⓑ ⓒ ⓓ | 66. ⓐ ⓑ ⓒ ⓓ | 100. ⓐ ⓑ ⓒ ⓓ |
| 33. ⓐ ⓑ ⓒ ⓓ | 67. ⓐ ⓑ ⓒ ⓓ | |
| 34. ⓐ ⓑ ⓒ ⓓ | 68. ⓐ ⓑ ⓒ ⓓ | |

# MILLER ANALOGIES

# PRACTICE TEST 8

**TIME:**    50 Minutes
             100 Analogies

---

**DIRECTIONS**: Read each of the following analogies carefully, and choose the BEST answer to each item. Fill in your responses in the answer sheets provided.

---

1.  I. M. PEI : (a. architecture b. sculpture c. education d. illustration) :: ALVIN AILEY : CHOREOGRAPHY

2.  NEMO : NAUTILUS :: AHAB : (a. Lusitania b. Nimitz c. Pequod d. Titanic)

3.  PALEOCENE : CENOZOIC :: TRIASSIC : (a. Cambrian b. Silurian c. Devonian d. Mesozoic)

4.  10 : 1,000 :: 4 : (a. 16 b. 24 c. 48 d. 64)

5.  COURAGEOUS : (a. pusillanimous b. victorious c. venerated d. vilified) :: VALOR : COWARDICE

6.  HYDROGEN BOND : PAPER :: (a. disulfide linkages b. Van der Waals forces c. metallic bonds d. electrostatic attraction) : RUBBER

7.  PRADO : MADRID :: HERMITAGE : (a. Paris b. New York c. St. Petersburg d. Vienna)

8.  MALE : FEMALE :: TENOR : (a. alto b. soprano c. mezzo soprano d. bass)

9.  STEER : COW :: GELDING : (a. horse b. mare c. foal d. colt)

10. COPERNICUS : SUN :: PTOLEMY : (a. Earth b. moon c. stars d. church)

11. *BROWN V. BOARD OF EDUCATION* : 1954 :: *ROE V. WADE* :
    (a. 1968 b. 1979 c. 1970 d. 1973)

12. (a. keratotomy b. demographics c. cartography d. topology) :
    MAPMAKING :: HAGIOGRAPHY : SAINTS

13. PERISSODACTYLA : HORSE :: ARTIODACTYLA : (a. pig b. cat
    c. monkey d. kangaroo)

14. SANCTION : PERMIT :: (a. argument b. tirade c. discussion
    d. debate) : HARANGUE

15. MCCARTHYISM : 1950 :: SALEM WITCH HUNTS : (a. 1730
    b. 1580 c. 1692 d. 1800)

16. PIAGET : COGNITIVE DEVELOPMENT :: (a. Freud b. Jung
    c. Maslow d. Marcuse) : HIERARCHY OF HUMAN NEEDS

17. GARLIC : CLOVE :: GEAR : (a. tooth b. machine c. spin d. transfer)

18. HOMOGENEITY : INDIVIDUALISM :: (a. comprehension
    b. indoctrination c. education d. impartiality) : LEARNING

19. SYMMETRY : H :: ASYMMETRY : (a. E b. O c. J d. M)

20. BUS BOYCOTT : ALABAMA :: KENT STATE : (a. Massachusetts
    b. New Jersey c. California d. Ohio)

21. TEAPOT DOME : (a. gold b. oil c. uranium d. railroads) :: CREDIT
    MOBILIER : RAILROADS

22. BLANK VERSE : RHYME :: FREE VERSE : (a. form b. theme
    c. meter d. tone)

23. THORAX : (a. insect b. heart c. brain d. eyes) :: DIGIT : HAND

24. JUTE : SISAL :: TWINE : (a. fabric b. rope c. cotton d. sail)

25. ORIGINAL : REPLICA :: PUZZLE : (a. riddle b. question c. enigma
    d. solution)

26. AMPLE : ABUNDANT :: ENTHUSIASM : (a. happiness b. pleasure c. calm d. frenzy)

27. 3/10 : 0.30 :: 4/3 : (a. 1 1/3 b. 1.3 c. 1.33 d. 0.67)

28. COLLOQUIAL : (a. idiomatic b. pretentious c. aloof d. amiable) :: ALACRITY : ENTHUSIASM

29. ERSATZ : SUBSTITUTE :: PSEUDO : (a. approximate b. false c. partial d. genuine)

30. (a. errant b. arbitrary c. ignoble d. phlegmatic) : GERMANE :: NEFARIOUS : RIGHTEOUS

31. EBULLIENT : ENNUI :: (a. lecherous b. lustrous c. parochial d. quiescent) : LASCIVIOUS

32. MICHIGAN : GREAT LAKES STATE :: INDIANA : (a. Treasure State b. Bluegrass State c. Hoosier State d. Garden State)

33. GEOLOGY : EARTH :: ERGONOMICS : (a. finances b. comfort c. health d. movement)

34. BURNS : ALOE :: (a. sneezing b. headache c. backache d. nausea) : PEPPERMINT

35. VERISIMILITUDE : TRUTH :: (a. apparent b. obvious c. unknown d. unaware) : ACTUAL

36. LANGUAGE : PHILOLOGICAL :: (a. snake b. rodent c. fish d. bird) : OPHIDIAN

37. Given   A = {1, 3, 4, 5, 7}

    B = {2, 4, 6, 8, 10}

    C = {4}

    D = {1, 2, 3, 4, 5, 6, 7, 8, 10}

    A ∩ B : C :: A ∪ B : (a. A b. B c. C d. D)

38. MYRMIDON : SYCOPHANT :: PROLETARIAT : (a. bourgeoise b. worker c. intellectual d. prolix)

39. GONG : CYMBAL :: (a. bass b. timpani c. bongo d. tom) : DRUM

40. SIMULACRUM : IMAGE :: ESTIMATE : (a. calculation b. guess c. opinion d. prospectus)

41. CRYPTOGRAPHER : CODES :: GLAZIER : (a. ice b. glass c. confections d. animals)

42. $3\frac{1}{4} : \frac{13}{4} :: 2\frac{1}{7} :$ (a. $\frac{14}{7}$ b. $\frac{10}{7}$ c. $\frac{15}{7}$ d. $\frac{22}{7}$)

43. CORNHUSKER STATE : NEBRASKA :: CONSTITUTION STATE : (a. Pennsylvania b. Massachusetts c. Connecticut d. Maryland)

44. NARCISSISM : CONFIDENCE :: FEAR : (a. apprehension b. worry c. welcome d. panic)

45. Given

| $f$ | $h$ |
|-----|-----|
| 1 | 3 |
| 2 | 5 |
| 3 | 7 |
| 9 | 9 |

$f : h - 1 :: 2 :$ (a. 5 b. 1 c. 4 d. 9)

46. (a. magnesium b. calcium c. strontium d. barium) : CHLOROPHYLL :: IRON : HEMOGLOBIN

47. PROTOSTOMES : SPIRAL :: DEUTEROSTOMES : (a. radial b. bilateral c. round d. helical)

48. UGA : CODON :: (a. TCG b. ACU c. UGT d. AAG) : ANTICODON

49. QUEBEC : (a. Edmonton b. Quebec City c. Winnipeg d. Toronto) :: BRITISH COLUMBIA : VICTORIA

50. SPIDER MONKEY : NEW WORLD :: (a. woolly monkey
    b. marmoset c. tamarin d. loris) : OLD WORLD

51. COMPLEX : FREUD :: ARCHETYPE : (a. Adler b. Jung c. James
    d. Campbell)

52. RENEGE : FULFILL :: RECANT : (a. declare b. absolve c. expose
    d. dissent)

53. $e^{2x}$ : $2x \log e$ :: $\sqrt{8}$ : (a. 1/2 log 8 b. 8 log 2 c. 2 log 8 d. 4 log 8)

54. NIELS BOHR : QUANTUM THEORY :: ANNIE CANNON :
    (a. astronomer b. stellar spectral classification system c. Harvard
    College Observatory d. probability theory)

55. PLAINTIFF : LITIGANT :: (a. igneous b. stone c. weathered
    d. ancient) : ROCK

56. $x$ : $1/x$ :: PERIOD : (a. amplitude b. 1/amplitude c. frequency, d. 1/
    frequency)

57. SET : ELEMENT :: EQUATION : (a. division b. axiom c. variable
    d. Venn diagram)

58. WATER : DAM :: (a. livestock b. gas c. hair d. beer) : SNOOD

59. NANKING : (a. Beijing b. Canton c. Hong Kong d. Guangzhou) ::
    KYOTO : TOKYO

60. BALEFUL : (a. angelic b. masochistic c. malefic d. doleful) ::
    DULCET : MELODIOUS

61. EXCULPATE : (a. absolve b. repay c. blame d. banish) :: EXALT :
    HONOR

62. PHILISTINE : (a. uncouth b. urbane c. laggard d. neophyte) ::
    ACRID : AROMATIC

63. BALTIMORE AND TEMIN : REVERSE TRANSCRIPTASE ::
    (a. Kornberg b. Newton and Leibniz c. Watson and Crick d. Thomson
    and Kelvin) : DNA

64. DEARTH : VACUOUS :: PENULTIMATE : (a. juxtaposition
    b. hiatus c. epitome d. terminus)

65. KR : KRYPTON :: CO : (a. chlorine b. copper c. cobalt d. carbon)

66. NASCENT : (a. incipient b. descant c. umbrage d. solace) ::
    INANIMATE : EXTINCT

67. GREGARIOUS : RECLUSIVE :: OBSEQUIOUS : (a. servile
    b. insolent c. petulent d. demure)

68. PROGENY : (a. genetics b. feminism c. genius d. offspring) ::
    PALLID : SALLOW

69. CREPUSCULAR : (a. twilight b. darkness c. sunrise d. noon) ::
    PEDAGOGICAL : EDUCATION

70. E : ECHO :: F : (a. fancy b. forest c. firefly d. fox-trot)

71. FRUCTOSE : (a. lactose b. sucrose c. glucose d. maltose) :: FRUIT :
    MILK

72. ANALOGOUS : (a. tautological b. tantamount c. similar d. opposite)
    :: LIQUESCENT : MELTING

73. PRIMA BALLERINA : BALLET :: DIVA : (a. opera b. art c. music
    d. dance)

74. ELUCIDATE : CLARIFY :: MAGISTRATE : (a. attorney b. police
    officer c. judge d. warden)

75. TRANSPOSONS : BARBARA McCLINTOCK :: (a. HIV b. HTLV
    c. AIDS d. DNA polymerase) : LUC MONTAGNIER

76. PROSELYTE : (a. devotee b. concubine c. convert d. expert) ::
    NOVICE : NEOPHYTE

77. Given

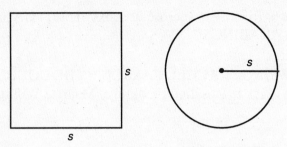

Then, $4s : s^2 :: 2\pi s :$ (a. $2\pi s^2$ b. $\pi s^2$ c. $(\pi/2)s^2$ d. $\pi(s/2)^2$)

78. MALE : INCUBUS :: FEMALE : (a. demon b. succubus c. distaff d. dowager)

79. $2x^2 + 4x + 3x^2 - 6x + 5 : 5x^2 - 2x + 5 :: 7x - 9x^2 + x^3 - 10x - 5 + 4x^4 + 7 :$ (a. $4x^4 + x^3 - 9x^2 - 3x + 2$ b. $5x^4 - 9x^2 - 3x$ c. $4x^4 + x^3 + 17x - 12$ d. $x^3 + 7x - 19x^2 - 2$)

80. *LAPSUS LINGUAE* : (a. tongue tied b. tongue twister c. lap dog d. slip of the tongue) :: *IN ABSENTIA* : IN ABSENCE

81. YATHRIB : MEDINA :: PERSIA : (a. Iraq b. Iran c. Saudi Arabia d. Mecca)

82. APOTHEGM : (a. touchstone b. maxim c. criticism d. praise) :: LAIRD : LORD

83. RED : BLUE :: (a. x-ray b. ultraviolet c. gamma radiation d. radio wave) : MICROWAVE

84. AMALIE NOETHER : PHYSICS :: ROSALIND FRANKLIN : (a. molecular biology b. x-ray crystallography c. organic chemistry d. transposons)

85. (a. voluble b. trite c. veracious d. accede) : FLUENT :: LACKADAISICAL : TARRY

86. DROMEDARY : CAMEL :: PACHYDERM : (a. ox b. tiger c. elephant d. whale)

87. TONI MORRISON : *BELOVED* :: (a. Jane Smiley b. John Updike c. Norman Mailer d. Alice Walker) : *RABBIT AT REST*

88. (a. glucose b. fructose c. sucrose d. deoxyribose) : GALACTOSE ::
    RIBOSE : ARABINOSE

89. *SILENT SPRING* : RACHEL CARSON :: THE DOUBLE HELIX :
    (a. Francis Crick b. Rosalind Franklin c. Maurice Wilkins d. James
    Watson)

90. SCURVY : VITAMIN C :: (a. beriberi b. zwitterion c. kwashiorkor
    d. ketosis) : PROTEIN

91. NIXON : FORD :: GOLDA MEIR : (a. Itzhak Rabin b. Menachem
    Begin c. Shimon Peres d. Yitzhak Shamir)

92. SYCOPHANTIC : PANDERING :: DOGMATIC : (a. authoritarian
    b. unprincipled c. karmic d. innocuous)

93. SEPTADEKAPHILIA : 17 :: ARACHNAPHILIA : (a. people
    b. spiders c. strangers d. insects)

94. OBDURATE : (a. tenacious b. tacit c. succinct d. obstinate) ::
    UBIQUITOUS : OMNIPRESENT

95. RECANTATION : AFFIRMATION :: DEFY : (a. rebel b. challenge
    c. acquiesce d. dare)

96. PINEAL : MELATONIN :: KIDNEY : (a. glucagon b. insulin
    c. renin d. calcitonin)

97. Given    A = {0, 1, 2, 3}

             B = {4, 5, 6, 7}

             C = {0, 1}

             D = {6, 7}

             E = {8, 9}

    C : A :: D : (a. A b. B c. C d. E)

98. CHOLERIC : CANTANKEROUS :: BOMBASTIC : (a. behoove
    b. affable c. turgid d. pious)

99.  APRIL : MAY :: (a. ruby b. sapphire c. garnet d. diamond) :
     EMERALD

100. PLUVIOMETER : (a. rainfall b. age c. blood pressure d. RPMs) ::
     CHRONOMETER : TIME

# Practice Test 8

## ANSWER KEY

| | | | | | | | |
|---|---|---|---|---|---|---|---|
| 1. | (a) | 26. | (d) | 51. | (b) | 76. | (c) |
| 2. | (c) | 27. | (c) | 52. | (a) | 77. | (b) |
| 3. | (d) | 28. | (a) | 53. | (a) | 78. | (b) |
| 4. | (d) | 29. | (b) | 54. | (b) | 79. | (a) |
| 5. | (a) | 30. | (b) | 55. | (a) | 80. | (d) |
| 6. | (a) | 31. | (c) | 56. | (d) | 81. | (b) |
| 7. | (c) | 32. | (c) | 57. | (c) | 82. | (b) |
| 8. | (b) | 33. | (b) | 58. | (c) | 83. | (d) |
| 9. | (a) | 34. | (d) | 59. | (a) | 84. | (a) |
| 10. | (a) | 35. | (a) | 60. | (c) | 85. | (a) |
| 11. | (d) | 36. | (a) | 61. | (a) | 86. | (c) |
| 12. | (c) | 37. | (d) | 62. | (b) | 87. | (b) |
| 13. | (a) | 38. | (b) | 63. | (c) | 88. | (a) |
| 14. | (b) | 39. | (b) | 64. | (d) | 89. | (d) |
| 15. | (c) | 40. | (a) | 65. | (c) | 90. | (c) |
| 16. | (c) | 41. | (b) | 66. | (a) | 91. | (a) |
| 17. | (a) | 42. | (c) | 67. | (b) | 92. | (a) |
| 18. | (b) | 43. | (c) | 68. | (d) | 93. | (b) |
| 19. | (c) | 44. | (d) | 69. | (a) | 94. | (d) |
| 20. | (d) | 45. | (c) | 70. | (d) | 95. | (c) |
| 21. | (b) | 46. | (a) | 71. | (a) | 96. | (c) |
| 22. | (c) | 47. | (a) | 72. | (b) | 97. | (b) |
| 23. | (a) | 48. | (b) | 73. | (a) | 98. | (c) |
| 24. | (b) | 49. | (b) | 74. | (c) | 99. | (d) |
| 25. | (d) | 50. | (a) | 75. | (a) | 100. | (a) |

# DETAILED EXPLANATIONS OF ANSWERS

1.  **(a)**  (a) is correct because I. M. Pei is an architect just as Alvin Ailey is an choreographer. All other answer choices are incorrect because I. M. Pei was not active in these disciplines.

2.  **(c)**  (c) is correct because Nemo was the captain of the *Nautilus* in Jules Verne's *20,000 Leagues Under the Sea,* just as Ahab was the captain of the *Pequod* in Herman Melville's *Moby-Dick*. All other answer choices are incorrect because they are actual ships, not fictitious ones.

3.  **(d)**  (d) is correct because the Cenozoic period marked the beginning of the Paleocene era, just as the Triassic period marked the beginning of the Mesozoic. All other choices were periods in the Paleozoic era.

4.  **(d)**  (d) is correct because 1,000 is 10 cubed, just as 64 is 4 cubed. All other choices are insignificant to this analogy.

5.  **(a)**  (a) is correct because courageous is the opposite of pusillanimous (meaning cowardly), just as valor is the opposite of cowardice. (b) is incorrect because it is an indirect synonym of courageous. (c) is incorrect because something that is venerated is revered. (d) is incorrect because to be vilified means to be defamed.

6.  **(a)**  (a) is correct because Hydrogen bonds provide the cross linkages of cellulose in paper, while Disulfide linkages provide the cross linkages in rubber. Van de Waals forces (b), metalic bonds (c), and electrostatic attraction (d) do not provide the cross linking forces in either of these situations and therefore do not provide a completion for the analogy.

7.  **(c)**  (c) is correct because the Prado is Madrid's most famous art museum just as the Hermitage is St. Petersburg's. (a) is incorrect because the most famous museum in Paris is the Louvre. (b) is incorrect because there are several famous museums in New York, including the Metropolitan and the Museum of Modern Art. (d) is incorrect because the most famous museum in Vienna is the Naturhistorices.

8.  **(b)**  (b) is correct because tenor is the highest normal male voice just as soprano is the highest female voice. (a) is incorrect because alto is a

lower female voice. (c) is incorrect because a mezzo soprano is lower than a soprano. (d) is incorrect because bass is the lowest male voice.

9.    **(a)**    (a) is correct because a castrated male cow is called a steer, just as a castrated male horse is called a gelding. (b) is incorrect because a mare is a female horse. (c) and (d) are incorrect because these are names for the offspring of horses.

10.  **(a)**    (a) is correct because in the Copernican model of the solar system, the Earth revolves around the sun, while in the Ptolemaic model, the sun revolved around the Earth. (b), (c), and (d) are incorrect because no credible scientist ever proposed that the Earth revolved around these bodies.

11.  **(d)**    (d) is correct because *Brown v. Board of Education* declaring segregation unconstitutional was decided in 1954 just as *Roe v. Wade* declaring prohibition of abortion unconstitutional was decided in 1973. All other answer choices are insignificant to this analogy.

12.  **(c)**    (c) is correct because cartography refers to the science of mapmaking just as hagiography refers to the study of saints' lives. (a) is incorrect because keratotomy is a corrective operation on the lens of the eye. (b) is incorrect because demographics refers to the study of population distribution. (d) is incorrect because topology refers to a branch of calculus.

13.  **(a)**    Pig is correct because a horse is an ungulate and like all perissodactyla has an odd number of toes, while a pig is also an ungulate but has an even number of toes like all artiodactyla. Cats (b), Monkeys (c), and kangaroos (d) are not ungulates and therefore do not fit the analogy.

14.  **(b)**    (b) is incorrect because permit and sanction are synonyms meaning to allow, just as harangue and tirade are synonyms meaning a bombastic rant. Argument (a), discussion (c), and debate (d) are incorrect because they convey a lesser degree of emotion.

15.  **(c)**    (c) is correct because in 1950, the nation was gripped by the panic of McCarthyism, just as in 1692 the community of Salem, Massachusetts, was paralyzed by the Salem witch hunts. All other answer choices are insignificant to this analogy.

16. **(c)** (c) is correct because Jean Piaget developed a theory of cognitive development just as Abraham Maslow developed a hierarchy of human needs. (a) is incorrect because Freud developed a theory of psychoanalysis. (b) is incorrect because Jung is famous for his theory of collective unconscious. (d) is incorrect because Marcuse is well known for his theories on work and labor.

17. **(a)** (a) is correct because a clove is a part of a garlic bulb as a tooth is a part of a gear. (b) is incorrect because a gear is part of a machine, and this reverses the whole : part relationship. (c) and (d) are incorrect because a gear spins (c) and by doing so transfers (d) power, however this is the function of a gear, not a part of its structure.

18. **(b)** (b) is correct because homogeneity, or conformity on a social level, is the opposite of individualism, in much the same way that indoctrination, or the insertion of another's ideas and opinions into one's mind, is the opposite of learning. (a) and (c) are incorrect because they have similar meanings to learning. (d) is incorrect because to be impartial is to be unbiased.

19. **(c)** The letter H is symmetric both horizontally and vertically; as such, only J (c) is not symmetric, or it is asymmetric. However, the other choices are symmetric as shown.

20. **(d)** (d) is correct because just as the bus boycott occurred in Montgomery, Alabama, a very influential student protest occurred at Kent State in Kent, Ohio. All other answer choices are insignificant to this analogy.

21. **(b)** (b) is correct because the Teapot Dome Scandal involved the transfer of naval oil reserves, and the Credit Mobilier Scandal involved railroad tycoons establishing slush funds to defraud the government. All other choices are irrelevant to this analogy.

22. **(c)** (c) is correct because just as blank verse poetry does not rhyme, free verse poetry has no set meter. (a) is incorrect because free verse is a form in itself. (b) and (d) are incorrect because there is nothing inherent in the term free verse that would suggest that theme or tone are absent.

23. **(a)** (a) is correct because the thorax is part of an insect just as the digit is part of a hand. (b), (c), and (d) are incorrect because these are too specific to complete the analogy.

24. **(b)**    (b) is correct because jute is a plant material used to make twine just as sisal is a plant fiber used to make rope. (a), (c), and (d) are incorrect because neither jute nor sisal are used to make these materials.

25. **(d)**    (d) is incorrect because an original is the opposite of a copy, just as a problem is the opposite of a solution. (a), (b), and (c) are incorrect because these are not antonyms of problem.

26. **(d)**    (d) is correct because abundant means ample (sufficient) to a greater degree, just as frenzy means enthusiasm to a greater degree. (a) and (b) are incorrect because they do not convey a greater degree. (c) is incorrect because calm is the opposite of frenzy.

27. **(c)**    The fraction 3/10 is rewritten as the decimal 0.30, with two decimal places. The fraction 4/3 can also be written as a decimal, 1.33. Choice (a) is incorrect because the number is still in fraction form. In choice (b), the decimal is written with only one decimal place. Choice (d) is not equivalent to 4/3.

28. **(a)**    (a) is correct because colloquial and idiomatic are synonyms meaning common just as alacrity and enthusiasm are synonyms for liveliness. (b) and (c) are incorrect because pretentious and aloof are opposites of colloquial. (d) is incorrect because amiable means friendly.

29. **(b)**    (b) is correct because ersatz and substitute are synonymous, just as pseudo and false are synonymous. (a), (c), and (d) are incorrect because these are all relative antonyms of pseudo.

30. **(b)**    (b) is correct because arbitrary, meaning unimportant, is the antonym of germane, meaning pertinent, just as nefarious and righteous are opposites. (a) is incorrect because errant means wandering, (c) is incorrect because ignoble means shameful, and (d) is incorrect because phlegmatic means without interest or emotion.

31. **(c)**    (c) is correct because parochial, meaning religiously moral, is the antonym of lascivious, meaning immoral, just as ebullient and ennui are opposites meaning excited and bored, respectively. (a) is incorrect because lecherous is a synonym for lascivious. (b) is incorrect because lustrous means radiant. (d) is incorrect because quiescent means inactive.

32. **(c)**    (c) is correct because the nickname for Michigan is the Great Lakes State just as Indiana is the Hoosier State. (a) is incorrect because

Montana is the Treasure State. (c) is incorrect because the Bluegrass State is Kentucky. (b) is incorrect because the Garden State is New Jersey.

33. **(b)**   (b) is correct because just as geology is the scientific study of the Earth's origin, history, and structure, ergonomics is the science of human comfort. (a) is incorrect because economics is the study of production, distribution, and consumption of goods. (c) is incorrect because the study of health would be medicine. (d) is incorrect because studies of movement include kinesiology and eurythmics.

34. **(d)**   (d) is correct because aloe is a natural treatment for burns just as peppermint is a natural treatment for nausea. All other answer choices are incorrect because peppermint is not used for an antihistamine or an analgesic, appropriate treatments for these ailments.

35. **(a)**   (a) is correct because the relationship between verisimilitude, meaning the appearance of truth, and truth is analogous to the relationship between apparent and actual. (b) is incorrect because obvious refers to something clearly known. (c) and (d) are incorrect because these terms imply a lack of knowledge rather than a perceived, though flawed knowledge.

36. **(a)**   (a) is correct because philogical is an adjective pertaining to literary study, just as ophidian is an adjective pertaining to snakes. (b) is incorrect because a rodent is an order of mammals. (c) is incorrect because an adjective meaning pertaining to fish would be ichtyian. (d) is incorrect because an adjective meaning pertaining to birds would be either ornithian or avian.

37. **(d)**   This analogy uses set theory. A ∩ B is interpreted as the intersection of sets A and B, which is set C. The element {4} occurs in both sets. A ∪ B is the union of both sets, which should include the elements of both sets. Only set D includes all the elements.

38. **(b)**   (b) is correct because both myrmidon and sycophant refer to someone who obeys an authority without question, just as proletariat refers to a member of the working class. (a) is incorrect because the bourgeoisie refers to the middle class. (c) is incorrect because there is nothing inherent in the term intellectual that would denote specifically a class standing. (d) is incorrect because prolix means wordy and tedious.

39. **(b)**   (b) is correct because a gong is a large version of a cymbal, just as a timpani is a large set of kettle drums. (a) is incorrect because while a

bass drum is a large version of this instrument, it is smaller than a timpani. (c) and (d) are incorrect because a bongo and a tom are smaller drums.

40. **(a)**  (a) is correct because a simulacrum is a vague image, just as an estimate is a vague calculation. (b), (c), and (d) are incorrect because they are all relatively synonymous with estimate.

41. **(b)**  (b) is correct because a glazier is someone who works with glass in the same way that a cryptographer is someone who works with codes. (a) is incorrect because it is irrelevant to this analogy. (c) is incorrect because someone who works with confections is a baker or pastry chef. (d) is incorrect because a zoologist, veterinarian, or farmer might work with animals.

42. **(c)**  (c) is correct because just as $^{13}/_4$ is the improper fractional representation of the mixed number $3^1/_4$, $^{15}/_7$ is the improper fractional representation of $2^1/_7$. (a) is incorrect because this improper fraction is equivalent to the whole number 2. (c) is incorrect because its mixed number representation is $1^3/_7$. (d) is incorrect because this is the fractional equivalent of $\pi$.

43. **(c)**  (c) is correct because Connecticut's nickname is the Constitution State, just as Nebraska's is the Cornhusker State. (a) is incorrect because Pennsylvania's nickname is the Keystone State. (b) is incorrect because Massachusetts nickname is the Bay State. (d) is incorrect because Maryland's nickname is the Old Line or Free State.

44. **(d)**  (d) is correct because narcissism is an extreme form of confidence just as panic is an extreme form of fear. (a) and (b) are incorrect because they convey a lesser degree of fear than panic. (c) is incorrect because welcome would be an opposite of fear.

45. **(c)**  The given table provides the relationship between $f$ and $h$. For the analogy, 2 is substituted for $f$, and $h$ is then 5, thus, $h - 1 = 5 - 1 = 4$. The choice (a) is the direct value of $h$ (5) in the table.

46. **(a)**  Magnesium is correct because magnesium is the central ion in the chlorophyll molecule, while iron is the central ion in the hemoglobin molecule. Calcium (b), strontium (c), and barium (d) all belong to the same group on the Periodic Table, but they cannot be effectively used in the chlorophyll molecule.

47. **(a)**   Radial is correct because protostomes have a spiral cleavage pattern at the third cleavage, while deuterostomes have a radial cleavage pattern at the third cleavage. Bilateral (b) is not a type of cleavage, but indicates a type of symmetry, but spiral is not a type of symmetry and therefore an analogy would not be formed. Round (c) is a shape but spiral is a twisting pattern. Helical (d) is a term similar to spiral and therefore would not complete an analogy.

48. **(b)**   ACU is correct because UGA is one codon of the possible 64 codons which can be found on messenger RNA. Because of the strict base pairing which occurs, ACU is the only transfer RNA anticodon which should fit with this codon. Therefore, the other three choices cannot be used to complete the analogy.

49. **(b)**   (b) is the correct answer because Quebec City is the provincial capital of the Canadian Province of Quebec, just as Victoria is the capital of British Columbia. (a) is incorrect because Edmonton is the capital of Alberta. (c) is incorrect because Winnipeg is the capital of Manitoba. (d) is incorrect because Toronto is the capital of Ontario.

50. **(a)**   (a) is correct because only the woolly monkey is an Old World monkey. All others are New World monkeys.

51. **(b)**   (b) is correct because Freud is noted for originating the psychological concept of a complex, just as Jung is credited with the concept of the archetype. All other answer choices are irrelevant.

52. **(a)**   (a) is correct because to renege is to go back on a promise, the opposite of fulfilling it. To recant is to reverse a decision about a belief, as to declare is to affirm it. (b) is incorrect because to absolve means to forgive. (c) is incorrect because to expose something means to reveal it. (d) is incorrect because to dissent from something is to go against a popular idea.

53. **(a)**   Another way of writing $e^{2x}$ is $2x \log e$, therefore, $\sqrt{8}$ can be written as $8^{1/2} = (1/2) \log 8$.

54. **(b)**   Stellar spectral classification system is correct because Bohr discovered quantum theorem, while Annie Cannon discovered the stellar spectral classification system. While Cannon was indeed an astronomer (a) and she did work at the Harvard College Observatory (c), these two

choices do not demonstrate the discovery analogy. Probability theory (d) was discovered by Pascal and Fermat.

55. **(a)**    (a) is correct because a plaintiff is a more specific type of litigant, or party in a lawsuit, just as igneous refers to a specific type of rock. (b), (c), and (d) are all adjectives that might describe a rock, but are too general to complete the analogy.

56. **(d)**    In this analogy, $1/x$ is the inverse of $x$. Likewise, the inverse of the period is 1/frequency.

57. **(c)**    A set is composed of elements, and thus an equation contains variables and coefficients. Division (a) is an operation done on variables. An axiom (b) is a statement, or a part of a theorem. A Venn diagram (d) is used to shown relationships between sets.

58. **(c)**    (c) is correct because a dam is built to confine water to a particular place just as a snood is designed to hold hair in a specific style. (a) is incorrect because a barn or stable would contain livestock. (b) is incorrect because gas is contained in tanks. (d) is incorrect because beer is contained in kegs.

59. **(a)**    (a) is correct because Nanking is the past capital of China and Beijing is the current capital just as Kyoto was once the capital of Japan; an office now filled by Tokyo. (b), (c), and (d) are all incorrect because although they are cities in China, they are not and have never been the capital.

60. **(c)**    (c) is correct because malefic and baleful both describe something evil and are synonyms just as dulcet and melodious are synonyms for that which is pleasant sounding. (a) is incorrect because angelic is the opposite of baleful. (b) is incorrect because masochistic describes someone who enjoys abuse. (d) is incorrect because dole means something given in small amounts.

61. **(a)**    (a) is correct because to exculpate means to remove blame, and so is synonymous with absolve. This is analogous to the synonomous relationship between exalt and honor. (b) is incorrect because to repay an offense would be to punish rather than absolve. (c) and (d) are incorrect because they are relative antonyms of exculpate.

62. **(b)**    (b) is correct because urbane, meaning cultured, is the opposite of philistine, meaning uncultured. Acrid, foul-smelling, is the antonym of

aromatic, which means pleasant in aroma. (a) is incorrect because uncouth is a synonym for philistine. (c) is incorrect because a laggard is a lazy person. (d) is incorrect because a neophyte is a novice or beginner.

63. **(c)**   Watson and Crick is correct because Baltimore and Temin worked cooperatively to discover the enzyme known as reverse transcriptase. Watson and Crick worked cooperatively to discover DNA. Kornberg (a) discovered the DNA polymerase enzyme, but he alone is credited with the initial discovery. Newton and Leibniz (b) discovered calculus, but independently of each other. William Thomson and Lord Kelvin (d) are the two names of the same individual.

64. **(d)**   (d) is correct because penultimate means next to last or near completion, and terminus is defined as completion or conclusion. Dearth means scarcity or shortage, followed by vacuous, meaning completely empty or void. (a) is incorrect because juxtaposition is the placement of something side-by-side. (b) is incorrect because a hiatus is only a break in activity, not an end. (c) is incorrect because epitome means typification.

65. **(c)**   (c) is the correct answer because the periodic abbreviation for cobalt is Co, just as Kr is for krypton. (a) is incorrect because chlorine's chemical abbreviation is Cl. (b) is incorrect because the periodic abbreviation of copper is Cu. (d) is incorrect because the periodic abbreviation for carbon is C.

66. **(a)**   (a) is correct because incipient and nascent both mean to come into being or existence just as inanimate and extinct are synonyms for lifelessness. (b) is incorrect because descant means to talk at length. (c) is incorrect because umbrage means resentful displeasure. (d) is incorrect because solace means comfort.

67. **(b)**   (b) is correct because obsequious, meaning overly attentive, and insolent, meaning overly rude and abrasive, are antonyms just as gregarious, meaning sociable, and reclusive, meaning solitary, are antonyms. (a) is incorrect because servile is synonymous with obsequious. (c) is incorrect because petulent means impatient. (d) is incorrect because demure means shy.

68. **(d)**   (d) is correct because progeny and offspring are synonyms for descendents just as pallid and sallow are synonyms for paleness. (a) is incorrect because genetics is the study of genes and chromosomes. (b) is incorrect because feminism is a political belief in gender equality. (c) is

incorrect because a genius is defined as an exceptionally smart person with a high IQ.

69. **(a)**   (a) is correct because crepuscular means pertaining to twilight, just as pedagogical means pertaining to education. All other answer choices (b), (c), and (d) are incorrect because they refer to states other than twilight.

70. **(d)**   (d) is correct because in the International Radio Alphabet, E is clarified as echo, just as F is clarified as fox-trot. All other choices are incorrect.

71. **(a)**   (a) is correct because fructose is sugar found in fruit as lactose is sugar found in milk. (b) and (c) are incorrect because sucrose and glucose are derived from sugar cane. (d) is incorrect because maltose is derived from malt.

72. **(b)**   (b) is correct because tantamount, meaning equal to, is synonymous with analogous, just as liquescent, meaning becoming liquid, is synonymous with melting. (a) is incorrect because tautological refers to an overstatement of the truth. (c) is incorrect because similar means close, but not necessarily equal to a given thing or idea. (d) is incorrect because, of course, it is the opposite of analogous.

73. **(a)**   (a) is correct because a prima ballerina is the lead female dancer in a ballet, just as a diva is the lead female voice in an opera. All other answer choices are incorrect because, traditionally, the term diva refers to operatic performers.

74. **(c)**   (c) is correct because elucidate and clarify are synonyms, just as magistrate and judge are synonyms. (a), (b), and (d) are incorrect because while these are court-related professions, they are not synonymous with magistrate.

75. **(a)**   Montagnier is correct because Barbara McClintock discovered the "jumping genes" or transposons, while Luc Montagnier discovered HIV, the causative agent of AIDS. AIDS (c) is an incorrect answer, because Montagnier did not discover the disease itself, but rather its causative agent. HTLV (b) is a virus which causes an AIDS-like illness, and DNA polymerase (d) is an enzyme which was discovered by Kornberg.

76. **(c)**   (c) is correct because a proselyte is a convert from one creed to another just as a novice and a neophyte both refer to a recent convert. (a) and (d) are incorrect because these terms do not imply conversion. (b) is incorrect because a concubine is a consort.

77. **(b)**   This relationship is the perimeter of the square to the area of the square. Therefore, the perimeter (or circumference) of the circle is $2\pi s$, and the area will be $\pi s^2$.

78. **(b)**   (b) is correct because an incubus is a male demon, just as a succubus is a female demon. (a) is incorrect because it is not gender specific. (c) is incorrect because while it means pertaining to a female, it has no demonic connotations. (d) is incorrect because a dowager is an older unmarried woman.

79. **(a)**   Part of the analogy, $5x^2 - 2x + 5$, is the simplified form of

$$2x^2 + 4x + 3x^2 - 6x + 5.$$

Thus simplifying

$$7x - 9x^2 + x^3 - 10x - 5 + 4x^4 + 7$$
$$= 4x^4 + x^3 - 9x^2 + 7x - 10x - 5 + 7$$
$$= 4x^4 + x^3 - 9x^2 - 3x + 2$$

80. **(d)**   (d) is correct because *lapsus linguae* is Latin for slip of the tongue, just as *in absentia* is Latin for in absence. (a), (b), and (c) are insignificant to this analogy.

81. **(b)**   (b) is correct because Yathrib is the old name of the city of Medina, just as Persia is the old name of Iran. All other choices are not significant to this analogy.

82. **(b)**   (b) is correct because both apothegm and maxim are defined as short, pithy sayings, just as laird and lord are synonymous. (a) is incorrect because a touchstone is some criterion against which something is judged. (c) and (d) are incorrect because neither an apothegm nor a maxim is inherently critical or praising.

83. **(d)**   (d) is correct because light in the red wavelength is long, whereas light in the blue wavelength is short. Radio waves are long, whereas the microwave is short. X-ray (a), ultraviolet (b), and gamma radiation (c) are long wavelengths and therefore do not complete the analogy.

84. **(a)**    Molecular biology is correct because the work of Amalie Noether became a guiding principle in the field of physics. The work of Rosalind Franklin led to the discovery of DNA structure which became the guiding principle in the field of molecular biology (a). X-ray crystallography (b) is a technique which Franklin used in her work. Organic chemistry (c) is a branch of science which deals with the chemical molecules which make up living matter. Transposons (d) are a type of genetic material which moves around within the DNA of a cell.

85. **(a)**    (a) is correct because voluble is a synonym for fluent, which means well versed or able to communicate. Lackadaisical and tarry both describe something lacking vigor or enthusiasm. (b) is incorrect because trite means commonplace. (c) is incorrect because veracious means accurate. (d) is incorrect because accede means to comply with.

86. **(c)**    (c) is correct because dromedary is another name for a camel just as pachyderm is another name for an elephant. (a) is incorrect because an ox is bovine. (b) is incorrect because a tiger is feline. (d) is incorrect because a whale is cetaceous.

87. **(b)**    (b) is correct because John Updike won the 1991 Pulitzer Prize for his novel *Rabbit at Rest*, just as Toni Morrison won the coveted award in 1988 for her book *Beloved*. (a), (c), and (d) are all incorrect because, although Smiley, Mailer, and Walker are all Pulitzer winners, they won for the books *A Thousand Acres, The Executioner's Song,* and *The Color Purple*, respectively.

88. **(a)**    Glucose is correct because glucose and galactose are diasteriomers. Ribose and arabinose are also diasteriomers. Fructose (b), sucrose (c), and deoxyribose (d) are not diasteriomers of galactose and therefore they do not fit the analogy.

89. **(d)**    James Watson is correct because *Silent Spring* is a book written by Rachel Carson about the care of the environment, while *The Double Helix* is a book written about the discovery of DNA by James Watson. Francis Crick (a), Rosalind Franklin (b), and Maurice Wilkins (c) all played a role in the discovery of DNA, but they did not write this book.

90. **(c)**    Kwashiorkor is correct because scurvy is caused by a vitamin C deficiency. Kwashiorkor is caused by a protein deficiency. Beriberi (a) is caused by a vitamin deficiency and is not associated with protein. Zwitterion (b) is not associated with vitamins, proteins, or deficiencies and

does not fit into the analogy. Ketosis (d) is associated with faulty fat metabolism and is therefore not protein related.

91. **(a)**    (a) is the correct answer because Rabin succeeded Meir as Prime Minister of Israel in 1974 until 1977. Nixon and Meir both served as leaders of their respective countries from 1969–1974 just as Ford and Rabin served from 1974–1977 for their countries, the U.S. and Israel, respectively. (b) is incorrect because Begin was Prime Minister from 1977–1983. (c) is incorrect because Peres was Prime Minister from 1984–1988. (d) is incorrect because Shamir was leader from 1988–1992. Rabin was re-elected in 1992.

92. **(a)**    (a) is correct because dogmatic and authoritarian are synonyms just as sycophantic and pandering are. (b) is incorrect because unprincipled is the opposite of dogmatic. (c) is incorrect because karmic describes actions seen as bringing upon oneself inevitable results. (d) is incorrect because innocuous describes something that is unlikely to cause damage.

93. **(b)**    (b) is correct because septadekaphilia means an affinity for the number 17, just as arachnaphilia refers to an affinity for spiders. (a) and (c) are incorrect because an affinity for people, especially strangers, would be xenophilia. An affinity for insects would be entophilia (d).

94. **(d)**    (d) is correct because both obdurate and obstinate mean stubborn or unwavering, just as ubiquitous and omnipresent mean everywhere at once. (a) is incorrect because tenacious means holding onto something. (b) is incorrect because tacit describes something that goes unexpressed. (c) is incorrect because succinct means concise.

95. **(c)**    (c) is correct because a recantation is a reversal of a past assertion, while an affirmation is a restatement of a previously held position. This relationship is analogous to that of defy, meaning to challenge (b), and acquiesce, meaning to concede. (a) and (d) are incorrect because these are synonymous with defy.

96. **(c)**    Renin is correct because the pineal gland secretes the chemical melatonin which helps to regulate biorhythms, while the kidney secretes renin, which helps to regulate blood pressure. Glucagon (a) and insulin (b) are secreted by the pancreas and calcitonin (d) is secreted by the thyroid, so none of these can complete the analogy.

97. **(b)**    C is a subset of set A, and thus D is a subset of set B. D is not a subset of any of the other choices, set A (a), set C (c), or set E (d). Set D is a subset of itself, but this choice is not given.

98. **(c)**    (c) is correct because bombastic and turgid are both adjectives describing pompousness just as choleric and cantankerous are synonyms for cranky. (a) is incorrect because behoove means advantageous. (b) is incorrect because affable describes friendliness. (d) is incorrect because pious is an antonym for bombastic.

99. **(d)**    (d) is correct because the birthstone for April is the diamond just as the birthstone for May is the emerald. (a) is incorrect because the ruby is the gem for July. (b) is incorrect because the sapphire is the birthstone for September. (c) is incorrect because the garnet is the birthstone for January.

100. **(a)**    (a) is correct because a pluviometer measures rainfall, just as a chronometer measures time. (b) is incorrect because there is no gauge that measures age. (c) is incorrect because blood pressure is measured with a sphygmomanometer. (d) is incorrect because in a combustion engine, revolutions per minute are measured with a tachometer.

# SECTION THREE

# *Subject Reviews*

# INTRODUCTION TO SUBJECT REVIEWS

Because of the wide scope of material covered by the Miller Analogies Test, the most reliable way to review the subject matter is to absorb as much information as possible before taking the test. Although you could study for years and not cover everything that *may* be encountered on the exam, you can study the subject reviews in this section to become familiar with the most frequently tested information. When deconstructing an MAT analogy, the more terms you are familiar with, the better your chance of discerning the relationship between the remaining elements. You need not memorize all the information included in the subject reviews. This would not be feasible for the average candidate. However, you can familiarize yourself with as much of the information as possible, so that you can confidently take the actual exam.

This section includes reviews in the following subject areas:

1. *Important Literary Figures and Terminology*
2. *Art and Architecture*
3. *Music*
4. *Commonly Tested Words*
5. *Word Parts – Prefixes, Suffixes, and Roots*
6. *Foreign Words and Phrases*
7. *Experts and Collectors*
8. *Animal Group Names*
9. *European History 1450–1648*
10. *European History 1648–1789*
11. *United States History 1789–1841*
12. *United States History 1841–1877*
13. *United States History 1877–1912*
14. *United States History 1912–1941*
15. *United States History since 1941*
16. *Important Scientists and Their Contributions*
17. *Classifications of Living Things*
18. *Summary of Animal Tissues*
19. *Periodic Table of Elements*
20. *Comprehensive Geography Review*
21. *Greek, Roman, and Norse Gods and Goddesses*
22. *Philosophy*
23. *World Religions*
24. *Mathematical Reference Table*
25. *The Metric System*

# 1. IMPORTANT LITERARY FIGURES AND THEIR MAJOR WORKS

**Homer**
(appx. 9th Cen. B.C.)
*Odyssey, Iliad*
—Products of a non-literate culture. 1st works of Western literature

**Sappho**
(appx. 612 B.C.—?)
Verse fragments
—Early Greek poetry

**Aeschylus**
(525 B.C.–456 B.C.)
*Oresteia (Agamemnon, Chophori, and Eumenides)*
—Responsible for the origin and development of Greek Drama; introduced 2nd speaking character and concept of conflict

**Sophocles**
(496 B.C.–406 B.C.)
*Oedipus Tyrannus, Antigone, Electra*
—Added 3rd speaking character and moved Greek drama further from religious commentary to more basic human interaction

**Euripides**
(485 B.C.–405 B.C.)
*The Trojan Women, Helen, The Bacchae*
—Chiefly responsible for introducing the technique of deus ex machina

**Aristophanes**
(450 B.C.–385 B.C.)
*Lysistrata, The Clouds, The Birds*
—Considered the father of Greek comedy

**Plato**
(428 B.C.–399 B.C.)
*Republic, Apology, Symposium*
—Father of Western philosophy

**Aristotle**

(384 B.C.–322 B.C.)

*The Poetics*

—Introduced and popularized the concept of literary criticism

**Virgil**

(70 B.C.–19 B.C.)

*The Aeneid*

—(Publius Vegilius Maro) Popularized the pastoral poem and the concept of civic virtue

**Ovid**

(43 B.C.–18 A.D.)

*Metamorphoses, Love's Remedy*

—(Publius Ovidius Naso) Brought erotic verse to popularity

## THE MIDDLE AGES AND THE RENAISSANCE

**Dante Alighieri**

(1265–1321)

*Divine Comedy (The Inferno, Purgatorio, Paridiso)*

—Considered to have single handedly founded modern European literature; perfected "terza rima" (rhyme in threes)

**Giovanni Boccaccio**

(1313–1375)

*The Decameron*

—Introduced the use of the vernacular in classically focused literature

**Francesco Petrarch**

(1304–1374 )

*The Canzoniere*

—His works provided the basis for love poetry and popularized the theme of humanism

**Geoffrey Chaucer**

(1340–1400)

*The Canterbury Tales, Troilus and Criseyde*

—Chiefly responsible for bringing literature to the middle class

## Nicolò Machiavelli
(1469–1527)
*The Prince, La Madrigola*
—*The Prince* outlined a governmental structure based on the self-inter-
est of the ruler. Such rule is still called Machiavellian

## François Rabelais
(1494–1553)
*Gargantua, Pantagruel*
—Introduced satiric narrative

## Miguel de Cervantes Saavedra
(1547–1616)
*Don Quixote*
—Wrote the 1st modern novel

## Edmund Spenser
(1552–1599)
*The Faerie Queen, Amoretti*
—Popularized the use of allegory

## Francis Bacon
(1561–1626)
Essays, *The New Atlantis*
—Founder of the inductive method of modern science and philosophical writings about science

## Christopher Marlowe
(1564–1593)
*The Tragedy of Doctor Faustus, Edward the Second*
—Author of 1st real historical drama and 1st English tragedy

## William Shakespeare
(1564–1616)
*Hamlet, King Lear, Macbeth, Romeo and Juliet, Twelfth Night, Richard
III, Julius Caesar, Much Ado About Nothing,* Sonnets
—Considered the greatest English poet and dramatist

## Ben Jonson
(1573–1637)
*Every Man in His Humour*
—English playwright

**John Milton**
(1608–1674)
*Paradise Lost, Paradise Regained*
    —Puritan poet noted for allegorical religious epics

## THE NEOCLASSICAL PERIOD

**Molière (Jean-Baptiste Poquelin)**
(1622–1673)
*Don Juan, Tartuff, The Misanthrope*
    —Perfected literary conversation and introduced everyday speech to theatre

**John Dryden**
(1631–1700)
*Alexander's Feast, Heroic Stanzas*
    —Influential in establishing the heroic couplet

**Jean Racine**
(1639–1699)
*Andromaque, Bernice and Phaedre*
    —Renowned for lyric poetry based on Greek and Roman literature

## THE ENLIGHTENMENT

**Jonathan Swift**
(1667–1745)
*Gulliver's Travels, Tale of a Tub*
    —Noted for his direct style, clear, sharp prose and critical wit

**Joseph Addison**
(1672–1719)
*The Tattler, The Spectator, Cato*
    —Outstanding poet, critic, and playwright whose numerous essays marked political free thinking of his time

**Alexander Pope**
(1688–1744)
*The Dunciad, The Rape of the Lock*
    —Classicist and wit who formulated rules for poetry and satirized British social circles

## Voltaire  (François-Marie Arouet)
(1694–1778)
*Candide, Zadig*
—Progressive philosopher and free thinker best known for synthesizing French and English critical theory

## Benjamin Franklin
(1706–1790)
*Poor Richard's Almanac, Observations on the Increase of Mankind,* numerous essays and state papers
—Scientist, educator, abolitionist, philosopher, economist, political theorist, and statesman who defined the colonial New World in his writings; principle figure of the American Enlightenment

## Jean Jacques Rousseau
(1712–1778)
*Social Contract, The New Heloise*
—Libertine whose focused prose inspired the French Revolution

## William Blake
(1757–1827)
*Songs of Innocence, Songs of Experience*
—Visual artist and poet who defied neoclassical convention with subjects of truth and beauty

# THE ROMANTICS AND TRANSCENDENTALISTS

## William Wordsworth
(1770–1850)
*The Prelude, Lyrical Ballads*
—Romantic poet who broke with neoclassical theory in much of his nature poetry

## Jane Austen
(1775–1817)
*Sense and Sensibility, Pride and Prejudice*
—Principally known for novels of manners and middle class English society

## Samuel Taylor Coleridge
(1772–1834)
*Rime of the Ancient Mariner*
—Foremost literary critic of the Romantic period

## George Gordon Lord Byron
(1788–1824)
*Don Juan*
—Major figure in Romantic movement, and inspiration for the Byronic hero

## Percy Bysshe Shelley
(1792–1822)
*Adonais*
—Romantic poet who mastered metaphor and metrical form

## John Keats
(1795–1821)
*Hyperion, On a Grecian Urn*
—Most versatile of the Romantics

## Mary Shelley
(1797–1851)
*Frankenstein, The Last Man*
—Romantic novelist whose liberal social and political views underscore her work

## Nathaniel Hawthorne
(1804–1864)
*The Scarlet Letter, House of the Seven Gables*
—American Transcendentalist

## Elizabeth Barrett Browning
(1806–1861)
*Sonnets from the Portuguese, Aurora Leigh*
—English poet

## Edgar Allen Poe
(1809–1849)
*Fall of the House of Usher, Tell Tale Heart, The Raven*
—American Transcendentalist who dealt with macabre issues of insanity and horror

## Harriet Beecher Stowe
(1811–1896)
*Uncle Tom's Cabin*
—American novelist, wrote the most important novel of the abolitionist movement

**Robert Browning**
(1812–1889)
*Bells and Pomegranates*
   —English poet

**Charles Dickens**
(1812–1870)
*Great Expectations, Oliver Twist*
   —English novelist

**Charlotte Brontë**
(1816–1855)
*Jane Eyre*
   —Victorian novelist

**Emily Brontë**
(1816–1848)
*Wuthering Heights*
   —Victorian novelist

**Henry David Thoreau**
(1818–1848)
*Walden*
   —American transcendentalist and social theorist

**George Eliot (Mary Ann Evans)**
(1819–1880)
*Mill on the Floss*
   —English author

**Herman Melville**
(1819–1891)
*Moby-Dick, Billy Budd*
   —American transcendentalist

**Walt Whitman**
(1819–1892)
*Leaves of Grass*
   —American poet

**Fyodor Dostoyevsky**
(1821–1881)
*Crime and Punishment, Notes From the Underground*
  —Russian novelist

**Gustave Flaubert**
(1821–1880)
*Madame Bovary*
  —French novelist

**Charles Baudelaire**
(1821–1867)
*Flowers of Evil (Les Fleurs du Mal)*
  —French Symbolist poet

**Henrik Ibsen**
(1828–1906)
*A Doll's House*
  —Norwegian Playwright and forerunner of the Expressionist movement

**Leo Nikolayevich Tolstoy**
(1828–1910)
*War and Peace, Anna Karenina*
  —Major Russian novelist

**Emily Dickinson**
(1830–1886)
*Because I Could Not Stop for Death*
  —American poet

**Christina Rossetti**
(1830–1894)
*Goblin Market*
  —English poet

**Mark Twain (Samuel Clemens)**
(1835–1910)
*Huckleberry Finn, Tom Sawyer*
  —American novelist, essayist, and satirist

**Oscar Wilde**

(1854–1900)

*The Importance of Being Earnest, Picture of Dorian Gray*
  —English novelist, dramatist, and social critic

**George Bernard Shaw**

(1856–1950)

*Arms and the Man, Saint Joan*
  —Irish born British author and playwright

**Joseph Conrad**

(1857–1924)

*Heart of Darkness, Lord Jim*
  —Ukranian born of Polish parents, major English post-colonialist novelist

**William Butler Yeats**

(1865–1939)

*The Wind Among the Reeds, The Winding Stair*
  —Irish poet and dramatist

**Robert Frost**

(1874–1963)

*Birches, The Road Not Taken*
  —Major American poet

**Gertrude Stein**

(1874–1946)

*3 Lives*
  —American modernist author

**Upton Sinclair**

(1878–1968)

*The Jungle*
  —American novelist and social critic, characterized as a "muckraker"

**James Joyce**

(1882–1941)

*Portrait of an Artist as a Young Man, Ulysses*
  —Premier Modernist novelist of Ireland, pioneered stream of conscious and non-linear narratives

**Virginia Woolf**
(1882–1941)
*A Room of One's Own, To the Lighthouse*
  —Modernist novelist and early feminist

**Franz Kafka**
(1883–1924)
*The Metamorphosis, The Castle*
  —Major Existentialist novelist

**Ezra Pound**
(1885–1972)
*The Cantos*
  —American poet

**D.H. Lawrence**
(1885–1930)
*Lady Chatterly's Lover, The Rainbow*
  —English novelist

**Sinclair Lewis**
(1885–1951)
*Babbitt, Elmer Gantry*
  —American novelist and social critic

**Eugene O'Neill**
(1888–1953)
*Anna Christie, The Hairy Ape*
  —Major American dramatist

**T.S. Eliot**
(1888–1965)
*The Waste Land*
  —Christian poet and theorist

**Henry Miller**
(1891–1980)
*The Tropic of Cancer, The Tropic of Capricorn*
  —Controversial American novelist

**e.e. cummings**
(1894–1962)
*Tulips and Chimneys*
—Known for non-traditional forms of poetry

**William Faulkner**
(1897–1962)
*The Sound and the Fury, Absalom! Absalom!*
—Major author of the American South

**Vladimir Nabokov**
(1899–1977)
*Lolita, Invitation to a Beheading*
—Russian novelist

**Ernest Hemingway**
(1899–1961)
*The Old Man and the Sea, A Farewell to Arms*
—Known for lean prose and ardently masculine themes and characters

**Zora Neale Hurston**
(1901–1960)
*Their Eyes Were Watching God, Tell My Horse*
—American novelist and folklorist

**John Steinbeck**
(1902–1968)
*Grapes of Wrath, Cannery Row*
—American novelist whose major theme was the life of the American worker

**Langston Hughes**
(1902–1967)
*Collected Works*
—Harlem Renaissance poet

**Samuel Beckett**
(1906–1989)
*Waiting for Godot, Happy Days*
—Irish-born French playwright and novelist; themes include existentialism and absurdity

**Elizabeth Bishop**
(1911–1979)
*Collected Works*
   —American poet

**Tennessee Williams**
(1911–1983)
*A Streetcar Named Desire, The Glass Menagerie*
   —American playwright

**Arthur Miller**
(1915–   )
*Death of a Salesman, The Crucible*
   —American Playwright

**Aleksander Isayevitch Solzhenitsyn**
(1918–   )
*The Gulag Archipelago*
   —Major Russian novelist and social critic

**Jack Kerouac**
(1922–1969)
*On the Road, Dharma Bums*
   —American Beat poet and novelist

**Nadine Gordimer**
(1923–   )
*A Sport of Nature*
   —South African novelist

**James Baldwin**
(1924–1987)
*The Fire Next Time*
   —American poet and novelist

**Allen Ginsberg**
(1926–1997)
*Howl*
   —American Beat poet

**Adrienne Rich**
(1929–   )
*Aunt Jennifer's Tigers*
   —American poet

**Toni Morrison**
(1931–   )
*The Bluest Eye, Song of Solomon, Beloved*
   —American novelist

**V.S. Naipaul**
(1932–   )
*Enigma of Arrival, House for Mr. Biswas*
   —Post-Colonialist novelist, born in Trinidad of Indian parents, raised in
   England

**Sylvia Plath**
(1932–1963)
*Ariel, The Bell Jar*
   —American poet and novelist

**Thomas Pynchon**
(1937–   )
*Vineland, Gravity's Rainbow, The Crying of Lot 49*
   —Reclusive American novelist

**Alice Walker**
(1944–   )
*The Color Purple, Possessing the Secrets of Joy*
   —American novelist

**Salman Rushdie**
(1947–   )
*The Satanic Verses, Shame*
   —Known for death sentence (*fatwa*) placed upon him by Ayatollah
   Khomeni because Khomeni believed Rushdie's subject matter to be
   blasphemous

# LITERARY TERMS

**allegory**—Poetry or prose in which abstract ideas are represented by individual characters, events, or objects.

**alliteration**—Rapid repetition of consonants in a given line of poetry or prose.

**allusion**—Reference to one literary work in another.

**anachronism**—A chronological error in which a relationship between events or objects is historically impossible.

**anapest**—A metrical foot where two unstressed syllables are followed by a stressed syllable.

**antagonist**—The character in a literary work that goes against the actions of the hero.

**antihero**—The protagonist of a literary work who has none of the characteristics associated with the hero.

**apostrophe**—Direct address to someone or something not present.

**assonance**—Rapid repetition of vowels in a given line of poetry or prose.

**ballad**—A poem, often intended to be sung, that tells a story.

**bathos**—Deliberate anticlimax used to make a definitive point.

**bildungsroman**—A coming-of-age story, usually autobiographical.

**blank verse**—Unrhymed poetry usually written in iambic pentameter.

**caesura**—A deliberate pause in a line of poetry.

**canto**—Analogous to a chapter in a novel, it is a division in a poem.

**climax**—The peak of action in a literary work.

**conceits**—Elaborate comparisons between unlike objects.

**consonance**—Repetition of consonant sounds with unlike vowels—similar to alliteration.

**couplet**—A pair of rhyming lines of poetry in the same meter.

**dactyl**—A metrical foot composed of one stressed syllable followed by two unstressed syllables.

**denouement**—The action following the climax in a literary work.

**diction**—Word choice or syntax.

**doggerel**—Crudely written poetry, in which words are often mangled to fit a rhyme scheme.

**elegy**—A poem lamenting the passage of something.

**enjambment**—In poetry, the continuation of a phrase or sentence onto the following line.

**epistolary**—Refers to a novel or story told in the form of letters.

**fable**—A story used to illustrate a moral lesson.

**foot**—A group of syllables that make up a metered unit of a verse.

**haiku**—A Japanese poetical form, having three lines and 17 syllables, five in the first line, seven in the second, and five in the third.

**hubris**—In tragic drama, the excessive pride that leads to the fall of a hero.

**hyperbole**—Exaggeration for effect.

**iamb**—A foot containing two syllables, a short then a long (in quantitative meter).

**irony**—A deliberate discrepancy between literal meaning and intended meaning.

**malapropism**—Often used for humorous effect, it is the substitution of a word for one that sounds similar but has radically different meaning.

**metaphor**—A form of comparison in which something is said to be something else, often an unlikely pairing.

**meter**—The combination of stressed and unstressed syllables that creates the rhythm of a poem.

**metonymy**—A phrase or statement that takes on larger meaning.

**motif**—The recurrence of a word or theme in a novel or poem.

**onomatopoeia**—A word whose sound suggests its meaning; for example, "crash."

**oxymoron**—Two contradictory words used together to create deeper meaning; for example, sweet sorrow.

**paradox**—A seemingly contradictory phrase, which proves to be true upon comparison.

**pathos**—An appeal that evokes pity or sympathy.

**scansion**—The annotation of the meter of a poem.

**simile**—Means of comparison using either "like" or "as."

**sonnet**—A verse form consisting of fourteen lines arranged in an octet (eight lines) and a sextet (six lines), usually ending in a couplet; in common English form, arranged in three quatrains followed by a couplet.

**spondee**—A metrical foot comprised of two stressed syllables.

**synecdoche**—The use of part of a thing to represent the whole; for example, "wheels" for a car.

**tone**—Attitude of the speaker, setting the mood for a given passage.

**trochee**—A metrical foot composed of a stressed syllable followed by an unstressed syllable.

**villanelle**—A verse form consisting of five tercets and a quatrain, the first and third lines of the tercet recur alternately as the last lines of the other tercets and together as the last lines of the quatrain.

# 2. ART AND ARCHITECTURE

## ARTISTS AND ARCHITECTS

**Henry Bacon** (1866–1924)—American architect: Lincoln Memorial

**Gustave Eiffel** (1832–1923)—French engineer: Eiffel Tower

**Donato di Niccolo Bardi** (1386?–1466)—commonly known as Donatello, leading sculptor in Italy, one of the founders of the new Renaissance style: bronze sculpture *David* (first nude David), *Mary Magdalen* in gilded wood

**Sandro Botticelli** (1445–1510)—Botticelli, Italian painter, known for concentration on line, depth of feeling, delicacy of style: *Birth of Venus* (Venus on a Half-Shell), tempera on canvas

**Filippo Brunelleschi** (1377–1446)—founder of Renaissance style in architecture: *Pazzi Chapel* in Santa Croce, Florence

**Jan van Eyck** (1385–1441)—Early Renaissance Flemish painter known for the naturalism, minute detail, and representation of atmospheric space in his works: *Ghent Altarpiece,* 20 panels, oil

**Leonardo da Vinci** (1452–1519)—High Renaissance Italian painter, sculptor, architectural engineer, inventor: *Last Supper,* mural, oil and tempera on plaster, *Mona Lisa,* oil on panel

**Raffaello Sanzio** (1483–1520)—commonly known as Raphael, High Renaissance Italian painter, his ideals of figural and compositional harmony became to be recognized as the High Renaissance principles: fresco *School of Athens,* panel painting *Madonna of the Meadows*

**Michelangelo Buonarroti** (1475–1564)—commonly known as Michelangelo, High Renaissance Italian painter, sculptor: marble sculpture *David,* ceiling fresco for the Sistine Chapel

**Francesco Mazzola** (1503–40)—commonly known as Parmigianino, Mannerist Italian painter, known for the distortion in his renderings: *Madonna with the Long Neck,* panel painting

**Tiziano Vecellio** (1490–1576)—commonly known as Titian, High Renaissance painter in Venice, established color as the major determinant in his paintings: *Venus of Urbino, Man with the Glove, Sacred and Profane Love,* all oil on canvas

**Albrecht Dürer** (1471–1528)—founder of German High Renaissance, known for his graphic art—woodcuts, copper engravings: *Four Horsemen of the Apocalypse,* woodcut, *Adam and Eve,* engraving, *Saint Jerome,* engraving

**Domenikos Thetokopoulos** (1541–1614)—commonly known as El Greco, born in Crete, recreated in contemporary Renaissance style the Byzantine pictorial tradition: *Resurrection, The Burial of Count Orgaz, Toledo,* all oil on canvas

**Michelangelo Merisi** (1573–1610)—known as Caravaggio, Baroque Italian painter, known for his naturalism, hard pictorial style, but mostly for his intense light and dark contrasts: *Conversion of St. Paul,* oil on canvas

**Peter Paul Rubens** (1577–1640)—Baroque Flemish Painter, in many of his paintings, the figures form a spiral up into the picture: center panel of a triptych *Raising of the Cross*

**Diego Rodriguez de Silva y Velázquez** (1599–1660)—known as Velázquez, Spanish Baroque painter, known for his optical method of painting, nature as revealed to human vision through light: *Las Merinas,* oil on canvas

**Rembrandt van Rijn** (1606–69)—Baroque Dutch painter, known for his spirituality in art, radiant light against and through warm, glowing, vibrant shadow: *Supper at Emmaus, Return of the Prodigal Son,* both oil on canvas

**Thomas Jefferson** (1743–1826)—American architect: *Monticello* in the style of a neoclassic temple

**Jacques Louis David** (1748–1825)—known as David, Rococo painter, revival of classicism: *Oath of the Horatii, Death of Marat,* oil on canvas

**Fransisco José de Goya y Lucientes** (1746–1828)—known as Goya, Romantic Spanish painter: *The Third of May, 1808, at Madrid: The Shootings on Principe Pio Mountain,* oil on canvas

**Edouard Manet** (1832–1883)—French Impressionist painter, forefather of Impressionism: *Luncheon on the Grass, A Bar at the Folies-Bergere,* oil on canvas

**Claude Monet** (1840–1926)—French impressionist painter painted outdoors, began with reality and painted into it the objective perception of color: *Nympheas* (Water Lilies), *Rouen Cathedral in Full Sunlight,* oil on canvas

**Pierre Auguste Renoir** (1842–1919)—French Impressionist painter, known for the warmth, physical delight, enjoyment of the moment of light and air in his paintings: *Le Moulin de la Galette,* oil on canvas

**Edgar Degas** (1834–1917)—French Impressionist painter, did not share the Impressionist interest in landscape, fascinated by the dance, known for his paintings of dance: *The Rehearsal,* oil on canvas

**Auguste Rodin** (1840–1917)—Impressionist sculptor: exclusively concerned with the human figure, particularly in moments of great physical and emotional stress: *The Age of Bronze, The Kiss* (in marble)

**Henry Moore** (1898–1986)—English sculptor, adaptation of empty spaces and Cubist Structure: *Interior-Exterior Reclining Figure,* in bronze

**Frank Lloyd Wright** (1867–1959)—American architect: *Solomon R. Guggenheim Museum*

**Mary Cassatt** (1845–1926)—American Impressionist painter: soft surface, snapshot vision in paintings, subjects almost exclusively female: *The Bath,* oil on canvas

**Paul Cézanne** (1839–1906)—French Post-Impressionist painter, used color to construct form, painted abstractly, "Father of Modern Art":

*Still Life with Apples and Oranges, Woman with the Coffeepot,* oil on canvas

**Georges Pierre Seurat** (1859–1891)—French Post-Impressionist painter, began with divisionism, in which each touch of the brush represents a separate color so the shades mix only in the eye, not on the palette, later developed into pointilism: *Sunday Afternoon on the Island of La Grande Jatte,* oil on canvas

**Vincent van Gogh** (1853–1890)—Dutch Post-Impressionist painter, used thick pigment, blazing color, strong strokes: *Starry Night, The Night Cafe,* oil on canvas

**Paul Gauguin** (1848–1903)—no formal art training, departed from Western artistic tradition, return to archaic, primitive styles: *The Day of the God, Vision After the Sermon,* oil on canvas

**Edvard Munch** (1863–1944)—Norwegian painter, forerunner of Expressionism, themes involving sex and death, psychological subjects: *The Scream,* oil on canvas

**Henri Matisse** (1869–1954)—French Expressionist, experimented with simplified figures, masses stated with bold areas of pigment, brilliant color: *The Green Stripe (Madame Matisse),* oil and tempera on canvas

**Pablo Ruiz y Picasso** (1881–1973)—father of Cubism: *Les Demoiselles d'Avignon, Seated Woman,* oil on canvas

**Constantin Brancusi** (1876–1957)—Rumanian pioneer of abstract sculpture: *Bird in Space,* in marble

**Piet Mondrian** (1872–1944)—Dutch painter, master of the De Stijl movement, reduced all formal elements to flat surfaces bounded by straight lines intersected at right angles, colors in black, white, gray, and primary colors: *Composition,* oil on canvas

**Salvador Dali** (1904–1989)—sexual symbolism, master of draftsmanship and color: *The Persistence of Memory* (the melting clock picture), oil on canvas

**Georgia O'Keeffe** (1887–1986)—American Modern painter, free flow of rhythmic shapes, known for her studies of flowers: *Blue and Green Music,* oil on canvas

**Jackson Pollock** (1912–1956)—American Abstract Expressionist painter, free motion of arm, drip painting, used gobs of color, "action painting": *Blue Poles,* oil, Duco, and aluminum paint on canvas

**Robert Rauschenberg** (1925–   )—American Pop artist, used objects in his works: *Trapeze,* oil on canvas with silkscreen

**Roy Lichtenstein** (1923–1997)—American Pop artist, "comic strip art": *Wham,* two panels, magna on canvas

**Andy Warhol** (1930–1987)—American Pop artist, specialized in the boring, impersonal, mechanized sameness: *Marilyn Monroe,* oil, acrylic, and silkscreen enamel on canvas

**Benjamin Latrobe** (1764–1820)—English American architect and engineer: Waterworks of Philadelphia, assisted in the design and construction of the Capitol at Washington

**Louis Le Vau** (1612–1670)—creator of the basic body of Versailles in France, later expanded and altered by others

**Robert Mills** (1781–1855)—American architect: *Washington Monument, U.S. Treasury*

**James Renwick, Jr.** (1818–1895)—American architect and engineer: St. Patrick's Cathedral in New York, Smithsonian Institution in Washington

**Louis Comfort Tiffany** (1848–1933)—American artisan, known for his Tiffany stained glass creations

**Gustav Klimt** (1862–1918)—greatest of Art Nouveau painters: *The Kiss*

**George Segal** (1924–   )—American Pop artist, began as painter, abandoned color almost entirely in his sculptural treatment of the human figure: *The Bus Riders,* plaster, metal, and vinyl

**Christo Javachef** (1935–   )—Bulgarian Earth artist, packages inert objects and nature in plastic and fabric: *Surrounded Islands, Biscayne Bay, Greater Miami, Florida,* woven synthetic fabric, 6 million square feet

## MOVEMENTS

**Paleolithic art** (Old Stone Age) (30,000–10,000 B.C.)—cave art, large-scale paintings in caves

**Gothic style** (about 1590 to 1750)—began in northern France before the middle of the 12th century and in the rest of western Europe slightly later, most distinctive are the Gothic cathedrals: *Notre-Dame* in Paris

**Early Renaissance art** (about 1400–1480)—in Italy: artists began to approximate reality in form, space, color

**High Renaissance** (about 1500–1580)—Central Italy: spatial depth and harmony, natural proportions, graceful poses

**Mannerism**—nervous, spaceless, crowded with twisting, turbulent figures, unnaturally lengthened

**Neo-classicism** (1775–1825)—held Baroque in abhorrence, return to discipline in form drawing and composition

**Rococo**—softness, vagueness, voluptuousness

**Romanticism** (about 1780–1825)—interest in the sublime, picturesque

**Realism** (about 1825–1870)—lowering of tonality of color, as well as action and emotion, insistence on priority of vision over abstraction, emotion

**Impressionism** (about 1860–1875)—considered photography false to the psychological perception of reality in color and motion, fascination with transformations wrought by light on natural objects, surfaces, atmospheric spaces

**Post-Impressionism** (about 1880–1890)—retained the bright palette of Impressionism, but acquired new shape and function, unique to the personal style of each painter

**Expressionism** (about 1900s)—daring treatment of unexpected and shocking themes, sharp contrast of colors and shapes, bold brushwork, arbitrary color, harshly unreal drawing

**Cubism** (about 1900s)—imposed formal structure of largely monochromatic planes upon an object; its chief exponents were Pablo Picasso and Georges Braque, who saw it as a stark expression of the impact of modernity

**Futurism** (about 1900s)—motion brought to Cubism: Umberto Boccioni (1882-1916)—*Orpheus*

**Surrealism** (began about 1930)—exploring illogic on Freudian principles to uncover and utilize for creative purposes the "actual" processes of thought

**Abstract Expressionism** (began about mid-1900s)—opposed to strict formalism that characterizes much of abstract art: Arshile Gorky (1904–48)—American artist, one of the founders

**Pop Art** (began about 1960s)—characterized by wit, anti-aestheticism, positive nihilism Op Art (Optical Art) (began about 1960s)—denies representation altogether, strong optical illusions of depth, mass, motion: Richard Anuszkiewicz, American artist: *Trinity*

**Minimal Art** (began about 1960s)—simple objects, shorn of all suggestion of meaning or of human receptiveness (e.g., bookshelves), Donald Judd, art based on pure proportion: *Untitled,* seven identical quadrangular cubic masses of galvanized iron

**Process Art** (began about 1960s)—any material was art, as long as it was shapeless and impermanent

**Earth Art** (began about 1960s)—creating art in nature: Robert Smithson (1938–1973)—*Spiral Jetty in Utah*

**Photo-Realism** (began about 1980s)—picture was painted, unaltered, with an airbrush from a photographic slide projected on the canvas, as long as the subject was as banal as possible: Richard Estes (1936– )—*Hotel Empirer* oil on canvas

**Performance Art**—intended to shock, combines theatricism with art, first performance artist: Allan Kaprow: *18 Happenings in 6 Parts*

# TERMS

**aqueduct**—artificial channel for conducting water, in Roman times, usually built overground and supported on arches

**atrium**—open entrance or central hall of an ancient Roman house

**basilica**—barn-like building form, central long space flanked by side aisles

**bungalow**—Indian (Bengali) word for single-storied house with veranda

**cameo**—a carving in relief upon a gem, stone, or shell

**cenotaph**—abstract monument to a person buried elsewhere: *Washington Monument*

**chiaroscuro**—painting term, the opposition of light and dark

**cinquefoil**—Gothic tracery pattern, reminiscent of a five-leaf clover

**cromlech**—circle of standing unhewn stones: *Stonehenge*

**crosshatching**—crossing sets of parallel lines to produce the effect of shading

**engraving**—print made by incising a design onto a copper plate, inking the plate, wiping off the excess ink, and pressing the plate onto a moistened piece of paper

**facade**—front or principle face of a building

**foreshortening**—in drawing, painting, the object seems to recede in space and conveys the illusion of three dimensions

**fresco**—painting on wet plaster with watercolors, so plaster absorbs colors and the painting becomes part of the wall

**fresco secco**—painting on dry plaster, less durable as the paint tends to flake off over time

**gargoyle**—roofspout in the shape of a grotesque human or animal figure, e.g., Gothic gargoyles of the Notre Dame

**genre painting**—scenes from everyday life for their own sake, usually with no religious or symbolic significance

**hatching**—in drawing or engraving, use of parallel lines to produce the effect of shading

**hieroglyphs**—characters in the picture-writing system of ancient Egyptians

**hypostyle**—in the style of ancient Egyptian temple architecture, a hall of many columns, e.g., *Parthenon* in Athens

**illumination**—decorating manuscripts, scrolls, with illustrations or designs in gold, silver, or bright colors

**lithograph**—print made by drawing with a crayon on a porous stone or metal plate, applying greasy printing ink which adheres only to the lines of the drawing, and pressing the plate on a moistened piece of paper

**megalithic architecture**—monuments made partially or wholly of giant stones

**mosaic**—surface decoration in which bits of colored stone or glass are laid in cement in a design or decorative pattern

**obelisk**—a tapering four-sided shaft of stone, usually monolithic, with a pyramidal apex, used as a freestanding monument, as in ancient Egypt, or as an architectural decoration

**perspective**—representation of three-dimensional objects on a flat surface so as to produce the same impression of distance and relative size as that received by the human

**relief**—sculpture that is not freestanding but projects from the background of which it is a part, can be high relief and low relief depending on the amount of projection, incised relief is when the background is not cut out, as in some Egyptian architecture

**stippling**—in painting, drawing, and engraving, a method of representing light and shade by the use of dots

**tempera**—widely used in Italian panel painting before the sixteenth century, ground colors mixed with yolk of egg, instead of oil

**triptych**—altarpiece or devotional picture consisting of three panels joined together, frequently hinged, so that the center panel is covered when the side panels are closed

**woodcut**—print made by cutting a design in relief on a block of wood and printing only the raised surfaces

**ziggurat**—tiered, truncated pyramid of mud brick

## SCHOOLS

**Bauhaus**—architectural design school opened in Germany in 1919, tried to blend art and architecture with industrial techniques

**École des Beaux-Arts**—in Paris, national French architectural school, architecture of l9th century France

**Chicago School**—around the middle of the nineteenth century, architects who became known as the Chicago School, their architecture more functional than artistic, characteristic new architectural forms were the factory, warehouse, office building, department store, apartment house

## REFERENCES

Art: A History of Painting, Sculpture, Architecture, Third Edition. 1989. Frederick Hartt. Harry N Abrams, Inc, New York.

The Architecture Book. 1976. Norval White. Alfred A Knopf, New York.

The History of Art. 1985. Ed. Bernard S Myers, Trewein Copplestone. Barnes & Noble Books, New York.

# 3. MUSIC

**Medieval Period** (500–1420)—Both secular (nonreligious) and sacred music were composed, although mostly sacred survived as monks transcribed the music used for worship in Christian mass.

**Gregorian chant**—Plainchant music. Monophonic, single melodic lines with no accompaniment. Vocal music of the church.

**Polyphony**—Two or more lines of melody; distinct thoughts performed together.

**Renaissance** (1420–1600)—A "rebirth" and revival of humanistic thoughts.

**Motet**—Vocal polyphony for use in church.

**Mass**—Polyphonic service.

**Giovanni Palestrina** (1525–1594)—Italian. Composed motets and masses.

**Madrigal**—Musical form which utilizes composed poetry and new music for each verse.

**Giovanni Gabrielli** (1557–1612)—Italian. Organist, teacher, and composer. Art song: poem set to music. Works: *Sonata Pian'e Forte*

**Baroque** (1600–1750)—Elaborate, intense and full of spirit. Opera was explored.

**Recitative**—Words and speech set to music. Pitches reflect the inflections of the voice.

**Claudio Monteverdi** (1567–1643)—Italian. Choirmaster at St. Mark's. Polyphonic church music, madrigals, and opera. Works: *Orfeo*

**Heinrich Schutz** (1585–1672)—German. Organist who composed opera and madrigals. Works: *Orpheus und Euridice*

**Jean-Baptiste Lully** (1632–1687)—Italian. Worked in France. Comedy ballets, lyrical tragedies, and overtures.

**Henry Purcell** (1659–1695)—English. Composed opera and church music. Known as a melodist. Works: *Dido and Aeneas*

**Arcangelo Corelli** (1653–1713)—Italian. Instrumental music. Concerto grosso-string orchestra and a group of solo instruments.

**Antonio Vivaldi** (1678–1741)—Italian. Ordained priest. Known for his concerto grosso. Works: *Four Seasons*

**Johann Sebastian Bach** (1685–1750)—German. Church musician, composer, and teacher. Works: *Mass in B minor; Little Fugue in G minor*

**Fugue**—Polyphonic. Two or more voices, with independent melodies, sounded together. Employed by Bach.

**Passions**—Choral. Oratorios based on the Crucifixion of Christ.

**George Frideric Handel** (1685–1759)—German. Oratorio, religious opera, voice, and orchestra. Works: *Messiah*

**Classical** (1750–1820)—Centered in Vienna. Stressed balance, form, and restraint in music.

**Orchestral symphony**—A sonata, usually with four movements.

**Franz Joseph Haydn** (1732–1809)—Austrian. Employed by the Esterhazy family. Composer and performer. Utilized symphonic form. Works: *Symphony No.94*

**Wolfgang Amadeus Mozart** (1756–1791)—Austrian. Worked in Vienna. Child prodigy with a natural gift. Composed with a lyrical touch. His work was rhythmic and inventive, and utilized melodic variety. Works: *Don Giovanni, The Marriage of Figaro*

**Ludwig van Beethoven** (1770–1827)—German. Innovative in his use of emotion and expressive human feelings; a bridge to the Romantic Period. Works: *Moonlight Sonata; Eroica; Fifth Symphony*

**Giuseppe Verdi** (1813–1901)—Italian. Known for opera. Nationalist. Used human emotion and drama. Works: *Aida; Otello*

**Gioachino Rossini** (1792–1868)—Italian. Known for opera.

**Romantic** (1820–1900)—Employed emotional feelings in music.

**Franz Schubert** (1797–1828)—Austrian. Melodic solo voice usually with piano. Works: *Der Doppelganger; Morning Greeting*

**Frédéric Chopin** (1810–1849)—Polish. Composed miniatures for piano. Considered the "poet of the piano."

**Felix Mendelssohn** (1809–1847)—German. Conductor and composer. Followed the classical ideas but his music conveyed the bold spirit of the Romantics.

**Robert Schumann** (1810–1856)—German. Intellectual, critic, and composer of art songs and piano music. Works: *Carnaval*

**Song cycles**—Works of music related by content or musical thoughts. Used by Schumann.

**Johannes Brahms** (1833–1897)—German. Stubborn use of classical intentions with Romantic nuances. Works: *Academic Festival Overture*

**Nationalism**—A patriotic influence, spirit, and flavor within the musical composition.

**Program music**—Descriptive music which represents ideas, thoughts, and feelings.

**Hector Berlioz** (1803–1869)—French. Compositions incorporated imagery and musical effects. Program music. Works: *Symphony Fantastique*

**Franz Liszt** (1811–1886)—Hungarian. Nationalistic style, symphonic poems, and tone poems. Works: *Hungarian Rhapsodies; Les Preludes*

**Richard Wagner** (1813–1883)—German. Poet, and musician. Musical drama. Innovated German opera. Works: *Lohengrin; Tristan and Isolde*

**Peter Ilyich Tchaikovsky** (1840–1893)—Russian. Romantic who combined Russian folk songs with a German style. Works: *Romeo and Juliet; The Nutcracker*

**Modest Moussorgsky** (1839–1881)—Russian. Nationalist who incorporated folk songs in compositions. Works: *A Night on Bald Mountain; Pictures at an Exhibition*

**Richard Strauss** (1864–1949)—German. His compositions often followed the classical form with Romantic emotions. Realistic symphonic poems and opera. Works: *Salome; Also Sprach Zarathustra*

**Tone poem**—Music which is dramatic and incorporates elements of a poetic nature

**Gustav Mahler** (1860–1911)—Austrian. Composer and conductor. Composed powerful and emotional symphonies which were influenced by folklore. Works: *The Song of the Earth; Symphony No. 2 Resurrection*

**Sergei Diaghilev** (1872–1929)—Russian. Created the Russian ballet, commissioned contemporary composers and choreographed ideas which were the beginnings of modern dance.

**Claude Debussy** (1862–1918)—French. Works involved musical impressionism which suggested an idea or feeling. Works: *Prelude to the Afternoon of a Faun*

**Absolute music**—Instrumental music with no text, or story. Abstract music which stands for itself.

**Igor Stravinsky** (1882–1971)—Russian. Used Primitivism which is uncivilized and exotic, with uninhibited rhythms and much dissonance. Works: *El Sacre du Printemps; Petrushka; The Firebird*

**Arnold Schönberg** (1874–1951)—Austrian. Used Expressionism which is emotional and often sounds disturbing. He was progressive and incorporated sprechstimme (speech voice). Works: *Pierrot Bunaire*

**Alban Berg** (1885–1935)—Austrian. Expressionist. Works: *Wozzeck*

**Maurice Ravel** (1857–1937)—French. Nationalist known for his orchestrational skills. Works: *Bolero; Daphnis and Cloe*

**Nicolai Rimsky-Korsakov** (1844–1908)—Russian. Orchestrator, also known for opera. Works: *Sheherazade; Russian Easter Overture*

**Charles Ives** (1874–1954)—American. An experimentalist who explored the possibilities of sound. His works combined melodies, hymns, and patriotic tunes. Works: *Decoration Day; The Circus Band*

**John Philip Sousa** (1854–1932)—American. Composer and band leader who popularized the march, patriotic songs, and band music. Works: *Stars and Stripes Forever*

**Jean Sibelius** (1865–1957)—Finnish. Nationalist who composed folk music, tone poems, and incidental music.

**Sergei Prokofiev** (1891–1953)—Russian. Conservative whose compositions were influenced by the Soviet power structure. Works: *Peter and the Wolf*

**Dmitri Shostakovich** (1906–1974)—Russian. His compositions were politically influenced.

**George Gershwin** (1898–1937)—American. Nationalist who composed symphonic and jazz music as well as musicals. The "American Sound." Works: *Rhapsody in Blue; Porgy and Bess*

**Béla Bartók** (1881–1945)—Hungarian. Neo-classical, nationalistic. Researched and revived Hungarian folk music. He made music for the people. Works: *Mikrokosmos; Music for Strings, Percussion and Celesta*

**Aaron Copland** (1900–1990)—American. Neo-classical and nationalistic. Used jazz, rhythmic variety and folk songs. Works: *Rodeo; Billy the Kid; Appalachian Spring*

**Cole Porter** (1891–1964)—American. Composed popular music, musical comedies and theater. Works: *Anything Goes*

**Scott Joplin** (1868–1917)—American. Considered the "King of Ragtime." Works: *Maple Leaf Rag*

**Paul Hindemith** (1895–1963)—German. Neo-classical composer. Influenced music education and composition. Works: *Mathis der Maler; Gebrauchmusik*

**Leonard Bernstein** (1918–1990)—American. Conductor, composer, educator and innovator. Composed for orchestras, broadway shows, and small ensembles. Works: *Candide; West Side Story; Age of Anxiety*

**Alfred Reed** (1921–  )—American. Composer and arranger with a worldwide influence on band music and education.

**Benjamin Britten** (1913–1976)—England. Composed patriotic music and operas. Works: *Peter Grimes; Billy Budd*

**Jazz** (1800s–  )—Truly "American" music. Originated from the black American musical traditions of folk music, ragtime and the blues. Contains a strong beat, relies on improvisation. Rhythmic with a swing feel.

**Louis Armstrong** (1900–1971)—American. Known as the "Father of Jazz." Used the Trumpet, scat singing, and call and response. Nickname: "Satchmo"

**Bessie Smith** (1894–1937)—American. Known as the "Empress of the Blues." Powerful vocal skills and expressive nature. Influenced by folksongs.

**Charlie Parker** (1920–1955)—American. Jazz saxophonist. Innovated the "Be-bop" style of jazz which used melody and improvisations based on chord progressions. Nickname: "The Bird"

**Dizzy Gillespie** (1917–1993)—American. Trumpet player, big band leader composer and performer. Utilized melodic and high register playing. Works: *A Night in Tunisia; Groovin' High*

**Miles Davis** (1926–1992)—American. Trumpet player. Flexible performer of cool jazz, modal jazz, and rock-fusion.

**Edward Kennedy "Duke" Ellington** (1899–1974)—American. Jazz pianist, big band leader and arranger. Innovated the jazz piano and defined African-American styles on the instruments.

**Count Basie** (1904–1984)—American. Created the "stride" style of piano playing which involved "comping" with a bouncy, flexible, and syncopated style.

**Benny Goodman** (1909–1986)—American. Clarinetist and big band leader. "King of Swing"

**Dave Brubeck** (1920–    )—American. "Cool Jazz" innovator. Used a classical style, with swing and unusual meter combinations.

**John Coltrane** (1926–1967)—American. Saxophonist who played hard bop. A composer, arranger, and performer known for a forceful, full, and dark sound. Experimented with modal music and researched African and Asian music to incorporate into his playing. Works: "Giant Steps"

**Emile Jaques-Dalcroze** (1865–1950)—French. Music educator. Used eurhythmics which entailed a physical response to music, ear training, and improvisation to teach music.

**Carl Orff** (1895–1982)—German. Concentrated on the rhythmic nature of music and developed percussion instruments to teach music to children Works: *Carmina Burana*

**Zoltan Kodaly** (1882–1967)—Hungarian. Believed that music is for all people so he centered his teaching on using nationalistic themes and folksongs. He combined efforts with Béla Bartók. Developed symbols and hand signals for music. Works: *Hary Janos Suites*

**Shinichi Suzuki** (1898–    )—Japan. Educator. Mother-tongue method of education. Learning by rote.

# 4. COMMONLY TESTED WORDS

**abaft** – *adv.* – on or toward the rear of a ship

**abdicate** – *v.* – to reject, denounce, or abandon

**abjure** – *v.* – to renounce upon oath

**abnegation** – *n.* – a denial

**abscond** – *v.* – to go away hastily or secretly often with the intention to hide; to avoid capture by the authorities

**abstemious** – *adj.* – 1. sparing in diet; 2. sparingly used

**abysmal** – *adj.* – bottomless; extraordinarily bad

**acerbity** – *n.* – harshness or bitterness

**acrimony** – *n.* – sharpness

**addle** – *adj.* – confused

**adjure** – *v.* – to entreat earnestly and solemnly

**adulation** – *n.* – praise in excess

**adulterate** – *v.* – to corrupt, debase, or make impure

**agrarian** – *adj.* – relating to land and the equal divisions of land

**alchemy** – *n.* – any imaginary power of transmitting one thing into another

**allegory** – *n.* – symbolic narration or description

**anachronism** – *n.* – representation of something existing at other than its proper time

**annihilate** – *v.* – to reduce to nothing

**apocalyptic** – *adj.* – pertaining to revelation or prophecy

**arrogate** – *v.* – to claim or demand unduly

**artifice** – *n.* – skill; ingenuity; craft; deception; trickery

**askance** – *adv.* – 1. sideways; 2. with suspicion

**assay** – *n.* – the determination of any quantity of a metal in an ore or alloy

**attenuate** – *v.* – 1. to make thin or slender; 2. to lessen or weaken

**avarice** – *n.* – inordinate desire of gaining and possessing wealth

**batten** – *v.* – to grow fat; to thrive

**beholden** – *adj.* – obliged; indebted

**bellicose** – *adj.* – warlike; disposed to quarrel or fight

**besmirch** – *v.* – to soil or discolor

**bestial** – *adj.* – having the qualities of a beast

**betroth** – *v.* – to promise or pledge in marriage

**blighted** – *adj.* – destroyed; frustrated

**bode** – *v.* – to foreshadow something

**boorish** – *adj.* – rude; ill–mannered

**brindled** – *adj.* – streaked or spotted with a darker color

**broach** – *v.* – 1. to pierce; 2. to introduce into conversation

**bucolic** – *adj.* – pastoral

**burlesque** – *v.* – to imitate comically

**cadaver** – *n.* – a dead body

**caliber** – *n.* – 1. the diameter of a bullet or shell; 2. quality

**callow** – *adj.* – immature

**calumny** – *n.* – slander

**canard** – *n.* – a false statement or rumor

**candid** – *adj.* – open; frank; honest

**captious** – *adj.* – disposed to find fault

**carnage** – *n.* – slaughter

**carte blanche** – *n.* – unlimited power to decide

**castigate** – *v.* – to chastise

**cataclysm** – *n.* – 1. an overflowing of water; 2. an extraordinary change

**catharsis** – *n.* – purgation

**cavil** – *v.* – to find fault without good reason

**celibate** – *adj.* – unmarried, single; chaste

**cessation** – *n.* – a ceasing; a stop

**chafe** – *v.* – to rage; to fret

**chaffing** – *n.* – 1. banter; 2. teasing

**chaste** – *adj.* – virtuous; free from obscenity

**choleric** – *adj.* – easily irritated; angry

**circumvent** – *v.* – to go around

**clandestine** – *adj.* – secret; private; hidden

**cogent** – *adj.* – urgent; compelling; convincing

**cohort** – *n.* – a group; a band

**collusion** – *n.* – secret agreement for a fraudulent or illegal purpose

**comport** – *v.* – to agree; to accord

**conclave** – *n.* – any private meeting or closed assembly

**connivance** – *n.* – passive cooperation

**consort** – *n.* – 1. a companion; 2. *v.* – to be in harmony or agreement

**contravene** – *v.* – to go against; to oppose

**contusion** – *n.* – a bruise; an injury where the skin is not broken

**copious** – *adj.* – abundant; in great quantities

**covenant** – *n.* – a binding and solemn agreement

**coy** – *adj.* – 1. modest; bashful; 2. pretending shyness to attract

**crass** – *adj.* – gross; thick; coarse

**cursory** – *adj.* – hasty; slight

**dally** – *v.* – to delay; to put off

**dauntless** – *adj.* – fearless; not discouraged

**debonair** – *adj.* – 1. having an affable manner; courteous; 2. suave; urbane

**decadence** – *n.* – a decline in force or quality; moral decay

**deciduous** – *adj.* – falling off at a particular season or stage of growth

**decry** – *v.* – to denounce or condemn openly

**defunct** – *adj.* – no longer living or existing

**deliquesce** – *v.* – to melt away

**delusion** – *n.* – act or process of deception

**deposition** – *n.* – 1. a removal from a position or power; 2. a testimony

**depredation** – *n.* – a plundering or laying waste

**descant** – *v.* – to comment at length on a theme

**despoil** – *v.* – to strip; to rob

**despotism** – *n.* – 1. tyranny; 2. absolute power or influence

**desultory** – *adj.* – without order or natural connection

**dexterous** – *adj.* – having or showing skill of hands, body, or mind

**diffidence** – *n.* – 1. lack of self-confidence; 2. distrust

**dilapidated** – *n.* – falling to pieces or into disrepair

**dilettante** – *n.* – an admirer of the fine arts; a dabbler

**dint** – *n.* – a blow; a stroke

**disarray** – *n.* – 1. disorder; confusion; 2. incomplete or disorderly attire

**divulge** – *v.* – to make known

**dormant** – *adj.* – as if asleep

**doting** – *adj.* – excessively fond

**doughty** – *adj.* – brave; valiant

**dregs** – *n.* – waste or worthless manner

**ecclesiastic** – *adj.* – pertaining or relating to a church

**edify** – *v.* – 1. to build or establish; 2. to instruct and improve the mind

**efface** – *v.* – to erase; to remove from the mind

**effrontery** – *n.* – impudence; assurance

**effusive** – *adj.* – pouring out or forth; overflowing

**egregious** – *adj.* – remarkably bad, outrageous

**egress** – *v.* – to depart; to go out

**elegy** – *n.* – a poem of lament and praise for the dead

**elucidate** – *v.* – to make clear or manifest; to explain

**emanate** – *v.* – to send forth; to emit

**embellish** – *v.* – to improve the appearance of

**enamored** – *adj.* – filled with love and desire

**encroach** – *v.* – to trespass or intrude

**encumber** – *v.* – to hold back; to hinder

**endue** – *v.* – to provide with some quality or trait

**enrapture** – *v.* – to fill with pleasure

**epilogue** – *n.* – closing section of a play or novel providing further comment

**epiphany** – *n.* – an appearance of a supernatural being

**epitaph** – *n.* – an inscription on a monument, in honor or memory of a dead person

**epitome** – *n.* – a part that is typical of the whole

**equinox** – *n.* – precise time when the day and night everywhere is of equal length

**equivocate** – *v.* – to be purposely ambiguous

**eschew** – *v.* – to escape from; to avoid

**estranged** – *adj.* – kept at a distance; alienated

**ethereal** – *adj.* – 1. very light; airy; 2. heavenly; not earthly

**euphemism** – *n.* – the use of a word or phrase in place of one that is distasteful

**euphoria** – *n.* – a feeling of well-being

**exhume** – *v.* – to unearth; to reveal

**expunge** – *v.* – to blot out; to delete

**exude** – *v.* – to flow slowly or ooze in drops

**faction** – *n.* – a number of people in an organization having a common end view

**fallible** – *adj.* – liable to be mistaken or erroneous

**fathom** – *v.* – to reach or penetrate with the mind

**fatuous** – *adj.* – silly; inane; unreal

**fealty** – *n.* – fidelity; loyalty

**feign** – *v.* – to invent or imagine

**ferment** – *v.* – to excite or agitate

**fervid** – *adj.* – 1. very hot; burning; 2. intensely fervent or zealous

**fester** – *v.* – to become more and more virulent and fixed

**fetish** – *n.* – an object to which one gives excessive devotion or blind adoration

**fidelity** – *n.* – faithfulness; honesty

**fissure** – *n.* – a dividing or breaking into parts

**flaccid** – *adj.* – 1. hanging in loose folds or wrinkles; 2. lacking force; weak

**flamboyant** – *adj.* – ornate; too showy

**foible** – *n.* – a slight frailty in character

**foist** – *v.* – 1. to put in slyly or stealthily; 2. to pass off as genuine or valuable

**foray** – *v.* – to raid for spoils, plunder

**forensic** – *adj.* – pertaining to legal or public argument

**fortitude** – *n.* – firm courage; strength

**fractious** – *adj.* – rebellious; apt to quarrel

**fraught** – *adj.* – loaded; charged

**froward** – *adj.* – not willing to yield or comply with what is reasonable

**fulminate** – *v.* – 1. to explode with sudden violence; 2. to issue thunderous verbal attack or denunciation

**galvanize** – *v.* – to stimulate as if by electric shock; startle; excite

**gamut** – *n.* – 1. a complete range; 2. any complete musical scale

**garish** – *adj.* – gaudy; showy

**gauche** – *adj.* – awkward; lacking grace

**gauntlet** – *n.* – a long glove with a flaring cuff covering the lower part of the arm

**germane** – *adj.* – closely related; pertinent

**glib** – *adj.* – smooth and slippery; speaking or spoken in a smooth manner

**gnarled** – *adj.* – full of knots

**gourmand** – *n.* – a greedy or ravenous eater; glutton

**gregarious** – *adj.* – fond of the company of others

**grisly** – *adj.* – frightful; horrible

**guffaw** – *n.* – a loud, coarse burst of laughter

**guise** – *n.* – 1. customary behavior; 2. manner of dress; 3. false appearance

**halcyon** – *adj.* – calm; quiet; peaceful

**hapless** – *adj.* – unlucky; unfortunate

**harangue** – *v.* – to speak in an impassioned and forcible manner

**heretic** – *n.* – one who holds opinion contrary to that which is generally accepted

**hiatus** – *n.* – an opening or gap; slight pause

**hoary** – *adj.* – very aged; ancient; gray or white with age

**homily** – *n.* – discourse or sermon read to an audience

**hybrid** – *n.* – anything of mixed origin

**idiosyncrasy** – *n.* – any personal peculiarity, mannerism, etc.

**igneous** – *adj.* – having the nature of fire

**ignominious** – *adj.* – 1. contemptible; 2. degrading

**immaculate** – *adj.* – 1. perfectly clean; perfectly correct; 2. pure

**imminent** – *adj.* – appearing as if about to happen

**impasse** – *n.* – a situation that has no solution or escape

**impenitent** – *adj.* – without regret, shame, or remorse

**impiety** – *n.* – 1. irreverence toward God; 2. lack of respect

**impolitic** – *adj.* – unwise; imprudent

**imprecate** – *v.* – to pray for evil; to invoke a curse

**imputation** – *n.* – attribution

**incarcerate** – *v.* – to imprison or confine

**incommodious** – *adj.* – uncomfortable; troublesome

**incorporeal** – *adj.* – not consisting of matter

**incorrigible** – *adj.* – not capable of correction or improvement

**incubate** – *v.* – to sit on and hatch (eggs)

**inculcate** – *v.* – to impress upon the mind by frequent repetition or urging

**indemnify** – *v.* – to protect against or keep free from loss

**indigenous** – *adj.* – innate; inherent; inborn

**indomitable** – *adj.* – not easily discouraged or defeated

**indubitably** – *adv.* – unquestionably; surely

**inimical** – *adj.* – unfriendly; adverse

**iniquitous** – *adj.* – unjust; wicked

**inordinate** – *adj.* – not regulated; excessive

**intrepid** – *adj.* – fearless; brave

**inured** – *adj.* – accustomed

**irascible** – *adj.* – easily provoked or inflamed to anger

**irreparable** – *adj.* – cannot be repaired or regained

**jettison** – *n.* – a throwing overboard of goods to lighten a vehicle in an emergency

**jocund** – *adj.* – merry; gay; cheerful

**lacerate** – *v.* – 1. to tear or mangle; 2. to wound or hurt

**lambent** – *adj.* – giving off a soft radiance

**lassitude** – *n.* – a state or feeling of being tired or weak

**lewd** – *adj.* – lustful; wicked

**libertine** – *n.* – one who indulges his desires without restraint

**licentious** – *adj.* – disregarding accepted rules and standards

**lithe** – *adj.* – easily bent; pliable; marked by effortless grace

**loquacious** – *adj.* – talkative

**lucent** – *adj.* – shining; translucent

**lugubrious** – *adj.* – mournful; very sad

**lurid** – *adj.* – ghastly pale; gloomy

**magnate** – *n.* – a very influential person in any field of activity

**malefactor** – *n.* – one who commits a crime

**malign** – *v.* – to defame; speak evil of

**marauder** – *n.* – a rover in search of booty or plunder

**maudlin** – *adj.* – foolishly and tearfully sentimental

**mendacious** – *adj.* – addicted to deception

**mercurial** – *adj.* – quick, volatile; changeable

**meretricious** – *adj.* – alluring by false, showy charms; fleshy

**mettle** – *n.* – high quality of character

**mien** – *n.* – manner; external appearance

**misanthropy** – *n.* – hatred of mankind

**mite** – *n.* – 1. very small sum of money; 2. very small creature

**modulate** – *v.* – 1. to regulate or adjust; 2. to vary the pitch of the voice

**mollify** – *v.* – to soften; to make less intense

**moot** – *adj.* – subject to or open for discussion or debate

**mordant** – *adj.* – biting, cutting, or caustic

**mutinous** – *adj.* – inclined to revolt

**nefarious** – *adj.* – very wicked; abominable

**nemesis** – *n.* – just punishment; retribution; one that inflicts relentless vengence

**nexus** – *n.* – a connection

**nostrum** – *n.* – a quack medicine

**noxious** – *adj.* – harmful to health or morals

**nugatory** – *adj.* – trifling; futile; insignificant

**obeisance** – *n.* – a gesture of respect or reverence

**obfuscate** – *v.* – to darken; to confuse

**objurgate** – *v.* – to chide vehemently

**obloquy** – *n.* – verbal abuse of a person or thing

**obtrude** – *v.* – to thrust forward; to eject

**odious** – *adj.* – hateful; disgusting

**oligarchy** – *n.* – form of government in which the supreme power is placed in the hands of a small exclusive group

**opalescent** – *adj.* – iridescent

**opprobrious** – *adj.* – reproachful or contemptuous

**palatial** – *adj.* – large and ornate, like a palace

**palindrome** – *n.* – a word, verse or sentence that is the same when read backward or forward

**paltry** – *adj.* – worthless; trifling

**pandemonium** – *n.* – a place of wild disorder, noise, or confusion

**parapet** – *n.* – a wall or railing to protect people from falling

**pariah** – *n.* – an outcast; someone despised by others

**parity** – *n.* – state of being the same in power, value, or rank

**parley** – *v.* – to speak with another; to discourse

**parry** – *v.* – to ward off; to avoid

**parsimonious** – *adj.* – miserly; stingy

**paucity** – *n.* – scarcity; small number

**peculate** – *v.* – to embezzle

**pecuniary** – *adj.* – relating to money

**pellucid** – *adj.* – transparent

**penury** – *n.* – lack of money or property

**perdition** – *n.* – complete and irreparable loss

**peremptory** – *adj.* – 1. barring future action; 2. that cannot be denied, changed, etc.

**perfidious** – *adj.* – violating good faith or vows

**perquisite** – *n.* – a fee, profit, etc., in addition to the stated income of one's employment

**peruse** – *v.* – to read carefully and thoroughly

**pied** – *adj.* – spotted

**pinioned** – *adj.* – 1. having wings; 2. having wings or arms bound or confined

**platonic** – *adj.* – 1. idealistic or impractical; 2. not amorous or sensual

**plenary** – *adj.* – full; entire; complete

**plethora** – *n.* – the state of being too full; excess

**pommel** – *n.* – the rounded, upward-projecting front of a saddle

**portend** – *v.* – to foreshadow

**potable** – *adj.* – drinkable

**prate** – *v.* – to talk much and foolishly

**precept** – *n.* – a rule or direction of moral conduct

**precocious** – *adj.* – developed or matured earlier than usual

**prefatory** – *adj.* – introductory

**preponderate** – *v.* – to outweigh

**prerogative** – *n.* – a prior or exclusive right or privilege

**prevaricate** – *v.* – to evade the truth

**prognosis** – *n.* – a forecast, especially in medicine

**prolific** – *adj.* – fruitful

**propagate** – *v.* – to reproduce or multiply

**propitiate** – *v.* – to win the good will of

**protocol** – *n.* – an original draft or record of a document

**provident** – *adj.* – prudent; economical

**proviso** – *n.* – conditional stipulation to an agreement

**pseudonym** – *n.* – a borrowed or fictitious name

**puerile** – *adj.* – childish; immature

**purloin** – *v.* – to steal

**purview** – *n.* – the range of control, activity, or understanding

**quaff** – *v.* – to drink or swallow in large quantities

**quagmire** – *n.* – a difficult position, as if on shaky ground

**qualm** – *n.* – sudden feeling of uneasiness or doubt

**quintessence** – *n.* – 1. the ultimate substance; 2. the pure essence of anything

**quixotic** – *adj.* – extravagantly chivalrous

**quizzical** – *adj.* – 1. odd; comical; 2. suggesting puzzlement; questioning

**ramification** – *n.* – the arrangement of branches; consequence

**rampant** – *adj.* – violent and uncontrollable action

**rancor** – *n.* – a continuing and bitter hate or ill will

**raze** – *v.* – to scrape or shave off

**recalcitrant** – *adj.* – refusing to obey authority

**recidivism** – *n.* – habitual or chronic relapse

**recumbent** – *adj.* – leaning or reclining

**recusant** – *adj.* – disobedient of authority

**redolent** – *adj.* – sweet–smelling; fragrant

**reminiscence** – *n.* – a remembering

**remonstrate** – *v.* – to exhibit strong reasons against an act

**rendition** – *n.* – a performance or interpretation

**repertoire** – *n.* – stock of plays which can be readily performed by a company

**reprehend** – *v.* – to reprimand; to find fault with

**reprieve** – *v.* – to give temporary relief

**resonant** – *adj.* – resounding; re-echoing

**resplendent** – *adj.* – dazzling; splendid

**resurgent** – *adj.* – rising or tending to rise again

**revile** – *v.* – to be abusive in speech

**risible** – *adj.* – able or inclined to laugh

**roseate** – *adj.* – bright, cheerful, or optimistic

**rote** – *n.* – a fixed, mechanical way of doing something

**rotundity** – *n.* – condition of being rounded out or plump

**rudimentary** – *adj.* – elementary

**ruminate** – *v.* – to muse on

**salutatory** – *adj.* – of or containing greetings

**sapid** – *adj.* – having a pleasant taste

**sardonic** – *adj.* – bitterly ironical

**savant** – *n.* – a learned person

**schism** – *n.* – a division in an organized group

**scourge** – *v.* – to whip severely

**scurrilous** – *adj.* – using low and indecent language

**sedentary** – *adj.* – 1. characterized by sitting; 2. remaining in one locality

**serendipity** – *n.* – an apparent aptitude for making fortunate discoveries accidentally

**shoal** – *n.* – a great quantity

**sloth** – *n.* – disinclination to action or labor

**slovenly** – *adv.* – careless in habits, behavior, etc.; untidy

**sordid** – *adj.* – filthy; foul

**specious** – *adj.* – appearing just and fair without really being so

**spelunker** – *n.* – one who explores caves

**splenetic** – *adj.* – bad-tempered; irritable

**staid** – *adj.* – sober; sedate

**stanch** – *v.* – to stop or check the flow of blood

**stigmatize** – *v.* – to characterize or brand as disgraceful

**stoic** – *adj.* – a person who is seemingly indifferent to joy, grief, pleasure, or pain

**stolid** – *adj.* – unexcitable; dull

**striated** – *adj.* – marked with fine parallel lines

**strident** – *adj.* – creaking; harsh; grating

**stymie** – *n.* – 1. to hinder or obstruct; 2. in golf, an opponent's ball lying in direct line between the player's ball and the hole

**succor** – *n.* – aid; assistance

**sumptuous** – *adj.* – involving great expense

**sundry** – *adj.* – 1. various; miscellaneous; 2. separate; distinct

**supplant** – *v.* – to take the place of

**suppliant** – *adj.* – asking earnestly and submissively

**surfeit** – *v.* – to feed or supply in excess

**swathe** – *v.* – to wrap around something; envelop

**tawdry** – *adj.* – gaudy or cheap

**teem** – *v.* – 1. to be stocked to overflowing; 2. to pour out; to empty

**tenet** – *n.* – any principle, doctrine, etc., which a person, school, etc. believes or maintains

**termagant** – *n.* – a boisterous, scolding woman; a shrew

**terrestrial** – *adj.* – pertaining to the earth

**tether** – *n.* – the range or limit of one's abilities

**thrall** – *n.* – a slave

**throe** – *n.* – a violent pang or spasm of pain

**timorous** – *adj.* – fearful

**tortuous** – *adj.* – pertaining to or involving excruciating pain

**traduce** – *v.* – 1. to exhibit; 2. to slander

**transmute** – *v.* – to transform

**travail** – *v.* – to harass; to torment

**trenchant** – *adj.* – 1. keen; penetrating; 2. clear-cut; distinct

**tribunal** – *n.* – the seat of judge

**troth** – *n.* – belief; faith; fidelity

**turbid** – *adj.* – 1. thick; dense; 2. confused; perplexed

**tutelage** – *n.* – the condition of being under a guardian or a tutor

**umbrage** – *n.* – shade; shadow

**uncouth** – *adj.* – uncultured; crude

**unfeigned** – *adj.* – genuine; real; sincere

**untrowable** – *adj.* – incredible

**uxoricide** – *n.* – the murder of a wife by her husband

**vagary** – *n.* – 1. an odd action or idea; 2. a wandering

**vantage** – *n.* – advantage; gain; profit

**vaunt** – *v.* – to brag or boast

**venal** – *adj.* – that can be readily bribed or corrupted

**veneer** – *n.* – 1. a thin surface layer; 2. any attractive but superficial appearance

**verbiage** – *n.* – wordiness

**verity** – *n.* – truthfulness

**vertigo** – *n.* – a sensation of dizziness

**vestige** – *n.* – a trace of something that no longer exists

**vicarious** – *adj.* – taking the place of another person or thing

**vicissitude** – *n.* – changes or variation occurring irregularly in the course of something

**vigilance** – *n.* – watchfulness

**visage** – *n.* – appearance

**vitriolic** – *adj.* – extremely biting or caustic

**vociferous** – *adj.* – making a loud outcry

**volition** – *n.* – the act of willing

**voracious** – *adj.* – greedy in eating

**vouchsafe** – *v.* – 1. to be gracious enough to grant; 2. to guarantee as safe

**wan** – *adj.* – pale; pallid

**wily** – *adj.* – cunning; sly

**wizened** – *adj.* – withered; shrunken

**wreak** – *v.* – to give vent or free play

**wrest** – *v.* – 1. to turn or twist; 2. usurp; 3. to distort or change the true meaning of

# 5. WORD PARTS

## PREFIX

| Prefix | Meaning | Example |
|---|---|---|
| *ab –, a –, abs –* | away, from | absent – away, not present<br>abstain – keep from doing, refrain |
| *ad –* | to, toward | adjacent – next to<br>address – to direct towards |
| *ante –* | before | antecedent – going before in time<br>anterior – occurring before |
| *anti –* | against | antidote – remedy to act against an evil<br>antibiotic – substance that fights against bacteria |
| *be –* | over, thoroughly | bemoan – to mourn over<br>belabor – to exert much labor upon |
| *bi –* | two | bisect – to divide<br>biennial – happening every two years |
| *cata –, cat –, cath –* | down | catacombs – underground passage-ways<br>catalogue – descriptive list |
| *circum –* | around | circumscribe – to draw a circle around<br>circumspect – watchful on all sides |
| *com –* | with | combine – join together<br>communication – to have dealing with |
| *contra –* | against | contrary – opposed<br>contrast – to stand in opposition |

| Prefix | Meaning | Example |
|---|---|---|
| *de –* | down, from | decline – to slope downward<br>decontrol – to release from government control |
| *di –* | two | dichotomy – cutting in two<br>diarchy – system of government with two authorities |
| *dis –, di* | apart, away | discern – to distinguish as separate<br>dismiss – send away |
| *epi –, ep –, eph –* | upon, among | epidemic – happening among many people<br>epicycle – circle whose center moves on the circumference of a greater circle |
| *ex –, e –* | from, out | exceed – go beyond the limit<br>emit – to send forth |
| *extra –* | outside, beyond | extraordinary – beyond or outside the common method<br>extrasensory – beyond the senses |
| *hyper –* | beyond, over | hyperactive – above the normal activity level<br>hypercritic– one who is critical beyond measure |
| *hypo –* | beneath, lower | hypodermic – pertaining to or injected beneath the skin<br>hypocrisy – to be under a pretense of goodness |
| *in –, il –, im –, ir –* | not | inactive – not active<br>irreversible – not reversible |
| *in –, il –, im –, ir –* | in, on, into | instill – to add or introduce slowly<br>impose – to lay on |
| *inter –* | among, between | intercom – a system allowing for communication between people<br>interlude – an intervening period of time |

| Prefix | Meaning | Example |
|---|---|---|
| *intra –* | within | intravenous – within a vein<br>intramural – within a single college or its student body |
| *meta –* | beyond, over, along with | metamorphosis – change in form or nature<br>metatarsus – part of foot beyond the flat of the foot |
| *mis –* | badly, wrongly | misconstrue – to interpret wrongly<br>misappropriate – to use wrongly |
| *mono –* | one | monogamy – marriage to one person at a time<br>monotone – a single, unvaried tone |
| *multi –* | many | multiple – of many parts<br>multitude – a great number |
| *non –* | no, not | nonsense – lack of sense<br>nonentity – not existing |
| *ob –* | against | obscene – offensive to modesty<br>obstruct – to hinder the passage of |
| *para –, par –* | beside | parallel – continuously at equal distance apart<br>parenthesis – sentence inserted within a passage |
| *per –* | through | persevere – to maintain an effort<br>permeate – to pass through |
| *poly –* | many | polygon – a plane figure with many sides or angles<br>polytheism – belief in existence of many gods |
| *post –* | after | posterior – coming after<br>postpone – to put off until a future time |
| *pre –* | before | premature – ready before the proper time<br>premonition – a previous warning |

| Prefix | Meaning | Example |
|---|---|---|
| *pro –* | in favor of, forward | prolific – bringing forth an abundance of offspring<br>project – throw or cast forward |
| *re –* | back, against | reimburse – pay back<br>retract – to draw back |
| *semi –* | half | semicircle – half a circle<br>semiannual – half-yearly |
| *sub –* | under | subdue – to bring under one's power<br>submarine – travel under the surface of the sea |
| *super –* | above | supersonic – above the speed of sound<br>superior – higher in place or position |
| *tele –, tel –* | across | telecast – transmit across a distance<br>telepathy – communication between mind and mind at a distance |
| *trans –* | across | transpose – to change the position of two things<br>transmit – to send from one person to another |
| *ultra –* | beyond | ultraviolet – beyond the limit of visibility<br>ultramarine – beyond the sea |
| *un –* | not | undeclared – not declared<br>unbelievable – not believable |
| *uni –* | one | unity – state of oneness<br>unison – sounding together |
| *with –* | away, against | withhold – to hold back<br>withdraw – to take away |

# ROOT

| Root | Meaning | Example |
|------|---------|---------|
| *act, ag* | do, act, drive | activate – to make active<br>agile – having quick motion |
| *alt* | high | altitude – height<br>alto – highest singing voice |
| *alter, altr* | other, change | alternative – choice among two things<br>altruism – living for the good of others |
| *am, ami* | love, friend | amiable – good-natured<br>amity – friendship |
| *anim* | mind, spirit | animated – spirited<br>animosity – violent hatred |
| *annu, enni* | year | annual – every year<br>centennial – every hundred years |
| *aqua* | water | aquarium – tank for water animals and plants<br>aquamarine – semiprecious stone of sea-green color |
| *arch* | first, ruler | archenemy – chief enemy<br>archetype – original pattern from which things are copied |
| *aud, audit* | hear | audible – capable of being heard<br>audience – assembly of hearers |
| *auto* | self | automatic – self-acting<br>autobiography – story about a person who also wrote it |
| *bell* | war | belligerent – a party taking part in a war<br>bellicose – war-like |
| *ben, bene* | good | benign – kindly disposition<br>beneficial – advantageous |

| Root | Meaning | Example |
|------|---------|---------|
| *bio* | life | biotic – relating to life<br>biology – the science of life |
| *brev* | short | abbreviate – make shorter<br>brevity – shortness |
| *cad, cas* | fall | cadence – fall in voice<br>casualty – loss caused by death, injury, or illness |
| *capit, cap* | head | captain – the head or chief<br>decapitate – to cut off the head |
| *cede, ceed, cess* | to go, to yield | recede – to move or fall back<br>proceed – to move onward |
| *cent* | hundred | century – hundred years<br>centipede – insect with a hundred legs |
| *chron* | time | chronology – science dealing with historical dates<br>chronicle – register of events in order of time |
| *cide, cis* | to kill, to cut | homicide – one who kills or the killing of one human being by another<br>incision – a cut |
| *clam, claim* | to shout | acclaim – receive with applause<br>proclamation – a public announcement |
| *cogn* | to know | recognize – to know again<br>cognition – awareness |
| *corp* | body | incorporate – combine into one body<br>corpse – dead body |
| *cred* | to trust, to believe | incredible – unbelievable<br>credulous – too prone to believe |
| *cur, curr, curs* | to run | current – flowing body of air or water<br>excursion – short trip |
| *dem* | people | democracy – government by the people<br>epidemic – affecting all people |

| Root | Meaning | Example |
|------|---------|---------|
| *dic, dict* | to say | dictate – to read aloud for another to transcribe<br>verdict – decision of a jury |
| *doc, doct* | to teach | docile – easily instructed<br>indoctrinate – to instruct |
| *domin* | to rule | dominate – to rule<br>dominion – territory of rule |
| *duc, duct* | to lead | conduct – act of guiding<br>induce – to overcome by persuasion |
| *eu* | well, good | eulogy – speech or writing in praise<br>euphony – pleasantness or smoothness of sound |
| *fac, fact, fect, fic* | to do, to make | factory – location of production<br>fiction – something invented or imagined |
| *fer* | to bear, to carry | transfer – to move from one place to another<br>refer – to direct to |
| *fin* | end, limit | infinity – unlimited<br>finite – limited in quantity |
| *flect, flex* | to bend | flexible – easily bent<br>reflect – to throw back |
| *fort* | luck | fortunate – lucky<br>fortuitous – happening by chance |
| *fort* | strong | fortify – strengthen<br>fortress – stronghold |
| *frag, fract* | break | fragile – easily broken<br>fracture – break |
| *fug* | flee | fugitive – fleeing<br>refugee – one who flees to a place of safety |

| Root | Meaning | Example |
|------|---------|---------|
| *gen* | class, race | engender – to breed<br>generic – of a general nature in regard to all members |
| *grad, gress* | to go, to step | regress – to go back<br>graduate – to divide into regular steps |
| *graph* | writing | telegram – message sent by telegraph<br>autograph – person's own handwriting or signature |
| *ject* | to throw | projectile – capable of being thrown<br>reject – to throw away |
| *leg* | law | legitimate – lawful<br>legal – defined by law |
| *leg, lig, lect* | to choose, gather, read | illegible – incapable of being read<br>election – the act of choosing |
| *liber* | free | liberal – favoring freedom of ideas<br>liberty – freedom from restraint |
| *log* | study, speech | archaeology – study of human antiquities<br>prologue – address spoken before a performance |
| *luc, lum* | light | translucent – slightly transparent<br>illuminate – to light up |
| *magn* | large, great | magnify – to make larger<br>magnificent – great |
| *mal, male* | bad, wrong | malfunction – to operate incorrectly<br>malevolent – evil |
| *mar* | sea | marine – pertaining to the sea<br>submarine – below the surface of the sea |
| *mater, matr* | mother | maternal – motherly<br>matriarch – female head of family or group |

| Root | Meaning | Example |
|------|---------|---------|
| *mit, miss* | to send | transmit – to send from one person or place to another<br>mission – the act of sending |
| *morph* | shape | metamorphosis – a changing in shape<br>anthropomorphic – having a human shape |
| *mut* | change | mutable – subject to change<br>mutate – to change |
| *nat* | born | innate – inborn<br>native – a person born in a place |
| *neg* | deny | negative – expressing denial<br>renege – to deny |
| *nom* | name | nominate – to put forward a name<br>anonymous – no name given |
| *nov* | new | novel – new<br>renovate – to make as good as new |
| *omni* | all | omnipotent – all powerful<br>omnipresent – all present |
| *oper* | to work | operate – to work on something<br>cooperate – to work with others |
| *pass, path* | to feel | pathetic – affecting the tender emotions<br>passionate – moved by strong emotion |
| *pater, patr* | father | paternal – fatherly<br>patriarch – male head of family or group |
| *ped, pod* | foot | pedestrian – one who travels on foot<br>podiatrist – foot doctor |
| *pel, puls* | to drive, to push | impel – to drive forward<br>compulsion – irresistible force |

| Root | Meaning | Example |
|------|---------|---------|
| *phil* | love | philharmonic – fond of or devoted to music<br>philanthropist – one who loves and seeks to do good for others |
| *port* | carry | export – to carry out of the country<br>portable – able to be carried |
| *psych* | mind | psychology – study of the mind<br>psychiatrist – specialist in mental disorders |
| *quer, ques, quir, quis* | to ask | inquiry – to ask about<br>question – that which is asked |
| *rid, ris* | to laugh | ridiculous – laughable<br>derision – to mock |
| *rupt* | to break | interrupt – to break in upon<br>erupt – to break through |
| *sci* | to know | science – systematic knowledge of physical or natural phenomena<br>conscious – having inward knowledge |
| *scrib, script* | to write | transcribe – to write over again<br>script – text of words |
| *sent, sens* | to feel, to think | sentimental – expressive or appealing to tender feelings<br>sensitive – easily affected by changes |
| *sequ, secut* | to follow | sequence – connected series<br>consecutive – following one another in unbroken order |
| *solv, solu, solut* | to loosen | dissolve – to break up<br>absolute – without restraint |
| *spect* | to look at | spectator – one who watches<br>inspect – to look at closely |
| *spir* | to breathe | inspire – to breathe in<br>respiration – process of breathing |

| Root | Meaning | Example |
|------|---------|---------|
| *string, strict* | to bind | stringent – binding strongly<br>restrict – to restrain within bounds |
| *stru, struct* | to build | misconstrue – to interpret wrongly<br>construct – to build |
| *tang, ting, tack, tig* | to touch | tangent – touching, but not intersecting<br>contact – touching |
| *ten, tent, tain* | to hold | tenure – holding of office<br>contain – to hold |
| *term* | to end | terminate – to end<br>terminal – having an end |
| *terr* | earth | terrain – tract of land<br>terrestrial – existing on Earth |
| *therm* | heat | thermal – pertaining to heat<br>thermometer – instrument for measuring temperature |
| *tort, tors* | to twist | contortionist – one who twists violently<br>torsion – act of turning or twisting |
| *tract* | to pull, to draw | attract – draw toward<br>distract – to draw away |
| *vac* | empty | vacant – empty<br>evacuate – to empty out |
| *ven, vent* | to come | prevent – to stop from coming<br>intervene – to come between |
| *ver* | true | verify – to prove to be true<br>veracious – truthful |
| *verb* | word | verbose – use of excess words<br>verbatim – word for word |
| *vid, vis* | to see | video – picture phase of television<br>vision – act of seeing external objects |

| Root | Meaning | Example |
|---|---|---|
| *vinc, vict, vang* | to conquer | invincible – unconquerable<br>victory – defeat of enemy |
| *viv, vit* | life | vital – necessary to life<br>vivacious – lively |
| *voc* | to call | provocative – serving to excite or<br>  stimulate to action<br>vocal – uttered by voice |
| *vol* | to wish, to will | involuntary – outside the control of<br>  will<br>volition – the act of willing or choos-<br>  ing |

## SUFFIX

| Suffix | Meaning | Example |
|---|---|---|
| *– able, – ble* | capable of | believable – capable of being believed<br>legible – capable of being read |
| *– acious, – icious,*<br>  *– ous* | full of | vivacious – full of life<br>wondrous – full of wonder |
| *– ant, – ent* | full of | eloquent – full of eloquence<br>expectant – full of expectation |
| *– ary* | connected with | honorary – for the sake of honor<br>disciplinary – enforcing instruction |
| *– ate* | to make | facilitate – to make easier<br>consecrate – to make or declare sacred |
| *– fy* | to make | magnify – to make larger<br>testify – to make witness |
| *– ile* | pertaining to,<br>capable of | docile – capable of being managed<br>  easily<br>civil – pertaining to a city or state |

| Suffix | Meaning | Example |
|---|---|---|
| *– ism* | belief, ideal | conservationism – ideal of keeping safe |
| | | sensationalism – matter, language designed to excite |
| *– ist* | doer | artist – one who creates art |
| | | pianist – one who plays the piano |
| *– ose* | full of | verbose – full of words |
| | | grandiose – striking, imposing |
| *– osis* | condition | neurosis – nervous condition |
| | | psychosis – psychological condition |
| *– tude* | state | magnitude – state of greatness |
| | | multitude – state of quantity |

# 6. FOREIGN WORDS AND PHRASES

*ad hoc* – Latin – literally, "to this" – for a specific purpose

*ad infinitum* – Latin – literally, "to infinity" – for a long time

*ad nauseum* – Latin – to the point of nausea

*alfresco* – Italian – out of doors, in the open

*alma mater* – Latin – literally "fostering mother" – the school one attended

*ars gratia artis* – Latin – literally, "art for art's sake"

*au naturel* – French – naked, unadorned

*avant-garde* – French – on the cutting edge

*bête noire* – French – literally "black beast" – a minor personal annoyance

*bon vivant* – French – someone who gets great enjoyment from life

*carpe diem* – Latin – literally, "seize the day"

*carte blanche* – French – literally, "white card" – complete freedom

*cause célèbre* – French – an infamous event or scandal

*comme il faut* – French – appropriate

*corpus delecti* – Latin – literally, "body of the crime" – evidence

*coup de grâce* – French – the death blow

*de facto* – Latin – literally, "in fact"

*deus ex machina* – Latin – literally, "god from the machine" – a solution created out of desperation because no plausible one exists

*enfant terrible* – French – an unmanageable child

*ex cathedra* – Latin – literally, "from the chair" – with unquestionable authority

*fait accompli* – French – literally, "accomplished fact"

*faux pas* – French – literally, "false step" – a breach in etiquette or social protocol

*flagrante delicto* – Latin – literally, "with the crime blazing" – caught red handed

*in vino veritas* – Latin – literally, "in wine, truth"

*ipso facto* – Latin – literally, "by the fact itself"

*joie de vivre* – French – literally, "joy of living" – high spirits, enthusiasm

*lingua franca* – Italian – literally, "the Frankish tongue" – a common language between people who do not speak the other's native language

*mea culpa* – Latin – literally, "my fault"

*noblesse oblige* – French – the obligation of those of noble heritage

*prima facie* – Latin – literally, "on the face of it" – at first glance

*quod erat demonstratum* – Latin – literally, "as has been demonstrated" – often abbreviated Q.E.D.

*raison d'être* – French – literally, "reason for being"

*savoir-faire* – French – literally, "to know what to do"

*status quo* – Latin – the current circumstances

***tabula rasa*** – Latin – literally, "erased tablet" – not yet affected by environment

***tempus fugit*** – Latin – literally, "time flies"

***tête-à-tête*** – French – literally, "head to head" – a private conversation

***veni, vidi, vici*** – Latin – literally, "I came, I saw, I conquered"

***verboten*** – German – forbidden

***Zeitgeist*** – German – the mood of the moment

# 7. EXPERTS AND COLLECTORS

**anatomist**—expert in dissection and body parts

**Arabist**—expert in Arabic language and culture

**arachnologist**—spider expert

**arlologist**—expert on primitive people

**astrophysicist**—an expert in astronomy in a branch dealing with the physical and chemical makeup of celestial matter

**bacteriologist**—expert in bacteria in medicine, industry, and agriculture

**botanist**—a specialist in plant life

**discophile**—expert on music that is recorded

**ecumenist**—expert in, or one who practices, principles and practices of religious groups, mostly Christian

**entomologist**—expert in insects

**epidemiologist**—expert in disease incidence, distribution, and control

**gastroenterologist**—expert in stomach diseases

**genealogist**—expert in tracing the descent of people

**ichthyologist**—fish expert

**metallurgist**—expert in the science of metals

**numismatist**—an expert in the study or collection of coins, tokens, and paper money and sometimes related objects (as medals)

**oncologist**—expert in tumors

**ophthalmologist**—expert in the structure, function, and disease of the eye

**ornithologist**—bird expert

**orthodontist**—expert in irregularities of teeth

**parasitologist**—expert in parasites

**pathologist**—expert in the changes caused by disease in tissues and body fluids

**periodontist**—expert in diseases of the supporting and investing teeth structures

**podiatrist**—foot doctor

**teratologist**—expert in the biological study of monsters

**thanatologist**—expert in death

**urologist**—expert in urinary or urogenital tract

**virologist**—expert in viruses

**vulcanologist**—expert in volcanic phenomena

# 8. ANIMAL GROUP NAMES

a herd of antelope, ass, buffalo, camel, cattle, crane, deer, elephant, giraffe, goat, horse

a drove of ass

a pace of ass

a cete of badgers

a sloth of bears

a swarm of bees

a hive of bees

a sounder of boars

a clowder of cats

a cluster of cats

a kindle of young kittens

a drove of cattle

a brood of chickens

a flock of chickens

a murder of crows

a team of ducks in flight

a paddling of ducks in water

a convocation of eagles

a swarm of eels

a gang of elk

a business of ferrets

a charm of finches

a shoal of fish

an army of frogs

a skulk of foxes

a tribe of goats (also flock or herd)

a skein of geese (on the wing; gaggle is on the water)

a convey of grouse (family only)

a pack of grouse (larger numbers)

a colony of gulls

a drove of hare

a trace of hare

a flight of hawk

a siege of heron

a glean of herring

a shoal of herring

a charm of hummingbirds

a band of jays

a troop of kangaroos

an exaltation of larks

a leap of leopards

a shoal of mackerel

a nest of mice

a barren of mules

a rake of mules

a watch of nightingales

a covey of partridges

a muster of peafowl

a nye of young pheasants

a herd of pigs

a school of porpoises

a bevy of quail

an unkindness of ravens

a crash of rhinoceros

a crash, herd, or pod of seals

a host of sparrow

a dray of squirrels

a chattering of starlings

a mustering of stork

a wedge of swans

a sounder of swine

a knot of toads

a rafter of turkeys

a gam of whales

a rout of wolves

a clew of worms

# 9. EUROPEAN HISTORY, 1450–1648

## THE RENAISSANCE, REFORMATION, AND THE WARS OF RELIGION

## THE CHURCH IN THE LATE MIDDLE AGES (1300–1500)

A. The church was a pyramidal organization with believers at the base, then priests, supervised by bishops. The pope ruled over the church and its clergy. Monks, nuns, and friars were also governed by the pope.

B. Papacy – the pope, as leader of the Western church, faced problems which reduced papal prestige and interfered with the church's ability to deal with problems.

1. Criticisms against the papacy were aimed at individuals and church practices but not the idea of the church or Christian beliefs.

   a. Corruption.

   b. Simony – the purchase of church positions.

   c. Pluralism – the holding of more than one office.

2. Critics of the church were often attacked and labeled as heretics. Some major critics were:

   a. John Wycliffe – an English friar, he believed the church should follow only the Scriptures.

   b. John Huss – a Czech priest, led Bohemian followers in their rejection of the pope's authority.

C. Lay persons attempted to find different ways of being pious both inside and outside the institution of the church.

1. Meister Eckhart – German mystic sought union with God through emotion.

2. Thomas à Kempis – German mystic sought direct knowledge of God through inner feelings.

3. Gerard Groote – began a semi-monastic life for lay persons in the low countries guided by Christian principles.

D. Babylonian Captivity – popes were subservient to French kings during this 68-year period and resided in Avignon.

E. Great Schism – two popes were elected; one resided in Rome, the other in France during this 40-year period.

1. The conciliar movement attempted to overcome the problems of two popes and proposed that the church be ruled by bishops, cardinals, abbots, and laity.
   a. Marsiglio of Padua urged that the church be governed by a general council.
   b. Church was reunited under Pope Martin V but failed to reform itself; the pope rejected the conciliar movement.

F. Renaissance popes were, for the most part, patrons of the arts (Jixtus IV and Julius II) but failed to reform the church.

# THE HUNDRED YEARS' WAR (1337–1453)

A. Causes – struggle between England and France over the French duchy of Aquitaine; England's king, Edward III, had a claim to the French throne through his mother, a French princess; French nobles sought power over France's king whose control over the wool trade was growing; kings and nobles on both sides seized the chance to put chivalric values into action.

B. The war, fought on French soil, involved sieges and raids. The French wore down the English invaders.
   1. Major battles of Crecy, Poitiers, and Agincourt were English victories.
   2. Technological advances included the use of the English longbow and stronger French armor for knights.
   3. Joan of Arc rallied the French for several victories, was captured by the French allies of England, and was sold to the English who tried her for heresy. Joan was burned at the stake in 1431.

C. Immediate results of the war –
   1. England lost all French possessions except Calais.
   2. French land was devastated.
   3. France and England spent huge sums of money on war.
   4. Population in France declined.
   5. Trade was disrupted.
   6. Peasants were taxed heavily.

D. Long-term results of the war –
   1. England's parliament became more powerful due to parliamentary approval of taxation.
   2. Nobles gained more power in England.
   3. Factional struggles resulted in England's War of the Roses (1450–1485).
   4. French king retained power, which he refused to share with noble assemblies.

5. Nationalism grew in each country fed by propaganda, hatred of the enemy, and military victories; national literatures expressed in the language of the people arose both in England and France in the works of Chaucer and Villon, respectively.

# HOLY ROMAN EMPIRE IN THE LATER MIDDLE AGES

A. The emperor's power declined in Germany and Italy.
  1. After 1326, seven German electors had the power to name the emperor.
  2. City-states or communes in Italy sought independence from the emperor.
     a. Despots (in Milan and Florence) or oligarchies (in Venice) ruled the city-states.
     b. Large cities came to dominate outlying territories.
B. Hapsburgs ruled the empire after 1272.
  1. Their main interest during this period was to create possessions in Austria and Hungary.
C. Ottoman Turks pressured the empire from their base in Constantinople.
D. Swiss cantons gradually threw off rule by the empire.

# GROWTH OF STRONG MONARCHIES (AFTER 1450)

A. Monarchs faced various challenges to their authority.
  1. Money had to be raised through new taxes.
  2. Nobles sought power over the monarch and other nobles and were often involved in internal conflicts.
  3. Weak kings hindered the growth of royal power.
  4. Noble clergy often sided with fellow nobles against kings.
  5. Newly independent towns were unwilling to obey the royal ruler.
B. Strong monarchies grew in France, England, and Spain.
  1. France defeated England in the Hundred Years' War; duchy of Burgundy was defeated, trade was expanded, Louis XI exerted ruthless control over nobles.
  2. War of the Roses in England wiped out many nobles; royal court controlled nobles via Star Chamber; standard procedures of law and taxation were developed.
  3. Spain was united under Ferdinand and Isabella; Navarre was added to kingdom; Muslims were driven out in 1492; sheep farming was encouraged; cities and towns were organized against nobles; the Inquisition reformed and controlled the church.

# SOCIAL PROBLEMS IN THE LATE MIDDLE AGES

A.  Black Death wiped out 25 to 40 percent of Europe's population by 1350; cities were most affected by the plague because of poor sanitation, overcrowding, and poor nutrition.
B.  Consequences of plague – economic decline, growth of pessimism in population and among intellectuals, anti-Semitism was prevalent.
C.  Decline of population after 1350 resulted in shortage of workers and a rise in wages, an end to serfdom in many places, guilds arose to protect merchants and artisans, trading leagues controlled international, regional trade, enclosures of fields in England forced many farmers off their land.
D.  Peasant revolts resulted as a consequence of higher taxes, a desire for higher wages, and hostility to nobles.
   1.  Peasants' Revolt in England (1381).
   2.  Jacquerie in France (1358).
   3.  Revolt of poor workers in Florence (1378).
   4.  Worker revolts in the low countries, Germany, Spain, and Sicily.

# THE RENAISSANCE (1300–1600)

A.  Began in the Italian city-states of Florence, Venice, Milan, Padua, and Pisa.
   1.  A secular movement.
   2.  Stressed the individual over the group – "man was the measure" of all things.
   3.  Developments were limited to the rich elites.
   4.  Announced the re-awakening or rebirth of interest in the classical past of Greece and Rome; stressed humanism and human abilities in all areas of life.
B.  Causes – Rich Italian merchants had wealth to invest in pursuits of new ideas in art and learning; they became patrons of artists and writers; independent city-states were free of control and could follow their own way in artistic areas; citizens were aware of their ancient past; new ideas entered Italy from the East; princes sought justifications for their wars and conflicts in the past; legalists studied Roman laws to support their disputes with popes and emperors.
C.  Literary Giants – included Dante (*Divine Comedy*), Petrarch (writer of sonnets), Boccaccio (*The Decameron*), and Castiglione (*The Book of the Courtier*).
D.  Art breakthroughs took place in painting, sculpture, and architecture.
   1.  Artists depicted secular themes and employed linear perspectives.
   2.  Sculptors celebrated the human form and non-religious subjects

and copied classical models.

    3. Architects copied classical styles in constructing buildings both religious and secular.

E. Leading Renaissance artists – included Giotto (father of Renaissance painting), Donatello (bronze *David*), Masaccio, Leonardo da Vinci (*Last Supper* and *Mona Lisa*), Raphael, Michelangelo (Sistine Chapel and *David*).

F. Leading Renaissance scholars – included Leonardo Bruni (first to use the term "humanism"), Lorenzo Valla (author of *Elegances of the Latin Language*), Machiavelli (author of *The Prince* and leading political analyst of his day).

## THE RENAISSANCE SPREADS

A. From its base in Italy, the ideas of the Renaissance spread northward and west to the Low Countries, Germany, France, Spain, and England.

    1. Renaissance innovations in Western Europe were made in art, literature, drama, and technology.

        a. Movable type – Gutenberg (1450).

        b. Rabelais' *Gargantua and Pantagruel*.

        c. El Greco's paintings.

        d. Van Eyck, Brueghel, and Rembrandt in painting.

        e. Drama as culminated in the works of Shakespeare.

## CHRISTIAN HUMANISM

A. Thinkers outside Italy focused on using the techniques of the Italian humanists to guide people in their behavior. They emphasized education and the power of the human intellect to bring about moral improvement.

    1. Desiderius Erasmus – most notable Christian humanist; wrote "In Praise of Folly."

    2. Thomas More – wrote *Utopia*.

    3. Jacques Lefeured "Etables" – produced five versions of the Psalms.

    4. Francesco de Cisneros – reformed the Spanish clergy.

## THE REFORMATION 1517–1560

A. Destroyed religion's unity in Europe, spread to England, and resulted in a Counter Reformation on the part of the Catholic church.

B. Abuses in the church led some to question the church's authority in determining the individual's role vis-à-vis God.

C. Martin Luther, an Augustinian friar and teacher, initiated the Reformation in his native Germany.

1. Luther questioned basic teachings of the church and held that salvation was possible only through faith.
2. He attacked the sale of indulgences.
3. He argued that the Bible and not traditions or papal bulls could determine correct religious beliefs.
4. Luther was excommunicated by the pope.
5. Luther wrote extensively about his beliefs and translated the Bible into German.

D. Lutheranism – Luther's teachings had wide impact in Germany and Europe.

1. Peasants revolted in Germany in 1524 and were supported by Luther.
2. Augsburg Confession of 1530 was a statement of Lutheran beliefs.
3. Church lands were often seized in lands where Lutheranism took hold.
4. Germany was divided into two religious camps: Catholic and Lutheran; the religion of a region would be that of the ruler of the region.

E. Other Reformers included Zwingli in Switzerland, Anabaptists in Switzerland and Germany, Calvin in Geneva, Switzerland.

1. Calvinism was noted for its stern and militant stance and its rejection of most of the medieval church's practices and traditions.

F. Church and king break in England – as a result of Henry VIII's divorce of his wife and the king's declaration of his control of the church in England.

1. Edward VI adopted Calvinism.
2. Mary restored Catholicism.
3. Elizabeth I restored Protestant beliefs.
4. The Church of England retained many Catholic practices, rules, and rituals. Many English remained Catholic in private.
5. Some Protestants wanted to purify the church of all Roman Catholic elements. They came to be known as Puritans.

G. Protestantism spreads

1. Landlords and people near Dublin in Ireland became members of the Protestant church.
2. John Knox set up Calvinist-style church in Scotland.
3. Huguenots in France made inroads among the French nobility.

# THE COUNTER REFORMATION

A. Efforts to reform the church included the establishment of new religious orders such as the Society of Jesus, the work of specific popes such as Paul III, the purge of certain abuses such as the sale of church offices, and councils (the Council of Trent) that settled doctrinal issues which had come under attack by Protestants.

## DIFFERENCES BETWEEN CATHOLICISM AND PROTESTANTISM

A. Protestants stressed the role of the Bible, priesthood of all believers, a clergy that preached, and denied the efficacy of some or all of the sacraments.
B. Catholics retained church hierarchy, sacraments, authority of the pope, and belief in good works.

## LONG-TERM RESULTS OF THE REFORMATION

A. Political rulers gained power over the church.
B. Religious enthusiasm grew.
C. Individualism grew.
D. All Christian churches remedied abuses of the clergy.

## WARS OF RELIGION (1560–1648)

A. Catholics and Protestants fought each other in France, the Netherlands, and Germany. They were aided by the use of powerful cannons, well-organized infantry, larger armies, and mercenaries.
  1. Spain vs. the Netherlands – Spain's devout ruler Philip II aimed to make Europe Catholic and led the attack on the Netherlands, ruled by Spain in the 1500s. Calvinists had sought refuge in the Netherlands after fleeing persecution in France.
    a. Sources of Spain's power – gold and silver from the New World and the world's largest navy.
    b. Dutch resisted Spain's attempt to assert a more centralized government on the Dutch provinces and rebelled. They flooded the land to stop the Spanish armies.
    c. Leaders – Spain's Duke of Alva executed Calvinists, imposed new taxes, and established the Inquisition. William of Orange led the Dutch.
    d. Results of the war – two sections of the Netherlands broke up into religious factions – Union of Utrecht (Protestant) and Union of Arras (Catholic); Spain was driven out of the northern Netherlands in the 1590s but retained control of southern provinces called the Spanish Netherlands.
  2. Civil war in France – each French king was a Catholic until 1589

and the monarch was willing to work with Catholics or Calvinists as it suited him.

   a. Nine wars took place between 1562 and 1589; the most bloody event was the St. Bartholomew's Day Massacre of 1572 in which 20,000 Huguenots were killed.

   b. Royal assassinations took place in the late 1500s and Spain intervened with troops to support Catholics in 1590.

   c. Henry of Navarre, a Calvinist, became king in 1589. His conversion to Catholicism helped unite the country. Henry issued the Edict of Nantes in 1589 which extended religious tolerance to Huguenots.

3. England and Spain compete for power – Mary, daughter of Henry VIII, sought to restore Catholicism in England. She married Philip II of Spain and promoted Spain's interests.

   a. Elizabeth I, after an attempt at compromise between Catholics and Protestants, countered moves to place the Catholic Queen of Scotland, Mary, on the throne of England.

   b. England defeated Spain's Armada in 1588 and crushed an attempt to enforce Catholicism on the nation.

4. The Thirty Years' War – Protestants fought Catholics across Europe. In addition, Protestants fought one another for control. Germany suffered major destruction since it was the main battleground and was weakened politically.

   a. Major battles – White Mountain (1620): Calvinist leader, Frederick, was defeated and Bohemia made Catholic; Breitenfeld (1630): Sweden defeats Hapsburgs.

   b. Ferdinand, Holy Roman Emperor, defeated Christian IV of Denmark and established a strong Hapsburg presence in northern Germany.

   c. Results of the war – Treaty of Westphalia (1648) reasserted the principles of the Peace of Augsburg and included the Calvinists; Swiss Confederacy achieved independence from Holy Roman Empire; over 300 German states obtained nearly complete independence from the Holy Roman Empire; Catholic crusade to reunite Europe failed; France entered a time of disunity; realistic political leaders came to dominate monarchies; Spain entered a period of decline.

# THE GROWTH OF THE STATE AND THE AGE OF EXPLORATION

A. Nation-states pursued different political systems: constitutionalism and absolutism in the period after the wars of religion.

    1. Constitutionalism – rules limited government; consent of the governed provided the basis for the legitimacy of the regime.

    2. Absolutism – kingship is often viewed as divine

B. English monarchs – needed support of Parliament to levy taxes.

    1. Charles I – trying to raise money for wars involved him in conflicts with Parliament.

    2. Open war between Charles and Parliament (Cavaliers vs. Roundheads) led to his execution.

    3. 1628 Petition of Right declared illegal the king's actions in raising taxes thus setting a precedent for parliamentary action.

C. French monarchs – proceeded from a France disunited and weakened by wars of religion, the rule of powerful ministers, and the attempts of nobles to control the capital to the absolutism of Louis XIV.

    1. Henry IV – duke of Sully was the strong minister who involved the state in mercantilism.

    2. Louis XIII – real power was held by Cardinal Richelieu.

    3. Louis XIV – Cardinal Mazarin ruled during Louis' minority. By 1652, Louis headed a strong, centralized government with himself at the helm.

D. Other constitutional states

    1. Holland – became a major trading nation under the guidance of the merchant class.

    2. Sweden – became a world power under Gustavus Adolphus while the government was dominated by rich and powerful groups.

E. Explorations and conquests – Europeans sought gold, silver, and spices to fuel their home economies.

    1. English settled North America.

    2. Spanish settled in South America.

    3. African slaves were taken to the Americas.

    4. Explorations by Spain, Portugal, England, and France opened up the New World to colonization.

       a. Portugal – Dias, da Gama, Henry the Navigator.

       b. Spain – Columbus, Magellan, Cortes, Pizarro.

       c. England – Cabot, Drake.

       d. France – Cartier.

    5. English colonies in the New World.

       a. Jamestown – 1607.

       b. Massachusetts Bay – 1620.

    6. Dutch – New Amsterdam.

# SCIENCE, LEARNING, AND SOCIETY

A. Revolutions in science – astronomy and scientific methodologies experienced great advances.
   1. Copernicus – heliocentric theory of universe placed humans in a vast system.
   2. Tycho Brahe – made important observations of the heavens that swept away age-old myths of the unchanging sky.
   3. Johannes Kepler – established the concept of the elliptical orbits of the planets.
   4. Galileo – discovered four moons of Jupiter and expanded the use of the telescope; his support of scientific observations brought him into conflict with the church.
   5. Francis Bacon – formalized empiricism and advocated useful knowledge.
   6. Rene Descartes – formulated analytic geometry and believed scientific laws could be found by deductive reasoning.
B. Results of scientific innovations – experienced throughout society.
   1. Schools of mathematics and physics established in European universities.
   2. Warfare became more precise as a result of mathematical measurements.
   3. Science of medicine employed new thinking to discover workings of human body.
   4. Scientific methods employed by philosophers to develop new ideas.
C. Innovations in Literature – led to masterpieces.
   1. Cervantes – *Don Quixote.*
   2. Shakespeare – drama.
   3. Milton – *Paradise Lost.*
D. Society underwent a change in which two groups of people lived – urban and rural.
   1. Urban societies – mainly merchant and artisan and mobile.
   2. Cities grew at a rapid rate in the 1600s; London and Paris were major cities with populations over 150,000.
   3. Trade increased within Europe and specialization took hold in industries such as textiles.
   4. Governments sought to export manufactures rather than import them thus increasing the need for colonies and world markets.

# 10. EUROPEAN HISTORY, 1648–1789

## INTERNATIONAL RELATIONS

A. Historical Setting in 1648 – Thirty Years War ended, Germany and Central Europe devastated, Bourbon dynasty stronger.
B. Peace of Westphalia (1648) – Dutch and Swiss republics recognized. Sweden, Prussia, France gain new territory.
C. Treaty of the Pyrenees (1659) – Spain cedes part of Spanish Netherlands to France. Louis XIV of France marries daughter of Phillip IV of Spain.
D. War of Devolution (First Dutch War), 1667–68 – Louis XIV claims Spanish Netherlands after death of Phillip IV. Triple alliance formed (England, Holland, Sweden)
    1. Treaty of *Aix-la-Chapelle* (1668) – France receives 12 towns on border, but loses Franche-Comte (Burgundy)
E. Second Dutch War (1672–78) – France invades Holland. Dutch open dikes and flood land to beat French. Peace of Nijmegan grants Holland all territory back.
F. Invasion of the Spanish Netherlands (1683) – France occupies Luxemburg and Lorraine. League of Augsburg formed in response (Holy Roman Empire, Holland, Spain, Sweden, Palatinate, Saxony, Bavaria, Savoy)
G. War of the League of Augsburg (1688–97) – France battles Holland and England on Rhine, in Low Countries, and in Italy.
    1. Treaty of Ryswick (1697) – Captured territories returned, French sovereignty over Alsace and Strasbourg acknowledged.
H. War of the Spanish Succession (1701–13)
    1. The Grand Alliance – England, Holland, Holy Roman Empire, and Prussia support Charles VI and oppose Phillip of Anjou for Spanish throne.
    2. War – Battle of Blenheim prevents French from dominating Europe. French and Spanish drive Allies from Spain and place Phillip on throne.
I. Treaty of Utrecht (1713) – Spanish empire partitioned, Phillip V crowned King, Hapsburgs gain Spanish Netherlands, England gains territory in New World.

J.  War of the Austrian Succession (1740–48) – Frederick the Great invades Silesia. England sides with Hapsburgs against Prussia, Bavaria, France, and Spain. Prussia emerges retains Silesia and emerges as great power.

K.  The Seven Years' War (1756–63) – Austria attempts to regain Silesia with help of France and Russia. Britain sends funds to Prussia.
1.  Treaty of Paris (1763) – France loses all New World possessions to Britain, Spain cedes Florida to Britain

L.  The American War for Independence as a European War, 1775–83 – France and Spain join Americans to regain territories lost to Britain
1.  Treaty of Paris (1783) – Britain recognizes U.S. and retrocedes Florida to Spain, France gets nothing

## ECONOMIC DEVELOPMENTS

A.  Traditional Economic Conditions – Subsistence farming the norm, contagious diseases decimated towns.

B.  Mercantilism – wealth measured in commodities, should increase power of government, favorable balance of trade important, colonies existed for mother country.

C.  Growth of Trade – Route around Africa to Asia discovered and opening of Western Hemisphere.

D.  Agricultural Changes – Growth of absentee landlords and commercial farms. All-metal plows came into widespread use.

E.  Improvements in Transportation – Canal lock invented. All-weather roads constructed.

F.  Industrial Technology – Steam engine developed and improved (1769), textile machines revolutionized industry (flying shuttle, spinning jenny, spinning frame, power loom)

## BEGINNINGS OF MODERN SCIENCE AND AGE OF THE ENLIGHTENMENT

A.  Scientific Revolution – leading figures included
1.  N. Copernicus – discovers planets revolve around Sun.
2.  J. Keppler – discovers orbits of planets are ellipses.
3.  G. Galilei – utilizes telescope, investigates gravity
4.  R. Descartes – develops deductive analysis, leader in math and physics
5.  I. Newton – discovers principle of universal gravitation

B.  Scientific Societies – Royal Observatory (Britain, 1675), Royal Society (Britain, 1662), Academie des Sciences (France, 1666), Berlin Academy of Sciences (Prussia, 1700), St. Petersburg Academy of Sciences (Russia, 1725)

C. The Age of the Enlightenment – secular view of the world, God created then was no longer involved
   1. Rationalists – stressed deductive reasoning or mathematical logic.
   2. Empiricists – inductive reasoning, emphasis on sensory experience.
   3. The Philosophes – teachers and journalists who popularized Enlightenment.
D. The "Counter-Enlightenment" – Diverse and disparate groups who opposed Enlightenment.

# BOURBON FRANCE

A. France Under Louis XIV (1643–1715)
   1. Government of France Under Louis XIV – Aristocracy kept out of government, orders transmitted to provinces by intendants, nullification of all institutions that might challenge Louis. Peasants not farming conscripted into army or workhouses. Growth of French trading companies and merchant marine.
   2. Palace of Versailles – Third of a mile long, 1400 fountains, 60% of taxes put toward upkeep of court and attendants.
   3. Louis XIV's Policies Toward Christianity – Pope has no temporal authority over French Church, Protestants persecuted, many flee to England and Holland.
B. France Under Louis XV (1715–74) – Inherits throne at age five. Leaves the same problems as he inherited.
C. France Under Louis XVI (1774–1792) – sought to make reforms, aristocracy refused to implement, married to M. Antoinette.

# SPAIN: HAPSBURG AND BOURBON

A. Spain in the Seventeenth Century – Continued expulsion of Moors, industry declines, Spanish navy ceased to exist by 1700.
B. Charles II – sick and timid, dies childless which leads to War of Spanish Succession.
C. Philip V (1700–1746) – Modernizes Spanish army, Industry, agriculture, and ship-building revived, his son, Ferdinand VI, rules 1746–59.
D. Charles III (1759–88) – continues to enact reforms, eliminates laws that restrict internal trade. Strongly Catholic, Spanish intellectuals ignore Enlightenment.

# AUSTRIAN HAPSBURG AND CENTRAL EUROPE

A. Government of the Austrian Empire – consists of remnants of Holy Roman Empire, no single constitutional system for all parts.

B. Feudalism in the Hapsburg Empire – lord of manor has absolute control over lives of peasants.

C. Music and Vienna – Leopold I is patron of music. People from around Europe come to Vienna to compose.

D. Emperor Leopold I (1658–1705) – Patron of arts, devout Catholic, drove Turkish army from Austria (1683).

E. Emperor Charles VI (1711– 40) – Takes throne after death of his older brother. Recognizes personal liberties of Hungarians (Treaty of Szatmar).

F. Maria Theresa (1740–80) – Increases army, centralized government of Empire in Austria.

G. Joseph II (1765–1790) – ruled with his mother for first fifteen years, expanded state schools, granted religious tolerance.

# PRUSSIA AND THE HOHENZOLLERN

A. Frederick William (1640–88) – increases army through heavy taxation, build canal to link Elbe and Oder Rivers. Settled Huguenots on his estates.

B. Frederick I (1688–1713) – Founds several universities, encourages intellectuals as well as tradesman to settle in Prussia.

C. Frederick William I (1713–40) – Fourth-largest army in Europe, paid off Prussia's debts, increased treasury, developed most efficient bureaucracy in Europe.

D. Frederick the Great (Frederick II: 1740–86) – Pondered questions of religion, morality, and power; read French poetry. First 23 years of reign spent at war, the second 23 spent rebuilding a population that had doubled in size and increased territory.

# THE DUTCH REPUBLIC

A. Historical Background

B. Government of the Netherlands – consisted of seven provinces, each with Stadholder, national policy decided by delegates from each province.

C. Dutch Economy – lacked government controls and monopolies, greatest mercantile nation in Europe, no natural resources so most income came from finishing raw goods.

D. Dutch Art – Rembrandt, Van Gogh, Vermeer paint scenes of everyday life.

# ENGLAND, SCOTLAND AND IRELAND

A. English Civil War (1642–49) – underlying issue was whether the King could govern without the consent of Parliament.

1. Charles I (1625–49) – Inherits English and Scottish thrones, demands money from Parliament, then forces loans upon wealthier citizens. Imprisons those who refuse to loan king money. Both houses of Parliament oppose king.

2. The Petition of Right (1628) – king bribed with tax grant in exchange for signing Petition of Right which stipulated that no loan or tax could be levied without parliamentary consent, no one could be imprisoned or detained without due process, and soldiers would not be billeted in homes of private citizens.

3. The Parliament of 1629 – King seeks to force adjournment of Parliament, but his messenger is detained and several resolutions were passed, when the messenger finally arrived the king dissolved Parliament (1629–40). Some Puritan leaders were imprisoned.

4. Religious Persecution – Church of England was only legal church under Charles I, others were harshly suppressed.

5. National Covenant of Scotland (1638) – Covenant affirmed loyalty of people to the Crown, but declared the king could not reestablish episcopate over church. Charles orders army into Scotland.

6. War in Scotland – The army leaves Scotland without a fight when faced with a superior force. Scottish granted right to determine constitution for themselves.

7. The Short Parliament – King reconvenes Parliament to vote new taxes to pay for Scottish war. When presented with list of grievances, he again dissolves it.

8. The Scots Invade – Scots invade northern counties and treaty with England leaves things exactly as they were.

9. The Long Parliament – King summons Parliament because he had no money, no army and no support. Trial begins against T. Wentworth, principal minister for the king, for treason against country. Charles signs the execution order fearing Parliament and mob violence.

10. Rebellion in Ireland and the Grand Remonstrance – Irish Catholics murder Protestants. House of Commons votes funds for army, but questions over parliamentary or royal army delays action.

11. The English Civil War Begins – Charles orders impeachment proceedings against leaders of Puritans in House of Commons. Charles arrives with 400 soldiers but is forced back to Hampton Court.

12. The Division of the Country – north and west side with king, east and south side with Parliament. Navy and merchant marine support Parliament.

13. The King Attacks London – King's sizable force takes Oxford, but is driven back from London.

14. Early Stages of the War – Royalist forces won early victories, but began losing ground when Scots persuaded by parliamentary forces to attack from the north. Charles defeated by O. Cromwell at Naseby and becomes fugitive. Surrenders to Scots in May 1646.

15. Controversy Between Parliament and the Army – Army ordered to disband without pay, when they refuse plan is devised to bring Scottish army to remove them. King arrested by the army as he is brought in from Scotland.

16. The Death of the King – Scots invade but are defeated by Cromwell. Charles I was tried and executed.

B. The Commonwealth and the Protectorate (1649–59)

1. The Commonwealth (1649–53) – Parliament institutes a Commonwealth governed by representatives to Parliament. The people, however, were not represented.

2. Opposition to the Commonwealth – Royalists and Presbyterians were against Parliament, army dissatisfied that elections not held. Russia imprisons English merchants, France is openly hostile, Holland allows royalist privateers to refit.

3. Ireland – Cromwell lands in Dublin and massacres Catholic/Protestant coalition at Drogheda. Roman Catholic lands confiscated to pay soldiers.

4. Scotland – Proclaims Charles II king. Scots defeated by Cromwell and army led by Charles II annihilated to almost the last man, Charles flees to France.

5. The Protectorate (1653–59) – When elections were not held, Cromwell took troops to Parliament and dissolved it. New elections were held and Cromwell became Lord Protector. With Cromwell's death, new Parliament elected under old systems.

C. The Restoration (1660–1688)

1. Charles II (1660–85) – New Parliament restores a limited monarchy. Charles agrees to abide by decisions of Parliament.

2. The Convention Parliament (1660) – Pardons given to all but 12 participants of civil war. Royalists allowed to recover their lands in court. Feudalism abolished.

3. The Clarendon Code – Cavalier parliament (1661) attempts to drive Puritans out. Several Acts passed with severe penalties for not following codes set up by Anglican church.

4. Scotland's Independence – Scotland gains independence with return of Charles II. Charles then disregards earlier agreements and begins religious persecution of Presbyterians. In 1666, armed re-

volt began. Charles II dies in 1685.

5. James II (1685–88) – Brother of Charles II. Strong Roman Catholic who sought to return England to Catholicism.

D. The Glorious Revolution of 1688 – Parliament invites William and Mary of Holland to assume the English throne. They do so, James starts to advance on them, then flees to France. William summons free Parliament. The English Bill of Rights was passed as well as several acts providing limited religious freedom.

E. Queen Anne (1702–14) – Weak and ineffective ruler. Does unite England and Scotland into one kingdom.

F. Eighteenth Century England – Monarchs now ruled as Kings-in-Parliament, which meant that support of Parliament was necessary for actions to be taken. In 1690, William lands in Ireland to put down rebellion started by James II. Scots offer throne to William and Mary in exchange for recognition as Presbyterian. James's son and grandson both attempted to incite Scottish Highlanders to rebellion and both were beaten.

## SCANDINAVIA

A. Swedish Empire – Baltic and German provinces too difficult to defend and were eventually lost.

B. Political Situation – after death of Gustavus Adolphus government ruled by oligarchy of the nobility. Brief return to absolute monarchy with Gustavus III, until his assassination (1792).

C. Scandinavian Relationships – Finland part of Swedish empire, and Norway was part of Denmark.

D. Denmark – Frederick III (1648–70) becomes absolute ruler, Frederick IV (1699–1730) fights in war with Russia against Sweden. Christian VII allows more civil liberties and economic freedoms.

## RUSSIA OF THE ROMANOVS

A. Background to 17th Century – Ivan the IV (1533–84) begins westernizing Russia, his death preceded by power struggles.

B. The Romanov Dynasty – Estates General elect M. Romanov as Czar. Annexes Ukraine (1654), westernization continues, many Westerners brought into Russia to train Russians.

C. Peter the Great (1682–1725) – Seven feet tall with great strength and boundless energy. Great drive to modernize Russia. Visits Europe in disguise to learn techniques and cultures. Sends many technicians and craftsmen back to Russia. Treaty of Nystad with Sweden grants Russia Livonia and Estonia. Builds St. Petersburg.

D. 18th Century Russian Czars after Peter the Great – ruled by one family member after the next from 1725–1762, until Catherine II takes over and continues to modernize Russia and annexes Crimea.

## ITALY AND THE PAPACY

A. The Papacy – Church loses influence over matters of state due to growth of Enlightenment and an inability of Papal leadership to counter anti-clerical feelings.
B. 17th and 18th Century Italy
1. Independent Italian States – Italy consisted of numerous independent states, most controlled by foreign powers.
2. Savoy – only state with native Italian dynasty. In 1713, awarded Sicily which it exchanged with Austria for Sardinia.

## THE OTTOMAN TURKISH EMPIRE IN EUROPE

A. Turkish Decline 17th and 18th Centuries – government finance based on spoils of war, tributes and sales of office.
B. Mohammedan IV (1648–1687) – Attempted to take Vienna, routed after arrival of Polish army.
C. Mustapha II (1695–1703) – Loses Hungary and Transylvania to Austria.
D. Ahmed III (1703–1730) – gained port of Azov in Black Sea after defeating Peter the Great (1711), lost Serbia and Belgrade to Austria (1718), abdicates in face of rebellion.
E. Mahmud I (1730–1754) – Russia regains Azov (1737), but Austria loses Belgrade, political governors begin to become independent of sultan.
F. Abdul Hamid I (1774–1789) – Catherine the Great of Russia forces Turks to surrender Crimea, Austria retakes Belgrade (1789).

## CULTURE OF THE BAROQUE AND ROCOCO

A. Age of the Baroque (1600–1750) – emphasized grandeur, spaciousness, unity, and emotional impact.
1. Baroque Architecture – G. Bernini creates colonnade for piazza of St. Peter's Basilica, Palace at Versailles designed on symmetry and balance.
2. Baroque Art – Peter Paul Rubens, Flemish painter.
3. Baroque Music – A. Vivaldi, G. Handel
B. Rococo – emphasizes elegance, pleasantness, more sentimental than emotional. Compositions of F. Haydn and W. A. Mozart contain characteristics.

# 11. UNITED STATES HISTORY, 1789–1841

## THE FEDERALIST ERA (1789–1800)

A. George Washington and John Adams elected in 1789 and again in 1792, with predominantly Federalist Congress.
   1. Judiciary Act of 1789 created Supreme Court and system of district and appeals courts.
   2. Executive departments created—state, treasury, war, attorney-general—became nucleus of cabinet.
   3. Bill of Rights, first ten amendments, adopted in 1791.
B. Treasury Secretary Hamilton presented his "Report on Manufacturers" and "Report on the Public Credit," outlining his program to build a strong central government and an economy based on industry and commerce. Jefferson opposed this program.
C. Emergence of Political Parties
   1. Hamilton supporters, Federalists, favored strong central government, "loose" interpretation of Constitution, and encouragement of business and urbanism.
   2. Jefferson and Madison's Republicans wanted small government, "strict" interpretation, and development of an agrarian, rural society.
D. Foreign Affairs
   1. French Revolutionary Wars (1792) prompted a Proclamation of Neutrality, but we traded with both sides.
   2. Jay Treaty (1794) with Britain settled few issues, but bought time for us.
   3. Pinckney Treaty (1795) with Spain opened the Mississippi River to American traffic and settled the northern boundary of Florida.
E. Battle of Fallen Timbers (1794) – Anthony Wayne defeated the British-backed Indians and cleared the Ohio territory
F. Whiskey Rebellion (1794) – Federal response in crushing the protest to the new whiskey tax strengthened credibility of the central government.
G. Election of 1796 – Adams and Jefferson elected. Split ticket produced conflict-ridden administration.
   1. XYZ Affair – French tried to bribe American diplomats. Anti-French sentiment surged at home.

2. Quasi-war with France (1798–1799) – Department of the Navy created to defend American shipping.

3. Alien and Sedition Acts promoted by Adams to suppress dissent and the growing power of Republican opposition.

4. Kentucky and Virginia Resolves – Jefferson and Madison protested the Alien and Sedition Acts by proposing a process of nullification of unpopular laws by injured states.

# THE JEFFERSONIAN ERA (1801–1825)

A. The Revolution of 1800 saw Jefferson elected president by the House, after electoral confusion with vice-presidential nominee Aaron Burr.
   1. Conflict with the courts – Adams' Judiciary Act of 1801 packed the court system with last-minute Federalist appointees.
      a. *Marbury v. Madison* – Marshall's court failed to seat Adams' appointee, and thus declared the right of judicial review for the court.
   2. Twelfth Amendment (1804) corrected the flaw in the electoral process.
B. Louisiana Purchase (1803)
   1. Napoleon's ambitions for a New World Empire died in Santo Domingo, and he was ready to sell.
   2. Jefferson violated his own "strict interpretation" stand and paid $15 million, doubling U.S. territory.
   3. Lewis and Clark were soon mapping the new lands (1804–1806); Zebulon Pike and others were also exploring the West.
C. The Burr Conspiracy
   1. Aaron Burr killed Hamilton in a duel. He became involved in a scheme to seize Texas from Mexico. Charged with treason in 1806.
   2. The Burr trial ended in acquittal, frustrating Jefferson's demands for "executive privilege" and helping to establish the guidelines for treason prosecutions.
D. Foreign Relations
   1. Barbary Wars ended in a stalemate.
   2. Napoleonic Wars drew America into conflict because we tried to trade with both sides.
   3. Chesapeake-Leopard Affair (1807) involved British violation of our neutrality at sea.
   4. Embargo of 1807 was Jefferson's attempt to stay out of war by shutting off all trade with Europe. Economic disaster.
E. Madison's Administration (1809–1817)
   1. Non-Intercourse Act and Macon's Bill No. 2 tried to regulate trade with Britain and France and avoid war.

2. Indian problems on the frontier were exploited by British.
3. War Hawks convinced Madison to ask Congress for a declaration of war in 1812.
4. In the North, U.S. invasion of Canada failed. The battle of Lake Erie in 1813 was an American victory, as was the battle of the Thames in Canada.
5. Battle of Horseshoe Bend (Alabama) (1814) put Andrew Jackson into the public eye.
6. British invasion of Chesapeake Bay was stopped at Fort McHenry, Baltimore, after Washington, D.C. was burned.
7. At New Orleans, January 1815, Jackson defeated the British, two weeks after the Treaty of Ghent was signed, restoring the prewar political status quo.
8. Hartford Convention (1814) – New England Federalists met and threatened secession if their commercial interests were not protected. This discredited the Federalists.

F. Monroe's Administration (1817–1825)
1. Known as the "Era of Good Feelings."
2. Rush-Bagot Treaty (1817) – A disarmament agreement to demilitarize the Great Lakes.
3. Adams-Onis Treaty (1819) – Spain sold Florida to the U.S.
4. Monroe Doctrine (1823) – Declared that the Western Hemisphere was closed to European colonization.

# INTERNAL DEVELOPMENT – POST–WAR OF 1812

A. The Marshall Court
1. Chief Justice John Marshall built the power of the central government and the Court.
   a. *Marbury v. Madison* (1803) – Established the right of the Court to rule on constitutionality of federal laws.
   b. *Fletcher v. Peck* (1810) – Court declared a state law constitutional.
   c. *Trustees of Dartmouth College v. Woodward* (1819) – Upheld the sanctity of contracts against state action.
   d. *McCulloch v. Maryland* (1819) – Established federal immunity from states' taxing power.
   e. *Gibbons v. Ogden* (1824) – Established federal control over interstate commerce.

B. The Missouri Compromise (1820)
1. Missouri's application for statehood raised the issue of slavery's extension into the territories.
2. Henry Clay's compromise admitted Missouri as a slave state, bal-

anced with free Maine, but drew a line to the Pacific Coast, limiting the extension of slavery.

C. The Economy
1. The Northeast, the South, and the new West were all booming, but following different tracks of development.
2. Immigration increased, as well as migration to the West which consisted of small farms.
3. The Cotton Kingdom was expanding into the new Gulf states.
4. Roads and canals were expanding, creating a national market.
5. The factory system was growing, built on textiles and Eli Whitney's interchangeable parts.
6. Unions developed very slowly.

D. Education
1. Public schools were slow to develop. Most schools were private and expensive.
2. Higher education was limited to private, usually church-related, male-dominated colleges. Professional schools were scarce.
3. Noah Webster's speller and the Bible formed the basis for literacy.
4. Washington Irving, Mercy Otis Warren, and "Parson" Weems were well-known authors.

E. Religion
1. The Second Great Awakening was a response to the secular influence of the Enlightenment and the Scientific Revolution. Revivals began in the South and swept across the nation, helping to spark the movement for reform.
2. Peter Cartwright was a prominent preacher in this movement.

## JACKSONIAN DEMOCRACY (1829–1841)

A. Election of 1824 went to the House, even though Andrew Jackson had the largest popular vote. John Quincy Adams won the election, and Jackson vowed revenge, claiming a "corrupt bargain" with Henry Clay. The Tariff of Abominations (1828), which imposed high import duties, was bitterly denounced by the South.

B. Election of 1828
1. Jackson elected handily on the Democratic ticket after a dirty campaign on both sides.
2. Jackson perceived as a "man of the people," promoted the spoils system and exercised his veto freely.

C. Indian Removal Act (1830) provided for the removal of all Indian tribes to lands west of the Mississippi River. Many tribes resisted, and the Cherokee "Trail of Tears" was one result.

D. Webster-Hayne Debate (1830) saw Senate arguments over federal land policy move into debate over the slavery issue in the territories.

E. Nullification Threat – John C. Calhoun resigned the vice presidency and drew up an Ordinance of Nullification, proposing a process by which a state could ignore a distasteful federal law. Jackson's response was the Force Bill, by which he threatened to enforce the tariff with the army. Calhoun backed down.

F. The Bank War – Jackson distrusted the U.S. Bank and vetoed its charter renewal. He then removed the government deposits and put them into his "pet banks," precipitating a recession. In 1836 his Specie Circular plunged the country into a long-term depression.

G. The Election of 1836 saw Martin Van Buren, Jackson's choice, take the presidency.

H. The Election of 1840 saw the first Whig president, William Henry Harrison, win with a "log cabin" appeal to the common man. He died within a month, and John Tyler took over.

I. Jacksonian Politics
  1. The beginnings of the modern party system, with its organization, platform, and conventions.
  2. The strong executive dominating his party
  3. New emphasis on states rights – Charles River Bridge Case (1837) – Returned the commerce power to the states, if in the public interest.
  4. The rise of the Whigs, with their support of commercial and industrial development, led by Clay, Calhoun, and Daniel Webster.
  5. Alexis de Tocqueville published his *Democracy in America* in 1835, giving us our most insightful contemporary look at America of the period.

# ANTE-BELLUM CULTURE

A. The Reform Impulse
  1. Sources were in European Romanticism and in the desire for control over the changing social scene.
  2. Centered in New England
B. Examples of the Movement
  1. Literature
      a. Northern writers: James F. Cooper, Walt Whitman, Henry W. Longfellow, Herman Melville, Francis Parkman, Nathaniel Hawthorne
      b. Southern writers: Edgar Allen Poe, William Gilmore Simms
  2. Fine Arts
      a. Painters: Hudson River School, George Catlin's Indians, John J. Audubon's birds

     b. Theater and minstrel shows
  3. Transcendentalists tried to gain unity with God outside organized religion – Ralph Waldo Emerson, Henry David Thoreau (Walden)
  4. Utopians tried to escape the industrial world by retreating to communal life.
     a. Secular communities: Brook Farm (Mass.), New Harmony (Indiana), Nashoba (Tenn.), Amana (Iowa)
     b. Religious communities: the Shakers, the Mormons (Joseph Smith and Brigham Young)

C. Political Reform Movements
  1. Temperance movement began in 1826; had strong anti-Catholic overtones.
  2. Public schools were scattered, Protestant-oriented, mostly Northern. Much early opposition. Horace Mann in Massachusetts was early advocate; Henry Barnard in Connecticut.
  3. Feminism had origins in the Seneca Falls meeting, 1848, and was linked with abolitionists (Elizabeth Cady Stanton).
  4. Abolitionism originated with William Lloyd Garrison's "The Liberator" (1831) and his New England Anti-Slavery Society (1832).
     a. Theodore Weld, Frederick Douglass
     b. The Liberty Party fielded a presidential candidate in 1840.

D. Educating the Public
  1. The age of oratory, patriotic holiday speeches
  2. Newspapers and magazines multiplied ("Godey's Ladies Book").
  3. Colleges sprang up from religious roots or local "boosterism."
  4. The Lyceum movement

# LIFE IN THE NORTH

A. Population Trends
  1. Total population grew from 4 million in 1790 to 32 million in 1860. The greatest increase was in the new West.
  2. Birth rate decreased along with family size. "Cult of Domesticity" shifted family rearing to the woman.
  3. Immigration increased after 1815, mostly from Britain, Germany, and Ireland.

B. Urban Growth
  1. Five-fold increase in urban population from 1790–1860.
  2. Services and quality of life lagged. Social unrest and crime.
  3. Anti-Catholic sentiments widespread.

C. Minorities
  1. Women limited in economic and political participation. Sojourner Truth and Lucretia Mott traveled and spoke for women's rights.

2. Blacks were at the bottom of the ladder, threatened by immigrant labor and legal discrimination. African Methodist Episcopal Church flourished in the cities.

D. Industry grew rapidly. The Northeast led the way, producing two-thirds of manufactured goods.
   1. Technology was ahead of Europe – Eli Whitney's interchangeable parts, Elias Howe's sewing machine, Samuel F. B. Morse's telegraph.
   2. Corporate form of ownership grew apace.
   3. Labor began to organize, worked for 10-hour day. Immigration spurred unions but weakened their bargaining position.

E. Agriculture increased in profitability as cities grew
   1. Technology was applied to farming, as in McCormick's reaper, John Deere's steel plow, and Case's thresher.
   2. Specialization and large-scale production equipped farmers for the international market.

F. Transportation – The railroad was assuming importance by 1840. Most lines ran east and west, tying the Atlantic coast to the Pacific coast.

G. Domestic life was still primitive for the rural or urban working man. Wage-earners first exceeded the self-employed in 1860.

# LIFE IN THE SOUTH

A. The Cotton Kingdom
   1. Population and economic power shifted to the newly opened Gulf states, for cotton cultivation.
   2. By 1850, 3 million bales annually, for two-thirds of the value of U.S. exports.

B. Class Society
   1. Planter class (50+ slaves) were the minority, but they dominated social and political life.
   2. One-half of slave-owning families owned fewer than six slaves.
   3. Yeoman farmers were the largest group, owned few or no slaves. They grew corn and foodstuffs, and raised pigs.
   4. Poor whites ("crackers") formed an underclass.

C. The Slave System
   1. Gang system used in lower South for staple crops. Hardest on the workers.
   2. Task system used on smaller farms. Much less oppressive for the workers.
   3. Domestic servants had it best, but more often exploited personally.
   4. Urban slaves often worked for wages, sometimes in industry. They were seen as threats to the stability of the system, so numbers

decreased.

D. The Slave Trade – Importation was illegal after 1808, but internal trade flourished. Movement was toward the new Gulf states from the old upper South.

E. The Response of Slaves
   1. Treatment varied but most probably enjoyed adequate nutrition and shelter.
   2. Rebellions were fairly frequent. Gabriel Prosser (1800), Denmark Vesey (1822), and Nat Turner (1831) were best known.
   3. Running away was a frequent solution, and many succeeded. Harriet Tubman helped 300 to escape.
   4. "Soldiering," avoiding work, was the most popular form of resistance.
   5. Black culture survived, family ties were strengthened in some cases, in the face of oppression.

F. Commerce and Industry
   1. The South developed an industrial base, but lagged far behind the North.
   2. Textiles, iron goods, and flour milling were profitable.
   3. Most were consumed locally; very little exported.
   4. Commerce was limited to the needs of the planters. Factors served as merchants and bankers.
   5. Some Southerners advocated change (DeBow's "Review") but were unheeded. The social system was built on the agrarian model, and cotton was profitable.

G. Domestic life
   1. The plantation wife served a vital role in running the farms.
   2. High birth and death rates
   3. Education was only available to the sons of the well-to-do. Few public schools.
   4. Average living conditions inferior to the North. Dietary deficiencies common.

H. Response to the Anti-Slavery Movement
   1. Dissent was suppressed in the South.
   2. After 1832, political discussion of emancipation ceased.
   3. Southern Congressmen imposed the "Gag Rule" in the U.S. House in 1836.
   4. John C. Calhoun's theory of the "concurrent majority" tried to preserve Southern power.

# MANIFEST DESTINY AND WESTWARD EXPANSION

A. Lewis and Clark Expedition opened the new West to traders, trappers, and settlers.

B. The Oregon country was jointly occupied by Britain and the U.S. by 1820. The Oregon Trail was carrying thousands west by the 1840s.

C. Texas had welcomed American settlers since 1820, and by 1835, 35,000 "gringos" were living there.

   1. In 1836, Texans declared independence from Mexico.

   2. Santa Anna tried to put down rebellion.

   3. After the loss of the Alamo, Sam Houston defeated Mexican army at San Jacinto, April 1836.

   4. U.S. Congress refused to annex Texas because of the slavery issue, so Texans formed an independent nation.

D. California was receiving increasing American immigration.

E. The Sante Fe Trail was opening up American trade with the Southwest.

F. Canadian boundary with Maine came under dispute over timber rights. The Aroostook War settled nothing, but produced the Webster-Ashburton Agreement with Britain in 1842, establishing the present boundary.

G. "Manifest Destiny," the belief that Americans should own land to the Pacific, divided the nation further. Democrats favored the use of force to expand; the Whigs were more conservative. The question of whether slavery would "follow the flag" became increasingly divisive.

# 12. UNITED STATES HISTORY, 1841–1877

## TYLER, POLK, AND THE WESTWARD EXPANSION

A. Tyler's Presidency
   1. Rejection of Whig program for national bank, high tariffs, and internal improvements leads to president's expulsion from party and attempted impeachment
   2. Before resigning from Tyler's cabinet, Secretary of State D. Webster negotiates Webster-Ashburton Treaty with Great Britain settling Canada-Maine boundary dispute
   3. Treaty annexing Republic of Texas rejected for being too pro-slavery
   4. Texas admitted to Union (1845) by joint resolution requiring only majority vote
B. Polk's Presidency
   1. Negotiates revenue-only tariff and establishes sub-treasury system that lasts until 1920
   2. Negotiates Oregon Treaty (1846) extending northern U.S. border westward to Pacific Ocean, thus splitting the Oregon Territory and avoiding war with Great Britain
   3. Westward migration of Americans to Oregon and California dwarfed by Mormon migration to what is now Utah—war over polygamy ends in Mormon defeat
   4. Causes of conflict between U.S. and Mexico
      a. Influx of Americans into Mexican territory
      b. Failure of Mexican government to protect property of American settlers
      c. Mexican resentment over Texas annexation
      d. Dispute over southern boundary of Texas
   5. Events of Mexican War (1846–1848)
      a. Americans divided over war—many in favor believe in America's destiny to spread freedom; many oppose war as conspiracy to expand slave territory; H. D. Thoreau, jailed for refusing to pay taxes to support war, writes "Civil Disobedience"
      b. Polk adopts three-prong strategy
         1) Westward land attack through New Mexico and into Cali-

fornia led by S. W. Kearny
   2) Naval attack on Monterey and subsequent capture of California
   3) Southward land attack into Mexico—Americans capture Mexico City (1847)
 c. Treaty of Guadalupe-Hidalgo (1848) increases U.S. territory by one-third, sets Texas-Mexico boundary at Rio Grande, and focuses attention on issue of slavery in the new territories

# AMERICA AT MID-CENTURY

A. Political Developments
 1. Wilmot Proviso prohibiting slavery in land acquired from Mexico passes House but is repeatedly rejected by Senate
 2. Differing points of view on issue of slavery in the territories
   a. Southern position, expressed by J. Calhoun, that Congress has no right to prohibit slavery
   b. Abolitionist position that Congress does have right to prohibit slavery
   c. Compromise position to extend 36°30' line of Missouri Compromise westward to Pacific
   d. Compromise position, favored by S. Douglas and known as popular sovereignty, that territory's residents should decide issue
 3. Election of 1848 won by Z. Taylor
 4. Anti-slavery Whigs and Democrats form Free Soil party
 5. Discovery of gold at Sutter's Mill leads to huge influx of gold-seekers into California, which petitions for admission to the Union as a free state in 1849, bypassing territorial stage
 6. Compromise of 1850
   a. Introduced by H. Clay
   b. Gains for North
     1) Admission of California as free state
     2) New Mexico to receive land in dispute between itself and Texas
     3) Mexican Cession outside of California to decide slavery issue by popular sovereignty
     4) Slave trade prohibited in District of Columbia
   c. Gains for South
     1) Enactment of tougher Fugitive Slave Law
     2) Federal government to assume Texas debt of $10 million
     3) Congress to have no control over interstate slave trade
     4) Congress to promise not to abolish slavery in District of Columbia

       d. Eight-month-long debate led by Clay, Webster, and Calhoun

       e. Death of Compromise opponent President Taylor and work of S. Douglas leads to adoption of Compromise

   7. Decline of existing two-party system

       a. Whig party, divided along north-south lines, loses 1852 election and falls apart

       b. Know-Nothing party develops out of nativist fears over German and Irish immigration—anti-Catholic as well as anti-foreign—becomes second-largest party in 1855 but then declines because it ignores slavery issue

**B. Economic Developments**

   1. Naval expedition by Commodore M. Perry opens Japan to U.S. trade

   2. President F. Pierce acquires Gadsden Purchase from Mexico (1854) to obtain land for southern route for transcontinental railroad

   3. U.S. railroad mileage grows ten-fold between 1840 and 1860, helping to create a nationwide market

   4. Water transportation develops with rise of steamboat on inland waterways and clipper ship on high seas

   5. Textile industry leads spread of mechanization

   6. Cotton surges as South's main crop

   7. Labor-saving machines such as McCormick's reaper help spread agriculture from Middle Atlantic states to Midwest

# THE COMING OF THE CIVIL WAR

**A. Continuing Sources of Tension**

   1. New Fugitive Slave Law not only denies trial by jury and due process of law to northern blacks claimed by slave catchers but also requires Northerners to assist slave catchers; some northern states experience protest riots and pass personal liberty laws that antagonize Southerners

   2. Harriet Beecher Stowe's *Uncle Tom's Cabin*, presenting evils of slavery, becomes best-seller in North

**B. Troubles in Kansas**

   1. Kansas-Nebraska Act (1854) repeals Missouri Compromise prohibiting slavery in area

   2. Northern Democrats, former Whigs and Know-Nothings form Republican party based on opposition to slavery in the territories

   3. Northerners send anti-slavery settlers to Kansas while Southerners send pro-slavery settlers

4. Large-scale election fraud leads to establishment of pro-slavery territorial government in Kansas
5. Free-soil Kansans form own government
6. Guerrilla warfare between two sides erupts
7. Violence spills over into Congress where southerner P. Brooks severely beats northerner C. Sumner for anti-slavery speech

C. The 1856 Election
   1. Southerners threaten to secede if Republican J. Fremont wins
   2. Democrat J. Buchanan wins but Republican party shows great strength

D. Dred Scott Case
   1. Slave Dred Scott sues for freedom on grounds that his owner took him into a free state
   2. U.S. Supreme Court rules that residence in a free state does not make a slave free and that Congress cannot exclude slavery from any territory

E. More Troubles in Kansas
   1. Fraudulently chosen convention at Lecompton approves pro-slavery constitution
   2. Free-soilers submit anti-slavery constitution to Congress
   3. Senate approves Lecompton constitution but House insists on state-wide referendum
   4. Kansas voters reject Lecompton constitution

F. Lincoln-Douglas Debates
   1. Illinois senatorial candidates S. Douglas and A. Lincoln hold seven debates on slavery
   2. Lincoln argues that Douglas does not recognize slavery as being morally wrong
   3. Douglas, who opposed Lecompton constitution, argues that democracy does not require having a moral standard about slavery; accuses Lincoln of favoring racial equality and race mixing
   4. Lincoln challenges Douglas to reconcile popular sovereignty with Dred Scott decision
   5. Douglas' "Freeport Doctrine" asserts that voters can get around Dred Scott decision by refusing to pass special laws to protect slavery
   6. Douglas wins re-election but alienates South
   7. Lincoln gains national attention as potential Republican candidate for president

G. Additional Sources of Tension
   1. John Brown's Raid
      a. Brown and 18 followers seize federal arsenal at Harpers Ferry

and attempt to start slave uprising
  b. Brown captured, tried, and hanged for treason
  c. Many Northerners consider Brown a martyr
  d. Southerners, frightened by northern reaction, see separate southern confederacy as only way to prevent future slave uprisings
  2. North Carolinian Hinton Rowan Helper's *The Impending Crisis in the South* argues that slavery is economically harmful to South and enriches large planters at expense of yeoman farmers
H.  The 1860 Election
  1. Democratic party splits
    a. Northern wing nominates S. Douglas on platform of popular sovereignty
    b. Southern wing nominates J. Breckenridge on platform of federal slave code in territories
    c. Constitutional Union party nominates J. Bell on platform of enforcing laws
  2. Republican party nominates A. Lincoln on platform of no further expansion of slavery
  3. Voters vote along sectional lines
  4. Lincoln, with plurality but not majority of popular votes, leads in electoral votes and becomes sixteenth president
I.  The Secession Crisis
  1. South Carolina secedes from Union on Dec. 20, 1860
  2. By Feb. 1, 1861, six more states (Alabama, Florida, Georgia, Louisiana, Mississippi, and Texas) follow suit
  3. Seven seceded states organize Confederate States of America with J. Davis as president
  4. Confederate constitution recognizes slavery, prohibits protective tariffs, and recognizes state sovereignty; president to serve for single, non-renewable six-year term and to have item veto in appropriation bills
J.  Fort Sumter
  1. Lincoln urges southern states to reconsider secession; vows to hold federal forts in South
  2. Confederates attack and capture Fort Sumter in harbor of Charleston, South Carolina
  3. Lincoln calls for volunteers to put down southern insurrection
  4. Four more slave states (Arkansas, North Carolina, Tennessee, and Virginia) secede
  5. Remaining slave states of Delaware, Kentucky, Maryland, and Missouri stay in Union

# THE CIVIL WAR

A. Relative Strengths
   1. Northern advantages
      a. Much richer than South and better able to finance war
      b. Much more industrialized than South and better able to manufacture weapons and other supplies
      c. Three times more populous than South
      d. Control of U.S. Navy enables North to blockade southern ports
      e. Advanced railroad system enables North to move men and supplies easily
   2. Southern advantages
      a. Large area makes conquest difficult
      b. Southern soldiers familiar with terrain and psychologically "up" to defend homes and families
      c. Defensive fighting at that time easier than offensive fighting
      d. Large number of highly qualified senior officers, such as R. E. Lee and J. E. Johnston, from U.S. Army
B. Early Battles
   1. First Battle of Bull Run (called First Manassas in South) (1861) forces Union army back to Washington, D.C.; shows war will be long
   2. North sets up increasingly successful naval blockade of South
   3. Naval forces under D. Farragut capture New Orleans (1862)
   4. Peninsula Campaign (1862)—G. McClellan advances toward Richmond but is forced to retreat by R. E. Lee and T. "Stonewall" Jackson
   5. Second Battle of Bull Run (1862)—Lee defeats J. Pope
   6. U.S. Grant captures Forts Henry and Donelson and most of the Mississippi River
C. Campaign for European Intervention
   1. South bans cotton exports in attempt to obtain British intervention on South's behalf
   2. Britain develops alternative sources of cotton in India and Egypt
   3. Britain more dependent on wheat imports from North than on cotton imports from South
   4. British public opinion opposes slavery
   5. Pushed by northern diplomacy, Britain and other European nations remain neutral
D. The War at Sea
   1. Captain C. Wilkes stops British ship *Trent* and removes Confederate emissaries; Lincoln releases envoys and smooths matters over

2. South develops ironclad ship—C.S.S. *Virginia*, built over hulk of U.S.S. *Merrimac*, destroys two wooden Union warships before being defeated by Union ironclad U.S.S. *Monitor*

E. The Home Front
   1. Homestead Act of 1862 gives 160 acres of free land to anyone farming it for five years; leads to settlement of much of West
   2. Morrill Land Grant Act of 1862 gives free land to states for "agricultural and mechanical" colleges—predecessors of many state universities
   3. North and South institute conscription
      a. Northerners avoid draft by paying $300 or hiring substitute
      b. Hundreds killed in anti-draft riots in New York City
      c. South exempts one overseer for every 20 slaves
      d. Large-scale draft-dodging and desertion by non-slaveholding southerners
   4. Shortages of food and other consumer goods in South lead to "bread riot" in Richmond
   5. Difficulties of financing war
      a. North institutes nation's first income tax, raises tariffs, issues unbacked currency known as "greenbacks," and expands credit
      b. South issues paper money that becomes almost worthless, prices skyrocket, impressment policy means virtual confiscation of livestock and food
   6. Questions of constitutional authority
      a. Lincoln suspends *habeas corpus* and jails suspected secessionists in Maryland without charges or trials
      b. J. Davis hampered by states' rights emphasis of many Confederate governors
   7. Lincoln issues Emancipation Proclamation (1863) freeing slaves in Confederacy

F. Later Battles
   1. Lincoln removes McClellan after he fails to destroy Lee at Battle of Antietam (known as Sharpsburg in South)
   2. A. Burnside, who replaces McClellan, is defeated at Fredricksburg
   3. J. Hooker, who replaces Burnside, is defeated at Chancellorsville, where T. Jackson is shot by his own men
   4. G. Meade, who replaces Hooker, defeats Lee at Gettysburg (July 1–3, 1863)
   5. Grant captures Vicksburg and Port Hudson and gains complete control of Mississippi River—named overall commander of Union forces in West
   6. Grant wins at Chattanooga—named commander of all Union armies

7. Sherman captures Atlanta—marches through Georgia to Savannah and into Carolinas; destruction of railroads, buildings, and farms in his path designed to show southerners that they cannot win war

8. Lee surrenders to Grant at Appomattox (April 9, 1865)

G. Lincoln assassinated on April 14 by pro-southern actor John Wilkes Booth while watching a play

# RECONSTRUCTION

A. Developments Under Lincoln
1. Establishment of Freedmen's Bureau (1865) to provide food, clothing, and education to recently freed slaves
2. Lincoln's Ten Percent Plan
   a. Provides that governments can be formed in former Confederate states as soon as ten percent of 1860 voters take loyalty oath to Union and accept end of slavery
   b. Arkansas, Louisiana, and Tennessee meet requirements but Congress refuses to recognize their governments
3. Wade-Davis Bill calls for oath saying person has never been disloyal to Union—designed to give blacks right to vote; Lincoln pocket vetoes bill

B. Developments Under Johnson
1. Follows Lincoln's approach but requires ratification of Thirteenth Amendment abolishing slavery; recommends that blacks receive right to vote
2. Most southern states reject Johnson's requirements; pass Black Codes restricting former slaves
3. Radical Republicans in Congress exclude southern representatives, pass Civil Rights Act, and extend powers of Freedmen's Bureau; Johnson vetoes bills but Congress overrides
4. Congress approves Fourteenth Amendment that reduces Congressional representation of states denying blacks right to vote
5. Military Reconstruction Act divides South into five districts to be ruled by military governors
6. Southern states told to give blacks right to vote and to ratify Fourteenth Amendment before being readmitted into Union
7. Tenure of Office Act forbids president from dismissing cabinet members without Senatorial approval
8. Johnson dismisses Secretary of War E. Stanton and is impeached in House but avoids being removed in Senate by one vote

C. Foreign Developments Under Johnson
1. Pressures France to withdraw troops from Mexico and supports Mexican revolutionary leader Benito Juárez

    2. Purchases Alaska from Russia

D. Post-War Life in South
    1. Economic difficulties—one out of ten men killed, great loss of capital, sharp drop in property values
    2. Corruption in Reconstruction governments
    3. Rise of Ku Klux Klan aimed at keeping blacks and white Republicans from voting

E. Developments Under Grant
    1. Approval by southern states of Fifteenth Amendment giving blacks right to vote
    2. Extensive government corruption, including Crédit Mobilier scandal and Whiskey Ring Fraud
    3. Panic of 1873 leads to retirement of greenbacks and return to gold standard
    4. Leading Radical Republicans die; North loses interest in Reconstruction

F. Compromise of 1877
    1. Democrat S. Tilden wins popular vote but lacks single electoral vote needed for victory
    2. Twenty votes from three southern states still run by Republican governors in dispute
    3. Congressional commission votes along party lines to give all 20 votes to Republican R. Hayes
    4. Hayes promises to end Reconstruction and withdraw remaining troops from South in exchange for Democratic acceptance of his election

# 13. UNITED STATES HISTORY, 1877–1912

## NEW INDUSTRIAL ERA, 1877–1882

A. Politics
1. 1876 Election: special electoral commission (1877); Rutherford B. Hayes (Republican) defeated Samuel J. Tilden (Democrat).
2. 1880 Election: James A. Garfield (Republican) defeated Winfield S. Hancock (Democrat); Garfield assassinated (1881); Chester A. Arthur became president.
3. Republican factions: Roscoe Conkling's "Stalwarts" favored "spoils system"; E. L. Godkin and Carl Schurz's "Liberal Republicans" (Mugwumps) supported civil service reform; James G. Blaine's "Half-Breeds" stood in between.
4. Greenback-Labor party: supported inflation and agricultural marketing cooperatives; active in elections of 1878 and 1880.
B. Economy
1. New South: textiles, steel, and cigarettes; Henry W. Grady advocate of industrialization.
2. Income distribution: standard of living rose; 10% of population controlled 90% of wealth; "social Darwinism"; "gospel of wealth."
3. Labor: National Labor Union (1866) and Knights of Labor (1869) supported worker's cooperatives; both ultimately failed.
4. Bland-Allison Silver Act: authorized monthly purchase of $2 million to $4 million of silver for coinage (1878).
5. Greenbacks: Congress declared that all greenbacks then outstanding were on a par with gold (1878).
6. Agriculture: Desert Land Act provided 640-acre lots at $1.25 an acre (1877); National Grange (1870s and 1880s) and Farmer's Alliances (1880s) formed; supported inflation, regulation of railroads, and cooperative farm marketing.
7. Mining: gold rush in Tombstone, Arizona (1879), and copper rush in Butte, Montana (1882).
C. Society and Culture
1. Immigration: 2 million immigrants in 1870s, mostly Northern European; 5 million immigrants in 1880s, mostly Southern and Eastern European, called "New Immigration."

2. Population: 40 million (1870); 80 million (1900); New York, Chicago, and Philadelphia became major urban centers.
3. Social gospel: Jane Addams; Washington Gladden; Walter Rauschenbusch; called for better social and education services in cities; applied Christianity to social problems.
4. New religions: Salvation Army (1878); Mary Baker Eddy's First Church of Christ, Scientist (1879).
5. African-Americans: Booker T. Washington led Tuskegee Institute in Alabama (1881); emphasized vocational education; George Washington Carver, agricultural chemist.
6. Literature: Mark Twain, *The Adventures of Tom Sawyer* (1876); William Dean Howells, *A Modern Instance* (1882); Henry James, *Daisy Miller* (1879); works represented turn toward "realism."
7. Social thought: Henry George, *Progress and Poverty* (1879), advocated "single tax."

D. Foreign Affairs
1. Latin America: International Bureau of American Republics (1889) which became Pan American Union (1910); frequent border disputes: Argentina and Paraguay (1876), Colombia and Chile (1880), Mexico and Guatemala, Argentina and Chile, and Peru and Chile (1881).
2. Pacific: U.S. signed treaty with Samoa (1878) for trading rights and naval base.
3. Japan: U.S. signed treaty giving Japan tariff autonomy (1878).
4. Korea: trade and diplomatic relations with U.S. began (1882).

E. Native Americans
1. Indian Wars: Sioux War (1876–1877); Nez Percé War (1877).
2. Reform movement: Helen Hunt Jackson, *A Century of Dishonor* (1881).

# CORPORATE INDUSTRIALISM, 1882–1887

A. Politics
1. 1884 Election: Grover Cleveland (Democrat) defeated James G. Blaine (Republican); "Mugwumps" favored civil service reform and shifted from Republicans to Democrats.
2. Presidential Succession Act: line of succession shifted from president pro tempore of the Senate to secretary of state and other members of the cabinet (1885).

B. Economy
1. Corporate leaders: John D. Rockefeller (oil); J. P. Morgan (banking); Gustavas Swift (meat processing); Andrew Carnegie (steel); E. H. Harriman (railroads).

2. Interstate Commerce Act: created commission to oversee railway rates; prohibited rebates, required annual reports and financial statements (1887).

3. Agriculture: land under cultivation doubled between 1870 and 1890; disastrous winters and end of range cattle industry (1885–1886); drought in West (1887); prices for agricultural products declined.

4. American Federation of Labor: combination of craft unions; concentrated on wages, hours, and working conditions; Samuel Gompers and Adolph Strasser founded A.F. of L. (1886).

5. Scientific management: Frederick W. Taylor; scientific approach to industrial engineering and management.

6. Tariff: protective duties lowered by 5% (1883).

7. Railroads: Santa Fe, Southern Pacific, and Northern Pacific routes finished (1882–1883).

C. Society and Culture

1. Newspapers: linotype machine (1886) made mass publication possible; Joseph Pulitzer published New York *World*.

2. Higher education: curriculum modernized; graduate study developed; women's colleges such as Bryn Mawr (1885) established.

3. Natural science: Albert Michelson studied the speed of light; won Nobel Prize (1907).

4. Social thought: Richard T. Ely, Henry C. Adams, and Simon Patten (economics) called for government regulation and planning; Lester Frank Ward, *Dynamic Sociology* (1883), opposed social Darwinism as expounded by William Graham Sumner; Woodrow Wilson *Congressional Government* (1885), criticized committee system.

5. Literature: Mark Twain, *Huckleberry Finn* (1884), William Dean Howells, *The Rise of Silas Lapham* (1885), and Henry James, *The Bostonians* (1886), continued development of realism.

6. Art: Thomas Eakins and Winslow Homer pursued realism while Mary Cassatt and James Whistler experimented with impressionism.

D. Foreign Relations

1. Asia: Chinese immigration to U.S. suspended (1882).

2. Navy: moved from 12th to 3rd in world ranking (1883–1903); Naval War College established (1884).

3. Africa: Berlin Conference (1884) addressed trade in the Congo; Third International Red Cross Conference.

4. Latin America: U.S. signed pact with Nicaragua for Isthmian Canal (1884).

5. Pacific: U.S. obtained Pearl Harbor Naval Base in Hawaii (1886).

    6. Missionaries: American Christian missionaries active in Pacific, Africa, Asia, Latin America, and Middle East.

E. Native Americans
    1. Apache War: capture of Geronimo ended war (1887).
    2. Dawes Act: attempted to establish private property among Native Americans (1887).

# EMERGENCE OF REGIONAL EMPIRE, 1887–1892

A. Politics
    1. 1888 Election: Benjamin Harrison (Republican) won in electoral college, although Grover Cleveland (Democrat) won the popular vote.
    2. Agriculture: Department of Agriculture raised to Cabinet status (1889).
    3. House of Representatives: Thomas B. Reed became speaker (1890) and changed rules to gain absolute control.
    4. Dependent Pensions Act: Congress granted pensions to Union veterans and dependents (1890).
    5. New states: North Dakota, South Dakota, Montana, Washington (1889); Wyoming, Idaho (1890).
    6. Oklahoma: first Oklahoma land rush (1889).

B. Economy
    1. Sherman Anti-Trust Act: prohibited combinations or conspiracies in restraint of trade (1890); Supreme Court eventually applied it to unions and farmer cooperatives as well as corporations.
    2. Sherman Silver Purchase Act: government authorized to buy 4.5 million ounces of silver monthly and issue Treasury notes redeemable in gold and silver (1890); repealed (1893).
    3. McKinley Tariff: compromise protective tariff; included reciprocal trade provisions and presidential retaliation for discrimination (1890).
    4. Railroads: Great Northern Railroad completed (1893).

C. Society and Culture
    1. Popular amusements: vaudeville; circus; Wild West shows; invention of roll-film camera by George Eastman.
    2. Sports: professional baseball; boxing; croquet; bicycle racing; basketball invented (1891); inter-collegiate sports emerged.
    3. Child-rearing: parents less authoritarian and restrictive; golden age of children's literature: Mary Wells Smith, Sidney Lanier, Howard Pyle, and Joel Chandler Harris.
    4. Religion: Dwight L. Moody, urban evangelist; growth of Roman Catholicism and Judaism.

5. Native Americans: Ghost Dance and Battle of Wounded Knee (1889–1890).

D. Foreign Relations
   1. Latin America: Secretary of State James G. Blaine noninterventionist during Haitian (1888–1889) and Chilean (1891) revolutions.
   2. Samoa: U.S., Germany, and Great Britain established joint protectorate (1889).
   3. Africa: U.S. refused naval bases in Portuguese colonies of Angola and Mozambique (1890).
   4. Hawaii: American sugar planters overthrew Queen Liliuokalani (1893).
   5. Theoretical writers: Josiah Strong, *Our Country* (1885), Alfred Thayer Mahan, *The Influence of Sea Power on History* (1890), Frederick Jackson Turner, "The Significance of the Frontier in American History" (1893), and Brooks Adams, *The Law of Civilization and Decay* (1895) argued for expansion.

# ECONOMIC DEPRESSION, 1892–1897

A. Politics
   1. 1892 Election: Grover Cleveland (Democrat) defeated Benjamin Harrison (Republican); inflationary McKinley Tariff played a major role.
   2. Populist party: the People's party nominated James Weaver for president (1892); advocated public ownership of railroads, coinage of silver at 16–1 ratio with gold, 8-hour work day, initiative and referendum, secret ballot, direct election of senators, and graduated income tax.
   3. 1896 Election: William McKinley (Republican) defeated William Jennings Bryan (Democrat); Populist party also nominated Bryan.

B. Economy
   1. Homestead Strike: iron and steel workers struck Carnegie Steel (1892); strike broken by Pinkerton security guards.
   2. Panic of 1893: followed recall of European securities from U.S.; stock market collapsed; gold exports increased; prices of gold, silver, and commodities fell; recovery came in 1897.
   3. Coxey's Army: Jacob Coxey led unemployed workers to Washington (1894); leaders arrested.
   4. Pullman Strike: American Railway Union struck Chicago's Pullman Palace Car Co. (1894); Cleveland sent in federal troops.
   5. Tariff: Wilson-Gorman Tariff (1894) and Dingley Tariff (1897) raised rates.

C. Society and Culture
   1. Literature: William Dean Howells, *A Hazard of New Fortunes* (1890), and Stephen Crane, *Maggie: A Girl of the Streets* (1892) and *The Red Badge of Courage* (1895), continued realism; Edward Bellamy wrote *Looking Backward*, projected a future corporate state.
   2. Social and behavioral thought: Lester Frank Ward, *The Psychic Factors of Civilization* (1893), favored social planning; William James wrote *Principles of Psychology* (1890), a foundational text.
   3. Temperance: Anti-Saloon League formed (1893).
   4. Immigration: declined 400,000 during depression; settlement houses provided aid: Jane Addams, Hull House (Chicago), Lillian Wald, Henry Street Settlement (New York), Robert Wood, South End House (Boston).
   5. Chicago World's Fair: emphasized beautifying cities (1893).
   6. Technology: first radio voice transmission (1892); Thomas Edison invented kinetoscope making motion pictures possible (1893).
D. Foreign Relations
   1. Cuba: Cubans revolted against Spain (1895); Assistant Secretary of the Navy Theodore Roosevelt advocated U.S. intervention.
   2. Venezuela: U.S. supported British claims in border dispute between Venezuela and Guiana; Britain recognized Monroe Doctrine.
   3. Sino-Japanese War: Japanese victory (1894–1895) revealed that China was open to colonization by industrial powers; led to Open Door policy.
   4. Hawaii: Cleveland rejected annexation of Hawaii (1894).
   5. Latin America: U.S. supported existing governments during revolutions in Brazil and Nicaragua (1894).

# EXPANSION, 1897–1902

A. Politics
   1. 1900 Election: William McKinley and Theodore Roosevelt (Republican) defeated William Jennings Bryan and Adlai Stevenson (Democrat). People's party, Socialist Democratic party, and Prohibition party also ran presidential candidates.
   2. McKinley assassination: anarchist Leon Czolgosz killed McKinley (1901); Vice President Theodore Roosevelt became president.
B. Economy
   1. Federal Bankruptcy Act: standardized procedures and rule of bankruptcy (1898).

2. Erdman Act: mediation provided for unresolved railroad controversies (1898).

3. Gold Standard Act: gold reserve established; gold amount in dollar established (1900).

4. Business: Standard Oil of New Jersey (1899) and U.S. Steel (1900) formed.

C. Society and Culture

1. Newspapers: Joseph Pulitzer's New York *World* and William Randolph Hearst's New York *Journal* competed fiercely.

2. Literature: Frank Norris wrote *McTeague* (1899) and *The Octopus* (1901) describing capitalist competition.

3. Social thought: Jacob Riis, *How the Other Half Lives* (1890), documented New York slums; Thorstein Veblen, *Theory of the Leisure Class* (1899), attacked "conspicuous consumption."

D. Foreign Policy

1. DeLôme Letter: Spanish minister criticized McKinley (Feb. 9, 1898).

2. U.S.S. *Maine*: battleship exploded in Havana harbor (Feb. 15, 1898).

3. Spanish-American War: war declared (April 21, 1898); Teller Amendment disclaimed any attempt to annex Cuba; Spanish fleet in Philippines destroyed (May 1); U.S. forces landed in Cuba (June 22); hostilities ended (Aug. 12).

4. Treaty of Paris: U.S. obtained Philippines, Puerto Rico, and Guam; Spain received $20 million; ratified (Feb. 1900).

5. Hawaii: annexed by U.S. (July 1898).

6. Anti-Imperialist League: supporters included Mark Twain, William James, William Jennings Bryan, Grover Cleveland, Charles Francis Adams, Carl Schurz, Charles W. Eliot, David Starr Jordan, Andrew Carnegie, and Samuel Gompers (1898).

7. Imperialism advocates: Theodore Roosevelt, Mark Hanna, Alfred Thayer Mahan, Henry Cabot Lodge, Albert Beveridge, William McKinley.

8. Philippines: Emilio Aguinaldo led rebellion against U.S. (1899-1902).

9. Open Door: Secretary of State John Hay called for equal opportunity of trade in China (1899).

10. Platt Amendment: made Cuba a virtual protectorate of the U.S. (1901).

11. Hay-Pauncefote Treaty: signed with Britain (1901); abrogated Clayton-Bulwer Treaty; allowed U.S. to construct isthmian canal.

12. Insular cases: Supreme Court said constitutional rights did not extend to territories (1901-1903).

# THEODORE ROOSEVELT, 1902–1907

A. Politics
1. State Progressives: Robert LaFollette (Wisconsin); Albert Cummins (Iowa); Charles Evans Hughes (New York); James M. Cox (Ohio); Hiram Johnson (California); William S. U'Ren (Oregon); Albert Beveridge (Indiana); Woodrow Wilson (New Jersey).
2. Urban Progressives: John Purroy Mitchell (New York); Tom L. Johnson and Newton Baker (Cleveland); Hazen Pingree (Detroit); Sam Jones (Toledo); Joseph Folk (St. Louis).
3. State political reforms: primary elections (Mississippi, Wisconsin); initiative and referendum (South Dakota, Oregon); overthrew state and urban political machines (New York, Ohio, Michigan, California).
4. City Commission: commission form of government adopted by Galveston, Texas (1903).
5. Elkins Act: reiterated illegality of railroad rebates (1903).
6. 1904 Election: Theodore Roosevelt (Republican) defeated Alton B. Parker (Democrat).
7. Hepburn Act: strengthened Interstate Commerce Commission (1906).
8. Food Regulations: Pure Food and Drug Act (1906); Meat Inspection Act (1906).
9. Immunity of Witness Act: Immunity no longer allowed for corporate executives when witnesses in their corporation's trials (1906).
10. Conservation: Federal irrigation projects; national parks and forests, Internal Waterways Commission; National Conservation Commission (1902–1908).

B. Economy
1. Anti-trust policy: Northern Securities Case; Standard Oil Company case; by 1909 Roosevelt brought indictments against 25 monopolies.
2. Coal strike: Roosevelt intervened in United Mine Workers action against anthracite mine owners (1902).
3. Department of Commerce and Labor: created (1903).
4. Panic of 1907: resulted from failure of the Knickerbocker Trust Company of New York and the Westinghouse Electric Company; stock market collapsed and banks failed; recovery occurred after U.S. Treasury and J.P. Morgan and Company loaned $25 million to New York banks.

C. Society and Culture
1. Muckrakers: investigative journalism; *McClure's; Collier's*; Lin-

coln Steffens, *The Shame of the Cities* (1904); Ida Tarbell, *The History of the Standard Oil Company* (1904); Thomas Lawson, "Frenzied Finance" (1904–1905); David Graham Phillips, "The Treason of the Senate" (1906).

2. Social thought: Ray Stannard Baker, *Following the Color Line* (1908); Herbert Croly, *The Promise of American Life* (1909); John Spargo, *The Bitter Cry of the Children* (1906) examined aspects of American society.

3. Literature: Upton Sinclair, *The Jungle* (1906), and Jack London, *Call of the Wild* (1903) and *The Iron Heel* (1907), portrayed the struggle for existence.

4. Airplane: Orville and Wilbur Wright performed first flight at Kitty Hawk, North Carolina (1903).

D. Foreign Relations
1. Panama Canal: Hay-Bunau-Varilla Treaty; Panamanian revolution, canal built (1904–1914).

2. Roosevelt Corollary to Monroe Doctrine: U.S. reserved right to intervene in Latin America; interventions in Venezuela, Haiti, Dominican Republic, Nicaragua, and Cuba.

3. Rio de Janeiro Conference: moved toward promotion of economic development in Latin America (1906).

4. Russo-Japanese War: Roosevelt negotiated Treaty of Portsmouth (1904).

5. Japan: Taft-Katsura Memo (1905) pledged open door in China; Gentleman's Agreement (1907) limited Japanese immigration to U.S.

6. Great White Fleet: U.S. naval fleet sent to Asia (1907).

7. International Conferences: Algeciras Conference guaranteed equality of trade for Morocco (1906); Second Hague Conference discussed disarmament and international court (1907).

# REGULATOR STATE, 1907–1912

A. Politics
1. 1908 Election: William Howard Taft (Republican) defeated William Jennings Bryan (Democrat).

2. Joseph Cannon: Republican Speaker of the House; Progressives sought to limit Cannon's power (1910); Taft did not support Progressives.

3. Ballinger-Pinchot Controversy: Gifford Pinchot, Chief Forester, charged Richard Ballinger, Secretary of Interior, with giving away natural resources; Pinchot fired (1909–1910).

4. Sixteenth Amendment: graduated income tax passed Congress (1909); ratified (1913).

5. Mann-Elins Act: extended power of ICC over cable, wireless, telephone, and telegraph (1910).

6. 1912 Election: Woodrow Wilson (Democrat) defeated Theodore Roosevelt (Progressive) and William Howard Taft (Republican). Wilson's "New Freedom" emphasized preserving competition while Roosevelt's "New Nationalism" advocated government regulation of business.

B.  Economy

1. National Monetary Commission (1908): recommended U.S. Treasury reserve and branch banks (1913).

2. Payne-Aldrich Tariff: amendments made bill a protective tariff; endorsed by Taft (1909).

3. Postal Savings Bank: certain U.S. post offices authorized to receive deposits and pay interest (1910).

4. Antitrust: Taft ordered 44 antitrust suits; American Tobacco Trust broken (1911).

5. "Rule of Reason" decisions: Supreme Court said that "all combinations in restraint of trade meant "all *unreasonable* combinations in restoration of trade" (1911).

C.  Society and Culture

1. Social programs: Illinois established aid to mothers of dependent children (1911); Massachusetts adopted minimum wage law (1912).

2. African-Americans: W.E.B. DuBois helped found Niagara Movement, calling for full equality (1905); National Association for the Advancement of Colored People concentrated on using the courts (1909).

3. IWW: Industrial Workers of the World or "Wobblies"; radical labor union included Carlo Tresca, Elizabeth Gurley Flynn, Daniel DeLeon, "Mother" Jones, Father Thomas Hagerty, and "Big" Bill Haywood (1905).

4. Mann Act: interstate prostitution a federal crime (1910).

5. Motion pictures: Hollywood became center for silent film production.

6. Literature: Theodore Dreiser's *The Financier* (1912) examined big business.

D.  Foreign Relations

1. Dollar Diplomacy: Taft encouraged investments in Latin America and elsewhere.

2. Root Takahira Agreement: reiterated status quo in Asia (1908).

3. Latin America: Latin American Division of State Department created by Secretary of State Philander Knox (1909); U.S. intervened militarily in Nicaragua (1911).

4. Mexican Revolution: Taft recognized revolutionary government of Francisco I Madero; stationed U.S. troops along Texas border with Mexico (1912).

5. China Consortium: U.S. joined Britain, France, and Germany to build railway in China (1909); withdrew (1913).

# 14. UNITED STATES HISTORY, 1912–1941

## I. WOODROW WILSON AND THE NEW FREEDOM

A. Election of 1912 – Republicans nominate incumbent President W.H. Taft, Democrats vote 46 times before nominating W. Wilson. T. Roosevelt forms Bull Moose party, Socialists nominate E. Debs. Wilson wins 41 states, but receives less than 42 percent of popular vote.

B. Implementing the New Freedom – Wilson calls for reduction of tariff, reform of banking laws, and improvements in anti-trust laws.

1. Underwood-Simmons Tariff Act of 1913 – tariff rates reduced and graduated income tax implemented.

2. Federal Reserve Act of 1913 – twelve regional Federal Reserve banks, Commercial banks owned Federal Reserve Bank, Fed Reserve held gold surplus, Fed loaned money to member banks, money loaned as Federal Reserve Notes, member bank checks cleared through Fed Bank, Fed serviced government, supervised by Federal Reserve Board.

3. Clayton Antitrust Act of 1914 – supplemented and interpreted Sherman Antitrust Act of 1890

4. Federal Trade Commission Act of 1914 – prohibited all unfair trade practices without defining them.

C. Triumph of New Nationalism – Democrats abandon New Freedom platform after numerous Republican gains in favor of broad economic and social reforms.

1. Brandeis Appointment – Wilson appoints L.D. Brandeis, an advocate of social justice, as an associate justice of the Supreme Court.

2. Federal Farm Loan Act of 1916 – twelve regional Federal Land Banks, make mortgage loans at reasonable rates.

3. Child Labor Act of 1916 – forbade interstate shipment of products whose labor involved children under the age of 14 or 16. Declared unconstitutional by Supreme Court.

4. Adamson Act of 1916 – Eight-hour workday, time and a half for overtime and maximum 16 hours in a shift for all interstate railroad workers.

5. Kerr-McGillicuddy Act of 1916 – workman's compensation for federal employees.

D. Social Issues – Wilson opposed a women's suffrage amendment and immigration restrictions. When treasury secretary and the postmaster general segregated some workers, many blacks protested when Wilson did nothing. Wilson gained reputation for being inimical to civil rights.

E. Election of 1916 – Democrats renominate Wilson, platform continues reforms and calls for neutrality in WWI, Republicans nominate C.E. Hughes. Wilson receives almost 52 percent of the popular vote, increasing his last election win by almost three million votes.

## II. FOREIGN POLICY AND ROAD TO WAR

A. Foreign Policy – Wilson promises more moral foreign policy, denouncing imperialism.
   1. Conciliation Treaties – Secretary of State Bryan negotiates treaties with 29 nations, agreeing to submit disputes for conciliation including provisions for cooling off period.
   2. Dollar Diplomacy – Wilson withdraws from six-power loan consortium in China.
   3. Japan – Wilson fails to prevent passage of California law prohibiting land ownership by Japanese aliens. War seemed imminent but was smoothed over. Lanshing-Ishii Agreement wherein Japan recognized Open Door in China and US recognized Japan's special interest in China.
   4. Caribbean – Wilson sought to protect Panama Canal. Marines sent to Nicaragua, Haiti, and Dominican Republic to maintain order. Wilson purchases Virgin Islands after fears Germans would annex Denmark.
   5. Mexico – Wilson refuses to recognize government of V. Huerta, American forces occupy Veracruz after several American seamen were arrested. July 1914, Huerta abdicates and V. Carranza comes to power. "Pancho" Villa, seeking to have US intervention undermine government, shoots 16 Americans on train in North Mexico and burns Columbus, N.M., killing 19 people. Gen. Pershing with 6,000 troops cross Rio Grande to capture Villa. After several clashes with Mexican troops, Pershing withdrew.

B. Road to War – Wilson issues proclamation of neutrality on Aug. 4, 1914. US drifted to closer ties with Allies, mainly Britain and France, while distancing itself from the Central powers.
   1. Submarine Crisis – Germans blockade Allies and attack unarmed British passenger ships. Passenger liners *Lusitania* and *Arabic* sunk in 1915. "Arabic" pledge stops attacks on unarmed passenger ships.

2. Gore-McLemore Resolution – prohibits Americans to travel on armed ships or on ships carrying munitions.

3. Sussex Pledge – After torpedoing of French ship *Sussex*, Germans agree to stop surprise attacks, but threaten to resume if British do not stop violations of international law.

4. House-Grey Memorandum – Col. House signs agreement with British foreign secretary Gray pledging to join Allies if Germans refuse to enter peace talks or are uncooperative.

5. Preparedness – National Defense Act of 1916 increases size of army and national guard, $500 million appropriated for naval construction.

6. Final Peace Efforts – Germans propose peace conference but refuse Wilson's attendance. Alludes to his "association of nations."

7. In January 1917, Germans announce unlimited submarine warfare in large zone off Allied coasts.

8. Zimmerman Telegram – British intercept telegram to A. Zimmerman, ambassador for Germany in Mexico. Germans propose Mexico join Central powers and attack US. Mexico promised US territory.

9. Declaration of War – Wilson signs declaration after it passes both houses of Congress on April 6, 1917.

## III. WORLD WAR I

A. Military Campaign
1. Selective Service Act – draft begun in May 1917, men aged 21 to 30 initially, changed to 17 to 46 later. Two million men drafted by war's end.
2. War at Sea – after convoy system begun in July 1917, Allied shipping losses drop drastically.
3. American Expeditionary Force – commanded by General Pershing, resisted efforts to amalgamate forces with the other Allies. Major engagements include: Chateau-Thierry, St. Mihiel, and the Meuse-Argonne offensive. Over 100,000 US dead and twice that wounded. Armistice signed November 11, 1918.
B. Home Front
1. Industry – War Industries Board allocates raw material, controls production and pricing of goods.
2. Food – Lever Act gives president broad control. H. Hoover institutes "Wheatless Mondays" and "Meatless Tuesdays."
3. Fuel – Fuel Administration institutes "Fueless Mondays" and "Gasless Sundays."
4. Railroads – Government pays rent for control of railroad system,

improving efficiency in the process.

5. Maritime Shipping – US Shipping Board buys, builds, leases, and operates merchant ships.

6. Labor – War Labor Board prohibits strikes and encourages higher wages.

7. War Finance – Income and luxury taxes increased, Liberty Bonds sold to cover costs of war.

C. Public Opinion and Civil Liberties

1. Committee on Public Information – voluntary censorship of press and organization of writers, artists, and lecturers for propaganda campaign.

2. War Hysteria – volunteer organizations begin terrorizing foreigners and people encouraged to report suspicious activity.

3. Espionage and Sedition Acts – imposed fines or prison sentences for giving false information which aided the enemy or criticizing government. Forms basis for "clear and present danger" clause.

D. Social Trends

1. Women – Many begin working to replace men at war. New found freedom leads to suffrage gains in several states.

2. Minorities – Many migrate from South. Race riots occur in 26 cities.

3. Prohibition – manufacture and sale of alcohol prohibited in amendment to Constitution passed by Congress, sent to states for ratification in 1917.

## IV. PEACE AND DOMESTIC PROBLEMS

A. Peacemaking

1. Fourteen Points – first five called for; open peace treaties, freedom of seas and trade, arms reduction, fair adjustment of colonial claims. Next eight covered national aspirations of European countries and adjustments of boundaries, last point called for "League of Nations."

2. Armistice signed Nov. 11, 1918, Germany withdraws to Rhine and surrenders military equipment.

3. Versailles Treaty – provisions were; League of Nations formed, Germany held responsible and ordered to pay reparations, new nations created, German colonies become mandates of the League. Germany forced to sign under threat of economic boycott.

4. US and the Treaty – Congress divided on treaty, unless changes made; Wilson, in an open letter, angers Republicans and the treaty fails to pass. War between US and Germany ended with resolution of Congress and separate treaty. Wilson's stroke, suffered on

speaking tour, may have impaired his judgment on issue.

B. Domestic Problems
1. Demobilization – AEF brought home from Europe quickly, Veterans Bureau established to aid wounded, wartime boards disbanded.
2. Final Reforms of Progressive Era – 18th Amendment prohibiting manufacture, sale or consumption of alcohol ratified. 19th Amendment providing women's suffrage ratified in 1919.
3. Red Scare – Russia's fall to communism prompted scare, which led to many being arrested and deported as undesirable foreigners or communists. J. Edgar Hoover named to Intelligence Division of Justice Department.

C. Election of 1920 – Republicans nominate Warren G. Harding with Calvin Coolidge as vice president. Democrats run James Cox with Franklin D. Roosevelt as vice president. Harding receives 61 percent of the popular vote.

# V. 1920s

A. Economy
1. Brief recession occurs in 1920–1921 due to reduction in European purchases.
2. Industry begins to grow with automobiles and electrical plants as the biggest gainers. Introduction of sound movies also created a boom in the movie industry.
3. Consumer credit expanded to meet the demand for big-ticket items such as cars. Advertising expenditures increased to promote the new consumer products.
4. Big business increases, receiving half the corporate profits. Federal regulation agencies are quiet during this time. Banking assets grow and the number of banks tops 25 thousand.
5. Influence of labor unions wanes, more people join company-sponsored unions.
6. Farmers fail to share in prosperity as income drops and costs increase.

B. American Society
1. Standard of living increases with improved technology and the movement of more people to urban areas. The increase is uneven, as 43 percent of population lives below poverty level.
2. Automobiles, new music and dance styles lead to increase in sexual promiscuity. "Flappers" are independent assertive women.
3. Women gain right to vote with 19th Amendment in 1920. Most women still limited to traditional jobs and lower pay.
4. Southern rural blacks continue movement to northern, urban areas.

Marcus Garvey calls for blacks to purchase only from blacks and a return to Africa.

5. Free elementary and high school education becomes more available. Growth in vocational schools. College enrollment almost doubles.

6. Church and synagogue membership increases. Roman Catholics and Jews find themselves under attack by the Ku Klux Klan.

7. Spending on commercial entertainment increases. *Jazz Singer* introduces sound to movies. Baseball attendance increases by 50 percent. One-third of families now have radio. Literary figures of the time include E. Hemingway, F.S. Fitzgerald, and E. Pound.

C. Social Conflicts

1. Ku Klux Klan membership rises to oppose rise in status of blacks and influx of Roman Catholics. Klan used terrorist tactics to intimidate and exerted control over some elections.

2. Emergency Quota Act limits immigration from each nation to 3 percent of total number currently in US. National Origins Act reduces it to 2 percent and imposes maximum of 150,000.

3. Prohibition imposed with 18th Amendment and Volstead Act. Growth of speakeasies and organized crime. Bootleg liquor came from many areas within the US and abroad.

4. Scopes Trial pits advocates of creationism and evolution. Trial became battle of words between W.J. Bryan and C. Darrow. Scopes found guilty of teaching evolution and fined.

5. N. Sacco and B. Vanzetti, immigrants and anarchists, convicted of murder in 1921. Protests arise due to a lack of conclusive evidence. Both executed in 1927. (Vindicated in 1977 by proclamation of Gov. M. Dukakis.)

D. Government and Politics

1. Harding Administration – Revenue Acts of 1921 and 1924 cut taxes to 50 percent and then 40 percent. Fordney-McCumber Tariff imposed high tariffs on farm products. Budget and Accounting Act provided Federal government with unified budget.

2. Scandals rocked Harding Administration; Teapot Dome (A. Fall accepts bribe for oil leases), Veterans Bureau (C. Forbes steals bureau funds), Attorney General Daugherty (accepts bribes from criminals in exchange for protection). As scandals first hit, Harding takes extended vacation and dies of heart attack in 1923. VP Coolidge finishes Harding term.

3. Election of 1924 – Republicans nominate Coolidge; Democrats run J. W. Davis; Progressives run R. LaFollette. Coolidge received more votes than his two opponents combined.

4. Coolidge Administration – Coolidge vetoes attempts at government operation of Muscle Shoals dam (later nucleus of Tennessee Valley Authority), Veterans' bonus based on length of service passed over Coolidge veto, Revenue Act of 1926 cut most taxes.

5. Election of 1928 – Republican candidate is H. Hoover, Democrats nominate A. Smith. Hoover carried all the northern states except Mass. and R.I. and seven states in the solid South.

6. Foreign Policy – Five Power Pact called for end of new naval vessel construction, scrap some existing ships, and maintain ratios of ships as agreed upon; Nine Power Pact upheld Open Door Policy in China; Four Power Pact bound US, Gr. Brit, Japan and France to respect each other's possessions in Pacific; Dawes Plan called for loans to Germany so it could pay reparations from WWI to Allies, who could then pay back debts to America. Kellogg-Briand Pact signed by almost all major nations in 1928 renounced war as an instrument of national policy, it contained no enforcement provisions.

# VI. GREAT DEPRESSION

A. Causes of Depression
1. Stock Market Crash – stocks selling at 16 times earnings, investors begin selling. On "Black Thursday" 13 million shares are traded. Investment banks try to boost prices by buying. On "Black Tuesday," Oct. 29, 1929, market falls 40 points.
2. Investors buying stock by borrowing 90 percent of price. When stocks lost more than 10 percent, investors sold.
3. Farm economy had been depressed throughout the decade; coal, railroads, and textiles had not been prosperous; new construction and auto sales slow.
4. Average consumers did not have money to continue purchasing after credit had been used up; this resulted in underconsumption.
5. Americans spent less on foreign products, depriving foreign governments of the money to repay loans to US.

B. Effects of Depression
1. Financial – Gross National Product fell by almost 50 percent; Unemployment hit 25 percent (excluding farmers); National income dropped 54 percent; by 1932, 22 percent of the banks had failed.
2. Human Dimension – People unable to continue credit payments, loss of homes, cars, and other possessions; families double up in houses and apartments; marriage and birth rates decline; public and private soup and bread lines set up throughout the nation.
3. Bonus Expeditionary Force – unemployed veterans who march on

Washington to lobby for early payment of veterans bonus, driven from shanties by army.

C. Hoover's Depression Policies

1. Agricultural Marketing Act – creates Federal Farm Board to lend money to agricultural cooperatives to buy and hold commodities for higher prices.

2. Hawley-Smoot Tariff – raised duties on agricultural and manufactured imports.

3. Public Works – money appropriated to build in order to stimulate employment.

4. Reconstruction Finance Corporation – provided loans to railroads, banks and other financial institutions.

5. Federal Home Loan Bank Act – loans to building and loan associations, savings banks, and insurance companies to help prevent foreclosures.

D. Election of 1932

1. Republicans nominate Hoover; Democrats support F.D. Roosevelt.

2. Roosevelt receives over 57 percent of the popular vote. Democrats also capture Senate and increase majority in House.

## VII. FIRST NEW DEAL

A. Roosevelt Administration

1. Brain Trust – Roosevelt's unofficial advisors, more influential than his Cabinet.

2. Repeal of Prohibition – Congress passes 21st Amendment to repeal prohibition in 1933.

3. Banking Crisis – runs occur on many banks just before inauguration, state governments in 38 states close banks.

4. Inaugural address – Roosevelt gives "nothing to fear but fear itself" speech. Two days later closes all banks and forbids export or redemption of currency for gold.

B. Legislation of the First Hundred Days

1. Emergency Banking Relief Act – provides additional funds for banks, forbade hoarding or export of gold.

2. Banking Act of 1933 – establishes Federal Deposit Insurance Corporation to insure deposits.

3. Truth-in-Securities Act – requires full information on stocks and bonds.

4. Home Owners Loan Corp. – borrowed money to prevent foreclosures.

5. Gold – nation taken off the gold standard, devaluation of dollar.

6. Federal Emergency Relief Act – appropriates money to aid the poor, distributed by the states.
7. Civilian Conservation Corp. – small payments made to families of young men who work on projects.
8. Public Works Admin. – builds schools, highways, and hospitals, goal was to create construction jobs.
9. Federal Farm Loan Act – consolidates all farm credit programs to make low interest loans to farmers.
10. Tennessee Valley Authority – experiment in regional public planning, built 20 dams at Muscle Shoals to prevent soil erosion, improve navigation, and generate hydroelectric power.

C. Programs after the First Hundred Days
   1. Securities and Exchange Commission – created to supervise stock exchanges.
   2. Federal Housing Admin. – insures long-term, low interest mortgages for home construction.
   3. Commodity Credit Corp. – make loans to cotton and corn farmers against their crops.
   4. Frazier-Lemke Farm Bankruptcy Act – allows farmers to defer foreclosure.

# VIII. SECOND NEW DEAL

A. Opposition
   1. American Liberty League – formed by conservatives to defend business interests and promote open shop.
   2. Old Age Revolving Pension Plan – Dr. F. Townsend proposes retired people over age 60 receive $200/month, under stipulation they spend it during month; millions of older Americans join Townsend clubs
   3. Share Our Wealth Society – founded by Sen. Long of Louisiana, called for confiscation of fortunes over $5 million, and 100 percent tax on income over $1 million; money would be distributed to poor. Long assassinated before he could run for president.
   4. National Union for Social Justice – founded by Father C.E. Coughlin, advocated an inflationary currency and was anti-Semitic.

B. Legislation
   1. Works Progress Administration – employed people for 30 hours work at pay double relief roles, but less than private employment.
   2. National Youth Admin. – provides part-time jobs for high school and college students, so they could afford to stay in school.

3. Rural Electrification Admin. – provided loans and WPA labor to electric cooperatives.
4. Resettlement Admin. – relocated destitute families.
5. National Labor Relations Act – reaffirmed right to unionize, prohibited unfair labor practices, created National Labor Relations Board.
6. Social Security Act – establishes retirement plan for persons over age 65 through taxes on wages and employers.
7. Banking Act of 1935 – creates strong Board of Governors for Federal Reserve System.
8. Public Utility Holding Comp. – restricts public utility holding companies to one natural region.
9. Revenue Act of 1935 – increases income tax on higher incomes.
10. Motor Carrier Act – extends control of ICC to interstate trucking lines.

C. Election of 1936
1. Democrats – Roosevelt nominated on first ballot.
2. Republicans – run Gov. A. M. Landon of Kansas.
3. Union Party – formed by opposition groups, run Congressman W. Lemke.
4. Roosevelt wins every state except Maine and Vermont, gaining almost 61 percent of the popular vote.

D. Last years of New Deal
1. Court Packing – Judicial Reorganization Bill to allow president to name a new federal judge for everyone over 70 1/2 that does not retire. Roosevelt opposed by both parties and the bill fails to pass.
2. Recession of 1937–1938 – when economy started to improve, relief programs reduced economy, slipped rapidly and Congress appropriates more money for programs.
3. Bankhead-Jones Farm Tenancy Act – continues loans to farmers.
4. National Housing Act – establishes US Housing Authority which could borrow money to loan to housing projects.
5. Second Agricultural Adjustment Act – appropriated funds for soil conservation.
6. Fair Labor Standards Act – provides minimum wage.

# IX. ROAD TO WAR

A. Early Foreign Policy
1. Good Neighbor Policy to improve relations with Latin America. US agrees to nonintervention in Latin America at Montevideo Conference.

    2. US recognizes USSR (1933).

    3. Reciprocal Trade Agreement Act gives president power to alter tariff rates.

B. Neutrality Legislation

    1. House and Senate investigate profiteering by bankers and munitions makers leading up to WWI.

    2. Johnson Act prohibits securities selling by any nation in default of WWI payments.

    3. Neutrality Acts embargo exports to belligerent nations for six months (1935), prohibit loans or credit to billigerents (1936), prohibited arms sales to billigerents, but allowed cash-and-carry sales of nonmilitary goods (1937).

C. Threats to World Order

    1. Japan invades Manchuria (1931) and the rest of China (1937).

    2. Ethiopia falls to Italy (1936).

    3. German army enters Rhineland (1936), Rome-Berlin Axis formed (Oct. 1936), Germany unites with Austria (Mar. 1938), takes Sudetenland from Czechoslovakia (1938), takes all of Czech. (1939), non-aggression pact with Russia (1939).

    4. Germany invades Poland (Sept. 1, 1939). Britain and France declare war (Sept. 3).

D. American Response – Roosevelt increases military appropriations

    1. Creates War Resources Board and Office of Emergency Management to prepare for outbreak of war.

    2. Neutrality Act of 1939 allowed cash and carry sale of arms to belligerents.

    3 Coastal patrol set up in Greenland (republic of fallen Dutch government).

    4. Council of National Defense begins awarding military contracts.

    5. First peacetime draft (1940) instituted for men 21 to 35.

    6. 99 year leases on British bases traded for 50 destroyers.

E. Election of 1940 – Republicans run Wendell L. Willkie, a critic of New Deal domestic policies. Democrats nominate Roosevelt on first ballot. Roosevelt receives almost 55 percent of popular vote and wins unprecedented third term.

F. American Involvement

    1. Lend-Lease Act allows for post-war payment by Britain.

    2. American navy begins patrolling Western Atlantic.

    3. Marines occupy Iceland.

    4. Atlantic Charter issued by Churchill and Roosevelt which endorsed self-determination for all nations after WWII.

    5. Lend lease extended to Russia after German invasion (1941).

    6. American military ordered to shoot on sight at any German or

Italian vessel in patrol zone (Sept. 1941).

7. Congress orders arming of merchant ships (Nov. 1941).

G. Road to Pearl Harbor

1. Embargo on gas, lubricants, iron, and steel imposed on Japan after station of troops in Indochina (1940).

2. Japan signs Tripartite Pact with Germany and Italy (Sept. 1940).

3. Japanese funds frozen, Panama Canal closed to Japan, embargo on oil and other products enacted after Japan takes control of Southern Indochina.

4. Negotiations in Oct. 1941 and Nov. 1941 between Japan and US unresolved.

5. Japanese attack Pearl Harbor on Dec. 7, 1941, inflicting heavy US naval losses; aircraft carriers spared; Dec. 8, Roosevelt gives "date that will live in infamy" speech to Congress; US declares war on Japan.

6. Germany and Italy declare war on US (Dec. 11).

# 15. UNITED STATES HISTORY, SINCE 1941

## WORLD WAR II, 1941–1945

A. Road to War
   1. Lend-Lease: Congress allowed President Roosevelt to "lend" or "lease" equipment to Great Britain and other nations under Nazi attack (March 1941).
   2. Atlantic Charter: Roosevelt and Winston Churchill, Prime Minister of Great Britain, signed commitment to postwar freedom (Aug. 1941).
   3. Pearl Harbor: Japan attacked from air (Dec. 7, 1941).
   4. Declaration of War: U.S. declared war on Japan (Dec. 8, 1941) and Germany (Dec. 11).
B. North African and European Theatres
   1. North Africa: Dwight D. Eisenhower's allied forces defeated Erwin Rommel's Africa Korps (November 1942–May 1943).
   2. Italy: Allied forces moved into Sicily and then Italy (July 1943–June 1944).
   3. Soviet Union: Soviet Union pushed into Eastern Europe (March 1944).
   4. D-Day: Allied forces invaded Normandy, France (June 6, 1944).
   5. Surrender: Germany surrendered (May 7, 1945).
C. Pacific Theatre
   1. Coral Sea: U.S. halted Japanese advance toward Australia (May 7–8, 1942).
   2. Midway: U.S. defeated Japanese navy in turning point of Pacific war (June 4–7, 1942).
   3. Island hopping: Allied forces began strategy of attacking selected islands (1943).
   4. Philippine Sea: Japanese navy defeated (June 19–20, 1944).
   5. Leyte Gulf: Japanese navy defeated (October 25, 1944).
   6. Okinawa: Japanese defenses destroyed (April–June 1945).
D. Atomic Bomb
   1. Manhattan Project: research on atomic bomb begun (Aug. 1942).
   2. Alamogordo: atomic bomb successfully exploded (July 16, 1945).

3. Hiroshima and Nagasaki: atomic bomb dropped (Aug. 6 and 9, 1945).
4. Surrender: Japan announced surrender (Aug. 14, 1945).

E. Diplomacy
   1. Casablanca Conference: Allies declared policy of unconditional surrender (Jan. 1943).
   2. Tehran Conference: Roosevelt, Churchill, and Stalin planned offensive against Germany (Nov. 1943).
   3. Yalta Conference: "Big Three" decided on United Nations and occupation of Germany.
   4. Potsdam Conference: Harry S. Truman, Clement Atlee, and Joseph Stalin demanded Japanese surrender (July–Aug. 1945).

F. Home Front
   1. War Production Board: established to regulate raw material usage (1942).
   2. Wages and prices: Office of Price Administration established (April 1942).
   3. Revenue Act: extended income tax to majority of population (1942).
   4. *Korematsu v. U.S.*: Supreme Court upheld relocation of Japanese-Americans to concentration camps (1944).
   5. 1944 Election: Franklin D. Roosevelt (Democrat) defeated Thomas E. Dewey (Republican); Roosevelt died (April 12, 1945); Vice President Harry S. Truman became president.

# THE COLD WAR, 1945–1960

A. Emergence of Containment
   1. Containment: George F. Kennan proposed counterforce to Soviet pressures (1946).
   2. Truman Doctrine: Truman requested aid for Greece and Turkey; announces U.S. policy to prevent Communist expansion (1947).
   3. Marshall Plan: Secretary of State George C. Marshall proposed economic plan for European recovery (1947); Congress passed European Recovery Program providing $12 billion (1948).
   4. Berlin crisis: After Soviet Union blockaded Berlin (June 1948), U.S. instituted airlift until blockade was lifted (May 1949).
   5. NATO: North Atlantic Treaty Organization created (April 1949).

B. International Cooperation
   1. Bretton Woods: international bank and world monetary fund agreed upon (July 1–22, 1944).
   2. United Nations: United Nations established at San Francisco meeting (April–June 1945).

C. Containment in Asia
1. China: Mao Tse-tung established People's Republic of China (1949).
2. Korea: North Korea invaded South Korea (June 25, 1950); U.N. authorized U.S. forces to invade; armistice signed (June 1953).
D. Eisenhower-Dulles Foreign Policy
1. Vietnam: Eisenhower declined to aid French at Dien Bien Phu (1954); Geneva Accords signed (July 1954) dividing Vietnam into two zones.
2. SEATO: Philippines, Thailand, and Pakistan signed Southeast Asia Treaty Organization (1954).
3. Suez Canal crisis: Egypt nationalized Suez Canal; France, Great Britain, and Israel attacked Egypt; U.S. convinced European powers to stop war (1956).
4. Eisenhower doctrine: Eisenhower announced that U.S. would use force against Communist advances in the Middle East (1957).
5. Atomic weapons: Soviet Union and the U.S. signed atmospheric test ban (1958).
6. Cuba: Fidel Castro overthrew Fulgencio Batista (1959) and moved politically toward the Soviet Union; U.S. broke off diplomatic relations (1961).
7. U-2 incident: American U-2 spy plane shot down over Soviet Union (1960).

# DOMESTIC POLICIES, 1945–1960

A. Truman
1. Employment Act: established Council of Economic Advisors and Congressional Joint Committee on the Economic Report (1946).
2. Atomic Energy: Atomic Energy Commission established (1946).
3. Taft-Hartley Act: Congress restricted union power, especially by outlawing "closed-shop" (1947).
4. Civil rights: Truman desegregated armed forces and banned racial discrimination in federal hiring (1948).
5. 1948 Election: Harry S. Truman (Democrat) defeated Thomas E. Dewey (Republican).
B. Anticommunism
1. Loyalty Review Board: established to review government employees regarding Communist sympathies (1947).
2. Alger Hiss: accused as a Communist spy (1948); convicted of perjury (1950).
3. McCarran Act: required Communist-front organizations to register with the government (1950).

    4. Joseph McCarthy: senator from Wisconsin charged Communists were working in State Department and army; censured by Senate (1950–1954).

C. Eisenhower

    1. 1952 Election: Gen. Dwight D. Eisenhower (Republican) defeated Adlai Stevenson (Democrat).

    2. Supreme Court: Earl Warren appointed Chief Justice (1953).

    3. Atomic Energy Act: private nuclear power plants allowed; established Atomic Energy Commission (1954).

    4. Public works: St. Lawrence Seaway (1954); Interstate Highway System (1956).

    5. NASA: National Aeronautics and Space Administration established (1958).

    6. NDEA: National Defense Education Act provided loans and grants for college students (1958).

    7. New states: Alaska and Hawaii became the forty-ninth and fiftieth states (1959).

D. Civil Rights

    1. *Brown v. Board of Education:* Supreme Court declared separate educational facilities inherently unequal (1954).

    2. Montgomery: Martin Luther King organized bus boycott (Dec. 1955–Dec. 1956).

    3. Little Rock, Ark.: National Guard sent to force desegregation of Central High School (1957).

    4. Civil Rights Acts: Justice Department authorized to enforce voting rights (1957) and federal courts received power to register black voters (1960).

    5. Sit-ins: Greensboro, North Carolina, sit-ins led to formation of Student Nonviolent Coordinating Committee (SNCC) (1960).

E. 1960 Election

    1. Television debates: debates between Vice President Richard M. Nixon (Republican) and Senator John F. Kennedy (Democrat) turning point in campaign.

    2. Kennedy victory: Kennedy became first Roman Catholic president after narrow victory over Nixon.

## SOCIETY AND CULTURE, 1945–1960

A. Economic and Demographic Trends

    1. GNP: gross national product nearly doubled between 1945 and 1960.

    2. Population growth: U.S. population grew by more than 28 million in 1950s.

3. Sun Belt: Florida, Southwest, and California grew rapidly.
4. Suburbs: suburbs grew six times faster than cities in the 1950s.
5. Middle class: number of families classified as middle class grew from 5.7 million in 1947 to over 12 million by the early 1960s.

B. Social Conformity
1. Employment: by 1960, 38% of work force employed by organizations with over 500 employees.
2. Homogeneity: David Riesman, *The Lonely Crowd* (1950), and William Whyte, *The Organization Man* (1956), regarded society as characterized by conformity.
3. Women: books and magazines promoted a "cult" of feminine domesticity.
4. Religion: church membership rose to 65% of population by 1960; Fulton J. Sheen, Billy Graham, and Norman Vincent Peale emphasized reassurance.

C. Social Critics
1. Intellectuals: John Kenneth Galbraith and James B. Conant sharply criticized American society.
2. Theater and Fiction: Arthur Miller, J.D. Salinger, and Saul Bellow emphasized conflict between mass society and the individual.
3. Art: abstract expressionism, emphasizing spontaneous expression of subjectivity, emerged in the art of Jackson Pollock and Mark Rothco.
4. Beats: Allen Ginsburg and Jack Kerouac led a literary movement expressing alienation from 20th century American life.

# DOMESTIC POLICIES, 1960–1968

A. Kennedy
1. Legislative successes: increased minimum wage, Area Redevelopment Act (1961); Housing Act (1961).
2. Mississippi: National Guard enabled James Meredith to enroll at University of Mississippi (1962).
3. March on Washington: 200,000 people demonstrated in support of Civil Rights bill; King delivered "I Have a Dream" speech (Aug. 28, 1963).
4. Kennedy assassination: Lee Harvey Oswald shot John F. Kennedy in Dallas, Texas (Nov. 22, 1963); Lyndon B. Johnson became president; assassination conspiracy theories popular.

B. Johnson
1. Tax cut: $10 billion tax cut (1964).
2. Civil Rights Act: outlawed racial discrimination by employees and

unions; created Equal Employment Opportunity Commission (1964).

3. Economic Opportunity Act: established Job Corps and Volunteers in Service to America and other programs to address poverty; created Office of Economic Opportunity (1964).
4. Voting Rights Act: authorized Federal involvement in voter registration (1965).
5. Medicare: provided medical care for retired persons (1965).
6. Elementary and Secondary Education Act: provided $1.5 billion to school districts; created Head Start for educationally disadvantaged children (1965).
7. Cities: Housing and Urban Development Act (1965); Department of Housing and Urban Affairs established (1966).
8. Appalachia: Appalachian Regional Development Act provided $1.1 billion (1966).

## FOREIGN POLICY, 1961–1968

A. Kennedy
   1. Bay of Pigs: CIA directed failed invasion of Cuba (April 19, 1961).
   2. Berlin Wall: Nikita Khrushchev, Premier of Soviet Union, closed border between East and West Berlin and ordered erection of wall (Aug. 1961).
   3. Peace Corps: program to send young Americans to serve on projects in developing nations (1961).
   4. Cuban Missile Crisis: U.S. spy planes discovered Soviet missiles being placed in Cuba; Kennedy announced blockade of Cuba, forcing dismantling of missile bases (Oct. 22–28, 1962).
   5. Nuclear test ban: major powers signed treaty banning atmospheric testing of nuclear weapons (1963).
   6. Alliance for Progress: aid provided to Latin America (1961).
   7. Vietnam: military advisors increased from 2,000 (1961) to 16,000 (1963).
B. Johnson
   1. Gulf of Tonkin: alleged North Vietnamese attack on American ships in Gulf of Tonkin; Johnson authorized to use military force (Aug. 1964).
   2. "Rolling Thunder": sustained bombing of North Vietnam ordered; combat troops committed (1965); 38,000 troops by 1968.
   3. Opposition to war: "Doves" objected to the war, beginning with teach-ins (1965); congressional investigation began (1966).
   4. "Tet Offensive": Vietcong waged major counterattack in various

places (January 31, 1968), winning psychological victory.

5. Eugene McCarthy: Senator from Minnesota became anti-war candidate (1967); nearly defeated Johnson in New Hampshire primary (1968).

6. Lyndon Johnson: Johnson withdrew from presidential race and announced cessation of bombing (March 1968); Vice President Hubert Humphrey became candidate for presidential nomination.

7. Robert Kennedy: entered race after New Hampshire primary; assassinated in California (June 1968).

8. 1968 Election: Richard M. Nixon (Republican) narrowly defeated Hubert H. Humphrey (Democrat).

# POLITICAL AND SOCIAL ACTIVISM, 1965–1970

A. Ethinic Activism
1. Racial riots: inner-city riots in Watts, Los Angeles (1965), New York and Chicago (1966), and Newark and Detroit (1967).
2. Black power: Stokely Carmichael, chairman of SNCC, called for black control of the civil rights movement (1966).
3. Hispanics: Cesar Chavez's United Farm Workers Organizing Committee recognized by AFL (1965).
4. Native Americans: American Indian Movement (AIM) founded (1968).

B. New Left
1. SDS: Students for a Democratic Society (1960) called for "participatory democracy" in Port Huron Statement (1962).
2. Free Speech: students at University of California, Berkeley, staged sit-ins, challenging campus political restrictions (1964).
3. Vietnam: students began focusing on the Vietnam War, 500,000 gathering in New York's Central Park (1967).
4. 1968: over 200 major campus demonstrations took place; thousands protested war in Chicago during Democratic convention (August).
5. Counterculture: "hippies" experimented with alternative lifestyles, often in urban or rural communes; Woodstock Music Festival in upstate New York was high point of counterculture movement (1969).
6. Women's liberation: Betty Friedan, author of *The Feminine Mystique* (1963), helped found the National Organization for Women (1966).
7. Sexual revolution: birth control pills and antibiotics allowed challenges to traditional taboos against pre-marital sex.

8. Homosexual rights: gay and lesbian rights activists forged a visible movement after police raid on Stonewall Inn, Greenwich Village (1969).

# DOMESTIC POLICY AND SOCIETY, 1969–1980

A. Nixon
   1. Supreme Court: Warren E. Burger appointed Chief Justice (1969); Harry A. Blackmun, Lewis F. Powell, Jr., and William Rehnquist appointed associate justices; death penalty (1970) and anti-abortion laws (*Roe. v. Wade,* 1973) declared unconstitutional.
   2. Right to vote: voting rights extended to 18 year olds (1970).
   3. Environment: Clean Air Act (1970); acts to control water pollution (1970, 1972).
   4. Worker safety: Occupational Safety and Health Act (1970).
   5. Revenue sharing: $30 billion in federal money distributed to the states over five years (1972).
   6. Election reform: Federal Election Campaign Act (1972).
   7. Economy: unemployment and inflation rose; gross national product declined; 90-day wage and price freeze (Aug. 1971); mandatory guidelines for increases then instituted; voluntary wage and price controls established; OPEC increased oil prices (1973).
B. Watergate
   1. Break-in: five men caught breaking into Democratic headquarters at Watergate apartment complex (June 1973).
   2. Revelations: beginning with James McCord's letter to Judge John J. Sirica, Republican party and White House increasingly tied to break-in and later cover-ups (1972–1973).
   3. Congress: the Senate established an investigating committee and the House Judiciary Committee began impeachment hearings (1973–1974).
   4. Indictments: grand jury indicted seven individuals in connection with cover-up (March, 1974).
   5. Spiro T. Agnew: Vice President Spiro T. Agnew resigned (Oct. 1973) because of legal problems. Congressman Gerald R. Ford became Vice President under provisions of 25th Amendment.
   6. Resignation: Richard M. Nixon's resignation took effect at noon (Aug. 9, 1974); Gerald R. Ford became nation's first unelected president.
C. Ford
   1. Nixon pardon: Ford pardoned Richard Nixon, although he had not been charged with a crime (1974).

2. Economy: Ford called for voluntary controls over inflation ("Whip Inflation Now"), but economy continued to decline (1974).
3. New York: Federal government guaranteed loans when New York neared bankruptcy (1975).
4. 1976 Election: James (Jimmy) Earl Carter (Democrat) defeated Gerald R. Ford (Republican).

D. Carter
1. Economy: by 1980 unemployment was 7.5%, inflation 12%, interest rate 20%.
2. Energy: Carter unable to obtain adequate energy legislation; Department of Energy created (1977); fuel crisis (1979).
3. Environment: "superfund" created for cleanup of chemical wastes.
4. 1980 Election: Ronald Reagan (Republican) defeated Jimmy Carter (Democrat).

E. Social Trends
1. African-Americans: two-tier social structure (middle class and "under class") emerged.
2. Hispanics: grew 61%, much through "undocumented" immigration.
3. Women: 50% of women over 16 employed outside home; Equal Rights Amendment approved by Congress (1972) but not ratified by states.
4. Population: shift from Northeast to "sun-belt," particularly Florida, Texas, Arizona, and California.
5. Religion: U.S. experienced a major revival of conservative Christianity; some preachers, such as Jerry Falwell, became politically active.

# FOREIGN POLICY, 1969–1980

A. Nixon
1. Vietnamization: Nixon increasingly turned war over to Vietnamese; withdrew 60,000 U.S. troops (1969).
2. Cambodia: Nixon ordered bombing and then invasion of Cambodia (1969–1970); four students killed by National Guard during protest at Kent State University (1970); several hundred colleges closed by strikes.
3. Draft: lottery system instituted (1970); draft abolished (1973).
4. Pentagon Papers: classified Defense Department paper published in 1971 revealed government misleading regarding Vietnam War.
5. Mining and bombing: Nixon ordered mining of Haiphong and other North Vietnamese ports; bombing of North Vietnam resumed (1972).

6. China: Nixon and National Security Advisor Henry A. Kissinger visited China.
7. Settlement: agreement reached with North Vietnam (Jan. 1973); last American troops left Vietnam (March 1973).
8. War Powers Act: required congressional approval for commitment of combat troops (1973).
9. SALT: Soviet Union and U.S. signed Strategic Arms Limitation Treaty (1972).
10. Détente: name given by Nixon and Kissinger to policy to reduce tensions between U.S. and China and Soviet Union.

B. Ford
1. Vietnam: Congress rejected Ford's request for aid to South Vietnam; Saigon fell to North Vietnam (April 1975).
2. *Mayaguez*: Cambodia seized merchant ship *Mayaguez* (May 1975); Marine assault freed ship (May 1975).

C. Carter
1. Panama: treaty provided for transfer of ownership of Canal to Panama in 1999 (1978).
2. Israel: Camp David Agreement signed between Israel and Egypt (1978).
3. China: People's Republic of China recognized (1979).
4. SALT II: treaty signed with Soviet Union but not passed by the Senate (1979).
5. Afghanistan: Soviet Union invaded Afghanistan (1979); Carter halted shipment of grain and withdrew SALT II treaty from Senate.
6. Iran: after 1978 revolution against American-backed Shah, Americans taken hostage at U.S. embassy (Nov. 4, 1979–Jan. 20, 1981).

# DOMESTIC POLICY AND SOCIETY, 1981–1993

A. Reagan
1. Budget Reconciliation Act: $39 billion cut from domestic programs; defense increased $12 billion (1981).
2. Economic Recovery Tax Act: reduced income taxes 25% over three years (1981).
3. Deficit: deficit mounted; Tax Equity and Fiscal Responsibility Act (1981) and Deficit Reduction Act (1984) increased various taxes.
4. Air traffic controllers: Reagan fired striking air traffic controllers, destroying union (1981).
5. 1984 Election: Ronald Reagan (Republican) defeated Walter Mondale (Democrat).

6. Tax Reform Act: lowered personal income taxes (1986).
7. Supreme Court: Reagan appointed conservatives; William H. Rehnquist as Chief Justice; Sandra Day O'Connor, Antonin Scalia, Anthony Kennedy as associate justices.
8. 1988 Election: Vice President George Bush (Republican) defeated Michael Dukakis (Democrat).

B. Bush
   1. Deficit: taxes raised and spending cut 10% over five years (1990); deficit reached $4 billion (1992).
   2. Savings and loan crisis: S & L industry in financial trouble; Resolution Trust Corporation established to oversee closures and mergings (1989).
   3. Environment: Exxon *Valdez* spilled 240,000 barrels of oil into Prince William Sound, Alaska (1989); Clear Air Act required emissions to be cut 50% by year 2000 (1990).
   4. Americans with Disabilities Act: barred discrimination against people with physical or mental disabilities (1990).
   5. Supreme Court: Bush appointed David Souter and Clarence Thomas; Thomas nomination stirred controversy after Anita Hill accused him of sexual harassment (1991).
   6. Economy: median household income fell 3.5% (1991); highest number of poor people since 1964 (1992); California began paying bills with "IOUs" (1992).
   7. Los Angeles riot: beating of Rodney King (1991); police officers acquitted (April 1992); riot erupted (April 29–May 1, 1992).
   8. Congress: House bank scandal; 27th Amendment prohibited mid-term pay raises for Congress (1992).
   9. 1992 Election: William (Bill) Clinton (Democrat) defeated George Bush (Republican); Ross Perot gained nearly 20% of vote as an independent candidate.

C. Social and Cultural Trends
   1. AIDS: discovery of Acquired Immune Deficiency Syndrome (1981); by 1990, 83,000 Americans had died of the disease.
   2. Abortion: *Webster v. Reproductive Health Services* (1989) shifted abortion issue to state legislatures.
   3. Religion: televangelist Jim Bakker convicted of fraud and conspiracy (1991).
   4. Education: "A Nation at Risk" issued in 1981; many states began educational reforms.
   5. Drugs: Bush declared "War on Drugs" (1989); anti-drug agreement signed with Bolivia, Colombia, and Peru (1990).
   6. Labor: labor union membership declined to about 19% of workforce.

# FOREIGN POLICY, 1981–1993

A. Reagan
1. Nicaragua: U.S. provided arms and other military aid to Contras which opposed leftist Sandinista government; Sandinistas and Contras signed cease fire (1981–1988).
2. Grenada: U.S. troops sent to overthrow Cuban-backed regime (1983).
3. Lebanon: U.S. troops sent on peacemaking mission (1982); withdrawn (1984).
4. INF Treaty: U.S. signed agreement with Soviet Union eliminating medium-range missiles from Europe (1987).
5. Iran-Contra: arms sold to Iranians; profits diverted to Nicaraguan Contras (1985–1986); congressional hearings and court cases (1987–1990).

B. Bush
1. Panama: U.S. troops invaded (Dec. 1989), overthrowing Manuel Noriega (Jan. 1990), later convicted and jailed in the U.S. for assisting in drug trafficking.
2. China: marshal law imposed after pro-democracy demonstrations; Bush follows policy of "constructive engagement" (1989).
3. Africa: U.S. troops sent into Liberia to evacuate Americans; sanctions lifted from South Africa (1991).
4. Communist Bloc: Eastern European and Soviet Communist governments collapse (1989–1991).
5. Persian Gulf War: Iraq invaded Kuwait (Aug. 1990); U.S. ordered troops to Saudi Arabia; Operation Desert Storm attacked Iraq with missiles and air attacks (Jan. 1991) and ground attack (Feb. 1991); war ended (April 1991).
6. Arms control: START II signed with Russia (1992).
7. Somalia: U.S. soldiers sent to enable delivery of relief aid; U.N. peacekeeping force replaces U.S. forces (1992–93).

# CLINTON PRESIDENCY, 1993–

A. Domestic Policy
1. Abortion: Clinton overturned Bush "gag" rule prohibiting abortion counseling in federally funded clinics (1993).
2. Homosexuals: after attempting to lift ban on homosexuals in the military, compromise "Don't ask, Don't tell" policy was adopted (1993).
3. Deficit: $496 billion reduction of budget deficit over five years; taxes raised on upper incomes (1993).

4. "Motor-Voter" bill: states to allow voter registration at time of driver's license application (1993).
5. "Family Leave" Act: large employers to provide up to 12 weeks unpaid leave for family and medical emergencies (1993).
6. North American Free Trade Agreement: originally negotiated by Bush administration; eliminated most tariffs between U.S., Canada, and Mexico by 2009.
7. Supreme Court: Ruth Bader Ginsberg (1993) and Stephen Breyer (1994) appointed Associate Justices.

B. Foreign Policy
1. Middle East: Israel and Palestine Liberation Organization and Israel and Jordan signed agreements (1994). U.S. helped broker a breakthrough land-for-security accord between the Palestinians and Israel (1999).
2. Bosnia, Kosovo, Somalia, Rwanda, and Haiti major world trouble spots.

# 16. IMPORTANT SCIENTISTS AND THEIR CONTRIBUTIONS

**Baltimore and Temin**—discovered RNA-dependent DNA polymerase reverse transcriptase, the enzyme which has enabled us to study the retrovirus infections such as AIDS

**Beadle and Tatum**—developed the "one-gene-one-enzyme" theory

**Bernoulli Family**—produced extensive works in the fields of calculus, geometry and astronomy

**Daniel Bernoulli**—derived the central formula of fluid dynamics

**Niels Bohr**—major contributor to quantum theory

**Annie Cannon**—astronomer who developed the stellar spectral classification system at the Harvard College observatory

**Rachel Carson**—20th century environmentalist who wrote *Silent Spring*

**Paul Ehrlich**—provided work leading to the theory of antibody production

**Rosalind Franklin**—prepared the X-ray crystallography which lead to the discovery of the DNA double helix by Watson, Crick, and Wilkins (she died before the Nobel Prize was awarded)

**Werner Heisenberg**—a founder of quantum mechanics, formulated the uncertainty principle

**Arthur Kornberg**—discovered the DNA polymerase enzyme

**Barbara McClintock**—discovered the moving genetic material known as transposons or "jumping genes"

**Èlie Metchnikoff**—developed the theory of cellular immunity

**Luc Montagnier**—isolated and identified the Human Immunodeficiency Virus (HIV) which causes AIDS

**Isaac Newton**—developed the "Law of Universal Gravitation"

**Isaac Newton and Gottfried Wilhelm Leibniz**—independently discovered the branch of mathematics known as calculus

**Amalie Noether**—a mathematician whose analysis of symmetry became a guiding principle of contemporary physics

**Pascal and Fermat**—cocreators of probability theory

**Max Planck**—his work led to the discovery that energy is quantitized

**William Konrad Röntgen**—discovered X-rays

**William Thomson (Lord Kelvin)**—formulated the absolute temperature scale

## GEOLOGICAL TIME SCALE

**Biogenous Deposit Dating**—cores of sediments containing foraminiferal ooze show changes in latitude in response to temperature change

**Cambrian Rocks**—Contain the oldest easily identifiable fossils

**Cenozoic Era**—meaning "recent life"—dominated by mammals and flowering plants

**Cretaceous Period**—time during which dinosaurs peaked and then died out

**Eons**—great spans of geologic time defined by major events

**Epochs**—a unit of geologic time, longer than an age and representing a subdivision of a period during which the rocks of a particular series were formed

**Eras**—a unit of geologic time that includes two or more periods grouped together

**Faunal Succession**—an upward sequential change in fossil types with those in the lowest layers being most dissimilar to present-day animals

**Foraminifera**—live mainly in the near surface waters of the ocean; their existence in core sediments is useful for dating and for correlation of the simultaneous existence of species

**Geochronology**—the science of obtaining isotopic dates for geologic materials and events

**Geologic Time Scale**—a method for establishing the time correlation of rock layers in widely separated areas

**Isotopic Time**—a fixed-rate process that establishes the actual ages of rocks, etc.; it is based on the fact that nuclear breakdown reactions occur at a constant rate which is not affected by changes in temperature, pressure, or chemical reactions

**Magnetic Reversal Dating**—based on polarity changes recorded in magnetic minerals within rocks and sediments

**Marine Sediments**—rocks, mud, and minerals which contain the record of past oceanic events and climatic conditions

**Mesozoic Era**—geologic era extending from the end of the Paleozoic era to the Cenozoic era, marked by the end of the era of the dinosaurs

**Paleoceanography**—the study of the past environmental conditions of the ocean

**Periods**—subdivisions of eras based on evolutionary changes which are less dramatic than those used to differentiate eras

**Phanerozoic Eon**—includes the time during which advanced life flourished on earth; time frame defined by major differences in dominant life forms

**Plate Tectonics**—the constant destruction and renewal of the Earth's surface by the motion of sections of the Earth's crust. Currently the Atlantic Ocean is opening while the Pacific Ocean is closing

**Superposition**—the sequence in which sedimentary strata are the oldest at the bottom and the youngest at the top

**Unconformity**—a break in the geological time record

**Volcanic Sea Floor Rocks**—dating techniques indicate that the youngest rocks are along the ocean ridge and the oldest rocks are away from the ridge

## BASIC ASTRONOMY

**Achromatic Lens**—lens of a telescope which is composed of two ground lenses from different kinds of glass that are used to bring two selected colors to the same focus while correcting for chromatic aberration

**Active Galactic Nucleus**—the central energy source of an active galaxy

**Associations**—scattered stars which move through space together but are not bound by gravity into clusters

**Asteroids**—collections of small rocks which are found mainly between Mars and Jupiter in an area known as the asteroid belt

**Astronomical Unit**—the average distance from the Earth to the Sun = $1.5 \times 10^8$ km or $93 \times 10^6$ miles

**Aurora**—a display of glowing lights which occurs because a magnetic field guides charged particles toward the north and south magnetic poles

**Autumnal Equinox**—the point on the celestial sphere where the Sun crosses the celestial equator moving toward the south and autumn begins in the Northern Hemisphere

**Binary Stars**—star pairs which orbit around a common center of mass

**Black Hole**—a mass which has collapsed to a very small volume so that its gravity prevents the escape of all radiation

**Blue Shift**—the shortening of the wavelengths of light observed as the source of light and the observer move toward each other

**Cardinal Points**—points on the horizon which are directly north, south, east and west of you as you stand on the Earth

**Celestial Sphere**—the picturing of the sky as a giant sphere surrounding the Earth

**Charge-Coupled Device**—an electronic imaging device formed by place about 250,000 light sensitive diodes into an array of less than 1 square inch. This device is far more sensitive than a photographic plate and can project images directly into computer memory

**Comet**—small icy bodies which orbit the sun and produce tails made of gas and dust as they come near to the sun

**Constellation**—a stellar pattern or the region of the sky which it occupies which has been identified by a name which is usually related to mythology

**Corona**—the faint outer atmosphere of the sun which is composed of ionized, low density, very hot gases

**Cosmic Rays**—atomic nuclei which enter the Earth's atmosphere at or near the speed of light

**Cosmology**—the study of the origin, nature, and evolution of the universe

**Doppler Effect**—the change in the wavelength of radiation cause by the relative radial motion of the source of the wavelength and the observer

**Diurnal Motion**—daily motion of the sky which is caused by the Earth's rotation as evidenced in the rising and setting of the sun or moon

**Electromagnetic Radiation**—changing electric and magnetic fields which travel through space and transfer energy from one place to another

**Evening Star**—any star visible in the sky just after sunset

**Hertzsprung-Russell Diagram**—a plot showing the intrinsic brightness of stars versus their surface temperature

**Light-Year**—the distance which light travels in one mean solar year (approximately 9.46 trillion km)

**Morning Star**—any star visible in the sky just before sunrise

**Main Sequence**—the area of the Hertzsprung-Russell Diagram which runs from the upper left to the lower right and contains nearly 90 percent of all stars

**Meteor**—a small piece of matter which is heated by friction and vaporizes as it falls to Earth

**Meteorite**—a meteor which does not fully vaporize and therefore strikes the Earth

**Missing Mass**—unobserved mass in clusters of galaxies which is thought to produce enough gravity to bind the cluster together

**Nadir**—the point of the celestial sphere which is directly opposite the zenith

**Nebula**—a cloud in space made of dust and gas

**Nova**—the sudden brightening of a star which is associated with eruptions on white dwarfs which are in binary systems, often making it appear as a "new" star

**Polaris**—the brightest star in the constellation of Ursa Minoris (the little bear or little dipper)

**Prominences**—eruptions on the Sun's surface which are visible during a total solar eclipse

**Protostar**—a cloud of gas and dust which is collapsing and is destined to become a star

**Pulsar**—the source of short and precisely timed radio bursts which are believed to be spinning neutron stars

**Quasar**—a small powerful source of energy which is thought to be the active core of a very distant galaxy

**Red Dwarf**—a cool star of low mass found on the lower main sequence

**Red Shift**—the lengthening of the wavelengths of light; occurs when the source and the observer are moving away from each other

**Resolving Power**—the ability of a lens system, such as that found in a telescope, to distinguish two points from each other

**Right Ascension**—a coordinate used on the celestial sphere (similar to longitude). The right ascension is measured eastward from the vernal equinox

**Sideral Day**—the period of rotation of the Earth with respect to the stars

**Summer Solstice**—the point on the celestial sphere when the Sun is at its most northern point and summer begins in the Northern Hemisphere

**Sunspots**—intense magnetic fields on the Sun which can be observed as very dark spots

**Supernova**—the explosion of a star which is caused by the collapse of a very massive star or by the transfer of matter to a white dwarf

**Vernal Equinox**—the point of the celestial sphere where the Sun crosses the celestial equator moving toward the north and spring begins in the Northern Hemisphere

**Winter Solstice**—the point on the celestial sphere when the Sun is at its most southern point and winter begins in the Northern Hemisphere

**White Dwarf Stars**—stars which have collapsed to the size of the Earth and are cooling off slowly

**Zenith**—the point on the sky which is directly overhead while standing on the Earth

**Zodiac**—the band of sky with twelve constellations that extends 8° to either side of the ecliptic and through which the sun, moon, and planets apparently pass during the year

## TEMPERATURE CONVERSION SCALE

**Absolute Zero**—the very limit of low temperature at which atoms and molecules contain no energy of motion

**Boiling Point** = 212°F or 100°C

**Celsius to Fahrenheit**: °F = 9/5 (°C) + 32

**Centigrade Scale**—scale on which there are 100 units between the freezing point and the boiling point

**Fahrenheit to Celsius**: °C = 5/9 (°F–32)

**Freezing Point** = 32°F or 0°C

**Human Body Temperature** = 98.7°F or 37°C

**Kelvin Scale**—the temperature in Celsius degrees which begins above absolute zero, 0°K is therefore equal to the lowest limit of temperature

**Temperature**—a measure of the velocity of the random motion of the atoms or molecules of a material

**Triple Point of Water**—the temperature and pressure at which solid, liquid, and water vapor coexist

**Zero-Point Energy**—a system's or substance's nonthermal energy at absolute zero

# 17. CLASSIFICATIONS OF LIVING THINGS

## MONERAN KINGDOM

Bacteria, blue-green algae, and primitive pathogens

**Characteristics**—prokaryotic organisms, single-celled; autotrophic though a few are heterotrophic

**Structures**—flagella capsules

**Functions**—food gathering, respiration, reproduction

**Systems**—none

**Growth**—cell membrane and availability of food set growth limit

**Reproduction Method**—binary fission

## PROTISTA KINGDOM

Animal-like organism, distinguished by method of locomotion

**Characteristics**—eukaryotes, mainly microscopic, single-celled or multi-cellular; some autotrophic and many heterotrophic

**Structures**—cilia, flagella, cell organelles membrane bound, photosynthetic

**Functions**—organelles function as organ systems

**Systems**—none

**Growth**—cell membrane and availability of food set growth limit

**Reproduction Method**—asexual or sexual

## FUNGI KINGDOM

**Characteristics**—eukaryotes, mainly multicellular, parasitic, symbiotic, mycorrhizae

**Structures**—root-like, caps, filaments, reproductive

**Functions**—digestive-like, respiration, reproductive

**Systems**—beginning to develop

**Growth**—based on food source and availability

**Reproduction Method**—asexual, sexual

## PLANTAE KINGDOM

**Characteristics**—eukaryotes, multicellular, nonmotile, autotrophic

**Structures**—cellulose cell walls

**Functions**—based on cell and tissue chemistry

**Systems**—all present and functioning

**Growth**—based on hormone action

**Reproduction Method**—asexual, sexual by spores, seeds, flowers, and cones

## ANIMALIA KINGDOM

**Characteristics**—eukaryotes, multicellular, heterotrophic, most are motile at some point in lifetime

**Structures**—all present and unique to organism

**Functions**—based on nutrition, cell and tissue chemistry, and individual demands

**Systems**—all present and functioning

**Growth**—based on hormone action and nutrition

**Reproduction Method**—asexual, sexual

# 18. SUMMARY OF ANIMAL TISSUES

| Tissue | Location | Functions |
|---|---|---|
| Epithelial | Covering of body<br>Lining internal organs | Protection<br>Secretion |
| Muscle<br>  Skeletal | Attached to skeleton bones | Voluntary movement |
|   Smooth | Walls of internal organs | Involuntary movement |
|   Cardiac | Walls of heart | Pumping blood |
| Connective<br>  Binding | Covering organs, in tendons and ligaments | Holding tissues and organs together |
|   Bone | Skeleton | Support, protection, movement |
|   Adipose | Beneath skin and around internal organs | Fat storage, insulation, cushion |
|   Cartilage | Ends of bone, part of nose and ears | Reduction of friction, support |
| Nerve | Brain | Interpretation of impulses, mental activity |
|  | Spinal cord, nerves, ganglions | Carrying impulses to and from all organs |
| Blood | Blood vessels, heart | Carrying materials to and from cells, carrying oxygen, fighting germs, clotting |

# THE PERIODIC TABLE

METALS — NONMETALS

## KEY

22 → Atomic Number
IVA / IVB → Group Classification
Ti → Symbol
47.88 → Atomic Weight

( ) indicates most stable or best known isotope

TRANSITIONAL METALS

| 1 IA / IA | 2 IIA / IIA | | | | | | | | | | | | 13 IIIB / IIIA | 14 IVB / IVA | 15 VB / VA | 16 VIB / VIA | 17 VIIB / VIIA | 18 VIII / 0 |
|---|---|---|---|---|---|---|---|---|---|---|---|---|---|---|---|---|---|---|
| 1 H 1.008 | | | | | | | | | | | | | | | | | | 2 He 4.003 |
| 3 Li 6.941 | 4 Be 9.012 | | | | | | | | | | | | 5 B 10.811 | 6 C 12.011 | 7 N 14.007 | 8 O 15.999 | 9 F 18.998 | 10 Ne 20.180 |
| 11 Na 22.990 | 12 Mg 24.305 | 3 IIIA/IIIB | 4 IVA/IVB | 5 VA/VB | 6 VIA/VIB | 7 VIIA/VIIB | 8 VIIIA/VIII | 9 VIIIA/VIII | 10 VIIA/VIII | 11 IB/IB | 12 IIB/IIB | | 13 Al 26.982 | 14 Si 28.086 | 15 P 30.974 | 16 S 32.066 | 17 Cl 35.453 | 18 Ar 39.948 |
| 19 K 39.098 | 20 Ca 40.078 | 21 Sc 44.956 | 22 Ti 47.88 | 23 V 50.942 | 24 Cr 51.996 | 25 Mn 54.938 | 26 Fe 55.847 | 27 Co 58.933 | 28 Ni 58.693 | 29 Cu 63.546 | 30 Zn 65.39 | | 31 Ga 69.723 | 32 Ge 72.61 | 33 As 74.922 | 34 Se 78.96 | 35 Br 79.904 | 36 Kr 83.8 |
| 37 Rb 85.468 | 38 Sr 87.62 | 39 Y 88.906 | 40 Zr 91.224 | 41 Nb 92.906 | 42 Mo 95.94 | 43 Tc (97.907) | 44 Ru 101.07 | 45 Rh 102.906 | 46 Pd 106.4 | 47 Ag 107.868 | 48 Cd 112.411 | | 49 In 114.818 | 50 Sn 118.710 | 51 Sb 121.757 | 52 Te 127.60 | 53 I 126.905 | 54 Xe 131.29 |
| 55 Cs 132.905 | 56 Ba 137.327 | 57 La 138.906 | 72 Hf 178.49 | 73 Ta 180.948 | 74 W 183.84 | 75 Re 186.207 | 76 Os 190.23 | 77 Ir 192.22 | 78 Pt 195.08 | 79 Au 196.967 | 80 Hg 200.59 | | 81 Tl 204.383 | 82 Pb 207.2 | 83 Bi 208.980 | 84 Po (208.982) | 85 At (209.982) | 86 Rn (222.018) |
| 87 Fr (223.020) | 88 Ra (226.025) | 89 Ac (227.028) | 104 Unq (261.11) | 105 Unp (262.114) | 106 Unh (263.118) | 107 Uns (262.12) | 108 Uno (265) | 109 Une (266) | 110 Uun (269) | | | | | | | | | |

Alkali Metals — Alkaline Earth Metals — Halogens — Noble Gases

### LANTHANIDE SERIES

| 58 Ce 140.115 | 59 Pr 140.908 | 60 Nd 144.24 | 61 Pm (144.913) | 62 Sm 150.36 | 63 Eu 151.965 | 64 Gd 157.25 | 65 Tb 158.925 | 66 Dy 162.50 | 67 Ho 164.930 | 68 Er 167.26 | 69 Tm 168.934 | 70 Yb 173.04 | 71 Lu 174.967 |
|---|---|---|---|---|---|---|---|---|---|---|---|---|---|

### ACTINIDE SERIES

| 90 Th 232.038 | 91 Pa 231.036 | 92 U 238.029 | 93 Np (237.048) | 94 Pu (244.064) | 95 Am (243.061) | 96 Cm (247.070) | 97 Bk (247.070) | 98 Cf (251.080) | 99 Es (252.083) | 100 Fm (257.095) | 101 Md (258.1) | 102 No (259.101) | 103 Lr (262.11) |
|---|---|---|---|---|---|---|---|---|---|---|---|---|---|

# INDEX OF ELEMENTS

| | | |
|---|---|---|
| 1. HYDROGEN | 38. STRONTIUM | 75. RHENIUM |
| 2. HELIUM | 39. YTTRIUM | 76. OSMIUM |
| 3. LITHIUM | 40. ZIRCONIUM | 77. IRIDIUM |
| 4. BERYLLIUM | 41. NIOBIUM | 78. PLATINUM |
| 5. BORON | 42. MOLYBDENUM | 79. GOLD |
| 6. CARBON | 43. TECHNETIUM | 80. MERCURY |
| 7. NITROGEN | 44. RUTHENIUM | 81. THALLIUM |
| 8. OXYGEN | 45. RHODIUM | 82. LEAD |
| 9. FLUORINE | 46. PALLADIUM | 83. BISMUTH |
| 10. NEON | 47. SILVER | 84. POLONIUM |
| 11. SODIUM | 48. CADMIUM | 85. ASTATINE |
| 12. MAGNESIUM | 49. INDIUM | 86. RADON |
| 13. ALUMINUM | 50. TIN | 87. FRANCIUM |
| 14. SILICON | 51. ANTIMONY | 88. RADIUM |
| 15. PHOSPHOROUS | 52. TELLURIUM | 89. ACTINIUM |
| 16. SULFUR | 53. IODINE | 90. THORIUM |
| 17. CHLORINE | 54. XENON | 91. PROTACTINIUM |
| 18. ARGON | 55. CESIUM | 92. URANIUM |
| 19. POTASSIUM | 56. BARIUM | 93. NEPTUNIUM |
| 20. CALCIUM | 57. LANTHANUM | 94. PLUTONIUM |
| 21. SCANDIUM | 58. CERIUM | 95. AMERICUM |
| 22. TITANIUM | 59. PRASEODYMIUM | 96. CURIUM |
| 23. VANADIUM | 60. NEODYMIUM | 97. BERKELIUM |
| 24. CHROMIUM | 61. PROMETHIUM | 98. CALIFORNIUM |
| 25. MANGANESE | 62. SAMARIUM | 99. EINSTEINIUM |
| 26. IRON | 63. EUROPIUM | 100. FERMIUM |
| 27. COBALT | 64. GADOLINIUM | 101. MENDELEVIUM |
| 28. NICKEL | 65. TERBIUM | 102. NOBELIUM |
| 29. COPPER | 66. DYSPROSIUM | 103. LAWRENCIUM |
| 30. ZINC | 67. HOLMIUM | 104. UNNILQUADIUM |
| 31. GALLIUM | 68. ERBIUM | 105. UNNILPENTIUM |
| 32. GERMANIUM | 69. THULLUM | 106. UNNIHEXIUM |
| 33. ARSENIC | 70. YTTERBIUM | 107. UNNILSEPTIUM |
| 34. SELENIUM | 71. LUTETIUM | 108. UNNILOCTIUM |
| 35. BROMINE | 72. HAFNIUM | 109. UNNILENNIUM |
| 36. KRYPTON | 73. TANTALUM | 110. UNUNNILIUM |
| 37. RUBIDIUM | 74. TUNGSTEN | |

# 20. GEOGRAPHY

## GEOGRAPHY

A.  Lines of Latitude (parallels)
1.  Run east – west
    a.  Measure the distance (in degrees, minutes, seconds) north and south of the equator (0 degrees latitude), the lowest latitude possible.
    b.  The highest latitude possible is 90 degrees north (North Pole) and south (South Pole).
2.  Specific Names
    a.  The Tropic of Cancer and Tropic of Capricorn lie at 23.5 degrees north and south, respectively.
    b.  The Antarctic and Arctic Circles lie at 66.5 degrees north and south.
    c.  Low latitudes occur between the Tropics of Cancer and Capricorn.
    d.  Middle latitudes occur between the Tropic of Cancer and the Arctic Circle in the Northern Hemisphere, and between the Tropic of Capricorn and the Antarctic Circle in the Southern Hemisphere.
    e.  High latitudes occur between the Arctic Circle and the North Pole and between the Antarctic Circle and the South Pole.
B.  Lines of Longitude (meridians)
1.  Run north – south
    a.  Measure the distance (in degrees, minutes, seconds) east and west of the Prime Meridian (0 degrees longitude).
    b.  The Prime Meridian is an arbitrary reference line that runs through Greenwich, England.
    c.  The highest longitude possible is 180 degrees (east and west), called the International Date Line.
C.  Map Projections
1.  Cylindrical projection – projection of the earth onto a cylinder (e.g., navigation uses).
2.  Conic projection – projection of a globe onto a cone (parallels are spaced evenly along the central meridian).

3. Planar (azimuthal) – projection of a globe grid onto a plane (used in atlases).
   a. Equidistant – can be centered anywhere, facilitating the correct measurement of distances from that point to all others.
   b. Gnomonic – all great circles appear as straight lines.
D. Patterns and Quantities on Maps
   1. Cartography – construction of maps
   2. Scale – ratio between the measurement of something on a map and the corresponding measurement on the earth (e.g., 1 inch to 1 mile).
   3. Topographical features – portray the surface terrain of small areas, usually in detail (e.g., routes, boundaries, streams).
      a. Contour line – line along which all points are of equal elevation above or below a datum (single) plane, usually indicating mean sea level.
      b. Contour interval – vertical distance separating two adjacent contour lines.

# PHYSICAL GEOGRAPHY – LAND FORMATION

A. Continents – great divisions of the land on the globe: Asia, Africa, North America, South America, Antarctica, Europe, Australia/ Oceania.
B. Geomorphology – the study of landform origins, characteristics, and evolutions and their processes.
C. Plate Tectonic Processes
   1. Responsible for mountain-building, volcanoes, and earthquakes.
   2. Portions of the earth's mantle and crust on separate slowly moving "plates."
   3. Pangaea represents a super continent of 200 million years ago – later separated into two large sections: Gondwana and Laurasia, which further separated into today's continents.
   4. Diastrophism
      a. Warping – gentle bending of the earth's crust
      b. Folding – more intense bending of the earth's crust – produces accordion effect – series of upfolds (anticlines) and downfolds (synclines), referred to as ridge and valley topography.
      c. Faulting – break in the earth's crust, break can occur as a rock mass is pulled apart (tensional or normal fault) by irresistible forces in the crust – compressional faults occur when a rock mass is pushed or compressed and a break occurs, usually causing one part of the rock mass to rise up over the other.
   5. Vulcanism

a. The outpouring of molten material from cracks in the earth.
b. Intrusive vulcanism – molten material hardens before it reaches the earth's surface (e.g., granite), not exposed on the earth's surface.
c. Extrusive vulcanism – molten material hardens on the earth's surface (e.g., basalt).
d. Pacific Ring of Fire – series of volcanoes surrounding the Pacific Ocean, includes 80% of the world's active volcanoes.

D. Earth Materials
1. Igneous rocks – formed by cooling and hardening of earth material.
   a. Magma – underground molten material
   b. Lava – above ground molten material
2. Sedimentary rocks – composed of particles of gravel, sand, silt (fine particles of soil), and clay that were eroded from other rocks (e.g., shale, coal, sandstone).
3. Metamorphic rocks – igneous and sedimentary rocks transformed due to heat, pressure, or chemical reaction (e.g., marble, slate).

E. Gradational Processes
1. Wear down high places and fill in low places.
2. Weathering – breaking down rock mass into smaller particles
   a. Physical (mechanical) – force or pressure
   b. Chemical – interaction between surface or underground water and chemicals present in rock mass.
3. Erosion – wearing away of the earth's surface by moving ice (glaciers), water, or wind.
4. Gravity transfer – the force of gravity is the attraction of the earth's mass for bodies at or near its surface.
   a. This force is constantly pulling on materials. Large boulders, not held back by more stable material, will fall down slopes (occurs in dry areas.)

F. Glaciation
1. Movement of continental and alpine ice and snow that rubs and shapes topography.
2. North America and Europe were shaped by this process during the Great Ice Age.
3. Loess – fine fertile soil that is transported by wind (in glaciated regions).

# PHYSICAL GEOGRAPHY – WATER

A. River Components
1. 71% of the earth's surface area is covered by water.

2. Source – place of origin
3. River system composition
   a. Main stream of the river
   b. Tributaries – small bodies of water that feed into the main stream of the river.
   c. Distributaries – channels carrying water off of the main stream of the river.
4. Mouth – where the river empties into another body of water.
5. Delta – triangular soil deposit at the mouth of a river.
   a. As the river empties into another body of water, the flow slows down and the river drops fine soil sediment it is carrying.
6. River Basin – area drained by a river system.

# PHYSICAL GEOGRAPHY – WEATHER

A. Air Temperature
   1. Controlled by the intensity and duration of radiation from the sun (solar energy).
   2. Angle at which the sun's rays strike the earth, the number of daylight hours, the amount of water vapor in the air, the degree of cloud cover, the elevation above sea level, and the degree of air movement all affect the air temperature at any given location.
   3. Generally, air temperature decreases with increasing elevation.
      a. lapse rate – 6.5°F decrease in air temperature per 1,000 ft. of elevation.
B. Air Pressure
   1. The weight of the air as measured at a point on the earth's surface (barometric pressure).
   2. Pressure gradients occur with differences in air pressure between areas that induce air to flow from areas of high to areas of low pressures.
   3. Convection results from the flow of air that replaces warm, rising air and the rapid movement of replacement air.
   4. Wind belts
      a. Prevailing surface wind movements responding to pressure gradients (e.g., jetstream, monsoon).
C. Ocean Currents
   1. Wind direction and the differences in density (of water) cause water to move in paths from one part of the ocean to another.
   2. Land masses are barriers to water movement (deflecting currents).
D. Atmospheric Moisture
   1. Precipitation is water (can be rain, sleet, snow, hail) deposited on the earth's surface.

    a. Convectional precipitation – caused by rising, heated, moisture-laden air (rain or hail can occur).

    b. Orographic precipitation – occurs as warm air is forced to rise because of some obstruction (hill or mountain).

    c. Cyclonic (frontal) precipitation – occurs in mid-altitudes as cool and warm air masses meet.

2. Storms

    a. Storms can occur whenever two air masses come into contact (cyclone, hurricane, tornado).

# PHYSICAL GEOGRAPHY – CLIMATE

A. Dry Climates

  1. Desert

    a. High daily temperature range.

    b. Less than 10 inches of annual precipitation.

    c. Sandy soils that lack humus (organic matter)

    d. Xerophytic vegetation, deep roots, thick bark and leaves.

  2. Steppe

    a. Soils are chernozems; thick, black earth rich in humus.

    b. Natural vegetation is short grasses (used for livestock grazing).

    c. Transition from dry to humid climates, semi-arid.

    d. Annual precipitation 10-20 inches.

  3. Dry-summer subtropical (Mediterranean)

    a. Mild rainy winters; hot, dry summers. Warm climate with long growing season.

    b. Lack of humus in soils.

    c. Vegetation (chaparral or maquis) with large roots and small leaves, to survive the summer drought.

B. Wet Climates (low latitudes)

  1. Tropical rain forest

    a. Generally centered on the equator, rainy and warm, and no distinct dry season.

    b. Vegetation is dense tree growth ("canopy" vegetation)

    c. Heavy rainfall causes leaching of soils. Soils (laterites) become thin and "rock-like" containing materials such as alumina and iron oxide.

  2. Tropical Savanna

    a. Soils heavily leached.

    b. Warm and wet, but not as much as rain forest. No distinct dry season.

    c. Natural vegetation, mainly tall grasses mixed with tropical deciduous trees.

C. Humid Climates (mid latitudes)
  1. Humid subtropical
     a. Soil may become leached and slightly acidic.
     b. Located on the southeast corner of large landmasses in middle latitudes.
     c. Mild winters; hot, humid summers.
     d. Vegetation is mixed forest (both deciduous and coniferous).
  2. Humid continental
     a. Soils vary greatly. Plenty of humus, but soils can be acidic.
     b. Found in the middle of large landmasses in the mid latitudes. Often broken into long summer and short summer types. No maritime influence here. Plenty of moisture, cold winters and hot summers are normal.
D. Cold Climates
  1. Sub-Arctic
     a. Temperatures above 50°F for at least 1-3 months. Heavy snowfalls can occur.
     b. Soils (mainly podsols) are low in humus and highly acidic.
     c. Coniferous forests (taiga or boreal forests) are plentiful.
  2. Tundra
     a. Land of the permafrost
     b. Monthly temperature averages below 50°F.
     c. Vegetation dominated by dwarf trees, lichen, mosses.
  3. Ice cap
     a. Constant cold; less than 10 inches of precipitation annually.

# POPULATION GEOGRAPHY

A. Demographic Transition Model – traces the changing levels of human fertility and mortality over time. Gives a relationship between population growth and economic development in stages.
  1. Stage 1 – High birth rate, high death rate, and minimal population growth.
  2. Stage 2 – High birth rate, but death rate drops dramatically.
  3. Stage 3 – Birth rate drops in response to high growth of Stage 2.
  4. Stage 4 – Birth and death rates continue to drop, coming closer together.
B. Measurement of Population
  1. Crude birth rate (CBR) – annual number of live births per 1,000 population (without regard to sex or age).
  2. Total fertility rate (TFR) – more accurate, since it gives the average number of children that would be born to each woman if during her child-bearing years she bore children at the current year's

rate for women her age.

3. Crude death rate (CDR) or mortality rate – annual number of deaths per 1,000 population.

4. Rate of natural increase – the crude death rate is subtracted from the crude birth rate (excluding the effects of immigrations or emigration).

C. World Population Distribution Facts
   1. 90% of all people live north of the equator.
   2. 66% of people dwell in mid latitudes (20°-60° north).
   3. Over half the people live on 5% of the land, 66% on 10%, and 90% on less than 20%.
   4. China accounts for 20% of the world's population (1.66 billion+).
   5. Europe/Russia contain 13% of the world's population.

D. Population Density
   1. Crude population density – the number of people per unit area of land, usually within the boundaries of a political entity.

E. World Population (1995) – 5,642,000,000

# CULTURE

A. Components of Culture
   1. Culture traits – the smallest distinctive items of a culture.
   2. Culture hearth – cultural innovation—ideas that diffuse from this origin to other places around the world (e.g., Mesopotamia was an early cultural hearth in southwest Asia.)
   3. Cultural landscape – part of the landscape modified by humans.

B. Cultural Ecology
   1. Environmental determinism – belief that the physical environment by itself shapes humans, their actions, and their thoughts.
   2. Possibilism – is the viewpoint that people are the dynamic forces of cultural development (more widely accepted).

C. Language
   1. Language family is a group of languages thought to have a common origin in a single, earlier tongue.
   2. Dialect – regional or socioeconomic variation of a more widely spoken language.
   3. The world has 2700 different languages and thousands of dialects.

D. Principal Religions
   1. Judaism – belief in single God, single ethnic group with strict laws and beliefs.
   2. Christianity – follows the teachings of Jesus.
   3. Islam – follows the Koran, the word of God dictated to Mohammed.

4. Hinduism – oldest religion, a complex set of social and economic beliefs (may believe in one god, many, or none).
5. Buddhism – derived from Hinduism. Involved more of a philosophy than religious beliefs (universalizing faith).

E. Ethnicity
   1. Social status attributed to a minority group within a national population. Recognized based upon cultural traits.
   2. Ethnocentrism – believing one's own people and culture as setting the proper standard for others.
   3. Assimilation – process of merging into a composite culture and becoming culturally homogenized (i.e., one culture).

# POLITICAL GEOGRAPHY

A. Political System Components
   1. State – an independent political unit occupying a permanent territory with full sovereign control over its internal and foreign affairs.
   2. Country (nation) – group of people with a common culture occupying the same territory, bound together by shared beliefs and customs.
   3. Nation-state – a state whose territory is identical to that occupied by a particular nation.
B. Geographical Characteristics of States
   1. Size, shape, and location
C. Boundaries
   1. General classifications
      a. Natural (physical) boundaries – follows topographical features such as rivers, valleys, or mountains.
      b. Geometric boundaries – are straight-lined or curved and follow some precise measurement.
      c. Anthropogeographic boundaries – show a change in the cultural landscape or dominant cultural or ethnic group.
   2. Cultural Classifications
      a. Antecedent – placed before the cultural landscape developed.
      b. Subsequent – set after the cultural landscape developed.
      c. Superimposed – set in place as a result of wars or colonialism.
      d. Relict – political boundary that has ceased to function but still has an imprint on the cultural landscape (e.g., former East/West German border).
D. Nationalism – sense of unity binding the people of a state together.
   1. Centripetal forces – bind together
   2. Centrifugal forces – destabilize and weaken a state.

E. There are presently 181 independent nations in the world.

# ECONOMIC GEOGRAPHY

A. Economic Activities – involve the occupational structure, or the proportion of workers found in each economic activity.
   1. Primary activity
      a. Agriculture, mining, and other extractive activities.
      b. Many developing nations still use primary activities as a source of employment and export earnings.
   2. Secondary activity
      a. Manufacturing and processing of primary products.
      b. This activity permeated the world with the Industrial Revolution.
      c. This activity is rapidly leaving the developed world in search of lower industrial wages in developing countries.
   3. Tertiary activity
      a. Called "service activity," retailing and other services.
      b. Most of the labor force in the developed world falls into this classification.
      c. Countries whose labor force is dominated by this activity are called "post-industrial."
   4. Quaternary activity
      a. Services related to information and research.
B. Types of Economic Systems
   1. Subsistence economy – goods and services are produced for the use of the producers. Little exchange of goods and marketing is limited.
   2. Commercial economy – producers market goods and services, laws of supply and demand set price and quantity, and marketing is essential for production decisions and distributions.
   3. Planned economy – communist-controlled society controls the development of goods and services and also supply and price.

# NATURAL RESOURCES

A. Resource Terminology
   1. Resource is a naturally occurring, recoverable material that a society perceives to be useful to its economic and material well-being (natural resource).
      a. Renewable resource – materials that can be regenerated in nature faster than society can recover them (biomass [living matter], wood, waste, hydroelectric power, solar power).

    b.  Nonrenewable resource – are generated in nature slowly and in small quantities (crude oil, natural gas, coal, synthetic fuels).

    c.  Resource reserves – nuclear energy (fission process).

B.  Distribution of Resources

  1.  World Energy Reserves

| Crude Oil | | Natural Gas | |
|---|---|---|---|
| Saudi Arabia | 28% | former U.S.S.R. | 38% |
| Iraq | 11% | Iran | 13% |
| Kuwait | 10% | U.A.E. | 5% |
| Iran | 7% | Saudi Arabia | 5% |
| Venezuela | 6% | U.S.A. | 4% |

# ENVIRONMENTAL GEOGRAPHY

A.  Ecosystem – population of organisms existing together in an area with the resources (air, water, soil, chemicals) upon which it depends.

  1.  Components of the biosphere – thin film of air, water, and earth within which people live.

    a.  Hydrosphere – surface and subsurface waters (e.g., oceans, lakes, groundwaters, glaciers) not immediately available for use.

    b.  Troposphere – the layer of air closest to the earth, extending upward about 7-8 miles.

    c.  Upper part of the earth's crust, containing soils, minerals, ores, and fossil fuels (coal, natural gas, oil).

  2.  An ecosystem involves the interdependence of organisms and the physical environment.

    a.  Food chain – transfer of energy and material from one organism to another.

  3.  Hydrologic cycle – involves the cycling of water in different forms and composition through evaporation and transpiration (emission of water vapor from plants).

    a.  Aquifer – layer of water-bearing, porous rocks lying between impermeable layers (e.g., Ogallala aquifer (midwest) – largest underground water supply in the U.S.

B.  Environmental Pollution

  1.  Introduction of wastes into the biosphere

  2.  Water pollution

    a.  Fertilizers – excess nutrients in water (eutrophication).

    b.  Biocides – herbicides and pesticides

    c.  Animal wastes

    d.  Industrial wastes, mining runoff, sewage, urban drainage (from detergents)

3.  Air Pollution
    a.  Acid rain (from burning of fossil fuels), generally with a pH < 5.
    b.  Ozone (formed from automobile and industrial gas emissions).
    c.  Greenhouse Effect – gases released concentrate in the atmosphere, thus providing an insulation barrier for heat, causing warming of the earth.

# URBAN GEOGRAPHY

A.  Urban Settlement
    1.  Urban functions
        a.  Manufacturing
        b.  Commerce (exchange of goods)
        c.  Administration
        d.  Defense
        e.  Cultural
        f.  Recreation
    2.  Types of urban settlements (agglomeration)
        a.  Town – single urban function dominates.
        b.  City – urban area acquiring a second important function.
        c.  Metropolis – a center of specified activities, including local, national, and worldwide.
    3.  Metropolitan Area – several urbanized areas, built up discretely, but economically coherent.

# FACTUAL ANALYSIS OF WORLD DEMOGRAPHY

A.  World is 66% adult and 51% female.
B.  Population increasing 90+ million per year = 1.7%/year.
C.  66% are without clean, safe drinking water.
D.  50% of the world is illiterate.
E.  73% of the population receives only 28% of the world's food grain production.
F.  16,000,000+ die from lack of food each year.
G.  Only 7% own 1 or more automobiles.
H.  Only 55% of the world's female married population use contraceptives.
I.  20% of the population receive 75% of the income, while 20% receive 2%.
J.  In developing countries, 36% of the population will be under 15 years of age in the year 2000; developed countries only 23% will be under 15 years of age.

K. Most populous nation is China (1.166 billion+).
L. Most densely populated city is Macao, 62,000/sq. mile, located at the mouth of the Pearl River on southern China.
M. Although the United States constitutes only 5% of the world's population, it consumes 40% of the world's annual production of goods.
N. World spends more on weapons and war than on education.

# 21. MYTHOLOGY

## GREEK AND ROMAN GODS AND GODDESSES

**Titans**—The first divine race. Ultimately honored as ancestors of humans. Credited with the invention of the arts and of magic.

**Cronus**—Son of titans. Married his sister, Rhea. They gave birth to three daughters—Hestia, Demeter, and Hera, and three sons—Poseidon, Hades and Zeus. Roman counterpart—Saturn.

**Prometheus**—Created humans from earth and water. Though a titan, he was allowed to live on Olympus.

**Pandora**—The first woman. Created by all the divinities. Unleashed terrible afflictions which spread over the earth.

**Zeus**—Supreme god. Unites in himself all attributes of divinity—omnipotent, omniscient, omnipresent. Ruled according to fate and his own will. Lived on Mount Olympus. Roman counterpart—Jupiter.

**Hera**—Zeus's wife. Woman deified, presided over all stages of feminine existence, primarily marriage and maternity. Represents idealized wife. Roman counterpart—Juno.

**Athena**—Warrior goddess, goddess of arts of peace, and goddess of prudent intelligence. Zeus's daughter, she was born, fully armed, out of his skull. Roman counterpart—Minerva.

**Apollo**—A sun-god, god of the light. Cultivated and protected crops. God of divination and prophecy. Associated with music. Represented as an archer. Son of Zeus and Leto. Roman counterpart—Apollo.

**The Muses**—Apollo's habitual companions. Goddesses of memory and poetic inspiration. Clio—history. Euterpe—flute. Thalia—comedy. Melpomene—tragedy. Terpsichore—lyric poetry and dance. Erato—love poetry. Polyhymnia—mimic art. Urania—astronomy. Calliope—epic poetry and eloquence.

**Artemis**—Agricultural deity. Goddess of the chase and of forests. Associated with moonlight. Represented as an archer. Apollo's twin sister, also daughter of Zeus and Leto. Roman counterpart—Diana.

**Hermes**—God of travellers. Conducted the souls of the dead to the underworld. God of commerce and profit. Tireless runner, messenger of Zeus. Son of Zeus and Maia. Roman counterpart—Mercury.

**Ares**—God of war, of blind, brutal courage, and of bloody rage and carnage. Son of Zeus and Hera. Roman counterpart—Mars.

**Aphrodite**—Goddess of love. Goddess of pure and ideal love as well as of marriage and of lust and venal love. Essence of feminine beauty. Daughter of Zeus. Roman counterpart—Venus.

**Eros**—Youngest of the gods, a winged child, gracious and rebellious. Armed with bow and arrows which would cause people to fall in love if hit by them. Son of Aphrodite. Roman equivalent—Cupid.

**Poseidon**—God of the sea. Personification of water—god of vegetation and fecundity. Son of Cronus. Roman equivalent—Neptune.

**Orion**—Beautiful giant, son of Mother Earth. Passionate hunter, accompanied by his dog, Sirius. Banished to live in the sky, and now an easily recognized constellation.

**Tritons**—Strange sea creatures, half-men, half-fish, with scales, sharp teeth, claws, fins and forked tails. Hedonistic and lascivious.

**Sirens**—Sea monsters with bird's bodies and women's heads. Sang sweetly and irresistibly to lure travellers and then killed them.

**Charybdis and Scylla**—Dwelt in same Sicilian sea as the Sirens. Charybdis, daughter of Poseidon and the earth, was a whirlpool who swallowed ships. Scylla, once a beautiful woman, was changed into a monster, with six ugly heads.

**Demeter**—Goddess of the earth and the underworld, represents motherhood and fertile, cultivated soil. Earth mother. Daughter of Cronus and Rhea. Roman counterpart—Ceres.

**Dionysus**—God of wine and pleasure. Son of Zeus. Roman counterpart—Bacchus.

**Satyrs**—Part of the retinue of Dionysus. Represented the elementary spirits of forests and mountains. Half-man and half-goat, they were sensual and lascivious.

**Pan**—Son of Hermes. Not a satyr, though he also was half-goat. Shepherd god of woods and pastures, protector of shepherds and flocks.

**Hades**—God of the underworld. Invisible, god of buried treasure and agricultural wealth. Son of Cronus and Rhea, brother of Zeus. Roman equivalent—Pluto.

**Persephone**—Daughter of Demeter, wife of Hades. Spent part of the world in the underworld and part on earth, and therefore associated with seasons of the year and myths of regeneration. Roman counterpart—Proserpina.

**Heracles**—Not a god, but a hero. Personification of physical strength. Founder of Olympic Games. Had to perform twelve superhuman labors. Son of Zeus and a mortal woman. Roman counterpart—Hercules.

**Theseus**—Not a god, but a hero. Like Heracles destroyed many monsters, including the Minotaur on Crete. Son of a mortal woman, a mortal man, and the god, Poseidon.

**Perseus**—Son of a mortal woman and Zeus, who impregnated her disguised as a shower of gold. Also a hero, not a god, who had many adventures. Killed the snake headed monster Medusa. Also killed a sea monster to save a beautiful princess named Andromeda.

**Helen**—Woman whose beauty launched a thousand ships and began the Trojan War. Wife to Menelaus, but carried off by lovestruck Paris.

**Oedipus**—Son of King of Thebes. Unwittingly killed his father and married his mother, which caused him to blind himself. Answered the riddle of the Sphinx.

**Orpheus**—One of the few Greek heroes not known for warlike exploits. Son of Apollo, sang and played the lyre so beautifully that trees and savage beasts would follow him. Performed miracles on the voyage of the Argonauts to find the Golden Fleece.

# NORSE GODS

**Odin**—Of the Aesir race. Principle god of Teutonic peoples. Our word "Wednesday" is derived from his name, which suggests frenzy and fury. Decided human's fates. Handsome and eloquent, magician god of the other world, god of spiritual life. Warlike, but did not fight in battles himself, intervened magically. Lived in great glittering hall of gold called Valhalla. Sometimes know as "Woden."

**Valkyries**—Supernatural women who lived in Valhalla. Guardians and servants to the gods. Had both domestic and martial duties—they mingled with combatants in wars. Rode on fiery chargers.

**Sigmund**—A hero, not a god. Mortal descendant of Odin. Pulled a magical sword out of a tree trunk in which Odin had placed it, and had many adventures with it. Died willingly at Odin's insistence.

**Sigurd**—Sigmund's son, inheritor of his sword. Also a hero not a god, also had many adventures. Sometimes known as "Siegfried."

**Frigg**—An Aesir. Odin's wife. Most revered of goddesses. Our word "Friday" is derived from her name. Possessed of great wisdom and foresight. Sometimes known as "Frija."

**Mimir**—A water demon. Odin's uncle and wisest counselor. Lived by the roots of the ash tree Yggdrasil known as "world tree." Lived in a fountain in which all wisdom and knowledge were hidden.

**Kvasir**—Made from the mingled saliva of the two races of gods—Aesir and Vanir. Surpassed all men in wisdom. He was killed and his blood was mixed with honey in a cauldron to make a liquid which would cause the drinker to become a sage and poet.

**Thor**—An Aesir. God of thunder and war. Our word "Thursday" is derived from his name. Much feared. It was believed that thunder was caused by his chariot wheels and that thunderbolts were his fiery weapons. Rude, simple, noble. Often represented with a hammer. Sometimes known as "Donan."

**Jord**—The earth goddess. Thor's mother.

**Magni and Modi**—Thor's sons. Magni was strength and Modi was anger. They would inherit Thor's hammer and replace him in a new-made world.

**Tiw**—Sky god and god governing battles. His spear was a sign of judicial power. Our word "Tuesday" is derived from his name. Sometimes known as "Tyr."

**Loki**—A superior demon. Always making mischief. Served the gods but also undermined their power whenever possible. Handsome and attentive to goddesses. Thor's blood brother.

**Idun**—The goddess who owned the magic apples which gave all of the gods and goddess eternal youth and immortality.

**Heimdall**—God of light. Presided over ambiguous beginnings of things. Guardian of all the gods.

**Balder**—Son of Odin and Frigg. So beautiful he shed radiance all around himself. Wisest and favorite of gods.

**Njord**—A Vanir rather than an Aesir. Peaceful, benevolent and mighty. The greatest of the Vanir. Provided fields and pastures with sun and rain. God of harvests, game, riches, commerce, and navigation. Guarantor of oaths.

**Frey**—Njord's son. Also peaceful, benevolent and mighty. Also a Vanir, though he lived among the Aesir. Had all the same qualities as his father. Had a powerful horse and sword and a golden boar.

**Freja**—Female equivalent of Frey—his sister. Lived in Folkvang, a rich dwelling in the sky where she received the deceased warriors and assigned them seats in her banqueting hall. First and supreme commander of the Valkyries.

**Skadi**—Njord's wife. Daughter of a giant.

**Gerda**—Frey's wife, also the daughter of a giant.

# 22. PHILOSOPHY

**the Pre-Socratics**—general term for all of the Greek philosophers before Socrates

**Pythagoras**—sixth century BC pre-Socratic philosopher and mathematician; as well as making many scientific and mathematical discoveries, he believed in the transmigration of souls

**Thales**—sixth and fifth century BC pre-Socratic philosopher; sometimes called "the father of Western philosophy"; held that the first principle of nature (the substance that everything in the universe is made out of) is water

**Parmenides**—fifth and fourth century BC pre-Socratic philosopher; denied the existence of time, plurality and motion

**Heraclitus**—fourth century BC pre-Socratic philosopher; said to have believed that everything is always in a state of flux

**Zeno**—fourth century BC pre-Socratic philosopher; famous for a set of paradoxes which are intended to show that plurality and motion do not really exist

**Socrates**—fourth century BC Greek philosopher; did not write any philosophical treatises; his ideas have survived only through the writings of his followers, most notably Plato, and it is unclear to what extent the views attributed to the character of Socrates in Plato's dialogs were the views of the actual historical Socrates

**atomism**—the belief that matter consists of atoms

**Leucippus**—fourth century BC Greek atomist philosopher

**Democritus**—fourth and third century BC Greek atomist philosopher

**Plato**—BC (427–347 BC) Greek philosopher; wrote dialogs, many of which have Socrates as their main character, which provided the starting point for many later developments in ethics, epistemology and metaphysics; his best-known theory is the theory of Forms (or Ideas), according to which the objects of knowledge are universals (such as The Good and The Just), and things in this world (such as a just person) are mere reflections of the Forms and can only be the objects of opinion

**Aristotle**—third century BC—extremely influential Greek philosopher; criticized Plato's theory of Forms; was the first to systematize logic

**Aristotelianism**—medieval study and development of Aristotle's philosophy

**Plotinus**—third century AD Neoplatonist philosopher

**neoplatonism**—the dominant philosophy in Europe from 250–1250 AD; begun by Plotinus; a combination of Plato's ideas with those of other philosophers including Aristotle and Pythagoras

**Augustine**—fourth and fifth century bishop and philosopher, Neoplatonist, had a profound influence on medieval religious thought

**Anselm**—eleventh century philosopher, best known for his ontological argument for the existence of God

**Aquinas**—thirteenth century philosopher, best known for his "Five Ways," which are five proofs of the existence of God

**Thomism**—the philosophy of Aquinas and his followers

**Ockham**—fourteenth century English philosopher and cleric; famous for Ockham's Razor, which is the dictum "Do not multiply entities beyond necessity"

**Hobbes** (1588–1679)—British materialist philosopher and political scientist; wrote *Leviathan*

**rationalism**—the view that knowledge of the external world can be derived from reason alone, without recourse to experience; notable rationalists include Descartes, Leibnitz, and Spinoza

**Descartes** (1596–1650)—extremely influential French rationalist philosopher and mathematician; held a view of the relation between mind and body which has come to be known as Cartesian dualism; famous for the statement "*coqito ergo sum*," or "I think therefore I am."

**Leibnitz** (1646–1716)—German rationalist philosopher; argued (in his *Theodicy*) that this is the best of all possible worlds

**Pascal** (1623–1662)—French philosopher, mathematician and theologian; most famous for an argument called "Pascal's Wager" which provides prudential reasons for believing in God

**Spinoza** (1632–1677)—Rationalist philosopher; best known for his *Tractatus Theologico-Politicus*

**empiricism**—the view that all knowledge is derived from experience; Locke, Berkeley, and Hume are notable empiricists

**Locke** (1632–1704)—English empiricist philosopher; wrote the *Essay Concerning Human Understanding*, an attempt to give an empiricist account of the origins, nature, and limits of human reason

**Clarke** (1675–1729)—English philosopher and theologian

**Berkeley** (1685–1753)—Irish philosopher; idealist; empiricist

**idealism**—the view that the so-called "external world" is actually a creation of the mind. Berkeley and Hegel are notable idealists

**Reid** (1710–1796)—Scots philosopher; defended the commonsense view that through our senses we can have knowledge of a mind-independent reality

**Hume** (1711–1776)—Scots philosopher; empiricist; drew attention to the problem of induction

**Rousseau** (1712–1778)—political philosopher and philosopher of education

**Smith** (1723–1790)—Scots philosopher and political economist; wrote *The Wealth of Nations*

**Kant** (1724–1804)—German idealist philosopher; most famous for putting forward the categorical imperative ("Act only on that maxim which you can at the same time will to become a universal law") as a test of moral principles

**Bentham** (1748–1832)—British philosopher of law; utilitarian

**Hegel** (1770–1831)—German idealist philosopher; famous for his theory of dialectic, a process of argument which proceeds from a thesis and its antithesis to a synthesis of the two

**Mill, James** (1773–1836)—Scots philosopher and economist; father of the better-known philosopher J.S. Mill

**Schopenhauer** (1788–1860)—German philosopher; Kantian; best known for *The World As Will and Idea*

**Mill, J.S.** (1806–1873)—English empiricist philosopher; best known for his *System of Logic* and for his ethical writings, which include *Utilitarianism* and *On Liberty*

**Kierkegaard** (1813–1855)—Danish philosopher; existentialist

**existentialism**—the view that the subject of philosophy is *being*, which cannot be made the subject of objective inquiry but can only be investigated by reflection on one's own existence. Kierkegaard was probably the first existentialist; Sartre is another notable existentialist

**Marx** (1818–83)— German social theorist; wrote *Das Kapital*

**Engels** (1820–1895)—Marx's collaborator; dialectical materialist

**Marxism**—the body of doctrines originally propounded by Marx and Engels; includes dialectical materialism

**dialectical materialism**—a metaphysical doctrine originally propounded by Engels and held by many Marxists, according to which matter (rather than mind) is primary, and is governed by dialectical laws

**Brentano** (1838–1917)—German philosopher and psychologist; remembered for his "doctrine of intentionality"

**Peirce** (1839–1914)—American philosopher; founder of pragmatism

**pragmatism**—originally (as used by Peirce) a theory of meaning; later (as used by James) a theory of truth according to which "ideas become true just so far as they help us to get into satisfactory relations with other parts of our experience"

**James** (1842–1910)—American philosopher and psychologist; empiricist; pragmatist

**Nietzsche** (1844–1900)—German philosopher; best known for introducing the concept of the *Ubermensch* (Overman)

**Bradley** (1846–1924)—English philosopher; idealist; wrote *Appearance and Reality*

**Frege** (1848–1925)—German philosopher and mathematician; founding father of modern logic, philosophy of mathematics and philosophy of language

**Husserl** (1859–1938)—German philosopher; phenomenologist

**phenomenology**—a method of inquiry which begins from the scrupulous inspection of one's own conscious thought processes; developed by Husserl

**Bergson** (1859–1941)—French philosopher; dualist; rejected mechanistic and deterministic approach to understanding reality

**Dewey** (1859–1952)—American pragmatist philosopher and educational theorist

**Santayana** (1863–1952)—American Platonist philosopher, novelist and poet

**Russell** (1872–1970)—British philosopher; with Whitehead, the author of the extremely influential *Principia Mathematica*; argued (in such seminal papers as "On Denoting" and "The Principles of Logical Atomism") that the structure of the world can be revealed by the proper analysis of language

**Moore** (1873–1958)—British philosopher; best-known for his *Principia Ethica*

**logical positivism**—a radical empiricist position; the doctrine that the meaning of a proposition consists in the method of its verification; also known as "logical empiricism"

**Vienna Circle**—the group of logical positivists which centered around the University of Vienna in the 1920s and 30s; included Schlick, Carnap and Neurath

**Schlick** (1882–1936)—logical positivist philosopher; a founding member of the Vienna Circle

**Neurath** (1882–1945)—Austrian logical positivist philosopher; member of the Vienna Circle

**Wittgenstein** (1889–1951)—Viennese-born philosopher who has had an enormous influence on later philosophy of language; his first and most famous work was *Tractatus Logico-Philosophicus*, in which he defended a picture theory of meaning, and which contains such often-quoted aphorisms as "The world is everything that is the case."

**Heidegger** (1889–1976)—German philosopher; commonly regarded as an existentialist although he claimed not to be one

**Carnap** (1891–1970)—German philosopher; logical positivist

**Ryle** (1900–1976)—British philosopher of language and philosopher of mind; proponent of logical behaviorism

**Nagel** (1901–  )—American philosopher of science; author of *The Structure of Science*

**Tarski** (1902–  )—American logician and mathematician; famous for his definition of the concept of truth for formal logical languages, which has been used extensively by philosophers of language as a basis for theories of meaning for natural language

**Popper** (1902–  )—philosopher of science; wrote *The Logic of Scientific Discovery*; best known for his claim that falsifiability is the hallmark of science

**Sartre** (1905–1980)—French philosopher; Marxist; existentialist

**Hempel** (1905–  )—German empiricist philosopher of science; his theories of confirmation and explanation have been extremely influential

**Goodman** (1906–  )—American philosopher; nominalist; wrote (most notably) *Fact Fiction and Forecast* and *Languages of Art*

**Merleau-Ponty** (1908–1961)—French philosopher; worked on ethics and on problems of consciousness

**Quine** (1908–  )—American empiricist philosopher of language and logician

**Ayer** (1910–  )—English philosopher; logical positivist; member of the Vienna Circle; wrote *Language, Truth and Logic*

**Austin** (1911–1960)—British philosopher of language; developed speech act theory

**Strawson** (1919–  )—British philosopher of language and metaphysician; best known for arguing (in "On Referring") that some meaningful sentences have no truth value

**Rawls** (1921–  )—American political philosopher and ethicist; best known for *A Theory of Justice*

**Chomsky** (1928–  )—American linguist and philosopher; argues that there is an innate universal grammar

**Davidson** (1930–  )—American philosopher of language and philosopher of mind; holds a theory of mind called anomalous monism

**Kripke** (1941–  )—American philosopher of language, philosopher of mind and logician; his most influential work is "Naming and Necessity," which launched the causal theory of reference

# 23. WORLD RELIGIONS

## MAJOR WORLD RELIGIONS AND THEIR GODS

**Hinduism** (although there are actually millions, these are the major Gods)

**Bhrama**—the creator of life

**Brahman (or Brahm)**—supreme all-powerful entity of the universe

**Kali**—a goddess of destruction, the bloodthirsting goddess of death

**Mitra**—the god of light

**Shiva (or Siva)**—a god of fertility and life, destruction, and death

**Vishnu**—the god who preserves life

**Shintoism** (there are over 8 million and the number is growing, here are most well known)

**Amatersau Omikami**—the sun goddess, principle god of Shinto

**Amenominakanushi-no-kami**—god of the universe, based on Christian God

**Takami-musubi**—the high-producing subordinate of universe god

**Emperor Hirohito**—W.W. II Emperor of Japan, said to be a descendant of sun goddess.

**Kami-musubi**—divine producing god, subordinate of universe god

**Taoism** (there are numerous gods, goddesses, fairies, and immortals)

**Pa Hsien/The Eight Immortals**—immortal ancestors of China

**Tsao Shen/The god of hearth**—god of fire

**Ch'eng Huang/city gods**—gods who protected ancient Chinese cities

**Men Shen/Guardians of the door**—spirits who protect the way to the spirit world.

## Judaism (a monotheistic religion)

**Yahweh (Jehovah)**—the creator of universe and every living thing. Worshipped by the Hebrews.

## Christendom (although Christians worship one God, they identify him three separate ways)

**Holy Trinity**—comprised of God the Father, Jesus the Son, and the Holy Ghost.

## Islam (a monotheistic religion)

**Allah**—creator of the universe and all mankind, worshipped by Muslims

# WORLD RELIGIONS AND THEIR MAJOR FIGURES

## Buddhism

**Siddharathma Gautama**—was to become the Buddha—or enlightened One, founder and teacher of Buddhism.

## Sikhism (off-shoot of Hinduism)

**Guru Nanak**—founder of Sikhism, taught the belief that all mankind are brothers and sisters and should treat one another accordingly.

## Jainism (off-shoot of Hinduism)

**Nataputta Vardhamana**—also known as Vardhamana Mahavira his title meant Great Hero. Founder of Jainism, he taught self-denial, self-discipline, and nonviolence.

## Taoism

**Lao-tzu**—"Old Master" founder of Taoism, taught that mankind should leave behind the world and become one with nature.

## Confucianism

**Confucius**—founder of Confucianism, taught moral codes and ethics. Confucius taught that everyone must learn what role they play in society, and live accordingly.

## Judaism

**Abraham**—(Abram) the forefather of the Israelites, he worshipped Yahweh (Jehovah) over 4,000 years ago. He believed in adherence to Divine commandment.

**Moses**—leader of the nation of Israel, Moses provided the Jews with a copy of "the law" from God.

## Christianity

**Jesus Christ**—founder of Christianity, son of the Hebrew God. Christ was born a Jew, however he directed the Israelites towards another way of worship.

## Islam

**Muhammad**—Founder of Islam, a prophet sent by Allah to teach followers the pure way of worship.

# MAJOR WORLD RELIGIONS AND THEIR HOLY CITIES AND OTHER LOCATIONS

## Judaism

**Jerusalem**—Up until 70 C.E., Solomon's temple in Jerusalem was the center of worship for the Israelites. The city is still acknowledged as a holy one, there is also a holy wall located in the city.

## Islam

**Mecca**—Holy city for Muslims. All male Muslims must journey to Mecca at least once in their lifetime.

## Hinduism

**Ganges River**—Hindus believe that this river has the power to cleanse, purify, and release its believers.

## Sikhism

**Amristar**—the Sikh holy city located in India.

## Christendom

**Rome**—Holy city where the Vatican is located, acknowledged mostly by Catholics.

# MAJOR WORLD RELIGIONS AND THEIR FESTIVALS OR HOLY DAYS

## Shinto

**Sho-gatu**—The New Year festival days. (January 1–3)

**Setsubun**—The tossing of beans in and outside of homes, done to keep the evil spirits out and good ones in. (February 3)

## Judaism

**Yom Kippur**—Day of Atonement, day of fasting and spiritual self-examination

**Sukkot**—Festival of Booths, celebration of the harvest, the end of an agricultural year.

**Pesach**—Passover Festival, commemorates Israel's deliverance from Egyptian captivity

## Christendom

**Christmas**—The celebration of the birth of the Messiah, mankind's redeemer

**Easter**—Celebration of the Messiah's death and subsequent resurrection

# MAJOR WORLD RELIGIONS AND THEIR HOLY WRITINGS

## Christianity

**The Bible**—The most widely published and read book in history. Is comprised of 66 small books translated from Hebrew, Aramaic, and Greek.

## Islam

**Koran**—Holy book of Muslims, is said to have superseded the Bible.

## Judaism

**Tanakh**—comes from the three divisions of the Jewish Bible, consisting of the *Torah* (five books of Moses), Nevi'im (the Prophets), Kethuvin (the Writings).

**Talmud**—given as a supplement to the original law of Moses.

## Hinduism

**Vedas**—the earliest of sacred writings of Hinduism

## Confucianism

**The Four Books:** The Great Learning, The Doctrine of the Mean, The Analects, The Book of Mencius. All collections of sayings and teaching of Confucius.

**The Five Classics:** The Book of Poetry, The Book of History, The Book of Changes, The Book of Rites, Annuals of Spring and Autumn. Writings that deal with poetry, rituals, and ancient Chinese history.

# MAJOR WORLD RELIGIONS AND THEIR PLACE OF WORSHIP

## Judaism

**Temple**—Place of meeting for Jews.

**Christianity**

> **Church**—Meeting place of worship for most Christian religions.

**Islam**

> **Mosque**—Place of worship for Muslims.

# 24. MATHEMATICAL REFERENCE TABLE

## SYMBOLS AND THEIR MEANINGS

| | | | |
|---|---|---|---|
| $=$ | is equal to | $\leq$ | is less than or equal to |
| $\neq$ | is unequal to | $\geq$ | is greater than or equal to |
| $<$ | is less than | $\parallel$ | is parallel to |
| $>$ | is greater than | $\perp$ | is perpendicular to |

## FORMULAS

| DESCRIPTION | FORMULA |
|---|---|
| **Area (A) of a:** | |
| square | $A = s^2$; where $s$ = side |
| rectangle | $A = lw$; where $l$ = length, $w$ = width |
| parallelogram | $A = bh$; where $b$ = base, $h$ = height |
| triangle | $A = \frac{1}{2} bh$; where $b$ = base, $h$ = height |
| circle | $A = \pi r^2$; where $\pi$ = 3.14, $r$ = radius |
| **Perimeter (P) of a:** | |
| square | $P = 4s$; where $s$ = side |
| rectangle | $P = 2l + 2w$; where $l$ = length, $w$ = width |
| triangle | $P = a + b + c$; where $a$, $b$, and $c$ are the sides |
| circumference (C) of a circle | $C = \pi d$; where $\pi$ = 3.14, $d$ = diameter = $2r$ |
| **Volume (V) of a:** | |
| cube | $V = s^3$; where $s$ = side |
| rectangular container | $V = lwh$; where $l$ = length, $w$ = width, $h$ = height |
| **Pythagorean Theorem** | $c^2 = a^2 + b^2$; where $c$ = hypotenuse, $a$ and $b$ are legs of a right triangle |
| **Distance (d):** | |
| between two points in a plane | $d = \sqrt{(x_2 - x_1)^2 + (y_2 - y_1)^2}$ where $(x_1, y_1)$ and $(x_2, y_2)$ are two points in a plane |
| as a function of rate and time | $d = rt$; where $r$ = rate, $t$ = time |
| **Mean** | mean = $\dfrac{x_1 + x_2 + \ldots + x_n}{n}$ where the $x$'s are the values for which a mean is desired, and $n$ = number of values in the series |
| **Median** | median = the point in an ordered set of numbers at which half of the numbers are above and half of the numbers are below this value |
| **Simple Interest (i)** | $i = prt$; where $p$ = principal, $r$ = rate, $t$ = time |
| **Total Cost (c)** | $c = nr$; where $n$ = number of units, $r$ = cost per unit |

# 25. THE METRIC SYSTEM

The prefixes commonly used in the metric system are:

| Prefix | Meaning |
|--------|---------|
| kilo– | thousand (1,000) |
| deci– | tenth (0.1) |
| centi– | hundredth (0.01) |
| milli– | thousandth (0.001) |

The basic unit of linear measure in the metric system is the *meter*, represented by m. The relationship among the commonly used linear units of measurement in the metric system is as follows:

| | | |
|---|---|---|
| 1 kilometer (km) | = | 1,000 m |
| 1 meter (m) | = | 1.0 m |
| 1 decimeter (dm) | = | 0.1 m |
| 1 centimeter (cm) | = | 0.01 m |
| 1 millimeter (mm) | = | 0.001 m |

The basic unit of measurement for mass (or weight) in the metric system is the *gram*, represented by g. The relationship among the commonly used units of measurement for mass in he metric system is as follows:

| | | |
|---|---|---|
| 1 kilogram (kg) | = | 1,000 g |
| 1 gram (g) | = | 1.0 g |
| 1 milligram (mg) | = | 0.001 g |

# REA's Test Prep Books Are The Best!
## (a sample of the <u>hundreds of letters</u> REA receives each year)

" I am writing to congratulate you on preparing an exceptional study guide. In five years of teaching this course I have never encountered a more thorough, comprehensive, concise and realistic preparation for this examination. "
*Teacher, Davie, FL*

" I have found your publications, *The Best Test Preparation...*, to be exactly that. "
*Teacher, Aptos, CA*

" I used your *CLEP Introductory Sociology* book and rank it 99% — thank you! "
*Student, Jerusalem, Israel*

" Your GMAT book greatly helped me on the test. Thank you. "
*Student, Oxford, OH*

" I recently got the French SAT II Exam book from REA. I congratulate you on first-rate French practice tests."
*Instructor, Los Angeles, CA*

" Your AP English Literature and Composition book is most impressive."
*Student, Montgomery, AL*

" The REA LSAT Test Preparation guide is a winner! "
*Instructor, Spartanburg, SC*

*(more on front page)*